MODERNIST COMMITMENTS

Modernist Latitudes

MODERNIST LATITUDES
Jessica Berman and Paul Saint-Amour, *Editors*

Modernist Latitudes aims to capture the energy and ferment of modernist studies by continuing to open up the range of forms, locations, temporalities, and theoretical approaches encompassed by the field. The series celebrates the growing latitude ("scope for freedom of action or thought") that this broadening affords scholars of modernism, whether they are investigating little-known works or revisiting canonical ones. Modernist Latitudes will pay particular attention to the texts and contexts of those latitudes (Africa, Latin America, Australia, Asia, Southern Europe, and even the rural United States) that have long been misrecognized as ancillary to the canonical modernisms of the global North.

Barry McCrea, *In the Company of Strangers: Family and Narrative in Dickens, Conan Doyle, Joyce, and Proust*, 2011

Jessica Berman, *Modernist Commitments: Ethics, Politics, and Transnational Modernism*, 2011

Modernist Commitments

ETHICS, POLITICS, AND
TRANSNATIONAL MODERNISM

Jessica Berman

 Columbia University Press   *New York*

Columbia University Press
Publishers Since 1893
New York   Chichester, West Sussex
Copyright © 2011 Columbia University Press
All rights reserved

Library of Congress Cataloging-in-Publication Data
Berman, Jessica Schiff, 1961–
  Modernist commitments : ethics, politics, and transnational modernism / Jessica Berman.
      p. cm.
  Includes bibliographical references and index.
  ISBN 978-0-231-14950-1 (cloth : alk. paper) — ISBN 978-0-231-14951-8 (pbk. : alk. paper) — ISBN 978-0-231-52039-3 (e-book)
  1. Literature, Modern—20th century—History and criticism. 2. Modernism (Literature)—History and criticism. 3. Politics and literature—History—20th century. 4. Literature and society—History—20th century. I. Title.
  PN56.M54B47 2012
  809'.9112—dc23

                                                                2011020709

Columbia University Press books are printed on permanent and durable acid-free paper.
This book is printed on paper with recycled content.
Printed in the United States of America

References to Internet Web sites (URLs) were accurate at the time of writing. Neither the author nor Columbia University Press is responsible for URLs that may have expired or changed since the manuscript was prepared.

CONTENTS

List of Illustrations — vii
Acknowledgments — ix

INTRODUCTION Imagining Justice — 1

PART I

ONE Intimate and Global:
Ethical Domains from Woolf to Rhys — 39

TWO Comparative Colonialisms:
Joyce, Anand, and the Question of Engagement — 90

PART II

THREE Modernism in the Zenana:
The Domestic Spaces of Sorabji, Hussain, and Ishvani — 139

FOUR Commitment and the Scene of War:
Max Aub and Spanish Civil War Writing — 184

FIVE Arising from the Cornlands:
The Working-Class Voices of Conroy and Le Sueur — 237

Afterword — 281

Notes — 287
Bibliography — 331
Index — 353

ILLUSTRATIONS

Figure 1.1.	Bernini, head of St. Theresa (1647–52) 52
Figure 1.2.	Caravaggio, *Death of the Virgin* (1605) 53
Figure 1.3.	"Orlando on her return to England" 54
Figure 1.4.	A page from *The Daily Worker*, displaying photographs of children killed in the Spanish Civil War (1936) 66
Figure 1.5.	Republican propaganda poster from the Spanish Civil War, in English 67
Figure 4.1.	Republican propaganda poster from the Spanish Civil War 219
Figure 4.2.	Republican tourist office poster from the Spanish Civil War 220
Figure 4.3.	Propaganda poster from the Spanish Civil War, responding to the bombing of Asturias 221
Figure 4.4.	Antifascist propaganda poster from the Spanish Civil War 222
Figure 4.5.	Falange propaganda poster from the Spanish Civil War 224
Figure 4.6.	Falange propaganda poster from the Spanish Civil War 225
Figure 4.7.	Republican propaganda poster from the Spanish Civil War, in English 226

ACKNOWLEDGMENTS

Common images of academia often portray the lonely scholar reading under a single light bulb and writing in quiet isolation, waiting for the "eureka" moment. The years of writing this second book have taught me quite a different lesson about the communal process of scholarly work. This book has been made possible by the published work and personal guidance of many scholars and friends, too numerous to list here. It is clichéd (but true) to say that it would have been impossible without them (though of course any errors are my own). I'd like also to acknowledge the special support of the following people who read portions of the book, discussed it with me, and otherwise aided and abetted what sometimes seemed like a long and crazy project. I only hope that I'll be able to offer them in return some approximation of the thoughtful and generous help they've extended to me: Erin Carlston, Pamela Caughie, Laura Doyle, Marian Eide, Jed Esty, Raphael Falco, Susan Stanford Friedman, Piotr Gwiazda, Christoph Irmscher, Jordana Mendelson, Gayle Rogers, Paul Saint-Amour, and Sonita Sarker.

I owe a debt of gratitude to the anonymous readers for Columbia University Press whose insightful comments improved the book immeasurably. I thank copy editor Michael Haskell whose lithe hand rescued me from many an infelicity of expression and a few downright errors. Thanks also to Philip Leventhal at Columbia for shepherding the book expertly through the publication process and for his ongoing interest in modernist studies. His was the spark that set off our book series, Modernist Latitudes—a venture I have the good fortune to share with my coeditor extraordinaire, Paul Saint-Amour.

I thank my wonderful undergraduate students at UMBC who have kept me on my toes by asking the hard questions and Emek Ergun and Jennifer Harrison, Ph.D. students in the Language, Literacy, and Culture Program who have pushed me in new directions.

I'm grateful to:

Susan Harrell, Norma Falk, and Patricia Bach in the UMBC English Department office for making it possible to be both department chair and active scholar. (We know who *really* runs the department!)

Shirin Vajibdar for permission to quote from the unpublished work of Mulk Raj Anand.

Richard Sorabji for permission to quote from the personal papers of Cornelia Sorabji.

UMBC for Special Research Initiative Support funding and former provost Art Johnson for a semester-long research fellowship.

Dean John Jeffries of UMBC's College of Arts, Humanities, and Social Sciences for a subvention in aid of publication.

The Newberry Library for a short-term fellowship to consult the Jack Conroy papers.

Librarians at the Library of Congress, the Department of Special Collections and University Archives, McFarlin Library, the University of Tulsa, the University of Delaware Library Special Collections, and the British Library (where I thank the person in special collections who took pity on me and allowed me to request many more than my daily manuscript allotment!).

My parents Ben and Ellyn Schiff Berman for never failing in their interest, support, and love.

Aaron, Emma, and Michael, well, just *because*. This book is for you.

An earlier version of part of chapter 1 appeared as "Ethical Folds: Ethics, Aesthetics, Woolf," *MFS: Modern Fiction Studies* (Spring 2004): 151–72, and was reprinted in Maren Linett, ed., *Virginia Woolf: An MFS Reader* (Baltimore, Md.: Johns Hopkins University Press, 2009), 257–80. Earlier versions of parts of chapter 2 were published as "Comparative Colonialisms: Joyce, Anand, and the Question of Engagement," *Modernism/Modernity* (Fall 2006): 465–85; and "Toward a Regional Cosmopolitanism: The Case of Mulk Raj Anand," *MFS: Modern Fiction Studies* 55, no. 1 (Spring 2009): 142–62. I am grateful to these publications for permission to reprint.

MODERNIST COMMITMENTS

Imagining Justice | INTRODUCTION

> Modernity is not a concept philosophical or otherwise but a narrative category.
> —Frederic Jameson, *A Singular Modernity*

> Let us define "ethical intention" as aiming at the "good life" with and for others, in just institutions.
> —Paul Ricoeur, *Oneself as Another*

> Justice is always a revision of justice and the expectation of a better justice.
> —Emmanuel Levinas, "Uniqueness," *Entre Nous*

In his first novel, *Untouchable* (1928), the celebrated Indian writer Mulk Raj Anand follows a day in the life of an untouchable boy named Bakha, whose travails in a small village raise complex questions about the ethical and political dimensions of modernity in late-colonial India. One of the first novels to feature the outcaste as hero, *Untouchable* documents the conflicts between Bakha's obligations as a sweeper and his rising ethical awareness, which grows over the course of the novel and infuses its subjective, highly focalized narration. The novel is stunning in its depiction of the corporeality of Bakha's existence, incorporating the sounds and smells of the village streets and the tactility of untouchable life. At the same time, it invites us to glimpse the complexity of Bakha's naïve perspective and the challenge it poses to received ideas about caste, class, and colonialism in early-twentieth-century India.

But in the novel's final pages, politics enters more directly, bringing the ethical dimension of Bakha's daily life into contact with global issues of colonialism and development while challenging the assumptions we as readers have made about the narrative's sphere of activity. Bakha stumbles into a crowd waiting for Gandhi to address a political meeting, and the narrative steps out of its narrow, focalized perspective to deliver Gandhi's speech and several reactions to it, almost verbatim. Bakha listens to Gandhi speak about the problem of untouchability, which he lives day in and day out, thrilled by the fact that the Mahatma "will talk about us,"[1] and he imagines himself rising onto the platform and sharing his woes with Gandhi. When Gandhi tells a story about a sweeper he has known, Bakha seems almost to enter the center of political life, identifying with that sweeper and taking part in his influence on such a powerful man. Yet the Mahatma's speech confuses him.

> "If there are any Untouchables here," he heard the Mahatma say, "they should realize that they are cleaning Hindu society." (He felt like shouting to say that he, an Untouchable, was there, but he did not know what the Mahatma meant by "cleaning Hindu society.") He gave ear to the words... "In order to emancipate themselves they have to purify themselves."... But, now the Mahatma is blaming us, Bakha felt. "That is not fair!"
>
> (148)

This passage echoes Bakha's discomfort during an earlier conversation with a missionary whose evocation of original sin also seemed to be blaming him for his condition ("everyone thinks us at fault" [133]). He feels conflicted about how to reconcile his gratitude for Gandhi's sympathy and his own clear sense, supported by all we have witnessed during this day-in-the-life narrative, that he is not at fault for his situation and cannot possibly "emancipate himself," as it seems Gandhi is asking him to do. In sorting through this conflict, he employs the language of ethics ("that is not fair!") and raises the question of Gandhi's focus on individual virtue as a first step toward political resistance, even as he thrills at Gandhi's ethical egalitarianism, his willingness to stand next to an untouchable on the platform, and his commitment to justice for those like Bakha.[2]

Immediately following Gandhi, however, a poet in the crowd offers another approach to the problem of untouchability and to India's status in the world, one that embraces the potential of modern technology and uses the language of political rights rather than ethical responsibilities. Gandhi is wrong to shut India off from the world and from the machine age, he argues. Not only will modern technology help alleviate India's poverty, it will also help liberate the untouchables from the labor that taints them, thus granting them political rights in civil society.

> When the sweepers change their profession, they will no longer remain Untouchables. And they can do that soon, for the first thing

we will do when we accept the machine, will be to introduce the machine which clears dung without anyone having to handle it—the flush system. Then the sweepers can be free from the stigma of untouchability and assume the dignity of status that is their right as useful members of a casteless and classless society.

(155)

For the poet, engaging with modernity carries with it potential access to a rational system of political rights, obviating the need for the broad discussion of virtue and personal responsibility proposed by Gandhi and generating a more recognizably political version of justice. For his part, Bakha, who has overheard this speech in the crowd, wonders at the miracle of the machine that can clear away dung and at the potential to improve his status without the ethical stigma of blame. He is attracted both to the strange power of the Mahatma, who has been willing to stand side by side with the untouchables, and by the promise of the flush toilet, which might mean political liberation from the age-old enslavement of sweeping. "Torn between his enthusiasm for Gandhi and the difficulties in his own awkward, naïve self" (157), Bakha dreams of a way to access both ethical and political forms of liberation, to revel in the Mahatma's wondrous recognition of the untouchables, even while dreaming that someday he will be able to find the miraculous machine that will grant him freedom.

Dropped into the end of Bakha's story, these episodes are often decried as failures of narrative continuity; surely they represent lacunae of sorts, moments when reported speech about public political issues seems to disrupt the progress of an otherwise personal narration. Yet we can also read them as important events of textual modernism, where gaps in narrative consistency can signal moments of alternate logic and where defamiliarization works on several levels at once, linking Bakha's naïve confusion in the crowd to the disruptive power of Indian politics and to the libratory potential of machine-age technology. They insinuate a complex narrative dynamic into the novel, one that unsettles its own temporal structure as the text swings from the static moment of the represented speech back to the progress of Bakha's day, even while gesturing toward the possible future of Indian modernity. Gandhi tells a story about an untouchable friend from his past, adding another layer of temporal disruption and embedded narration into the novel, which propels Bakha not only into Gandhi's orbit but also, when he identifies with the protagonist of Gandhi's story, into the center of a broader conversation about the place of tradition in the future of Indian modernity. The episode of the speech thus disrupts, supplants, and rewrites the action of *Untouchable*, inscribing into the level of the text a key problematic of modernity, which we might describe as an encounter with "a substantive range of sociohistorical phenomena [including] capitalism, bureaucracy, [and] technological development," as well as the accompanying "experiences of temporality and historical consciousness"[3]—or what Foucault calls an attitude toward time. At the same time, this day-in-the-life narrative is also infused with the temporal twists and uneven development of economic and political modernization.[4] As we reach the end of the novel, sinking back into Bakha's point of view, the sweeper's role has been transformed from naïve to perspicacious and from a position irrevocably bound to the past to one that pivots toward an uncertain future. His ethical perspective has intersected the most pressing matters of modernity and political justice for India even as, at the end of the narrative, he turns toward his family, his village, and the day-to-day challenge of his own untouchable status.

In this way, *Untouchable* brings to the fore the intertwined problems of untouchability and modernity while demonstrating the role of narrative in linking ethics and politics. The situation of Bakha, our naïve hero, is from the beginning of the novel one that entails him in ethical encounters, raises questions about his obligations to others (and of others toward him), and discloses the narrative dimension of the ethical problem of untouchability, even as it prompts us as readers to respond to that problem. E. M. Forster's classic preface to the novel puts the claim succinctly: "The sweeper is worse off than a slave,"[5] but over the course of his day that slave is nonetheless plagued by concern about his duty to do his job as sweeper and about his obligations to his father, his sister, and his neighbors. A key event in the novel concerns Bakha's attempt to help an injured high-caste boy whose mother reviles the sweeper's touch more than she cares about her son's welfare and berates Bakha for having picked up her stricken child and brought him to her. "What had he done to deserve such treatment?" Bakha asks himself, in outrage, pointing out his ethical obligation: "He loved the child . . . it was impossible not to pick him up" (116). This statement becomes an ethical pivot in the narrative, drawing a stark contrast between Bakha's thoughtful but naive perspective and the callousness of the townspeople, who feel no obligation, ethical or otherwise, toward an untouchable.

From this moment on, "untouchability" in this novel stands for not only ethical responsibility and its primordial obligations but also for its motivating position in the narrative of (a) modern Indian life. When, in the scene that follows, the missionary tells Bakha "we are all sinners" (130) or Gandhi asks the untouchables to purify themselves, the text highlights the disjunction between the public discourse surrounding the problem of untouchabilty and Bakha's ethical subjectivity, which throws the future into doubt. We might say that the untouchable boy represents the very principle of ethical obligation to an other—or, as Simon Critchley puts it (reading Derrida), the "infinite responsibility of unconditional hospitality"—and marks this obligation as a structuring principle of narrative, both fictional and national-historical.[6] The dilemma the novel seems to address, then, in both its content and its form, is how to place the ethical potential of the sweeper boy at the center of the story of untouchability and build from it new narratives of justice for India.

This episode also clearly foregrounds the political problem that arises from the complex temporalities of modernity in late-colonial India, where matters of independence and nation building gesture toward both the power of India's pre-British, agricultural past and also the new social models made possible by commerce, modernity, and the machine. Gandhi's political program of Swadeshi (self-reliance) is linked to the past and can seem in many ways antimodern. It encouraged Indians to throw off their colonial status by refusing to play their assigned role as consumers of British goods and by turning to previous modes of production and technologies, such as the traditional spinning wheel, that would help them become independent of British commodity capitalism and its commercial technology. At the same time, the legacy of Swadeshi, as scholars from Sumit Sarkar to Dipesh Chakrabarty have made clear, is not wholly antimodern.[7] If Ashis Nandy calls Gandhi's position "critical traditionalism," Chakrabarty will argue that the examination of the self (and its virtues) within an inexorably public realm, which accompanies the program of Swadeshi in India, creates a new version of subjectivity we might call the "Gandhian modern."[8] Bakha's dilemma—how to access a Gandhian modern subjectivity without relinquishing the liberating elements of technology and commerce or the access they might provide to political freedoms—represents the often-paradoxical dimensions of political modernity in late-colonial India.

In this way, *Untouchable* also brings to the fore one of the central arguments of this book: that narrative can play a crucial role in bridging the gap between ethics and politics, connecting ethical attitudes and responsibilities—ideas about what we ought to be and do—to active creation of political relationships and just conduct—what is right and possible within the power structures and discourses of our social life and institutions.[9] In narrative we put ethics into play and begin to imagine justice, acting to generate and respond to the social relationships and obligations that shape the future of our common world.[10] The ethical demands of alterity infuse the narrative situation and the process by which we attempt to respond to it even as the narrative itself takes place as an ethical event between writers and readers that responds to, intervenes in, and changes its rhetorical and social situation. As Derek Attridge puts it, "The distinctiveness of the ethical in literature . . . is that it occurs as an *event* in the process of reading, not a theme to be registered, a thesis to be grasped, or an imperative to be followed or ignored."[11] Problems of chronology, emplotment, voice, and structures of address all extend the question of how we narrate our ethical responsibility to others and foreground not only the "ethical consequences" of narration but also the "reciprocal claims binding teller, listener, witness, and reader" and the actions that arise from them.[12] Yet if we consider how narratives come into being, take up the matter of who narrates and from what location, or examine the rhetorical exigence within which a narrative is situated, we immediately verge on worldly questions of history and politics.[13]

Our political being-in-common and the structures of justice to which it gives rise develop out of our understanding of our responsibilities and obligations to ourselves and others within both the moral and social realms, and they emerge in the ways that we account for ourselves to others in narration. Hannah Arendt makes clear that this act of narration, which goes on between and among people, constitutes a "web of human relations" in which political action takes place.[14] As a genre or mode, narrative arises in conjunction with particular rhetorical situations or exigences that call forth its action in the world.[15] At the same time, by reordering, recasting, and reconfiguring events, characters, and stories, narrative functions as the site of innovation and re-creation of the world, the intersection of the aesthetic and epistemological in the creation of new "facts" or ways of viewing them, the construction of a new narrative world as an object of knowledge and sensation, and the work of language and the imagination to figure and transform this world.[16] "Such a position . . . does not imply that the universe is merely the product of our interpretations," to quote Kenneth Burke, but rather emphasizes the inescapable situatedness of the narrative text, whose "'discoveries' are nothing other than revisions made necessary by the nature of the world itself."[17] In arguing this point, I do not claim that imaginative narratives always intervene directly in the public sphere (though they may) or inevitably carry real-world political power. Rather, I recognize, along with Gayatri Spivak, that in order to have such power, the event of narration, which takes place "as an indeterminate sharing between writers and readers," would need a public arena and an audience predisposed to attend to it.[18] Yet, like Dipesh Chakrabarty, I want to "contemplate narrative . . . as a form of political intervention."[19] Our imaginative narratives, whether in the form of memoir, reportage, fiction, or essay, create what Paul Ricoeur calls a realm of "as if," where the world can be both described and redescribed[20] and where new possible worlds make ethical and political claims upon our understanding of this one.[21] When the imaginative re-creation of the world takes place within the narrative web of human situations and relationships, narrative engages with politics and the possibilities of future justice.

Further, as I will argue, whether written in the metropolitan centers of Europe, the long-marginalized spaces of late-colonial India, Civil War Spain, or the proletarian neighborhoods of the American Midwest, modernism brings to the fore narrative's role in helping us imagine justice. Modernism, I will claim, stands for a dynamic set of relationships, practices, problematics, and cultural engagements with modernity rather than a static canon of works, a given set of formal devices, or a specific range of beliefs. As Susan Stanford Friedman has argued, it escapes nominal definition, even as a plurality, and exceeds our efforts to describe it through its difference from what came before or after.[22] Even where modernism seems to exhibit certain formal preoccupations, such as textual defamiliarization, refusal of strict verisimilitude, or play with the vagaries of space and time, it is clear that these are neither necessary nor ubiquitous conditions but rather signs or symptoms of a particular attitude toward a specific literary horizon of expectations. Nor can we pretend that such a list of preoccupations stands in for the practices, relationships, or problematics that motivate the great variety of modernisms as they emerge worldwide.

Rather, I would argue, modernist narrative might best be seen as a constellation of rhetorical actions, attitudes, or aesthetic occasions, motivated by the particular and varied situations of economic, social, and cultural modernity worldwide and shaped by the ethical and political demands of those situations.[23] Its rhetorical activity exists in constant and perpetual relationship to the complex, various, and often vexing demands of the social practices, political discourses, and historical circumstances of modernity and the challenges they pose to systems of representation—even as its forms and attitudes sometimes hide this fact. Further, the aesthetic dimensions of modernist narrative enlist the play of imagination in creating possible worlds that emerge from, correct, revise, and re-create these social and political situations and do so through their "vigorous and persistent attempts to multiply and disturb modes of representation."[24] The very term "modernity" seems to inaugurate an aesthetic attitude of contingency that privileges the present, like Baudelaire's perpetual search for the "transitory, fleeting beauty of our present life." [25] Yet its investment in the "new" also gestures toward the possibility of a (political) future, even while remaining suspicious of historical teleologies, thereby opening a potential sphere of activity for even the most experimental or disruptive modernist texts.[26]

Emerging in a multiplicity of languages, locations, cultures, and social temporalities, as Spivak, Arjun Appardurai, and Chakrabarty remind us, modernism's local situations and commitments modulate the possible global meanings of modernism and modernity even as they remind us of the political challenges to which they respond. To be sure, when we move beyond the European centers that are the source for most common Euro-American definitions of modernism, we will find a wider range of formal preoccupations as well as a broader set of attitudes toward modernity than those we are used to recognizing. Many of the texts I will take up in this book, for example, test the boundaries between reportage and fiction or between memoir and bildungsroman as a means of rewriting the experience of reality under the pressure of economic and social modernization. They often foreground folkways and the marks of the vernacular as part of their encounter with the public discourses of modernity, and they experiment with narrative modes like *skaz* (or the sketch) as a means of unsettling the linear temporalities and narrative expectations of representative prose fiction. They sometimes begin from an intimate, embodied sensibility, which may exist in contact and concert with cosmopolitan attitudes toward ethics and justice, thus creating a fiction both intimate and global.

In other words, in ways often more dramatic than in the canonical modernisms of metropolitan Europe and the United States, the texts I will explore over the course of this book destabilize the division between partisanship and aesthetics—indeed, often challenging the distinction between these two terms, using narrative experimentation as a force of social activity and grounding their formal resistance to consensus-based realism in their oppositional political engagement. In this way, as I will argue, reading modernism transnationally shifts our perspective on the forms and commitments of modernism, asking us to recognize the rhetorical action its forms undertake and the continuum of political engagement that undergirds its worldwide emergence. In particular, this book will look to explicitly political writing in several global locations in an effort to challenge the distinction usually drawn between politically engaged writing and self-consciously aesthetic or experimental modernism; to resist the segregation of so-called thirties or overtly political writing from what was once called "high" modernism; and to emphasize situated political commitment as a narrative concern central to the many varieties of transnational modernism.

Scholars of postcolonialism have described how the "links between writings in different parts of the Empire, and at different times in the colonized or ex-colonized world" bring into play the problematics of empire in varied locations.[27] In a similar way, this book argues that the specific ethical and political imperatives of worldwide modernisms link works to one another, forming nodes of interconnection that, in turn, help to extend and illuminate modernism's political commitments and its varied roles in imagining justice around the globe. We have long taught ourselves to see the formal lines of influence that tie modernist texts to one another, linking Joyce or Proust to Woolf and (more recently) Ocampo, much as the gossamer webs link characters across London in *Mrs. Dalloway*. Jahan Ramazani has reminded us that modernist writers rarely fit neatly into national paradigms, and he argues for an alternate literary history in which "transnational creolization, hybridization, and interculturation become almost as basic to our understanding of modernism as they are of the postcolonial."[28] But rarely do we recognize that the social and political situations of modernism create alternative global lines of contact and association, which are equally important, unusual, and complex, such as the links between Joyce and Anand that I will explore in chapter 2. Frederic Jameson argues that modernism "must be seen as a project that re-emerges over and over again with the various national situations as a specific and unique national-literary task or imperative, whose cross cultural kinship with its neighbors is not always evident."[29] This book seeks to make that kinship visible, even when lines of direct influence or formal affinity are absent. Transnationalism, in my use of the term, becomes not just an adjective describing a particular cosmopolitan attitude among a specific set of texts or authors (though it is that, too)—it describes a web of social and textual interrelationships linking modernisms worldwide as well as an optic through which to see these links.

In this way my use of the term "transnational" bears some affinities with Ramazani's "transnational poetics" even as it also hopes to extend the term beyond the specific travels, influences, or allegiances of writers and their texts, focusing instead on the ethical, social, and political domains in which texts arise and circulate.[30] Ramazani argues convincingly that, "modernists translated their frequent geographic displacement and transcultural alienation into a poetics of bricolage and translocation, dissonance and defamiliarization."[31] Yet if Mulk Raj Anand devises *Untouchable* somewhere in the hybrid spaces between London, England, and Sabarmati, India, it is not this fact that creates his work as transnational. Rather, Anand's very literary practice, in which the category of "untouchability" becomes the nexus not only of narrative and linguistic innovation but also of deep engagement with the specific social, historical, and political problematics of Indian modernity, links his novel to modernisms engaged with similar problematics elsewhere. In this sense he participates in the spaces of "exchange and participation wherever processes of hybridization occur . . . without necessary mediation by the center" that Françoise Lionnet and Shu-Mei Shih attribute to "minor Transnationalism."[32] The interconnection of narrative experimentation with commitment to the representations of subaltern experience that we see in Anand's work, as much as his use of irony, defamiliarization, or internal points of view, ties Anand to Joyce and, in more oblique ways, to Woolf and the other modernists I consider in this book. Indeed, Anand foregrounds this connection in his *Conversations in Bloomsbury*, remembering that it was in recognizing, during the General Strike of 1926, the similarities between London's workers and India's downtrodden that he became able to imagine a politically committed modernism for India.[33] In other words, the text need not be explicitly preoccupied with themes of dislocation, hybridity, or transculturation, nor the author an exile or itinerant, for a narrative to function transnationally. Even when resolutely local in its concerns or national in its literary ambitions, a narrative may also illuminate and engage the many nodes of interconnection, both literary and political, that interlink modernisms worldwide.

I also employ the term "transnational" as a critical optic that shares the oppositional valence of the prefix "trans-" in such words as "transgress" and "transform." In addition to simply meaning "across, over, and beyond," the prefix "trans-" can imply "on the other side of," representing not only a crossing of boundaries but also a challenge to the normative dimension of the original entity or space. Most prominently, the prefix has this valence in contemporary transgender and transsexual theory, where, as scholars like Judith Halberstam and Susan Stryker employ it, "trans-" has come to stand not only for gender or sexual identities that have crossed from one side of a binary field to the other but also for "anything that disrupts, denaturalizes, rearticulates and makes visible" the links we assume to exist between a sexual body and the social roles it is expected to play. Transgender studies thus engages with the ethical and moral dimensions of the fact that "people experience and express their gender in fundamentally different ways" and concerns itself with combating the political "injustices and violence that often attend the perception of gender nonnormativity."[34] In a similar way, the "trans-" dimension of the transnational critical optic I employ in this book seeks to denaturalize the connection between modernist narrative and its Euro-metropolitan contexts as, more generally, between the nation-state and literary forms; to raise the ethical dimensions of texts that operate both within and across national horizons of expectation; and to highlight the political implications of this nonnormative movement on both local and global levels. This book thus seeks not simply to accommodate modernism's less-explored Spanish, Indian, or Caribbean versions, or to illuminate the sometimes oblique or effaced lines of contact between and among them, but also to mark their importance to a reconceived transnational model of modernism and a revised critical practice. By examining the forms, attitudes, and commitments of a variety of transnational modernist narratives, whether memoir, reportage, fiction, or essay, I hope to discover the extraordinary engagement with matters of public justice that infuses global literary modernism and the nodes of contact and interconnection that generate its commitments.

From Ethics to Politics

Contemporary critics rarely mention ethics and politics in the same breath. Levinas is notoriously reticent on matters of politics while contemporary democratic theorists from John Rawls to Amartya Sen avoid bringing ethics into the conversations about modern, liberal notions of justice.[35] Yet the connection between ethics and politics extends back to Aristotle, who defined ethics as "knowledge of the

Good" and politics as a corollary of ethics: "instances of morally fine and just conduct" and the social systems that encourage them.[36] For Aristotle, ethics seems to be preliminary to politics, concerned as it is with the development of virtues among individuals, while justice becomes the exercise of virtue "in relation to somebody else," and political justice in particular "obtains between those who share a life for the satisfaction of their needs as persons free and equal"—in other words, as citizens.[37]

Philosophers have made many attempts since Aristotle to calibrate the relationship between ethics and politics and the status of justice between them, which often hinges on epistemology and the matter of experience in the world. Hume, for example, begins by arguing for a clear distinction between morality, which arises from "passions, motives, volitions, and thoughts" and comes to us by way of our "impressions or sentiments," and matters of material fact that can be "discovered by the understanding" or experienced directly.[38] The importance of morality is not diminished by this fact/value split; for Hume, impressions, sentiments, and passions are crucial to the way that we apprehend and make sense of the world. However, Hume objects to accounts that attempt to derive the matter of "ought," or ethics, from propositions about matters of fact (3.1.1 469), and this objection has become something like a law (called Hume's Guillotine) for philosophy: there can be no ethical conclusions that arise from premises of fact—no "ought" follows from any discussion of what "is."[39] Hume considers justice to be an artificial "social virtue," an aspect of morality that develops from human experience of the world and that primarily concerns conduct among individuals in society. Since it is governed by the principle of "utility" rather than some innate moral quality, justice depends "on the particular state and condition, in which men are placed," with its merit being its "usefulness to the public." Justice, therefore, may be seen in Hume to connect what "is" to what "ought to be" in society, belonging both to the realm of morals and to the domain of politics, war, and peace.[40]

Kant clearly distinguishes ethics from politics, defining ethics as "the totality of unconditionally mandatory laws according to which we ought to act" and politics as "the art of using [the] mechanism [of nature] for ruling men," seen primarily through deeds and actions.[41] Since ethics responds to universal or a priori principles while politics concerns practical rules based on "mere experience," only laws that move beyond experience to accord with universal principles may be termed ethical. Yet Kant argues for the compatibility of ethics and politics and the integration of theory with practice. It would "be absurd" to propose a theory of ethics without supposing that it is possible to act among men in the sphere of politics in accord with our ethical duty.[42] Rather, we might hope for a moral politician, bound by the demands of the categorical imperative and the universal law of right and able to bring those principles to bear on his response to experiences in the world.[43] Further, Kant will claim in "On Perpetual Peace" that "true politics can never take a step without rendering homage to morality. . . . All politics must bend its knee before the right."[44] The goal in politics, then, must be to develop actions that accord with the principles of ethical duty and instantiate what we might call justice. Clearly, for Kant, ethics takes priority over politics and determines the very possibility of justice, which in turn guides our experiences of the world.

Many theorists since Kant, however, separate ethics from politics more definitively, arguing, on the one hand, that ethics need not concern itself with the practical power relations of politics and, on the other, that political justice should not be bound by a normative morality. For example, the early-twentieth-century Cambridge philosopher G. E. Moore, whose system of aesthetics was deeply influential in Bloomsbury, developed an analytical metaethics concerned primarily with understanding the nature of ethical statements and judgments. His *Principia Ethica* distinguishes the matter of ethics from that of politics (and from other metaphysical questions) by claiming that ethics is a science concerned with the question of defining the "good" and distinguished from inquiry into the more complex notion of "good conduct."[45] Moore calls the "good" a "simple" notion that cannot be further broken down or explained; "just as you cannot, by any manner of means, explain to anyone who does not know it, what yellow is, so you cannot explain what good is."[46] It is a particular sort of fact in the world that cannot be proven with reference to scientific principles and has no necessary connection to motivations, actions, or individual virtues. Thus Moore and other analytic philosophers who followed him would argue that their reflections on the status of moral reasoning or the nature of the good have few immediate consequences for our practical understanding of conduct in society or for politics.

In a different way, the contemporary ethical theory of Emmanuel Levinas notoriously avoids describing the relationship between ethics and politics and clearly "favors" ethics over politics.[47] For Levinas, ethical responsibility for an other predates the individual's consciousness of self and freedom. Rather than explore the ontology of being or its conduct in the world, Levinas argues that the "first and final question" is not "how being justifies itself" but how it responds to a preexisting ethical responsibility to another.[48] In other words, for Levinas ethics "does not supplement a preceding existential base; the very mode of the subjective is knotted in ethics understood as responsibility."[49] His writing insists upon the other as "infinitely foreign"—the responsibility one feels in the face of the other must arise from beyond the call of the known. This is the radical challenge that Levinas's thought poses to philosophy—the refusal not just of a primary ontology, preceding ethics, but of a philosophy where the other is understood with reference to what is the same. It inheres in the very definition Levinas gives to ethics: "A calling into question of the same . . . brought about by the presence of the other."[50] Politics does not intercede at this level and must be considered secondary.[51]

On the other side of the question, for contemporary liberal political theorists such as John Rawls—whose *Theory of Justice* has been immensely influential over the past forty years—politics is also a second-order formation, but one entered into by self-complete and primarily self-interested individuals. An individualized ethics serves as the background for politics and as a means of generating a political conception of justice concerned with individual rights and freedoms.[52] Rawls's important 1985 essay "Justice as Fairness: Political Not Metaphysical," argues that "a political conception of justice is, of course, a moral conception, it is a moral conception worked out for a specific kind of subject, namely for political, social and economic institutions." Because Rawls's liberalism presumes deep pluralism on matters of religion and morality within the private sphere, he argues that "no general moral conception can provide a publicly recognized basis for a conception of justice in a modern democratic state."[53] Justice concerns the "assignment of rights and duties" and the regulation of "social and economic advantages" within the social structure that is set up in order to provide equality of opportunity and citizenship to individuals.[54]

Yet Rawls's model of justice depends on the assumption that rational self-interest will lead toward broad consensus around the mutually advantageous principle of fairness in the public sphere. He argues that despite the fact that people may harbor different notions of the good, which may raise competing demands, they will nonetheless recognize that "to pursue their own different conceptions of the good they need the same . . . basic rights, liberties and opportunities." He also claims that from an original, position-blind standpoint, these citizens will agree that all goods be distributed equally, unless an unequal distribution benefits the least advantaged.[55] As Amartya Sen points out, Rawls's notion of the principle of fairness seems to ignore the fact that a number of ethical choices about how and when to apply the distributive principle are central to its implementation. I would add that it is grounded on assumptions about the commensurability of persons that have deep ethical implications.[56] Rawlsian liberalism remains a resolutely political system, based on a contractual notion of justice that separates itself from the matter of ethical subjectivity and that sidesteps important questions about the status of individuals and their differential positioning that affects the matter of fairness among them.

This critical disjunction between ethics and politics makes a rapprochement not only more difficult but also, I would argue, more crucial.[57] It is this rapprochement that we can see nascent in *Untouchable* and that will be the subject of this book.[58] If ethics along either analytical or Levinasian lines steps away from the pragmatic, political situation of subject-citizens, it nonetheless carries implications for the conceptions of justice and the political structures that arise from that situation. As several contemporary feminists have pointed out, there are many reasons to regard the intimate, ethical domain as also important for the political development of matters of justice, community, and citizenship.[59] The citizen's extension of care to a neighbor, the child's response to a filial demand, even the lover's welcoming gesture toward her partner can raise matters of ethical awareness that carry with them not only the kinds of concerns of self and other, responsibility and obligation, that Levinas assigns to ethics but also implications for the surrounding relationships that undergird our notions of political community. This is what Derrida alludes to in his work on the reciprocity of the guest and host; each is caught up in a relationship of ethical responsibility, made no less complex or politically demanding (or perhaps more so) for being outside the existing domain of public laws or institutions.[60]

Indeed, we might argue that the Levinasian ethical subject, preengaged by the experience of the call of the other, opens the way toward a social notion of subjectivity that has clear implications for the matter of justice defined as the exercise of virtue "in relation to somebody else."[61] Jean-Luc Nancy elaborates just such a vision, arguing for a "between us as first philosophy" that might be seen as a parallel to Levinas's "ethics as first philosophy" within the political domain. Rather than presuppose some sort of original social antagonism, or a responsibility to an other who remains outside the self, Nancy posits plurality as a primary condition of being, or "being singular plural."[62] In a challenge to the "virile subject"—that is, the contained punctual self at the core of most conceptions of individual rights within Western political theory (Rawls included), Nancy describes a self that coexists with those around it in a primordial situation of being-with that Nancy calls community and that marks the beginning of justice.[63] As a consequence, for Nancy justice must always be cognizant of the ethical obligations between and among individuals and is dependent on the political communities they form. It cannot be separated out as belonging either to ethics or politics. Kelly Oliver makes a similar claim, arguing that if we understand the subject to be eminently social rather than isolated or punctual, then human relationships become the core of both ethical and judicial decision making.[64]

Thus, I would claim, the ways we describe our political being-in-common, or community[65] and the rights and privileges we grant within it grow inexorably out of our understanding of our responsibilities and obligations to ourselves and others within a moral realm even as they respond to the situations, experiences, actions, and forms of our being among others in the world.[66] Our commitment to fairness or justice begins with our attitudes toward being among others and our understanding of the ethical demands of plurality. Anthony Appiah reminds us that "the ethical task each of us has—our life making—is inevitably bound up with the ethical life of others."[67] Ethics as an attitude or activity within the sphere of community, rather than a set of common principles or a normative domain, becomes essential to the ordering of our lives together, and to the "ensemble of human relations in their real, social structure" that we might call politics.[68]

But when it privileges the practical sphere of publicly recognized, legal conceptions of justice, contemporary political theory often avoids grappling with the ethical assumptions about identity, community, and citizenship that lie at its core.[69] Clearly, the conception of the free and equal citizen at the heart of liberal thought grows out of assumptions about individuality, the moral commensurability of persons, and the secondary nature of the political contract that carry implications for the definition of justice. But the assumption of sameness or commensurability as the basis for equality can be deeply problematic for women and others marginalized by the construction of the citizen in the Western political tradition[70] while the problem of who counts as a member with standing within any political community raises questions, in the context of a globalizing world, that challenge liberal assumptions about the distribution of goods and benefits within the bounded polity of a nation-state.[71]

This problem has been of particular concern to feminists, who point out that in the past women's experiences have rarely figured into the ethical scenarios of philosophers (Levinas included) or into the construction of the universal citizen-subject of Western thought. Hegel's reading of *Antigone* is a case in point here, as Irigaray makes clear, for Antigone serves Hegel not only as the "the other of reason, ethics, and knowledge" but also, in both her commitment to family and her marginalization, as a measure of the incompatibility of the activity of caring with public ethics or justice.[72] For Hegel, Antigone's actions represent the woman's "intuitive awareness of what is ethical" but do not pass "over into the consciousness of universality" that is required for participation in the realm of law and justice.[73] Clearly, as David Harvey puts it, "like space, time and nature, 'justice' is . . . socially constituted" and "expressive of social relations and contested configurations of power."[74] There cannot be a position-blind, universal position, except as an experiment in thought, nor can we assume that justice flows without regard to the variable positions of its subjects or sweeps them into a common body of consensus.

The challenge for current theory, liberal or otherwise, is to understand the moral and political implications of what Charles Taylor calls our "modern social imaginaries," which organize "the ways people imagine their social existence, how they fit together with others, how things go on between them and their fellows, the expectations that are normally met, and the deeper normative notions and images that underlie these expectations."[75] These social imaginaries provide the grounds for our construction of communities, as well as our understanding of our situation in the world, among others. Rather than being simply normative or constitutive of a common morality, social imaginaries should be understood, I would argue, as spheres of moral activity and attitudes toward justice that guide our actions in the world and generate rhetorical situations and narrative exigence. At the same time, the notions of being-in-common or community at the heart of any social imaginary carry implications for regimes of justice and of power, as well as for the constitution of publicly recognized structures of political society. The possibility of a radical democratic politics understood as based on contingent identities and dispersed antagonisms and allegiances depends upon just such a model of the social imaginary, one that understands community as primordial and inescapable but not derived from a single universalized experience, predicated on normative unity, or dependent on a singular consensus for its model of justice.[76]

Further, I would argue, imagination and the aesthetic lie at the heart of this socially constitutive activity. The imaginary domain takes us beyond the given, beyond the situation of our political being-in-common and its demands,[77] and toward a realm of "as if" that can move towards greater freedom and justice.[78] This is not simply a matter of creating an imaginative realm parallel or analogous to the political, without connection to the world or transformative potential. The philosopher Hans Vaihinger points out that fictive activity undergirds many of our most important insights "in all branches of thought,"[79] helping the scientist or the philosopher construct knowledge about the world by way of arguments and scenarios. The fictionalizing process of positing an "as if" thus becomes a means of making claims about the world rather than some sort of escape from it. Similarly, I'd argue, the social imaginary can be the place where the demands of the world become configured, contested, and reconfigured and where new situations, relationships, and attitudes are created, tested, and put into play. We can approach this notion from a number of different directions—from Drucilla Cornell's assertion that only in the "as if" space of the imaginary domain can we demand a reorientation of the public construction of justice; from Alan Badiou's insistence that only when we think beyond specific social and political circumstances can we hope to "invent a new way of being and acting in the situation;" from Nancy Fraser's focus on the imagination as crucial to the process of realigning political space beyond the borders of the nation-state in a globalizing world; or simply from Jacques Rancière's definition of politics as a "cluster of perceptions and practices that shape [our] common world."[80] "Imagination" as the overarching name for these perceptions, practices, and expectations can carry the power to revise and reconfigure the world.

And narrative is at the heart of this constitutive process of imagination.[81] In narrative we open the reciprocal process of accounting for ourselves to others by asking and answering the question "who are you?" which unites teller and listener in a mutual relationship of responsibility, though not necessarily in similarity, normativity, or consensus.[82] As we read, we are invited to respond to the challenge of each narrative and to its singularity in a way that acknowledges not only its otherness and its claims on us but also how the narrative asks us to understand it as acting in the world and its implications for how we imagine structures of social and political responsibility.[83] Chantal

Mouffe has argued that within a democracy the variety of discourses of justice will emerge as articulated "nodal points" around which we attempt to fix our social relations, however provisionally.[84] Narratives, I'd argue, can operate as just such nodal points, generating models of association and accountability that order our social and political relationships in connection with surrounding (and perhaps competing) discourses and in response to the demands of historical and political situations. The encounter between reader and text thus becomes a politically situated one, where the reader is responsible not only to the narration proper, or to its narrator, but also to the rhetorical demands of the time/space[85] of its creation and the political imperatives that set the reading in action, which are invariably social. In other words, through narration the social imaginary moves irrevocably beyond the bounds of the individual ethical encounter to play an active role in the imaginative construction of a common justice within the political domain.

Narrative Action

This kind of situated understanding of narration relies upon the connection between word and deed, which gives rise to action and, according to Hannah Arendt, becomes the basis of both ethics and politics.[86] As a process rather than a substantive thing, action (or acting) expresses the intersubjective identity of people who always exist in the realm of company or politics.[87] These relationships inform our process of ethical judgment: "We judge and tell right from wrong by having present in our mind some incident and some person ... that have become examples ... our decisions about right and wrong will depend upon our choice of company, of those with whom we wish to spend our lives." From this notion of profound intersubjectivity Arendt develops what she calls "enlarged thinking" or the "enlarged mentality," a mentality that acknowledges the perspectives and voices of those around us and is derived from the web of stories in which we are situated.[88] It is this mentality that creates our profound *sensus communis*, or "common sense," and that begins the movement toward politics.

But Arendt closely links enlarged thinking and action to speech, discourse, stories, and narrative. Acting and speaking become paired activities that present human identity through the creation of stories. We can think of these stories as human life stories; as she puts it,

"Every individual life between birth and death can eventually be told as a story." Human history is made out of a myriad of these stories, which are generated through human utterance and action. But they may also become part of the aesthetic realm of narrative. "It is because of this already existing web of human relationships . . . in which action alone is real, that it 'produces' stories with or without intention. . . . These stories may then be recorded in documents and monuments, they may be visible in use objects or art works, they may be told and retold and worked into all kinds of material."[89] Thus, for Arendt action and the process of creating stories, including those stories found in artworks, are not only irretrievably linked but also crucial for the human sphere of politics.

These human stories, I would add, also have the constitutive power to generate an ethical relation within the web of human interaction. The self that is produced in and through life stories and narration—what Adriana Cavarero calls the "narratable self"—exists always in relation to others, in response to their questioning gaze and our attempts to account for ourselves to others in narrative. As Cavarero puts it, "One always appears to someone. One cannot appear if there is no one else there." Or, in the context of narration, it is clear that one always tells one's story to an audience, real or imagined, which is irrevocably other from oneself yet crucial to the possibility of the story. "The altruistic ethics of relation does not support empathy, identifications, or confusions. . . . No matter how much you are similar and consonant, says this ethic, your story is never my story."[90] At the same time, each story intersects with other stories, and we can see that Arendt's web of relationships can also be described as a web of stories, each contingent on the others, none self-complete, all in irrevocable ethical relationship to one another.

But as soon as we are situated within a plurality—that community or company whose perspectives or stories we consider when we reason or judge, or that web of stories that surrounds the narratable self—we are in the realm of politics. As Arendt makes clear, "I am only with my own self or the self of another when I am thinking, whereas I am in the company of the many when I start to act. Power for human beings . . . can only reside in one of the many forms of plurality."[91] We can describe the transition from ethics to politics in this way: We begin to reason morally by entering into company with others, expanding the realm of our thinking from the self or other to the several. We judge by imagining the positions of others, interacting with them, as in a community. We act by disclosing ourselves to others in speech and narration—"in sheer human togetherness"—and we act *politically* when we imagine that human togetherness to be a polity, however ephemeral.[92] The transition to politics and action from ethics is thus one of degree rather than of kind, moving from the one to the several and finally into the realm of a potential polity. Arendt's theory helps us understand that in order to exert power in the world, or to move from ethics to politics, one would not only strive toward being otherwise, as Levinas suggests, or, following Nancy, acknowledge the primacy of being-with, but one would also seek to create in the world a version of ethical company or community. Thus Kant's *sensus communis*—the "sense that fits us into a community with others, makes us members of it, and enables us to communicate things"[93]—becomes a call to political action, a call to create communities, however provisional, where we can communicate our ethical positions and where they matter.

But we can also take Arendt's notion of the interconnection of action and story further into the realm of the imagination, which exists in tandem with action in the world.[94] On the one hand, we might say that imaginative narrative provides a laboratory of action where we "try out" our ability to act.[95] On the other hand, as I have claimed, it may be understood as a form of action whose power is predicated on its very distinction from life and the impossibility of a one-to-one referentiality or direct mimesis. It is just this sort of active power that modernism explores and expands and that flows directly from its narrative experimentation. According to Paul Ricoeur, fiction has "a double valence with respect to reference: it is directed elsewhere, even nowhere; but because it designated the nonplace in relation to all reality, it can directly sight this reality . . . this new reference-effect is nothing but the power of fiction to *redescribe* reality."[96] In other words, by creating an imaginative version of characters, relationships, stories, and events within the realm of human affairs, the narrative text becomes a laboratory for action in the world, committed not to mirroring reality but to redescribing and reworking it.[97]

Thus, along with Arendt, Cavarero, and Ricoeur, I will argue that imaginative prose narrative offers a place where selves can account for their being among others in the world and where the process of acting in the world may be recorded, instantiated, and reimagined. If the stories people tell are the ways that they create and communicate their being in the world, then narrating becomes a crucial form of activity, one that expresses subjectivity as it unfolds over time, among and to others, in the human sphere or social imaginary, and in active response to rhetorical and social exigence. In the guise of a "laboratory," or the realm of "as if," narrative can provide the space for the exercise of ethical and imaginative freedom and, by virtue of its social situatedness, can also anticipate or rework relationships in the world.

Because of its position "at the crossroads" of theories of rhetoric, action, ethics, and politics, narrative becomes the place where matters of responsibility and ethical encounter intersect with the imaginative refiguring of the world.[98] The narrative text, like any example of a genre or mode, acts in response to "situational 'demands'" and presents a recognizable fusion of motive and narrative "action."[99] The singularity of the literary text puts in play a set of actions, readings, and relationships conditioned in many ways by regimes of conduct and power. Yet if we understand the singularity of the text as exceeding "pre-existing determinations" or moving beyond "the possibilities pre-programmed by a culture's norms," then the actions and relationships invited by the text also have the potential to exceed predetermined expectations of conduct or ideologies and to generate alternate patterns of political community and justice.[100]

To return to the example of *Untouchable*: it is clear at the end of the novel that Bakha's ethical subjectivity and his political situation are at odds. While the text highlights the ethical dimension of Bakha's relationships and behavior toward others, it emphasizes the absolute disenfranchisement he faces and the disappearance of his everyday concerns from the political debates that dominate the end of the novel. If Gandhi's ethical egalitarianism and the uprising that we glimpse among the "millions of faces" in the crowd seem to offer Bakha little hope for change (at least for the time being), what does the poet's version of politics offer him? As his speech makes clear, laws alone will not change Bakha's untouchable status.[101] But at the end of the novel the socialist vision of "a casteless and classless society" also seems unreachable, a dream of a future world, perhaps, but not one that will liberate Bakha in the near term. Still, the text makes clear that the problem of untouchability is both an ethical and a political concern, imbricated in complex ways with the matter of India's colonial status and its modernity and concerned with the "socially constituted set of beliefs, discourses, and institutionalizations expressive of social relations and contested configurations of power" that, according to David Harvey, marks the terrain of justice.[102]

Further, as we have seen, the novel generates this ethicopolitical connection at the textual level, weaving modernity's uneven development into Bakha's oscillation between Gandhi and the machine and generating the possibility of justice from the combined naïveté and perspicacity of Bakha's meandering point of view. The novel's innovative narrative voice and its multiplication of styles, voices, and perspectives help unsettle the consensus view of untouchability and to disperse responsibility for Bakha's condition, and for the condition of India at large, throughout the text. Derek Attridge claims that "there is a sense in which the formally innovative work, the one that most estranges itself from the reader makes the most sharply challenging ... ethical demand."[103] While I do not believe that formal experimentation in and of itself generates ethical or political engagement, or that less innovative narratives make fewer claims on our moral sensibilities, I will argue that the experimentalism of *Untouchable* and the other narratives I will take up in this book is crucial to their ethicopolitical power, exhibiting the incommensurate experiences, uneven relationships, disrupted perspectives, and political uncertainties that characterize Bakha's modernity. I will not dwell longer on this complex and deeply moving novel here; chapter 2 will return to Anand and to the dimensions of his modernism. Still, the end of the novel hints at the way that narrative focalization, defamiliarization, refusal of closure, and play with the boundaries of fact and fiction both participate in the novel's response to the challenge of caste behavior, the geopolitics of colonialism, and the politicization of everyday life that marks Indian modernity and also help generate an Indian modernism that is at once formally innovative and deeply politically engaged.

Modernist Commitments

This is not to claim that we must remake the modern novel into a vehicle for narrative morality or describe it as providing "equipment for living," in Kenneth Burke's famous phrase.[104] Nor need we claim that modernist narrative always exhibits the direct political communication that Sartre, for example, describes in committed writing. For Sartre, prose writing is essentially communicative and utilitarian in that it displays the world for its audience and asks the audience to respond.[105] The prose writer (as opposed to the poet or painter) acts through his or her language; "he designates, demonstrates, orders, refuses, interpolates, begs, insults, persuades, insinuates" in a manner that can provoke political indignation or enthusiasm.[106] The focus then is on the position or, to use existential language, the "choice" of the writer, which is communicated through words to the reader. While the poet makes words into objects, the prose writer uses words to signify or indicate his commitment in relation to a condition of the world. Thus for Sartre, prose seems irrevocably tied to the mimetic function of realism, its political activity linked to the communication or disclosure of the writer's political position vis-à-vis the world.[107] This disclosure or unveiling of the world with the purpose of changing it, of course, requires the writer to develop new modes and techniques. Sartre does not suggest that only the most direct or most straightforward prose serves this purpose. But in distinguishing prose from poetry (at least modernist poetry), Sartre indicates his allegiance to transparency of form in literature, to *meaning* as such: "The writer deals with meanings."[108] Anything that gets in the way of meaning or the communication of the author's action, including the creation of aesthetic objects or the manipulation of form, is therefore suspect.

But certainly the author does not only deal with meanings. This is the central point of Adorno's celebrated critique of Sartre: "Although no word that enters into a work of literature divests itself fully of the meanings it possesses in communicative speech, still, in no work, not even the traditional novel, does this meaning remain untransformed."[109] Sartre's theory of the committed writer does not fully take into account the political ramifications of the transformations of form—the ramifications that I have been exploring throughout this chapter and that will be the focus of this book. Contra Sartre, Adorno claims that "there is no content, no formal category of the literary work that does not, however transformed and however unawarely, derive from the empirical reality from which it has escaped. It is through this relationship, and though the process of regrouping its moments in terms of its formal law, that literature relates to reality."[110] From this perspective, only in *rejecting* transparency and direct relationship to reality can art become politically engaged.

It is not surprising that Adorno will turn to modernism to find examples of the kind of political resistance through form that he calls "engagement." It bears stopping for a minute, then, to consider the implications of his aesthetics for understanding the political potential of modernist narrative. For Adorno, what matters most in considering the literary text's engagement is understanding the dialectical relationship between world and artwork. Rather than existing in some sort of complementary or mirroring relationship, art is defined by its essential otherness from reality and its efforts to differentiate or "seclude itself from the world." In its form, writing not only distinguishes itself from the reality it inhabits but also in doing so critiques that reality.

"Even the most sublime work of art takes up a definite position *vis à vis* reality by stepping outside of reality's spell, not abstractly once and for all, but occasionally and in concrete ways, when it unconsciously and tacitly polemicizes against the condition of society at a particular point in time."[111] So, we might say, the moments where a modernist text foregrounds its technique or steps out of a mimetic mode become the moments of tacit critique and opposition to the status quo.

These moments are not unlike what I have been calling "redescription"—places where the text casts a new version of the world or intervenes in its unfolding in a manner that resists or revises social reality. The crucial addition, however, that comes to us through Adorno is the notion that this redescription need not be bound to a wishful verisimilitude or a utopian version of a realistic future. Rather, the disruption of mimetic realism is precisely where the possibility of redescription emerges, and moments of linguistic or textual nontransparency open up the text not just away from reality but also toward critique. Thus, we might imagine, in the Woolfian context, the critique of advertising and propaganda in the opening pages of *Mrs. Dalloway* as the aeroplane spells its nearly indecipherable message of consumption across the London sky, or, in the Joycean context, the critique of bourgeois Dublin and commodity culture that inheres in the formal anomalies of the "Circe" chapter, where, as Franco Moretti reminds us, commodities literally come to life,[112] or, as I will discuss in chapter 3, the opposition to British imperialism that emerges through the use of language in *Ulysses* and *The Portrait of the Artist as a Young Man*. Adorno points out that Kafka's resistance to monopoly capitalism is made more salient because it is not addressed directly as a matter of theme but rather emerges in the interrelationship between social content and language use: "By zeroing in on the dregs of the administered world, he laid bare the inhumanity of a repressive totality, and he did so more powerfully and uncompromisingly than if he had written novels about corruption in multi-national corporations."[113] Thus, engagement emerges obliquely through form's departure from everyday reality and its opposition to a given social world.

But there is reason to distance ourselves from Adorno's assumption that the social significance of modernist art, or art more generally, is its "opposition, at the level of artistic form, to the existing world and . . . its readiness to aid and shape that world."[114] Though his theory helps us understand the possibilities of a noninstrumental politics, the way back to the world that emerges out of radically experimental texts, and the potential for critique in the fractured forms and languages of many varieties of modernism, it posits the work's autonomy and its disengagement from reality as a first principle.[115] As I have argued, literary modernism knits together aesthetics and the ethicopolitical experience of modernity so that the world becomes the problematic to be addressed, transformed, configured, and reconfigured, rather than refused. The text is inseparable from the rhetorical exigence that calls it into being; it cannot refrain from acting in the world. Further, Adorno seems to privilege the work of art as an autonomous element arising out of history rather than being produced within it. Its potential to resist arises from this separate status. Yet we must heed Raymond Williams's reminder that "the analysis of representation is not a subject separate from history . . . the representations are part of the history, contribute to the history, are active elements in the way that history continues; in the way people perceive situations, both from inside their own pressing realities and from outside them."[116] Across its worldwide range of practices, locations, and temporalities, modernist narrative not only inscribes the pressing realities of historical modernities but is inseparable from them.

Further, as Williams also points out, modernists' efforts to disconnect themselves from the bourgeois culture in Europe at the end of the nineteenth century often put them in contact with movements of social and political opposition.[117] Thus, the processes of disconnection and critique become two sides of the same coin. The disassociation from reality instigated by antirealist form or by efforts to bring the disruptions of modernization into the realm of aesthetics was often part of a broader attempt to disengage from dominant culture and to construct an alternative social imaginary. Symbolism and anarchism grew up together; manifestos of futurism or vorticism are manifestos of both aesthetic and political movements; feminism operates in the political and aesthetic domains at once. Yet the codification and canonization of modernism at midcentury erased the political allegiances of modernism, and its ultimate commercial success brought it safely into the fold of dominant culture.[118] Therefore, if we are to rethink modernism's role in imagining justice, we need to re-create the social and political implications of its refusal of verisimilitude, its blurring of fact and fiction, its disruption of conventions of genre or narrative structures of address, its display of uneven temporalities, its destabilization of the fact/value split, and other styles and attitudes as they arise around the world.

Further, in his celebrated essay "When Was Modernism?," Williams makes clear that the delimiting of modernism—as a formal movement requiring avant-garde technique; as a product of a particular period from the late nineteenth century to the mid-twentieth century; as a select and self-referential canon of "works of radical estrangement"; and, finally, as a universalized commodity that passes easily back into the mainstream of late capitalism—must be seen as an act of ideology that erases the complex relationships between modernisms and cultures and that silences modernist critique.[119] Clearly, the selection of a period for modernism has always been arbitrary, disputed, and tied to particular critical categories and national literary histories. Williams points out that if we privilege texts that are "outriders, heralds, and witnesses to social change" then we may ask why the "metaphoric control and economy of seeing discovered and refined by Gogol, Flaubert or Dickens from the 1840s on, should not take precedence over the conventionally modernist names of Proust, Kafka, or Joyce."[120] A similar point may be made about the usual periodization of modernism. When we segregate so-called thirties literature from the mainstream of American and European modernism, we necessarily define modernism against social and political engagement.[121] The means by which scholars separated work by George Orwell, Rebecca West, the radical American writers of the 1930s, or the members of the so-called Auden generation from canonical modernism was precisely the degree of political commitment in evidence in their writing—and the means of recuperating them for modernism, as many scholars have recently begun to do, is often to argue for their formal complexity. Commitment that seems to take precedence over form remains a sort of marker for "that-which-is-not-modernism."

Yet if we resurrect the long tradition of engaged, antibourgeois writing within the history of literary modernisms, and we recognize the role of experience in relation to both ethics and politics in the development of modernism, then we will not mistakenly presume that to be *engagé* means being less interested in form or that the avant-garde need fetishize form to such an extent as to extinguish the language of political commitment. Further, the principle of "radical estrangement" so often applied to modernism as a formal criterion, at least in its early-twentieth-century, European version, or as an element of Adornian negative dialectics, can also have strong political implications. In Orwell's *Homage to Catalonia*, which I will discuss in chapter 4, the experience of the Spanish Civil War becomes one of ongoing estrangement or defamiliarization, which disrupts our assumptions about both British and Spanish politics and produces a genre that acts in the world by mediating between memoir and propaganda.

For the Spanish writer Max Aub, the tortured geographies of wartime Spain give rise to a labyrinthine novel cycle that bears witness to the horror of total war while challenging the boundaries between home and battle fronts. In Anand's work, as we have seen, estrangement on the level of language, marks not only the site of ethics but also the place of potential resistance to colonialism. The novel's challenge to the tradition of the bildungsroman emerges from its translocation of the genre into the time/space of a colonial untouchable and confrontation with the demands of that geography.

Transnational Optics

The problem of delimiting modernism, which Williams ties to the matter of periodization, clearly also has a geographical dimension. Williams is careful to locate his analysis in Europe and particularly in what he calls the "great imperial capitals of Paris, Vienna, Berlin, and Petersburg," as well as London and New York.[122] The specific histories of these cities and the movements of people and capital between and among them within the economy of late capitalism are crucial for modernism in Europe in the early to mid-twentieth century, and to Williams' critique of it. But, it must be said, specifying the locations of modernism and its histories risks the same pitfalls as too strict periodization. For one, there is always another city to add to the list or another that falls to the wayside. As Susan Stanford Friedman has pointed out, any attempt to define modernism metonymically, by reference to a select set of canonical texts that might stand in for the whole or, as here, by listing key locations that represent modernism's relationship to the metropolis and to capitalist modernity, always raises the question of who or what is left out.[123] It is fundamentally impossible to represent a multivalent collection of texts and locations by a short list of canonical figures or metropolitan "hotbeds." And though Williams singles out these cities in order to highlight the connections between the development of modernism and the rise of late-capitalist imperialism—a connection also famously raised by Edward Said—his work nonetheless cements the relationship between modernism and the European metropolis.

Instead, if we step outside the hypercanon of European modernism, beyond the domain of the metropole and its associated "republic of letters," and into the worldwide sphere of textual activity, we discover a multiplicity of transnational modernisms that foreground their ethical and political dimensions as essential horizons for modernist experimentation, inseparable from their other purposes and commitments.[124] Rather than conceive of the political imperatives of modernist narrative in an additive fashion, as a second-order formation or a vagary of context appended to a formally innovative text, we can recognize narrative's construction of an "as if" realm of justice as a crucial aspect of its challenge to realist epistemologies and a sign of its disruption of the Humean fact/value split. Further, if we understand the text as on every level socially, historically, and rhetorically situated, then we cannot help but see its formal and political attitudes as deeply motivated and inseparable from the exigencies surrounding it. Modernism's formal and political demands operate within the local context, to be sure, but at the same time also function transnationally, placing Anand's *Untouchable*, for example, in contact with anticolonial or working-class writing elsewhere. For Jack Conroy, writing his novel *The Disinherited* in the Depression-era Midwest, the need to represent the political voices of unemployed workers within the brutal context of 1930s America, necessitates his use of a decentered narrative structure, a style inflected by orality and a political recasting of the mode of *skaz* (the sketch). As chapter 5 will elaborate, this reworking of voice from a working-class perspective sometimes bears more affinity to the politically engaged modernism of the Harlem Renaissance than to the hardboiled socialist realism to which it is usually compared. In this and the many other examples gathered in this book, whether written from Madras, India, or Madrid, Spain, the imbrication of modernist experimentation and politics demonstrates the role of narrative in revising ethical experience, resituating social action, and imagining a future justice within its local and global situations.

Thus, it will be my argument that if we take up a comparative perspective on transnational modernism, one that brings previously marginalized languages and literatures into view and shuttles among the variety of locations, temporalities, languages, and histories of modernism, then we will also finally dismantle the sway of a universal modernist canon, complete with the mythology of its inward turn or its dissociation from politics. Further, if we conceive of modernities and the modernisms that arise in conjunction and response to them as modes (for Lodge), ideologies (for Jameson), or groups of problems or contradictions (for Moretti) rather than a substantive set of attitudes, formal attributes, or texts, then our reading will seek to organize and compare these problems and responses rather than to assimilate them into a universal answer.[125] Transnational modernism will emerge as a dynamic series of aesthetic relationships or responses to the problematics of modernity in which we can see worldwide textual correspondences and intersections among its social and political commitments.[126]

This model responds to Gayatri Spivak's call, in her book *Death of A Discipline,* for a method that takes each literary work in its specificity and as nearly as possible from within its own cultural contexts rather than assuming that it will travel or translate easily into Euro-modernist frameworks. Still, this process need not overvalorize the local. As I have been arguing, we can attend to the cultural activity of a text in its geographical specificity without foreshortening its range. Certainly, if we imagine the cultural, communal, and geopolitical contexts of a work as multiple—potentially both local and global at once—then our reading practice ought follow suit, following the activity of texts as they gesture beyond their immediate contexts, helping us see the possibility of movement beyond the purely local, and asking us to imagine the ways that the many versions of texts become new in new contexts and vary according to how and where they are read. This is in part what I mean to indicate as a transnational "optic," a mode of reading that marries close attention to the local activity of the work in its specific contexts with a willingness to follow the nodal lines of interconnection that spin out from each text to its broader sphere of engagement. This transnational mode of reading would thus accommodate the "transversal movements of culture" that, according to Françoise Lionnet and Shu-mei Shih, characterize the complex ways in which "minor cultural articulations" circulate "in productive relationship with the major (in all its possible shapes, forms, and kinds), as well as [in] minor-to-minor networks that circumvent the major altogether . . . and produce . . . new forms of identification that negotiate with national, ethnic, and cultural boundaries."[127] We must, however, acknowledge that reading beyond the original context is a transformative matter. Texts are altered as they are viewed through this optic—first contexts may begin to seem less "original," and the sphere of the text's activity may shift dramatically when seen in a global light. Yet transnational modernism demands to be read as operating both at home and abroad at once, sometimes operating as what Rebecca Walkowitz calls "comparison literature"—texts that "do not belong to any one national, ethnic, or linguistic tradition"[128]—at other times operating as what other scholars have described as writing born to travel.[129] Placing James Joyce and Anand together, as I will do in chapter 2, allows us to see Joyce's anticolonial politics in a new light, even as it shows us how to place Anand in one key node of anticolonial modernist work.[130] Reading Max Aub's Spanish-language narrative about the Civil War in concert with Orwell's *Homage to Catalonia* and the film *The Spanish Earth*, as I will do in chapter 4, highlights the political commitments of Aub's deeply experimental, labyrinthine texts at the same time as it traces the fine line between engagement and propaganda in international multimedia responses to the Civil War.

Further, as I described earlier in this chapter, the transnational optic I employ in this book implies more than an ability to follow the lines of international textual travel or transculturation. It seeks to unsettle our assumptions about the European nexus of modernism and its national spheres of literary activity while highlighting the nonnormative dimension of the text as it operates both locally and globally. In calling attention to the "trans-" dimension of this way of reading—rather than characterizing it as "international" or "global"—I thus hope to highlight the interlocking ethical and political commitments that suffuse and connect modernist texts worldwide and to allow their potentially transgressive power to infuse our critical practice.[131] The transnational critical optic thus challenges us to attend, "to the political production of transnational texts," but also to recognize the political activity inaugurated by our transnational ways of reading them.[132]

Franco Moretti plays the provocateur by pushing for what he calls "distant reading."[133] Spivak argues that the text's activity begins in the local. The transnational optic that I have described here helps us reconcile these positions by insisting that both near and distant reading are necessary. The cultural activity of a text in its original context may be at odds with its global circulation, but together they create a new textual geography that claims our attention by arguing for close reading in the original language where possible but in the context of the transformative work of translocation, and by focusing on the many nodes and circles of interconnected social and political activity among global modernisms rather than on a single homogenizing worldwide literary sphere. As we shift to a nodal model of transnational modernisms, as scholars such as Friedman, Ramanzani, Hart, Walkowitz, Laura Doyle, Laura Winkiel, and Anita Patterson have, in various ways, begun to do,[134] we'll see wider patterns of intertextual exchange and global correspondence rather than simply the transmission of influence from metropole to colony or from colony back to the center.[135] We will also begin to see the socially and politically transformative potential of these nodes as they become articulated with discourses of justice and politics worldwide and begin to shift texts, languages, social imaginaries, and political realities.[136] These nodal correspondences will create oppositional and revisionary connections among modernist texts and practices, generating novel patterns of association and responsibility while demanding a new transnational critical practice that recognizes transversal movements of culture and reorients modernism around its multiple local and global commitments. In the chapters that follow I trace several transnational lines of connection, especially where they take us to modernisms mistakenly seen as marginal, ancillary, or belated, hoping to capture the energy of their narrative commitments, both aesthetic and political, and their singular claims on us as readers.

Frederic Jameson's exploration of modernism and modernity begins from the assumption that there can be no correct use of the word "modernity."[137] Susan Stanford Friedman argues that in reading modernism "dissonance matters." The approach to transnational modernism I elaborate in this book takes these caveats to heart, exploring modernism and modernity as a dynamic set of relationships, problematics, or cultural responses to modernity rather than a static canon of works or a given set of formal devices. If modernity is a "practice-based label," as Eric Rothstein has argued—a term used for a variety of experiences, habits, practices, and ideologies that accompany the political, social, and technological shifts of the development of global late capitalism, rather than these developments themselves—then so, too, is modernism, and we must therefore attend closely to its diverse activities and practices as they emerge in a variety of locations around the world.[138] In describing how modernist narratives generate both ethical being-in-the-world and the action of imagining justice, this book also privileges the "as if" potential of our thinking about modernism and modernity. Narrative engagements with social imaginaries worldwide generate new literary and political synergies that might have looked incorrect, dissonant, or out of time in relation to the old modernist canon. If the transnational optic shows us the otherwise-effaced political valences of modernist narrative and highlights the complex relationships among modernist texts and the streams of discourse, political imperatives, rhetorical situations, and social ideologies in which they are immersed, both locally and globally, it also demonstrates the futility of building a new, global canon or strictly delimiting the temporal-spatial boundaries of modernism. Rather, by describing transnational modernism as a mode that arises in conjunction with impending modernity in many places, guises, attitudes, and temporalities, and demonstrating the continuum of political engagement that helps to motivate it, I hope to offer not only an expanded account of modernist texts and commitments but also a new way of thinking about what modernism is and can do.

This book is divided into two parts. The two chapters that follow in part 1 are deliberately comparative. They read the canonical modernisms of Virginia Woolf and James Joyce in conjunction with the work of Jean Rhys and Mulk Raj Anand, writers who were born outside the Euro-metropolitan nexus of modernism and whose work foregrounds the complex geographies of empire. Reading these writers comparatively offers us a new optic for viewing the correspondences between anticolonial writers from a variety of locations; it also helps us to situate Anand and Rhys with Joyce and Woolf within an important node of transnational modernism.

Chapter 1, "Intimate and Global: Ethical Domains from Woolf to Rhys," begins by exploring the development of a feminist, intimate ethics across the gaps of lived experience in Woolf's *Orlando* and *To the Lighthouse* by way of the figure of the fold. Whereas in these novels the fold signals an ethical leap into the lives of others, in *Three Guineas* the narrative gaps, interruptions, ellipses, and detours take on more conspicuously political weight, providing the link between word and deed and serving as the vehicle for Woolf's political engagement with the Spanish Civil War. Thus, I will argue, Woolf's experimental style pushes us constantly beyond the personal, to a re-perception of the folds of ethics and experience that make accounting for ourselves and for others a matter of progressive, feminist politics.

In Jean Rhys's early novels *Quartet, Good Morning Midnight*, and *Voyage in the Dark*, this narrative self-accounting always takes place within the geographical spaces of empire. For Rhys's heroines, the question, "who are you?" calls up the uneven development and disrupted futurity of colonialism, which conditions both their corporeal experiences and their ability to disclose themselves to others in narrative. Rhys's heroines struggle to account for themselves in narratives with shifting perspectives, distorted temporalities, and uncertain plots. They walk the borderland between colony and metropolis, back room and sidewalk cafe, playing a geopolitical game that has at once no end and no future. Rhys thus shows us not only, like Woolf, the potential of narrative folds and gaps to generate ethical relations and resist their political foreclosure but also the power of convoluted life stories to refuse the political imperatives of twentieth-century colonial geographies.

Chapter 2, "Comparative Colonialisms: Joyce, Anand, and the Question of Engagement," takes up the transnational connection between James Joyce and the politically engagé Indian writer Mulk Raj Anand, whose reading of Joyce's *A Portrait of the Artist as a Young Man* inspired his own novels of Indian resistance. This chapter begins by examining the profound geographical sensibility that inhabits Joyce's work and the importance of questions of geography to modernist engagement with the sociopolitical spaces of modernity. Positioning Joyce within the contours of modernist geography, I argue, helps reorient our understanding of Joyce's confrontation with colonialism even while it foregrounds the global politics of location within his work.

In the second section of the chapter I show how this modernist geography helps Anand build a new Indian literary tradition that responds both to his Joycean inspiration and to the exigencies of his Indian locations. Anand crafts a cosmopolitan Indian modernism rooted, as we have seen, in matters of caste, poverty, national identity, and colonial status in late-colonial India. This chapter ends by highlighting the way that both Joyce and Anand revise the tradition of the bildungsroman, using narrative experimentation to challenge the political model of the exemplary, representative man within the geographical spaces of colonial modernity.

Part 2 of this book steps away from the explicitly comparative framework of the first chapters to delve more deeply into less studied transnational modernisms in three different settings: late-colonial India, Civil War–era Spain, and the United States of the 1930s. I examine modernism's textual encounter with the problem of justice and the ways in which experimental narratives in a variety of genres (novel, memoir, reportage, short story, creative essay) bridge the gap between ethics and politics. These chapters are, to a certain extent, case studies: each one represents a different geographical location, political imperative, or modernist textuality. Certainly, other situations and texts might have figured here. I must leave it to other scholars with different language skills to explore Bengali, Portuguese, or Japanese modernisms.[139] But with this book I hope to engage in a conversation about the stakes and aims of modernism worldwide that will continue well beyond its pages.

Chapter 3, "Modernism in the Zenana: The Domestic Spaces of Sorabji, Hussain, and Ishvani," explores the writings of several little-studied women writers of late-colonial India whose work presents an intersecting critique of gender and genre that realigns women's social and political identities while opening a space for an alternative narrative modernism. By masquerading as autobiography or reportage, Cornelia Sorabji's narratives about servants, children, and women living under conditions of purdah not only trouble the distinction between autobiography and fiction but also employ that liminal zone as a place of ethical encounter across irremediable gaps of knowledge and experience. In her later work, Sorabji employs the trope of the intermediary who intervenes between a secluded woman and the external world in order to recast the rhetoric of domestic and political spheres and develop modern citizenship for Indian women. Such writers as Iqbalunnisia Hussain, G. Ishvani, and Kamala Sathianadhan—whose work is mostly unknown and almost entirely out of print—plunge us more directly into the women's world of the zenana—the part of the Indian house often reserved for women among both Hindus and Muslims—yet they refuse the absolute dichotomy of home and world, individual and community. They resist the reinscription of the traditional model of "mother India" into the site of the zenana and, I argue, raise politics as a matter of communal responsibility and voice, even within seclusion.

Chapter 4, "Commitment and the Scene of War: Max Aub and Spanish Civil War Writing," seeks to bring Spanish narrative about the Civil War into the mainstream of discussion about modernism and politics rather than segregating it within the Spanish tradition or in the category of war writing. By allowing for the continuity between experimental narrative and war writing, this chapter challenges the assumption that choosing sides dooms narrative to what has been called a "ruined naturalism." The chapter first focuses on the writing of Max Aub, whose six-novel Civil War cycle, *El laberinto mágico* (*The Magic Labyrinth*) is at once a tour de force of narrative innovation and a chronicle of war that rarely travels to the front. It clearly demonstrates the possibility that modernist styles and perspectives can rise to the task of bearing witness. The chapter then shifts attention to the question of propaganda as the corollary or obverse of committed writing. By exploring the role of propaganda in multimedia responses to the war, including the vast visual record of Civil War posters and magazine covers and the films *The Spanish Earth* (directed by Joris Ivens and narrated by Ernest Hemingway) and *L'espoir* (directed by Andre Malraux and adapted from his book by Max Aub), as well as George Orwell's *Homage to Catalonia*, this section highlights the link between the manipulation of perspective, play with verisimilitude in propaganda, and the aesthetic construction of political attitudes within narrative modernisms.

Finally, chapter 5, "Arising from the Cornlands: The Working-Class Voices of Conroy and Le Sueur," argues that the narrative strategies that allow many radical writers in the United States during the 1920s and 1930s to incorporate working-class voices, rhythms, and experiences into narrative fiction have affinities with the projects of modernist writers. It reads the restless, shifting narrative perspective of Jack Conroy's *The Disinherited*, for example, or the floating, collective voices of a group of women in Meridel Le Sueur's *The Girl*, as aesthetic responses to the conditions of modernity in the United States, particularly for working-class people in and out of employment, as well as key aspects of the ways that the texts register resistance to those conditions. Conroy's work uses an episodic narrative structure that creates *skaz*, or sketches from "overheard" stories and interrupted autobiography, and then assembles those sketches into a communal tale of political disenfranchisement and burgeoning consciousness. In *The Girl*, the suffering of female bodies in hard labor, hunger, childbirth, or partner abuse generates an iterative style that rejects the authority of a presiding narrator and emphasizes the narrative dimension of the "contact" between the embodied lives of working-class women. These working-class narratives thus take us beyond the conventions of either narrative realism or a modernism characterized by interiority and aestheticism in order to allow orality, folk culture, and the materiality of everyday life, especially as it is displayed through the bodies of working women and men, to emerge as the locus of a politically engaged, experimental narrative tradition.

Finally, in the afterword of the book, I reflect on the connections among narrative, politics, and justice by way of Barack Obama's 2010 Nobel Peace Prize speech. By challenging us to recognize the tension between what is and what ought to be, Obama retells the story of the interrelationship between ethics and politics and brings this book full circle.

Part I

Intimate and Global | ONE
Ethical Domains from Woolf to Rhys

> Ethical Feminism is, for me, an ethical, aesthetic imperative.
> —Drucilla Cornell, *Moral Images of Freedom*

> Action and speech are so closely related because the primordial and specifically human act must at the same time contain the answer to the question asked of every newcomer: "Who are you?"
> —Hannah Arendt, *The Human Condition*

> Madrid not fallen. Chaos. Slaughter. War surrounding our island.
> —Virginia Woolf, *Diary*

In her posthumously published satiric essay, "Middlebrow," Virginia Woolf writes, "In whatever company I am I always try to know what it is like—being a conductor, being a woman with ten children and thirty-five shillings a week, being a stockbroker, being an admiral, being a bank clerk, being a dressmaker, being a duchess, being a miner, being a cook, being a prostitute."[1] Imagining herself into these many identities, with their various habits, conditions of existence, and distinct ways of riding "at a gallop across life,"[2] provides Woolf with food for thought and material for fiction. But it also presents her with an ethical imperative tied to aesthetics: the imagination may help us know other lives despite their distance from our own, but its aesthetic process ought not erase that distance or deform those lives, which beckon because, not in spite of their alterity. Marooned in the category of the "highbrow," Woolf acknowledges that not even her imagination can grant her full access to the daily, embodied experiences of "those who can deal successfully with what is called real life." As she put it in another context, "After all the imagination is largely the child of the flesh. One could not be Mrs. Giles of Durham because one's body had never stood at the wash-tub; one's hands had never wrung and scrubbed and chopped up."[3] The attempted leap into the lives of the conductor, the woman with ten children, or the prostitute represents not only Woolf's recognition of her responsibility toward people radically different from herself but also her effort, through narrative imagination, to explore the possibilities and limits of ethical connection across irrevocable distance.

Her fiction also famously begins with this premise. As she puts it in "Mr. Bennett and Mrs. Brown," "All novels begin with an old lady in the corner opposite" of the train compartment who beckons to the writer, "My name is Brown. Catch me if you can."[4] Fiction becomes the domain where lives might be "caught," spun out, responded to, and narrated in a manner that acknowledges their ethical claims upon both writer and reader. But Woolf offers no assurance that Mrs. Brown will allow herself to be caught, and her writing returns again and again to the moments when she seems to slip further away. The limitations of what feminist scholars would call one's "lived body"[5] constrain what can be known about an other, despite one's infinite responsibility toward that person or the necessity of judging from an "enlarged" perspective.[6] Mrs. Ramsay must imagine as she can the lighthouse keeper and his son. Her moment of insight into their lives comes as an imaginative extension of her own experiences. Even Orlando as woman cannot retain the embodied life experience of Orlando as man. These experiences slip away as she returns to London, artifacts of an embodied existence obviated by her change of sex.

For Woolf, this gap between the known life and the unknown life becomes a vital component of the ethical encounter in narrative rather than a difference to be concealed or a problem to be overcome, and it forms a crucial part of the imaginative leap toward another subjectivity. Her writing often creates what I will call, drawing on Deleuze, a "fold" in the text that brings subjects into relationship with other subjects across this gap without conflating them, assuming their commensurability, or eliminating their distance.[7] Further, the intimacy and care generated by these enfolded relationships harbors an ethics no less profound, I will argue, than that which rests on the obligation to radical alterity. Ethics in Woolf's work inhabits the fold between the incommensurable experiences of separate beings; this fold brings them into a kind of intimate relation, though not necessarily into a realm of similarity, normativity, or consensus. Woolf demonstrates that a powerful, nonnormative, feminist ethics can arise not only from the difficult leap toward the life of a stranger but also from the possibilities and limits of intimacy, eros, and care, which supplement but do not erase the challenge of alterity. In the experimental structures of *Orlando*, *To the Lighthouse*, and *Mrs. Dalloway* and in Woolf's play with the nature and limits of narrative coherence, we can see this intimate ethics at work, challenging our assumptions about the sphere of ethical relations and demonstrating the role of narrative in enfolding ethics.

In Woolf's late essay *Three Guineas*, however, gaps, interruptions, and moments of narrative incoherence carry more conspicuously political weight. Rather than emphasizing the ability of narrative to enfold lives and perspectives, *Three Guineas* builds its political argument from what we might call the hidden involutions of narrative, those moments when an unfathomable space opens up that the narrative cannot easily cross and that force it to proceed by other routes. If politics implies the promise of a future to which our relationships, actions, and words gesture, and follows a trajectory toward that future, no matter how distant or impossible it seems, then we might expect it also to demand fidelity to plot and narrative coherence.[8] Yet *Three Guineas* does the opposite, generating a radical democratic politics and a vision of the future by dismantling narrative unity and calling attention to the impossibility of a consensus point of view.[9] In other words, *Three Guineas* broaches the political by way of, rather than in spite of, its incoherence, elaborating a version of engagement that works against consensus and uniformity of opinion and that begins from the impossibility of a fixed point of view. Woolf's narrative involutions, gaps, and detours challenge the efficacy of a complete and coherent accounting for oneself, contest the documentary claims of war reporting, and interrupt the kind of teleological, unitary perspective that characterizes propaganda. Woolf's narrative detours, her efforts to give an account of herself, and the complexity of the narrative structure of address in *Three Guineas* all provide what Hannah Arendt has described as the link between "word and deed," which begins with the answer to the (ethical) question, "Who are you?" and ends with Woolf's trenchant critique of the politics of patriarchal authority and the Spanish Civil War.[10]

But for Jean Rhys, writing at about the same time, the same fraught question inevitably raises other questions about postcolonial political geographies that Woolf conspicuously avoids in *Three Guineas*. Caught up in the uneven relations, mistaken bodies, tortured geographies, and convoluted trajectories of colonialism, Rhys's heroines struggle not only to account for themselves to others but also to constitute a future for themselves. From beginning to end, the convoluted life stories of the heroines of *Good Morning, Midnight* (1939) and *Voyage in the Dark* (1934) are interrupted by their efforts to survive within a world governed by disembodiment, dissociation, and temporal-spatial dislocation. The narrator of *Good Morning, Midnight* enters the novel already un-homed—a shop girl who feels out of place in the shop, a British woman bent on staying out of Britain. Anna Morgan in *Voyage in the Dark* struggles against her situation. A chorus girl who hates the show, she continues to inhabit the Caribbean landscape of her past even as she cycles through a season's worth of cheap lodgings and empty encounters across Britain. Rhys's characters are not prostitutes yet are often labeled as such, and even their names are often in question. Identity in these novels is always bound to the matters of class and location, yet neither of these is easily pinned down for Rhys's itinerant, downwardly mobile heroines, who become border walkers between the middle and lower classes as well as between metropolis and colonial outpost.

Yet the voices of Rhys's heroines, emerging from cheap hotel rooms, railway stations, and the back corners of cafes, call us to see not only the ethical difficulty posed by their experience of cultural and economic dislocation but also the political implications of their struggle for self-disclosure within the context of both intimate and global geographies. Their fraught relationship to dominant discourses of race and gender disrupt any presumption that ethical responsibility comes smoothly, coherently, or without peril to the self while they also question the assumption of a future guided by the protocols of imperial geography and the uneven development of postcolonial modernity. In fact, we might say, the difficulties Rhys's heroines face in navigating a life trajectory and the convoluted narratives that result demonstrate the extent to which they are defined and limited by their global positioning.

In considering Rhys's late novel *Wide Sargasso Sea*, Gayatri Spivak writes, "In the figure of Antoinette . . . Rhys suggests that so intimate a thing as a personal and human identity might be determined by the politics of imperialism."[11] In Rhys's early novels, I claim in this chapter, the interfolding of colonial and metropolitan experience creates an uneven, unruly set of relationships that brings the intimate and global inexorably together but that also makes the progress of self-narrative impossible. Lee Edelman has argued that the refusal of a future may be seen as a political act that disrupts normative assumptions about social relations and their reproduction.[12] In their unwillingness to posit a future for their heroines or to reorient their waywardness, Rhys's novels may thus be seen to act politically. Her work not only questions the possibility of a Woolfian leap into the lives of others when from the subaltern rather than the dominant position but also challenges the ease with which an interrupted narrative may be simply resumed or reoriented. Rather than resonate with the productive potential of an involuted or disrupted structure of address, generating a new narrative future beyond the propaganda of war and patriarchy, Rhys's early novels resist the assumption of both continuity and progress. They spiral constantly back to the possibility of the question, "Who are you?" and make the viability of its future a matter of both intimate ethics and global politics.

It has been said that the novel comes of age with empire and that modernism marks its moment of crisis.[13] Still, it has not always been easy to situate metropolitan modernism in relation to twentieth-century geopolitics or to recognize its presence at the level of form.[14] The problematic question, "Who are you?" which is always lurking within narrative, initiates, in the writing of Woolf and Rhys, an encounter with global positioning that marks the matter of narrative hiatus or interruption as a sign of the politics of empire. Reading Woolf and Rhys together, as this chapter does, helps us see not only the ethical significance of the intersubjective encounters that are staged within their texts but also the political action created by their narrative gaps, folds, and refusals. This chapter, then, comes full circle, folding back on itself as it reconnects politics to ethics, Rhys to Woolf; demonstrating the role of narrative experimentation in tracing the terrain between intimate ethics and the politics of the global; and marking the complex role of modernist narrative between the two.

Intimate Ethics

Ethics, as I am positing it here, begins from the intersections of intimacy and experience. It emerges from the account of a self that not only is called into being by the demands of strangers around her, as Levinas would claim, but also is situated in relationship to friends, family, lovers, neighbors, and communities. These intimate relationships enmesh the subject in a web of responsibility and obligation that preconditions self-hood and that initiates ethical being-toward-the-other, even if they do not convey the shock of alterity so important to Levinas. If the self comes into being intersubjectively, in and through her response to those around her, then "this responsibility is an ontological responsibility" built on ethical relationships.[15] But these ethical relationships also emerge from embodied experiences of the world—from a touch that sets in motion the demand of an other, a caress that initiates her act of care, or even a fleeting contact with a neighbor in the street that can function, like the appearance of a face, as a reminder of the shared space of being. If Levinas will argue that "the relationship with an other begins not with intentional consciousness," or conscious knowledge of an other, but rather emerges from the primordial proximity of human beings, then embodiment and the experience it brings are essential to intimate ethics.[16]

Levinas insists on the shock of radical alterity so as to ensure that ethics not give way to any incorporation or usurpation of the other by the self, even in terms of an attempt to understand its suffering. Should the self become intimate with the other, he argues, the other will become an object of knowledge possessed by the self as a matter of consciousness and epistemology, rather than presenting the phenomenological challenge of alterity. The intimate scene of a lover's embrace is explicitly excluded from the realm of ethics for this very reason. The lover, Levinas would say, takes the beloved as the object of affection, to be known and incorporated into the lover's understanding, thereby mitigating her challenge as an other. Though Levinas discusses the importance of paternity as an opening toward ethics and often refers to the other as a neighbor, it is only when those relationships raise the specter of radical alterity that the ethical relation is engaged.

But as many feminist theorists have claimed, there is reason to suspect that intimate relations, which we might designate, along with Irigaray, by the figure of the caress or the presumption of care, also provide the experience of awakening to ethical responsibility and relationship without incorporating the other into the self or creating her as an object of epistemology.[17] And as Luce Irigaray and Tina Chanter have argued, the ethical intimacy of care, whether between parent and child or between lovers, not only moves ethics into the personal sphere but also brings women to the center of ethics, where the Western philosophical tradition has rarely placed them.[18] The moment of the caress, whether of mother, lover, or friend, is the moment of recognition of one's being toward the other in a bodily sense, cognizant of sexual sameness or difference. It offers a bodily instantiation of the profound coming together in intimacy that need not objectify or absorb the other but indeed can accomplish the reverse, making otherness intimate and procreative without usurping it.[19] We can thus begin to conceive an ethics that builds from intimacy but does not eliminate the challenge of alterity.

It is also possible to take this claim a step further, situating ethics within the realm of family, social affiliation, or community—so long the realm of women and so often the focal point for both Woolf and Rhys—and thereby also shifting our conception of the self and the role of experience in ethical understanding. As I have claimed, if we understand the subject to be eminently social rather than isolated, "punctual," or "virile," then human relationships rather than the individual self become the site of ethical thought and action. The notion of virtue becomes located in the quality of the exchanges between and among people and in the ways that they work out their (endless and primordial) obligations to one another. Kelly Oliver's notion of "family values" presumes just such a social sphere at the core of ethics, which revolves around a subject who is "neither opposed to nor identified with the other." Ethical attitudes, values, and decisions that flow from this model of a social self perched between intimacy and alterity must be cognizant of the "relationships between people and the conditions that make these relations possible."[20] They cannot arise from a presumed idea of independent individual agency or an assumption about the commensurability of experience. Jean-Luc Nancy's theoretical work on intersubjectivity and community makes a similar point. For Nancy the "essence of Being is only as co-essence"; the self coexists with those around it in the primordial being-with that Nancy calls community. The isolated or individual self is a self in exile from this community and from the original scene of intimacy. Thus "the co-existent—the other person . . . appears inaccessible to 'me' because it is withdrawn from the 'self' in general, and because it is as the self-outside-itself."[21] But the work of intimacy and proximity reasserts the ongoing dialectic between self and other that Nancy marks by the term "being-with" and becomes the proving ground for justice.[22] The experience we have of an intimate or local community becomes crucial to our recognition of this dialectic and the ethics that arises from it.

It is clear, then, that when ethics emerges from the self-in-community it is not only intimate but also dependent on embodied experience and material circumstances. The philosopher Adriana Cavarero points out that a coexisting or relational self that must respond to a distinct and material other in the here and now is very different from the "anonymous face of an indistinct and universal alterity" that emerges out of Levinasian thought.[23] The self emerges within a plurality where all beings appear to others, asking and responding to the same questions about identity, exhibiting and gazing upon one another's physical presence in the world. People "appear to each other reciprocally—first of all in their corporeal materiality and as creatures endowed with sensory organs."[24] In asking and answering the question, "Who are you?" each person becomes unique and distinct but only in relation to the others to whom she discloses herself. Thus, we might say, the ethical, relational self begins from the reciprocity of our material appearance among others in the world and our embodied experiences of community.

But the scene of intimate ethics may also be understood as the scene of narration, which makes its reciprocal, ethical claims on teller and listener.[25] In asking and answering the question, "Who are you?" the self becomes what Cavarero calls a "narratable self," beginning a life story that exposes her to others and elicits not only their responses but also their own life stories. The endless and endlessly incomplete process of narration provides the means of self-disclosure as well as the place of engagement with others. "The narratable self thus re-enters into what we could call a relational ethic of contingency . . . there lies at the center of the narrative scene a *who* which—far from enclosing herself within the pride of a self-referential ego meant to last forever . . . wants, gives, receives and offers, *here and now*, an unrepeatable story."[26] As Cavarero sees it, this process is unavoidable, integral to the matter of identity seen as always intersubjective and "entwined in other lives." Yet the practice of reciprocal narration exhibits each subject uniquely and creates an endless series of singular events of recognition and engagement with alterity. Rather than succumb to the danger of objectification or usurpation of an other, the ethics of the narratable self constantly restages plurality and recognition even as it situates ethics in the intimate connection between teller and listener or between narrator and reader.

At the same time, this experience of reciprocal narration also raises the question of the interconnection between ethics and aesthetics. Though Cavarero does not describe it as such, this ongoing process of self-narration claims our attention as an aesthetic practice. Like other aesthetic practices, it organizes the form and processes of imaginative and sense experiences while raising the question of what can be done or made within a community.[27] Though the text may be inessential to the narrative capacity of the self, its process of creation is necessary, ineluctable, and irremediable.[28] Its unity and form carry consequences for the identities and relationships that emerge from it and for the connection between the maker and the perceiver that is essential to the aesthetic experience.[29] And, as Cavarero suggests in reading Homer, Sophocles, and Shakespeare, narrative texts focalize the production of heroes or protagonists and construct our understanding of the shape of their lives. Thus, though the narrative of self may not always emerge as an aesthetic object per se, it nonetheless operates through what we might call its aesthetic properties as a human creation that also helps create subjectivity and that instigates ethical and aesthetic experiences on the part of a listener or perceiver. The narrative gives form to the experience of a relational selfhood and to the self and other locked together in a process of making, doing, and perceiving. It takes meaning from its role in this process.[30]

This focus on narrative as crucial to the aesthetic construction of a life is in many ways inimical to the tradition of Kantian idealism, which presumes disinterestedness as the sine qua non of aesthetics. The beauty of an aesthetic object, for Kant, must be separate from one's need or use for it—and not be caught up in the desire for self-disclosure that Cavarero's philosophy emphasizes. Yet for Kant the aesthetic rests on a subjective process of imagination and judgment that does not inhere in the object in the world but rather emerges from the universally shared feeling of pleasure that it produces. We take pleasure in the aesthetic qualities of an object not because we perceive some inherent virtue in it but because we recognize a characteristic in it whose appreciation we can share with others: "The pleasure that we feel is, in a matter of a judgment of taste, necessarily imputed by us to everyone else, as if, when we call a thing beautiful, it is to be regarded as a characteristic of the object."[31] The operant phrase here is "as if"; the shared experience of a common (because based in a priori categories) judgment of taste is what produces the pleasure of the object but it *seems as if* it were a factual matter of the object itself. From a different direction, then, Kant helps us recognize the importance of an imagined, shared experience or state of mind as the basis for aesthetics.

But by the end of the discussion of aesthetics in his *Critique of Judgment* Kant famously brings the domain of aesthetics back toward ethics by claiming that the aesthetic object gives this kind of shared pleasure because "the beautiful is the symbol of the morally good."[32] Taste or the judgment of aesthetic objects is analogous to morality because they both demonstrate the "imagination in its freedom,"[33] which moves us beyond mere experience toward this "as if"—the place where we judge in concert not only with a priori principles but also in connection with the subjective experience we imagine that we share with others. Both aesthetic and moral judgment depend upon the capacity to produce pleasure from disinterestedness, to link individual sense perception to universal principles (aesthetics) or concepts (morality), and to represent the active power of the freedom of the imagination (aesthetics) or will (morality) in structuring human life. Thus it is clear that aesthetics verges on ethics (if only analogically) by virtue of its reliance on shared subjective experiences created by the imagination in an "as if" realm and not because of the objective reality of the aesthetic object.

The question of the experience of the aesthetic object, however, becomes the crux of the problem in twentieth-century revisions of Kant, especially within the Cambridge/Bloomsbury world that surrounded Woolf and, to a lesser extent, Rhys. If the Cambridge realist philosopher G. E. Moore announced the "refutation of idealism"[34] around the same time as he published his influential *Principia Ethica*, he began his career as a Kantian, and his version of philosophical realism remains indebted to Kant.[35] "Significant form" as an aesthetic principle of philosophical realism may be seen, in many ways, as synonymous with Kantian conceptions of disinterested beauty. Like Kant, the realists focus on form as the immediately apprehensible aspect of aesthetic beauty, but they diverge in their understanding of the process and source of aesthetic judgment. While Kant claims, on the one hand, that only the secondary process of reflection and judgment (which is separate from sensation) produces the pleasure of the form of an object, the realists argue, on the other hand, that the form of a perceived object directly ignites aesthetic emotions.[36] Further, Moore's key claim in *Principia Ethica* is that what is good can not be broken down into concepts or properties but is good in and of itself, thus implying that it can be perceived directly through experience of the world. The good, he claims, is unanalyzable in the same way as is a color, which we perceive and recognize directly rather than as a consequence of a definition. Thus, by likening our apprehension of the good to our perception of color, Moore brings the aesthetic not only closer to the empirical but also back toward the realm of ethics.[37]

Ethical Folds

But Roger Fry will explicitly reject this connection between ethics and aesthetics for postimpressionism. His influential expressionist theory defines the graphic arts as nonrepresentational and beyond moral action as well as beyond communication. In his great theoretical statement "An Essay in Aesthetics," he claims that "in art we have no . . . moral responsibility—it presents a life freed from the binding necessities of our actual existence."[38] For Fry beauty of the kind seen in plastic art is "supersensual, and concerned with the appropriateness and intensity of the emotions aroused." Thus Fry at once moves beyond *l'art pour l'art* and rejects Ruskinian moralism while still elaborating a formalist aesthetic. The experience of the artwork is the first step toward the arousal of emotion by the formal aspects of its design.[39] Unity, rhythm, mass, space, light, shade, and color all generate imaginative reactions that directly arouse emotions but not moral action.

I dwell here on Fry's aesthetics because it is so often evoked (along with Clive Bell's less complex concept of "significant form") as the basis for Bloomsbury aesthetics in general and as a major influence on Woolf.[40] But what does this mean for the question of ethics and aesthetics in Woolf's work? On the one hand, if we follow the argument that she was almost completely indebted for her notions of art to Fry, who was her dear friend and an object of deep admiration, then there seems little room for any deep association between aesthetics and morality or ethics. The question of writing as a rhetorical process that enlists its audience's response, or of action as a possible outcome of its work in the world, becomes nearly impossible. On the other hand, Woolf commented in a 1940 letter that her "own point of view [was] entirely different from [Fry's]."[41] Jane Goldman has also argued persuasively that Fry's influence on Woolf's aesthetics was much more limited and that Woolf was connected to postimpressionism more directly through her sister Vanessa Bell, who stands in her own right as an aesthetic thinker, experimenter, and colorist and to whom Woolf remarked that her pictures had "changed her view upon aesthetics."[42] Further, while Fry's ideas about aesthetics and their relationship to the world become more conservative in the period between the first postimpressionist exhibition in 1910 and the second exhibition in 1912, Vanessa Bell's and Virginia Woolf's ideas do not. Their aesthetics bear striking affinities with the radical poster art of the suffrage movement, linking both Bell and Woolf much more directly to political art practices.[43] But this connection between postimpressionism and political engagement has been obscured by the dominance of the concept of "significant form" in the discussion of Bloomsbury aesthetics and by our continuing assumption that modernist aesthetics of the sort Woolf espoused were antithetical to overt political engagement.

The connection between ethics and epistemology for the problem of aesthetics is also crucial for the study of Woolf's work because so much of her writing takes up the question of ethical reality. For example, Andrew's description of Mr. Ramsay's philosophy in *To the Lighthouse* ("think of the kitchen table . . . when you're not there") begins Lily's ruminations on the table, which land it upside-down in her thoughts, lodged in a pear tree. As Ann Banfield puts it, the table here brings together the philosopher and the artist: "the impersonal truth it reveals imparts its austerity to the gazer . . . it imposes on the observer a discipline that lies in its very unobservability."[44] But Martha Nussbaum points out that *To the Lighthouse* is about problems that are "both epistemological and moral."[45] The kitchen table of importance here is *neither* Mr. Ramsay's unobservable one nor Lily's surrealist vision of a table upside-down in a tree. The tables in this novel are made real in being populated and made ethical in forcing human connection and obligation into that reality.

Woolf's writing, I would argue, elaborates the ways that narrative can be the bridge between these realms, bringing the epistemological and moral into conversation with each other, using aesthetics to make an ethical realm—a fold—between the potentially universal and the personal or between the face of the other as stranger and the call of the ethics of intimacy. In the experimental structures of *Orlando*, *To the Lighthouse*, and *Mrs. Dalloway*, we can see Woolf develop a version of intimate ethics that is poised between radical alterity and the ethics of care and that revolves around the figure of "the fold."[46] In Woolf's work the "fold" as both metaphor and narrative structure performs a mediating function, bringing characters into relationship across gaps of lived experience and confronting readers with the ethical imperatives of the text. The structural folds of *To the Lighthouse* enable Lily Briscoe to discover her responsibility to both Mrs. and Mr. Ramsay, despite her resistance to the regime of marriage. The rhetorical folds of *Orlando* enjoin us as readers to grapple with the ethical dimensions of gender even as they illuminate the gaps and shifts between gendered experiences. Ethics inhabits these folds between subjectivities in Woolf's work, bringing them into intricate and compelling relation, though not necessarily into a realm of familiarity, normativity, or consensus.[47]

As Mieke Bal employs it, the Deleuzian notion of the fold can be not only "a powerful tool for overcoming the dichotomy between epistemology and ontology" but also, because it highlights questions of representation, a means of bringing together subject and object or, as I will claim, subject and subject.[48] Bal speaks of a literal fold as she analyzes the drapery in a Caravaggio painting, which extends the bodies of its figures past the literal confines of their forms and creates a vortex at the center of the painting, where the vanishing point should be, that "enfolds what it resists, encapsulating the expectation of linear perspective" and refusing its illusion of objectivity.[49] But, following Deleuze, she also uses the fold to suggest a figurative enfolding of material, whether a gathering of associated ideas or expectations, a folding back of time upon itself, or a bend in the surface of experience that can bring objects into immediate relationship with subjects and subjects into contact with others. "Through the fold, subject and object become codependent, folded into one another, and this puts the subject at risk." For Bal this risking of the subject obligates us to focus our attention on point of view, whether in a painting by Caravaggio, a sculpture by Louise Bourgeois (her examples), or a modernist novel by Woolf or Rhys. Further, I would argue, if the putting at risk of the subject makes "the divide between ontology and epistemology untenable," then it also opens up the potential for a radically new ethical encounter across difference and distance.[50]

Deleuze's notion of the fold grows out of Leibniz's understanding of the self, which, like Jean-Luc Nancy's much later thought, assumes sociality as the core of subjectivity. For Leibniz, the community of monads and its relationship to bodily possessions that are always in flux, coming and going, mine and then someone else's, require what Deleuze calls an "interindividual" way of being.[51] This inter-individuality—or the fabric that forms the temporary and convoluted boundary between bodies even as it creates new ways of perceiving the body's relationship to the world—Deleuze calls "the fold." The fold is the monad's turning back on itself and its bodily possessions or the folding between the "levels" separating the soul and the body, as well as between "'species' of monads in the sense of souls." The fold "links the soul that possesses a body to other souls that body possesses." In the baroque it is also the movement of the finite body toward the infinite, made concrete by the representation in baroque painting and sculpture of voluminous folds of material extending past the vanishing point. Consider Bernini, whose marble "seizes and bears to infinity folds that cannot be explained by the body," Deleuze suggests (figure 1.1).[52] Consider Caravaggio, whose draped curtains "dictate a cyclical look without outcome," Bal adds (figure 1.2).[53]

Consider Orlando. Think for a minute about one of the pictures of *Orlando*—"Orlando on her return to England" (figure 1.3)—draped

Figure 1.1. Gian Lorenzo Bernini, head of St. Theresa, detail from *The Ecstasy of St. Theresa*, 1647–52. *Source:* Alinari/Art Resources, New York.

not only in beads but also in actual drapery (a dress, we are meant to presume). The beads loop around and then disappear, leading our eyes not only off the page but downward toward the edge of Orlando's clothing. Certainly these folds of clothing and loops of beads cannot be fully explained by her body nor contained by the frame of the picture. This is, then, a fold that verges on the baroque, working to take our eye beyond the frame of the possible and toward the infinite

Figure 1.2. Michelangelo Merisi da Caravaggio, *Death of the Virgin*, 1605. *Source*: Erich Lessing/Art Resources, New York.

Figure 1.3. "Orlando on her return to England." *Source*: Used by permission of the Hogarth Press and the Random House Group Limited.

cycles "without outcome" that the long history of Orlando's life suggests. It is also a provocative picture in this sense, one that mobilizes the desires of its viewers to follow those beads out into infinity or inward toward an engagement with their wearer. We do not read them as a series of atoms strung on a string, the primary building blocks of the perceived world as the early-twentieth-century realists described it. The drapery in this photo contributes to the effect as its folds deepen at the edges of the photo, its convoluted surfaces draw our eyes into their shadows and thus again shatter the surface of the image, insisting that we enter into connection with this sitter and her folds. These folds are like those that Bal analyzes in a painting by Caravaggio—folds that in our efforts to comprehend them work to incorporate into the everyday a movement toward the infinite and to bridge the subject/object rift. As she puts it, "Through the fold, subjectivity and the object become co-dependent, folded into one another."[54] The drapery extends the lived body in time and space, catching it up in the perpetual circulation of the baroque image but also pushing out beyond the picture plane, drawing the viewer into the circular vortex that replaces the verisimilitude of the vanishing point at the center of the image.

We must also consider that what we are looking at is "Orlando on her return to England"—in other words, Orlando as woman. That the text enfolds us by means of this image even as it broaches questions of Orlando's subjectivity as woman further dismantles our distance from the text, no matter our gender, for the key issue here is that of Orlando's woman-/manliness—or manly woman-ness. The page facing the photo, for example, reads, "She was censuring both sexes equally, as if she belonged to neither; and indeed for the time being she seemed to vacillate; she was a man; she was a woman; she knew the secrets, shared the weaknesses of each."[55] Thus the ethical dimension emerges not only in the text proper, the word "censuring" here implying an ethical judgment of each sex, but also in our connection to Orlando as both man and woman, which insists that we not succumb to any of the ethical failings that this passage names. If, by way of the folds in this image, we are brought into an intimate encounter with the multisexed being that is Orlando, despite our almost certain lack of shared experience with her/him, then we are also forced to acknowledge the demands that this being-together makes upon us. We are placed into an ethical encounter that expands the boundaries of our selves beyond their conventional limits at the same time as it asks us to acknowledge the gaps in shared experience and the ethical constraints on both thought and conduct made salient by that encounter. In other words—the folds of this image bring us face to face, as Levinas might put it, with the demands of otherness and place us into relationship with it. But because this otherness is beyond the conventional bounds of sexed beings, we are also here forced to "face" its challenge to the normative morality associated with sexual difference and to move toward an alternative ethical response to the multiplicity of Orlando.

In this way, in this passage of *Orlando*, ontology, in the form of potentially universalizable ethics based on the status of the subject, and epistemology seem to meet. Orlando censures as though from a priori values, according to which such behavior as denying "a woman teaching lest she may laugh at you" or being the "slave to the frailest chit in petticoats, and yet to go about as if you were the lords of creation" (158) is seen as immediately and obviously wrong. But, on the other hand, this censoriousness shifts according to experience, and especially according to gendered experience. The awareness of this "wrong" only emerges in Orlando as woman; the universalizable character of these values becomes clear only when experience makes gendered behavior into an ethical concern.

This ethical dilemma moves beyond the literal level of the text, where moral maxims may be presented as self-evident, to the domain of the relationship between the reader and Orlando, the folding of subject and subject across gaps of identity and experience within the textual encounter. Here, ethical feeling is not derived from a universalized maxim, as in the realm of morals, or simply from empathy;[56] rather, it emerges as a situated response of the imagination, which does not depend on commonality or consensus and looks more like aesthetic judgment. If aesthetic judgment may be seen as a reflective pleasure that begins from sensory experience but also requires a move beyond it to the realm of imagination, then this encounter between reader and Orlando operates in a similar manner. We may take pleasure in our apprehension of Orlando transformed into a woman and suddenly able to judge as a woman/man, but it is in our imaginative leap toward that subject position, while remaining cognizant of our distance from it, that we understand the ethical demands placed upon us by this moment in the text. The aesthetic demands of this image and of the surrounding text insist on an imaginative leap that is, from its outset, an ethical one.

But the notion of the fold need not remain tied to a photograph appearing as an aesthetic object in the text. There are many other textual images in Woolf's work that approximate the visual fold in Orlando's drapery and make the same ethical-aesthetic demands. To take one example among many: in the "Window" section of *To the Lighthouse* we encounter the image of the "crumpled glove," which prompts Lily to ruminate on the question of Mrs. Ramsay's being: "What was the spirit in her, the essential thing, by which, had you found a crumpled glove in the corner of a sofa, you would have known it, from its twisted finger, hers indisputably?" (49). Lily's twisting thoughts about Mrs. Ramsay end with her refusal of the moral injunction to marry—"gathering her desperate courage, she would urge her own exemption from the universal law" (50). Thereupon the image of the glove returns: Lily "had recovered her sense of her now—this was the glove's twisted finger"—and we begin the familiar passage where Lily wonders about the extent of her connection to Mrs. Ramsay: "Could loving . . . make her and Mrs. Ramsay one?" (51). The twisting of the glove throughout this passage marks not only the particularity of a singular being—we could know Mrs. Ramsay by her glove's twisted finger—but also the experience of otherness tinged with the desire for intimacy made clear here by Lily's narrating perspective. The twisted fabric conflates terms even as it connects subject (Mrs. Ramsay) and object (the glove) or folds subject (Mrs. Ramsay) onto subject (Lily) onto subject (reader). The twisted glove exists as an object of apprehension for us and for Lily that makes possible our engagement with the ontological question of singular being and with the profound intimacy across gaps in sensibility and experience, seen between Lily and Mrs. Ramsay, that, I have argued, can be the first move toward ethics.

This passage in *To the Lighthouse* thus demands to be read against Levinas's ethics, which would reject the possibility that Lily's embrace of Mrs. Ramsay gives rise to an ethical response to the call of the other—or that the relationship here might be an example of a profoundly ethical experience between intimate subjects. What we understand is that Lily's recognition of Mrs. Ramsay's alterity emerges directly out of Lily's intimacy with and desire to love Mrs. Ramsay. This love comes close to what Irigaray describes in *The Ethics of Sexual Difference* as the encounter with otherness in the experience of eros itself.[57] To be clear, Lily's desire for intimacy is not a desire to lose her self in Mrs. Ramsay or to ignore the constant reminders of the differences in their lives and experiences. Indeed, *To the Lighthouse* abounds with reminders not only of Mrs. Ramsay's singularity but also of the profound distinction of Lily's lived experience, outside of Mrs. Ramsay's Victorian marriage. Yet when Levinas describes being-otherwise as the ongoing process of being and articulation, he invokes precisely the kind of shifting, adjusting, and rearticulating of relationship that takes place between Lily and Mrs. Ramsay.[58]

Not incidentally, the unsettling tendency also appears in Woolf's use of color in the novel. If for Levinas the aesthetic work of art is problematic in its exhibition of pure essence in the beautiful object or phrase, it is also the place where that essence "recommence[s] being," turning back upon itself in a way that transforms it from a substantive to a verb. Color is crucial in painting; as "red reddens and green greens, forms are produced as contours and vacate with their vacuity as forms." Thus, as Levinas puts it, "the palette of colors, the gamut of sounds, the system of vocables and the meandering of forms are realized as a pure *how*" in which being resounds.[59] As many have pointed out, Lily Briscoe is a colorist painter. The famous description of her painting in the first section of the novel shows her as committed to the principle of color in a way that resists the fashion, here presented as masculinist, of black and white. "She would not have considered it honest to tamper with the bright violet and the staring white, since she saw them like that, fashionable though it was since Mr. Paunceforte's visit, to see everything pale. . . . Then beneath the color there was the shape" (18). The shadow of Mrs. Ramsay and James becomes, in Lily's work, a small purple triangle, set off against the white open space and violet of the flowers. That triangle almost vibrates with being through the novel, encapsulating the intensity of Mrs. Ramsay's existence as well as the problem posed by it: "How to connect this mass on the right hand with that on the left" (53). Color, then, is set to do the work of "being-toward," deepening, even blurring, as in Lily's final version ("it was blurred . . . it was done" [209]). It becomes the impetus for Lily's renewed connection to Mrs. Ramsay in the "Lighthouse" section, as well as her recognition of the huge leap of imagination it will require.

The intervening pages of the "Time Passes" section make even clearer the active force of colorism and the vibrant resonance of imagery in the novel as a whole. We are used to seeing this section as an inscription of time itself; its onward rush of sentences is broken up only occasionally by those declarative statements of human events, showing us the broader forces and rhythms of the natural world. Yet this section is also where, as Levinas would put it, the "green greens." That is, a profusion of colors and images—the rusted saucepan (137), "tortoise-shell butterflies" (137), "black ravens" (140), "pale mushrooms"(140), and, of course, "green suffused through leaves" (141), to name only a few—brings the verbal quality of language to the fore. Thus the copula created by this section of the novel is also a copula in another sense—an inscription of the verbal quality of narrative language and its constant push beyond singularity. The folding of the novel at this point, where the "Lighthouse" section presses on top of the "Window," Lily can be seen to be painting almost on top of her previous canvas, and the trip to the lighthouse beckons again, is thus a folding of ethical significance.

The fold between incarnations of Lily's painting also brings the question of aesthetics and the lived experience that surrounds it into contact with the more conventionally moral realm of Lily's understanding. "The question of relation" (148) is, of course what she is trying to paint, the remembered pattern in the cloth makes the fold in time that allows Lily to understand not only her aesthetic power but also the ethical lesson of benevolence, learned from Mrs. Ramsay as a personal not a public virtue. As she puts it in the "Lighthouse" section, after having resumed her painting and then having been interrupted by Mr. Ramsay, "she would give him [Mr. Ramsay] what she could" (152). This is a nonuniversalized ethical statement; it is not a maxim Lily will extend to her behavior with all others or one that might be based in any abstracted, position-blind sense of justice. I would argue that it is nonetheless a viable ethical position—that she ought give Mr. Ramsay what she could whether he deserved it or not. But it is a position made viable by Lily's understanding of her obligation to Mrs. Ramsay, rather than any ordinary feeling about Mr. Ramsay, which is brought into being by the folds of the text, the memory of tablecloth folded upon cloth, clean canvas folded onto the place where original canvas had been. Thus *To the Lighthouse* ventures to enfold subject and subject (Lily and Mrs. Ramsay, Lily and Mr. Ramsay); object and object (the two incarnations of Lily's painting); and subject and object (Lily and her painting) by way of the doubled action of its structure, which also draws together matters of epistemology, ontology, and ethics.

But let's return to the twisted glove as it appears and reappears throughout the passage with which we began. This moment is complex not only in its inscription of the potentially ethical connection between these two women but also as a reinscription of the distance between them, the eruption of Lily's resistance to the universal law of gender, and Mrs. Ramsay's representation of it in marriage. Here we see the series of attributes assigned to Mrs. Ramsay through the vehicle of her glove culminate in the injunction to marry and Lily's rejection of it. "All this [Mrs. Ramsay] would adroitly shape, she would maliciously twist . . . half turn back . . . insist that she must, Minta must, they all must marry" (49). Lily's feeble remonstrance, however inconsequential to Mrs. Ramsay, disrupts the universal claim: "She would urge her own exemption from the universal law; plead for it; she liked to be alone; she liked to be herself; she was not made for that" (50). It can be argued that this resistance is finally what propels

Lily's triumph in the "Lighthouse" section, for her painting reemerges out of her memory of Charles Tansley's comment that women "can't paint can't write" (159) and out of her rumination on Mrs. Ramsay's injunction about marriage. "For a moment Lily, standing there . . . triumphed over Mrs. Ramsay . . . how she stood here painting, had never married . . . Mrs. Ramsay had planned it. Perhaps, had she lived, would have compelled it" (175). In this sense the twist of the glove, like the fold in Orlando's fabric, brings us to the crux of the relationship among gender, ethics, and aesthetics, asking us again to link our notions of ontology and ethics to reflective judgments of our specific, lived experiences of the world.

Mrs. Dalloway offers another example in which the fold appears not in draped fabric as in *Orlando* or in a crumpled glove as in *To the Lighthouse* but rather in the shape of window curtains, folded back to allow us to see inside the house across the street. Here the aesthetic dimension of the fold is less as a convoluted surface that invites us to follow it into perpetuity, as Bal reads Caravaggio's folds, and more like the fold that Deleuze describes in Leibniz and Bernini, a membrane that exists between bodies, that subsumes collections of monads but is also flexible, fluctuating, and "interindividual."[60] This kind of a fold brings relationship into play as a question of movement through the membrane or the opening and closing of the curtain. In *Mrs. Dalloway* we see Clarissa's neighbor, the old lady "in the room opposite," glimpsed only fleetingly through the parted curtains at the window, not in the deep relationship of Lily and Mrs. Ramsay. When this old lady first appears in the novel she stands in Clarissa's mind for resistance to the dogmas of "love and religion" and for a certain laissez-faire: "Did she not wish everybody to be merely themselves? And she watched out of the window the old lady opposite climbing upstairs. Let her climb upstairs if she wanted to; let her stop; then let her, as Clarissa had often seen her, gain her bedroom, part her curtains and disappear into the background."[61] The ethical obligation in the face of this neighbor (neither an intimate nor a stranger) is to respond directly while resisting the temptation to incorporate her into some normative realm. The possibility is, however, that Clarissa will complacently consider this modest engagement through the curtain to be enough—and never acknowledge the further obligation this face might imply. By turning away from the mutual connection implied by the membrane and from the obligation imposed by being-with, she would fail to attain ethical understanding.

However, when the neighbor next appears, through another one of Woolf's temporal folds in the text, it is at the pivotal moment when Clarissa has been overwhelmed by the news of Septimus's death, which she feels to be her own disgrace (185). This is the moment of ethical awareness in the novel—a moment of response to an other—but also a moment when Woolf's emphasis on the private realm makes clear its constant implications for public morality. Septimus's shell shock is everyone's shell shock; his war death engages us all in the confrontation with death and our responsibility for it. The vision of the old lady is thus transformed: no longer is Clarissa content simply to watch and let be. She glances out, feeling "something of her own in" the view of the night sky (185), and is met with the sight of the old woman also looking out at the sky and straight back at Clarissa. "Could she see her?" Clarissa wonders, thus for the first time extending to the woman across the street an agency of her own and a demand to be recognized as a subject with a call for more than laissez-faire. The possibility that her neighbor, too, might find "something of her own" in the sky or in the view from the window back at Clarissa, and that this might then engage them in a relationship of mutuality, becomes real. That it is this sight that enables Clarissa to make sense of the importance of the death of Septimus and return to the world of her party further underscores it as a moment of ethical recognition.

Thus if we shift our attention from the celebrated final moment of Mrs. Dalloway's party to the one that slightly precedes it, we see a more direct inscription of ethical obligation and its aesthetics than is usually discussed in this novel.[62] What appears in *To the Lighthouse* primarily as the confrontation between intimate ethics and the social and moral injunction to marry here emerges as a matter not only of being-otherwise but also of the public good. War and its repercussions, class division and the difficulty it poses to Septimus and Rezia, the status of women and its significance for the old lady in the room opposite, for Clarissa, and for the other women in the novel all enter this moment through the curtain's folds. The parted curtain reveals not only the personal face of Mrs. Dalloway's neighbor, calling forth in Clarissa her recognition of the intersubjectivity of being, but also, and importantly, the public face of social life, marking even these private moments as politically significant.

We thus return to the question of ethics and its connection to aesthetics and politics. One might argue that the lesson Mrs. Dalloway presents us with here is much like Jean-Luc Nancy's claim that being-with-the-others is inseparable from being. Thus, our obligation toward subjectivity or toward another always takes part in our obligation toward our community—they are folded into each other. But once we have arrived at the status of the community and our obligations in and to it, we also verge on the matter of sovereignty, politics, and the operations of power. The notion of a community of beings who "co-appear" (to use Nancy's phrase) by its very nature challenges any hierarchical distribution of rights and privileges. The recognition of the face of the other as both private subject and public citizen makes responsibility a matter of both ethics and politics. Thus, the matter of being otherwise cannot be held apart from the demands of public discourse on, for example, women's rights or war.

Woolf believed one must "leave the ivory tower of ethics," which she considered the official domain of her father's work and far too abstract for her own writings.[63] Yet in *Mrs. Dalloway*, *Orlando*, and *To the Lighthouse* she creates a new ethics outside of that ivory tower. Resting in the folds between ontology and epistemology, intimacy and public responsibility, ethics in Woolf's work responds not only to the singular expression of alterity but also to the shared situation of community. Her novels illuminate the interconnection of ethics and aesthetics, even while bringing the claims of ethical intimacy, or the obligation toward being-otherwise, into the shared dimensions of our lived, embodied experiences.

War Interrupted: *Three Guineas* and the Challenge of Spain

In *Three Guineas*, however, Woolf's experimentation with narrative voice and structure of address link this intimate ethics more closely to public politics. Woolf creates a radically experimental new essay genre that generates political opposition from its play with documentary sources and photographs, its resistance to an overly personal partisan appeal, and its repudiation of narrative continuity. The vehemence of Woolf's rhetoric in *Three Guineas* has been the subject of much critical commentary, from Jane Marcus's "'No More Horses'" to Brenda Silver's "The Authority of Anger: *Three Guineas* as Case Study."[64] Yet the essay's mock epistolary form and disrupted structure of address participate more in its anti-war and feminist politics than has been noted and become crucial to Woolf's efforts to resist the conflation of home front and battlefront and the equation of noncombatant and soldier caused by modern total warfare, therefore also interrupting the continuity of political violence. Rather than build from the interconnective folds we have seen in her fiction, the political argument of *Three Guineas* works by an obverse logic, opening up narrative gaps and involutions that prevent the forced fusion of sensibility that characterizes propaganda and serves to perpetuate war. By refusing to emphasize the anonymity of war casualties, to heighten the effect of their atrocity, to personalize heroism on home or battlefront, or to individualize connection to the struggle, Woolf demonstrates how gaps in shared experience and narrative self-accounting can help constitute an ethical response to the intertwined politics of war and patriarchy.

First of all, Woolf's essay distinguishes itself from her earlier work by its apparent documentary impulse. Footnotes make up nearly a quarter of the total length of *Three Guineas*; it cites ninety-two books and forty-nine periodical sources.[65] Woolf's voluminous *Three Guineas* scrapbooks attest to her efforts to build an argument of reference and allusion and to ground her claims in the documentary materials that she clipped and saved between 1932 and 1938.[66] At the same time, Woolf alludes to reports, propaganda, and photographs from the Spanish Civil War that are not only absent from her notes and bibliographies but are also famously excluded from the essay itself, and she includes images that are never referenced. Photographs may seem to be "simply statements of fact addressed to the eye"(9) that attest to the reality of war and the horror of its effects. Yet among the five photographs included in *Three Guineas* ("A General," "Heralds," "A University Procession," "A Judge," and "An Archbishop"), none comes from Spain or depicts a war scene. What Woolf describes as the most efficacious documentation of the war—the evidence of atrocity and of violence that can clear up our confusion about the meaning of war—is neither reprinted in the volume nor footnoted.[67] Instead, she presents unnamed images of British patriarchal power. They appear as stand-ins for the images from Spain, their meaning generated metonymically through this substitution, which juxtaposes British domestic life with the state of total war in Spain without conflating their different material conditions or rhetorical situations.

In this sense, Woolf's essay immediately undermines its own evidentiary impulse and posits a narrative politics of hiatus, involution, and substitution.[68] Even as these photographs are crucial to Woolf's argument about the violence of the British patriarchal state, they also become part of a rhetorical strategy that asks readers to recognize the difficulty of responding to the images from the home front *as if* they were images from the battlefield and the danger of eliding the distinction between noncombatants and soldiers. The missing photographs introduce an occluded space or involution, which diverts the forward progress of Woolf's argument, asking us to stop and imagine the images that are not there, to understand them as objects of knowledge about the specific conditions in Spain as well as aesthetic elements crucial to the progress of the political argument of *Three Guineas*. Though she does not reproduce them or document their source, Woolf describes the missing photos for us:

> Here then on the table before us are photographs. The Spanish Government sends them with patient pertinacity about twice a week. They are not pleasant photographs to look upon. They are photographs of dead bodies for the most part. This morning's collection contains the photograph of what might be a man's body or a woman's. It is so mutilated, that it might, on the other hand be the body of a pig. But those certainly are dead children, and that undoubtedly is the section of a house. A bomb has torn open the side.
>
> (10)

Clearly, the photographs do not create the kind of immediate pleasure that an aesthetic object may be said to produce. Nor, at first glance, do they seem to generate the secondary reflection that Kant requires for judgments of taste. Woolf's comment about them ("they are not pleasant") appears to be an everyday sensation, akin to the kind common in response to food or drink. Yet when we consider them as aesthetic elements in Woolf's narrative rather than as external objects, the photographs we imagine spread out before us generate a shared reflective judgment both about the pleasure (or disgust) that they produce and about their connection to the "good," which becomes crucial to our encounter with the text and its ethical claims.

Certainly, as Susan Sontag points out, Woolf's use of these images also makes clear that "photographs are not 'simply' anything, and certainly not regarded just as facts, by Woolf or by anyone else."[69] As vectors both for information about the "reality" of Spain and for ethical and aesthetic judgment, they therefore challenge the fact/value split epitomized by Hume's law, raising the matter of the "ought" from the force of what "is." Further, Woolf's decision to omit the images from Spain also undermines the use of the documentary photograph as a sort of narrative trump card, one that appears to represent the truth about the war as though rhetoric-free. By leaving the Spanish images out of her volume, Woolf works to subvert "the photographic essay, which had emerged in newsprint as an objective framer of events," replacing it with her new narrative-essay hybrid whose power to reframe events develops from its refusal of transparent referentiality, its use of substitution and hiatus, and its emphasis on the constructive process of aesthetic imagination.[70]

In *Regarding the Pain of Others*, Susan Sontag takes Woolf to task for this passage, claiming the seemingly generic description of the photographs, which does not mention particular battles or name the victims, demonstrates that Woolf was disengaged from the actualities of the war and its politics and that she did not recognize the specificity of the Spanish people and the particularity of their struggle.[71] But Woolf describes precisely the kinds of anonymous images that flowed out of Spain during the height of the Civil War and that often show no more detail or focus on individual loss than Woolf here displays. In fact, it is likely that Woolf based this passage on photographs she had in hand. In a letter to her nephew Julian Bell she mentions "a packet of photographs from Spain all of dead children, killed by bombs."[72] Surprisingly, Woolf did not include those photographs in her scrapbooks, but they might have been images such as those on the many propaganda posters that were disseminated in Great Britain and France in 1936, which often blended documentary photographs with poster art and text (see figure 1.5). Or she might be referring to the five photographs of dead Spanish children that appeared in *The Daily Worker* on 12 November 1936 during the siege of Madrid, alongside "a contrasting picture of an English child at play in her peaceful garden"[73] (see figure 1.4), prompting Woolf to comment in her diary, "The Daily Worker article. Madrid not fallen. Chaos. Slaughter. War surrounding our island."[74] Though we cannot know whether Woolf was looking at British photojournalism or propaganda images sent out of Spain, both kinds of photograph would have played with the tension between the singular death of individuals and the forced anonymity of casualties under circumstances of total war, emphasizing the extent to which the war in Spain blurred boundaries between combatants and civilians, partisans and patriots. The images also erase many of the specific signs of class, location, or even national identity, making the Spanish dead iconic rather than particular. In both groups of images the status of individual children or the particularity of Spanish politics becomes secondary to the representation of an atrocity that could happen anywhere.

Indeed, both sets of images deploy the nameless dead as a form of Republican propaganda. Though Sontag remarks that Woolf's pho-

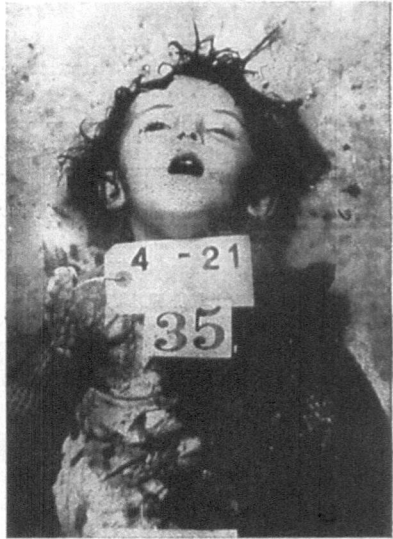

Twelve days ago THEY played as SHE does—
NAZI BOMB KILLS SEVENTY SPANISH CHILDREN

Why We Print This Page

BY WALTER HOLMES

WE DISCUSSED LONG AND SERIOUSLY WHETHER OR NOT TO PRINT THIS AWFUL PAGE.

PREVIOUSLY, DURING THIS SPANISH CIVIL WAR, WE HAVE RECEIVED PICTURES SHOWING AUTHENTICATED EXAMPLES OF THE MUTILATION OF MEN AND WOMEN BY FRANCO'S SAVAGE FORCES.

We have refrained from publishing these because it seemed that mere horror would not serve our great purpose, which is to harden the determination to fight Fascism and defend democracy.

BUT THE PICTURES ON THIS PAGE ARE NOT OF MERE HORROR. THEY TELL THE TALE OF THE MOST FEARFUL SIDE OF THE CONFLICT INTO WHICH FASCISM HAS HURLED THE SPANISH PEOPLE.

They do not tell the full tale. They only hint at the reality.

I write this explanation because it has been my lot to see death reap its ghastly harvest of powerful populations in these modern wars of aeroplanes and poison-gas.

I HAVE SEEN DAINTY DOLL-LIKE CHINESE CHILDREN AND COMICAL LITTLE MONGOLS REDUCED TO GHASTLY REMNANTS SUCH AS YOU SEE ON THIS PAGE.

I HAVE SEEN MUSSOLINI'S BOMBS COME HISSING DOWN AND BLOT OUT THE WARM, BROWN NAKED LITTLE BODIES OF ABYSSINIAN CHILDREN AS THEY PLAYED ROUND THEIR NATIVE HUTS.

But I know it does no good merely to tell tales of horror. War has abominations so foul that they are only for those who have had to see them.

Why, then, do we print these pictures. To shock? Certainly. But to shock all who look at them into realising that these dead children are the cost of brutal, militaristic aggression against peaceful people.

Planes and pilots from Mussolini and Hitler did this dreadful work. And behind them the whole machine of Fascism which capitalism has made as its last defence in Europe.

This same price of death will have to be paid until the death-dealers are themselves destroyed.

Look on these pictures and resolve, blow for blow, man for man shall be our reply until the arms of democracy have won the only war to peace.

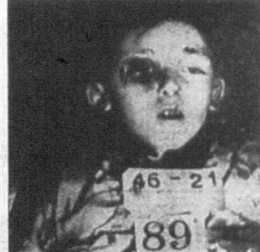

WHAT HAPPENED...

... when death fell among the schoolchildren playing in a quiet street of Telde, near Madrid, on October 15.

Three of Franco's Nazi Junker planes flew over the little town. They dropped a bomb on the street where the children played.

That bomb killed 70 schoolchildren. A British reporter wrote: "I saw parents searching for bodies. The bodies had been placed in a small delivery lorry belonging to local grocers. I tried to look in, but the sight was too gruesome."

Photos show the broken bodies of Fascism's little victims, and (below, left) the dead children, lying later in the school which they attended.

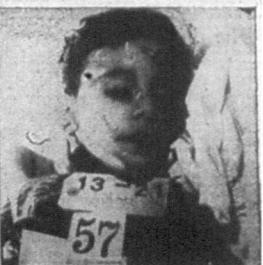

Figure 1.4. A page from *The Daily Worker,* displaying photographs of children killed in the Spanish Civil War. *Source: The Daily Worker,* 12 November 1936.

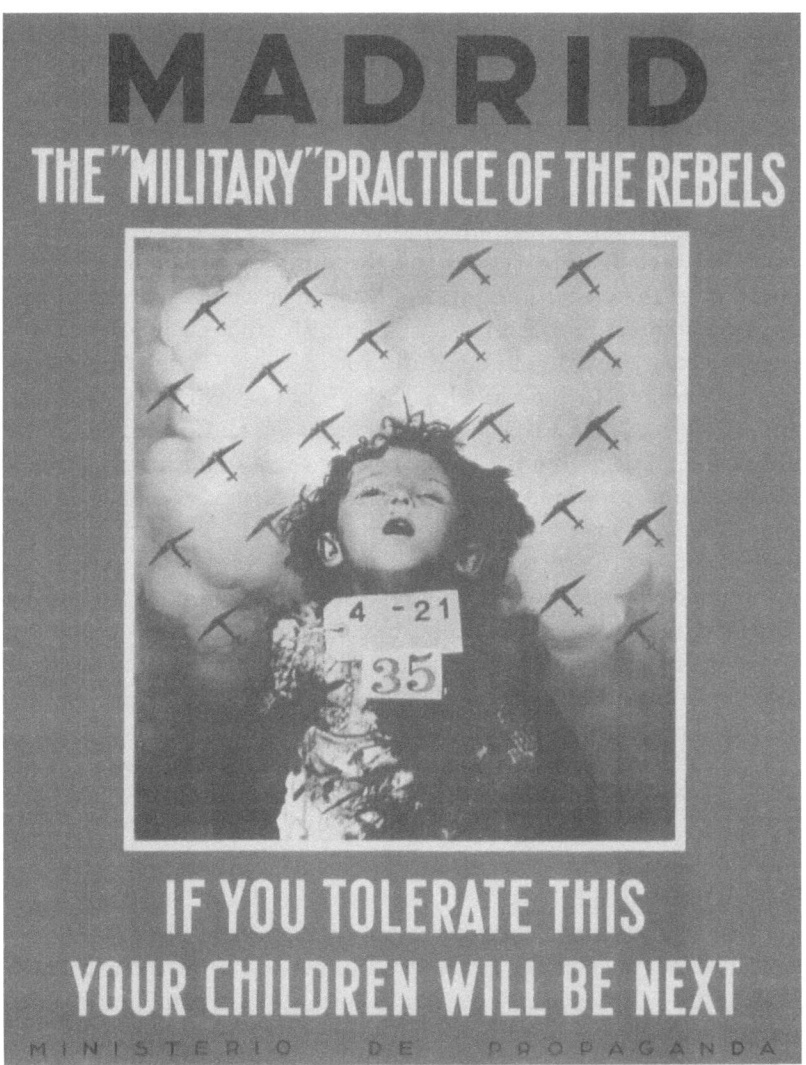

Figure 1.5. A Republican propaganda poster from the Spanish Civil War, in English. Madrid, Ministerio de Propaganda. *Source*: Spanish Civil War poster collection, POS-SP. CIV. WAR-.S656, no. 108. Library of Congress, LC-USZC4-7466.

tographs from Madrid seem "improbably not to be labeled," in fact, most of the images sent out of Spain carried only the kind of generic identification seen in figure 1.5.[75] *The Daily Worker* clearly published these atrocity photos to shock the British populace into opposition to the nonintervention pact.[76] The Republican propaganda posters highlight the deaths of anonymous children in order to emphasize their numbers rather than their individuality, thereby erasing the distance between British viewers and the suffering Spaniards. The implication of the poster in figure 1.5 is not that citizens abroad should respond with care for the particular Spanish children who have suffered but that they should be fearful for their own. The same reduction of children to the nameless dead, without individual claims as ethical subjects, that was begun by the bombing raids continues in the use of their images both in a journalistic setting and in propaganda. Contra Sontag, I would claim, Woolf is not further complicit in this generalizing, propagandistic use of the atrocity images. Rather, her efforts to subvert the particular power of this photograph as an "objective framer of events"—by leaving it out of the volume yet requiring readers to exert a process of moral and aesthetic judgment upon it—is a gesture of refusal in the opposite direction, toward its inevitable mobilization within an immoderate, emotional, and, in many ways, unethical propaganda argument.

Ironically, the Spanish Civil War marked a founding moment for what we now call "photojournalism," which grew out of the total warfare that merged home and battlefront in the streets of Madrid and Guernica. As Sontag remarks, "Ever since cameras were invented in 1839, photography has kept company with death," but Spain's was the first war in which there were photographers in place with portable cameras to take documentary images and send them back to print in the general press.[77] Advances in the 1920s, including the development of better hand-held cameras, faster shutters, new film, and better flash had made it possible to shoot in poor light and to capture bodies in motion.[78] Photojournalists were already on the ground during the siege of Madrid, having been sent by the European press to cover what was expected to be Franco's quick victory. They sent back images of street fighting, bombed out houses, and fires set by falling explosives and were among the first to display the results of Franco's raids over Guernica.

The photographers brought the world images of the dramatic consequences of aerial bombardment and demonstrated the effect of total warfare on the civilian population. Even though the photographs of

Guernica were used to buttress the conflicting claims on both sides, the degree to which photojournalism might participate in the heightened rhetoric of propaganda or be manipulated to elicit a particular political response was not often acknowledged.[79] The photographs coming out of Spain were censored and selected, but at the time they appeared to offer an unmediated, objective perspective on the war. Woolf's refusal to reprint the images or to treat them as simple bearers of facts disrupts this objective appearance. Her description of the photos highlights the combined home and battlefront that makes them significant as testimony to total warfare: a bomb has torn open the side of a house where children lived; those children, clearly noncombatants, have been killed in their homes. The horror of this scene is inescapable, the devaluation of human life it signals is clear. Yet Woolf neither issues incendiary language nor offers us an image that might generate an immoderate, emotional response.

Woolf's description also stands in marked contrast to Louis Delaprée's pamphlet "The Martyrdom of Madrid," which Woolf read and pasted into her scrapbook and likely used as another source for this section of *Three Guineas*. Delaprée, a reporter who was covering Madrid for the French newspaper *L'Humanité* provides a lengthy eyewitness account of the siege. He insists on his being dispassionate and objective, emphasizing again and again the unmediated quality of his narrative images. As with the photojournalists, his ability to see firsthand becomes crucial to his believability: "All the images of Madrid suffering martyrdom, which I shall try to put under your eyes . . . I have seen them. I can be believed. I demand to be believed." On another page he writes, "I am only an accountant of horror, a passive witness."[80] But as George Orwell would later say, in relation to Civil War writing, "on such an issue as this . . . consciously or unconsciously everyone writes as a partisan."[81] The possibility of writing with absolute objectivity, of bearing "passive witness" to atrocity is suspect. In Delaprée's case, the comment is disingenuous since he employs such words as "massacre," "martyrdom," and "atrocious." "I care nothing about propaganda literature" he says, "I do not follow any orders of parties or churches. . . . You shall yourselves draw your conclusions." But Delaprée not only selects the scenes he describes for particular effect but also focuses on the destruction of the streets of Madrid and the disruption of everyday life by the bombing of ordinary civilians. The insistence on the eye-witness as truthful and nonpartisan is belied by the horror Delaprée expresses and his insistence that the sight of the "child lying dead on the breast of a dead woman, in the middle of a pool of black blood" changes everything forever.[82] The indiscriminate violence of total war is represented by Delaprée's mobilization of sentimental images of women and children and the polemical manipulation of perspective and emotion.

Indeed, Delaprée's journalism, like the photo-reporting coming out of Madrid, bears strong affinities to propaganda, despite his protests to the contrary. The Spanish Civil War gave rise to an extraordinary amount and variety of propaganda, which I will explore at greater length in chapter 5. What is important to remark on here is the impossibility of separating documentary, evidentiary efforts to picture or describe the war from the use of those images to script an emotional response in readers or viewers. Propaganda, the "planned dissemination of news, information, special arguments, and appeals designed to influence the beliefs, thoughts, and actions of a specific group,"[83] infiltrates Delaprée's account, colors the photos printed in *The Daily Worker*, and clearly underlies the posters created by the Spanish Republicans to warn the British families that if they did nothing to intervene, their children might be the next victims of fascism. The Republican government and other partisan groups on the left mobilized the images of wounded children and terrified women in an effort to create an inescapable emotional response—in other words, to manipulate through propaganda without acknowledging the partisan nature of the message or attempting to mitigate the horror of the images presented. Thus, in these cultural products of the war, we can see the boundaries among war reporting, art, and propaganda being contested and their narrative dimensions restricted and manipulated. Perhaps we might say that those divisions are as specious as the rigid separations of public and private, home front and battlefront that are forever destroyed by the indiscriminate bombing of civilian populations. In other words, even as photojournalists and other observers like Delaprée were proclaiming their objectivity, the propaganda makes clear that there can be no presentation of pure "facts." Delaprée's attempt to define himself as an expert distributor of truth and his reader as an objective judge of that truth cannot sustain itself in the face of the events he witnesses, the atrocities he describes, and his conviction that we must respond to them with horror and political action.

We know that while drafting *The Years* Woolf was also concerned about these very boundaries, writing in her diary, "As this fiction is dangerously near propaganda, I must keep my hands clear." In fact, critics have claimed that the vehemence of *Three Guineas* defines it as a positive example of feminist propaganda, operating, in Jane Marcus's words, as a "socialist, pacifist, and feminist polemic."[84] Yet the essay's refusal to represent atrocity directly along with its rejection of the personalization of violence, as evidenced in what Sontag calls its lack of specificity, work together to undermine rather than generate the kind of unmodified, emotional responses that propaganda is designed to produce. Again discussing the photographs that she has both represented in and excluded from her essay, Woolf addresses this emotional response directly: "When we look at those photographs some fusion takes place within us; however different the education, the traditions behind us, our sensations are the same and they are violent. . . . For now at last we are looking at the same picture; we are seeing with you the same dead bodies, the same ruined houses" (*Three Guineas*, 10–11). She implies that viewing the photos creates a fusion of sensibility across lines of class, education, and tradition, smoothing over the differences of experience and perspective that are so important to Woolf's feminist argument throughout *Three Guineas*. If in the essay "Middlebrow," with which I began this chapter, Woolf seeks to imagine the lives of others across these boundaries, and if in her fiction the folds between subjects generate an ethical intimacy despite the gaps between perspectives, then here the forced commonality is reductive and potentially disempowering. Brutality in the photo creates an unavoidably violent sensation, leaving the viewer no choice in what to feel or believe—much as if she were looking at an image of explicit propaganda. The unanimity the image seeks to produce is also the goal of propaganda and is exactly what Woolf seeks to modify. If the Republican government and other partisan groups on the left mobilized photographs of wounded children and terrified women in an effort to create an inescapable emotional response that would lead toward scripted political action, Woolf, on the other hand, will evade and resist using war images to produce that "fusion" of sensibility.

The mock epistolary structure of *Three Guineas*, in which Woolf refuses again and again the political assumptions of the person writing to her, and describes the gaps between their lives, perspectives, and politics, also works to undermine any immoderate fusion of sensibilities. The structure of the essay is crucial to its power, rescuing it from the relentless movement toward some goal that Susan Suleiman has argued is crucial to ideological or propagandistic narratives and inscribing the possibility of reciprocity, which Janet Gurkin Altman calls the core of the epistolary pact, within even the most vehement passages of the essay.[85] Altman defines this reciprocity as "the call for response from a specific reader within the correspondent's world," and she reminds us that "even when the internal reader's interpretation of the letter does not constitute part of the represented action of the epistolary work, . . . this reader is nonetheless a determinant of the letter's message."[86] Yet the guiding assumption of *Three Guineas* is that gaps of lived experience preclude the completion of this reciprocal relationship in Woolf's essay and intervene in the structure that guides letter and response, thereby also interrupting its determinative power as propaganda.

Indeed, the gaps in lived experience between Woolf and her imagined interlocutor intervene directly in their epistolary relationship, limning the interpretive divide that emerges between the letter that Woolf receives and the response she writes. The way Woolf and her interlocutor respond to the photographs also intervenes in the way they read each other's letters and helps determine the involuted shape of what Woolf places before us in the text. If the anonymous letter writer hopes that the documentary images of the siege of Madrid will spur Woolf to join his efforts to prevent war, Woolf sees these images as evidence that it is impossible to join his cause or even answer his question "How in your opinion are we to prevent war?" (3). Rather than engage with the question, she stops the argument and interrupts herself, saying, "Let us give up for a moment, the effort to answer your question" (10). Here, in one of the many hiatuses of Woolf's text, in which she interrupts her narration, begins again, or switches to another generic mode, she mitigates the power of the image to determine her response and to act like propaganda on her or on us. Woolf uses narrative fragmentation, heteroglossia, and hiatus not only to elaborate an (interrupted) poetics of epistolary relationship but also to interrupt the forced fusion of sensibility in both image and text. Indeed, the experimental form of *Three Guineas* works to point out that, within the contexts of twentieth-century European patriarchy, the demand for uniformity of perspective participates in the same violent erasure of differences among lived experiences as the equation of soldier and civilian under circumstances of total war.

In the last section of the book, in her famous passage about the tyrant or dictator, Woolf once again returns to the occluded photograph to demonstrate this point:

> It seems . . . as if we were looking at the photograph again . . . but it is not the same picture. . . . Another picture has imposed itself on the foreground. . . . He is a man certainly. His eyes are glazed; his eyes

glare.... Behind him lie the ruined houses and dead bodies—men, women and children, but we have not laid that picture in front of you in order to excite once more the sterile emotion of hate. On the contrary it is in order to release other emotions such as the human figure ... arouses in us who are human beings

(141–42)

In her description Woolf has interposed the figure of the dictator where we expected to see the bombed out houses and dead bodies, once again substituting one image for another and arguing metonymically. She disrupts the emotion incited by the war photographs by interrupting our view of them and transfers our attention to the body of the man who by both argument and association becomes linked to this carnage. His glare is apparent; his eyes are mentioned twice. The dictator's face demands a nuanced, ethical response, an address by the reader, who must acknowledge both his personhood and the danger it poses. In the photographs from Madrid the subjects have been deprived of the ethical claim of the individual, embodied human; the images are of "what might be a man's body, or a woman's; it is so mutilated that it might, on the other hand, be a body of a pig" (10). They subside into objects of sympathy despite the despair they might evoke. Yet Woolf here personalizes the dictator's face in a way that the Spanish photos do not. The dictator's glare supplants those dead bodies, along with the easy sentimentality of a scripted emotional response to images of dead children. By insisting on the personhood of the foreign dictator, Woolf asks her readers to recognize both his singularity and his similarity to the British patriarchal authorities whose photographed faces are interleaved in the text. Yet in recognizing his singular glare, Woolf also ensures that we do not conflate the fields of home and battlefront or repeat the war's violent merging of noncombatant with soldier. In structuring this passage as she does, Woolf asks us not only to correlate the two images but also to respond to the distinctions between them, in which her politics emerges.

But I also want to connect Woolf's interruption of our view of the war photograph and its expected emotional response to her other famous interruption in *Three Guineas*—the interruption of her address to the first letter writer that appears in the opening pages—and therefore back to the mock epistolary structure of the narrative. Here, too, Woolf uses the figure of her interlocutor to interrupt a planned response (3). After describing what she has in common with this letter writer, Woolf shifts. "But," she writes, then stops and inserts the famous three ellipses that, she says, mark a "precipice" between them (4). This passage makes the structure of address of *Three Guineas* explicit—the Woolfian narrator will "give an account of herself" to each of the writers adumbrating her unwillingness to join their ventures. But Woolf's account of herself begins with the difficulty of that gulf, those ellipses, that makes simple common cause, empathy, or fused emotions, as is seemingly demanded by the photographs, impossible and that therefore precludes the reciprocity implied by the epistolary relationship.

As I have suggested, giving an account of oneself is a crucial aspect of narration that highlights both its ethical engagement and the limits of that engagement. In seeking to tell one's own story in and though narrative, one always exceeds the limits of what is known by the self since one cannot narrate one's own birth or death or account for the social relations in which one is irrevocably situated. For Judith Butler, the possibility of self-narration is always suspect, and the account we give of ourselves is always interrupted, involuted, incomplete. In fact, she argues, once we have been called to give an account for ourselves, narrative coherence disappears. Like Cavarera, Butler highlights this narrative incoherence as a possible source of an ethical subject position: "Our 'incoherence' establishes the way in which we are constituted in relationality: implicated, beholden, derived, sustained by a social world that is beyond us and before us."[87] The impossibility of even the personal act of narrating one's self becomes interrupted by the primacy of our relationships and obligations to others and by the structure of address to others within every narrative situation.

But Cavarera makes the ethical implications of intersubjective self-accounting more salient. In narrative we answer a demand from an audience, real or imagined, intimate or foreign, that asks, "What is this about?" But rather than respond with a self-reflexive statement or a coherent narrative that supplies the answer to the "what" of the question—that is, a substantive rather than an open narration of subjectivity—Cavarero would say that narratives gesture toward the other or audience by also asking, "Who are you?" This gesture marks the beginning of altruism and the recognition of the situation of relationship and reciprocity that surrounds the narratable self. "The relational status of Identity always posits *an other* as necessary," whether embodied as spectator or listener or by the narrator who tells the story.[88] The narratable self thus comes into being as a moment of exposure to the "you" who is listening, to others, to the outside of the story, in what Paul Ricoeur would call the "dialectic of selfhood and otherness," or what Hannah Arendt would describe as the "web of relationships" into which we inevitably fall when we speak.[89]

This reciprocal exposure of the self to others through the mutual question, "Who are you?" also constitutes an action in the world that immediately becomes political. As Arendt describes them, speech and action are intricately linked and indispensible to the political nature of human beings:

> With word and deed we insert ourselves into the human world and this insertion is like a second birth. . . . If action as beginning corresponds to the fact of birth . . . then speech corresponds to the fact of distinctness and is the actualization of the human condition of plurality, that is, of living as a distinct and unique being among equals. Action and speech are so closely related because the primordial and specifically human act must as the same time contain the answer to the question asked of every newcomer: 'Who are you?'"[90]

Answering this question not only reveals the singularity of each individual's identity but also instantiates her status as equal and unique within the public realm of politics. Indeed, it is within the sphere of human community, or "sheer human togetherness," that speech and action take place and within the realm of warfare that we see its limit.

> Whenever human togetherness is lost, that is, when people are only for or against other people, as for instance in modern warfare, where men go into action and use means of violence in order to achieve certain objectives for their own side and against the enemy. . . . Speech becomes . . . simply one more means towards the end, whether it serves to deceive the enemy or to dazzle everybody with propaganda.[91]

Arendt points out the importance of openness and reciprocity in the communal process of self-disclosure. If this process is foreclosed, then narration becomes merely an instrumental means toward an indiscriminate goal rather than an act of political freedom and community.

Thus, when Woolf uses the ellipses in *Three Guineas* to foreground the question, "Who are you?" she is using narrative hiatus as an antidote to war and calling us back from an instrumental use of speech akin to propaganda. The political power of the book is predicated not only on its physical dismissal of the images of Spanish atrocity but also on its structural disruption of the dominant ways of understanding who is speaking, about what, and to whom, which forecloses the kind of processual, ongoing disclosure of agency that Arendt calls necessary for freedom and politics. Woolf's manipulation of the structure of address—her foregrounding of her position vis-à-vis the letter writers, her constant self-reference, her acknowledgment of her scrapbooks or her pile of photos—undergirds Woolf's efforts to disrupt the scripted emotional responses to war that leave no room for exchange between narrating voice and imagined listeners or for a variety of responses to the question "Who are you?"

Yet the challenge of the Spanish Civil War, or perhaps of war in general, is that it erases the ongoing character of the question of "who," instead reifying and fusing the identities of its participants into the categories of witness, victim, partisan, and enemy, without regard to distinctions of attitude, experience, or geographical location. And as Sontag points out, the reification of these categories, aided and abetted by generic images and the forced, unitary perspective of propaganda, produces a level of disengagement with the specificity of Spanish history and politics that even Woolf finds difficult to resist.[92] At the same time, the actuality of total warfare confounds the distinctions between soldier and civilian, extending its unremitting violence to the very possibility of the category of the noncombatant. Woolf's manipulation of structures of address in *Three Guineas*, her disruption of the documentary impulse, and her unwillingness to use propaganda photos to motivate a scripted emotional response to the war work to defy both the fusion of identities and the erasure of their singularity. By insisting on the variety of faces, experiences, perspectives, and narrative responses to war, Woolf's essay works to reestablish the very category of the noncombatant and therefore to disrupt the power of total warfare. Like the Society of Outsiders that Woolf imagines at the end of *Three Guineas* (97–105), the essay's involuted and interrupted narrative logic not only brings intimate ethics to bear on the public politics of antiwar activism but also acts as a political refusal of the very categories of identity created by and perpetuated in war and patriarchy.

Modernist Exposure: Rhys's Border Walkers

Yet if we take up the early novels of Jean Rhys, written at about the same time, we begin to recognize another way of looking at the narrative politics of interruption and refusal. If Woolf's essay resists war and patriarchy by interrupting the assumption of shared identities, perspectives, or experiences, for Rhys gender, poverty, and colonial status intervene to prevent those very assumptions and disrupt their promise of a communal future.[93] Caught up in the uneven relations, mistaken bodies, tortured geographies, and disrupted futurities of colonialism, Rhys's heroines struggle to account for themselves to others and to maintain their existence in a world of dislocation and physical deprivation. The problem of narrative self-disclosure and community that in Woolf's work binds ethical intimacy to antipatriarchal politics becomes a matter always conditioned in Rhys's early novels, *Voyage in the Dark*, *Good Morning, Midnight*, and *Quartet*, by the locations of identity, and the uneven relations of coloniality. In these novels the matters of race, gender, and subaltern status seem to predetermine the possible responses to the reciprocal narrative question, "Who are you?" while the problem of belonging falls victim to the irregular development and foreclosed identities of colonialism.

We might here recall Sontag's criticism of *Three Guineas* as disengaged from the specificity of Spanish politics and the geopolitics of the Civil War. In claiming the Spanish struggle as her own, Woolf also seems to wish away the asymmetrical global, political relations that helped fuel the conflict and doom the Republic and to transport us through her antipatriarchal narration to another space, where her new Society of Outsiders will someday reign. Her political refusal is in this way productive, imagining as it does a new location for an oppositional politics of identity. But it is clear that Rhys's heroines cannot escape with Woolf to a space outside contemporary politics. Even as they struggle to account for themselves in narratives of shifting perspectives, distorted temporalities, and uncertain plots, Rhys's characters are irrevocably located within their specific circumstances of poverty, subaltern status, and coloniality. They walk the borderland between colony and metropolis, back room and sidewalk cafe, playing a geopolitical game that has at once no end and no future. Rhys takes Woolf's narrative gambit a step further, showing us not only, like Woolf, the potential of narrative folds and gaps to generate ethical relations and resist their political foreclosure but also the power of a convoluted life story to illuminate the spatial constraints on the narratable self and to refuse the political imperatives of twentieth-century British colonial geography.

Thus, while Rhys's narrative foreclosure does not produce Woolf's hopeful and at times almost utopian vision of a future politics, it is not apolitical. Lee Edelman has argued that queer theory "dispossesses the social order of the ground on which it rests" by refusing a belief in the "paramount value of futurity" and its structuring of social reality.[94] Within the context of the postcolonial politics of race, class, and gender, Rhys's narratives do the same. Her heroines are constantly on the move, shuttling between geographical locations, spaces, and identities, hoping that a change of territory will also dislodge the social relations and geographical assumptions that work to determine their futures. Her narrative convolutions, interruptions, and refusals question the possibility of personal growth under conditions of uneven colonial development. By refusing to posit a productive potential future for their heroines, utopian or otherwise, these novels challenge the viability of the very categories of identity that have created them. Thus, what Judith Butler points out as the ultimate impossibility of self-narration, its inscription within social relations and temporalities that define and exceed its own narrative power, becomes in Rhys's work a specific and pointed critique of the historical and political geographies that undergird her characters' lives, both in twentieth-century Britain and in Dominica. Rhys extends the implications of Woolf's refusal to participate in the culture of war and partriarchy by also questioning the viability of its future. Though the narratives revolve around a world of intimate relations, they give rise to few moments of ethical recognition or community and refuse to gesture toward an "as if" future where social realities might tend toward justice. Reading Rhys and Woolf together, then, shifts our perspective on the politics of narration, making clear not only the global positioning that conditions the very possibility of intimate ethics and social relation but also the potential of narrative incoherence, hiatus, and refusal to reorient the future.

Rhys's narratives famously interrupt themselves or jump around in time and space, sometimes devolving into a series of fragments separated by gaps on the page or a series of chapters linked only by juxtaposition. They have often been perceived as being quickly written or without craft. Yet in her autobiography Rhys comments, "A novel has to have a shape,"[95] and we know from her later work with her editor, Diana Anthill, that she was particular about word choice and revised her writing seriously.[96] These vagaries in Rhys's work, I would argue, display the challenge that accounting for human relation, especially across geographical, gender, and class identities, poses to narrative progress. Indeed, Rhys's work rarely exhibits the kinds of folds that can bridge the incommensurable in Woolf's novels or mark its future possibility. Her characters often exist in enclosed isolation, spending their days alone in bed-sit rooms or waiting in cafes. If Arendt argues for the importance of community as the threshold for human action, then Rhys's heroines exist on the margin of that possibility and of the potential link between word and deed. Their fragmentation and dislocation show much more than the troubled psychological state often ascribed to them, whether described as neurotic symptom or response to trauma. *Voyage in the Dark*, *Good Morning, Midnight*, and *Quartet* foreground narrative ethics as irresolvable, endless, and problematic and highlight the difficulty of narrative self-exposure, especially on the margins of community.

At the same time, as Gayatri Spivak points out, "the politics of imperialism" suffuses all of Rhys's novels, and the question of the global always lurks beneath the inconsistency and self-interruption of her main characters.[97] The profound dislocation that Rhys's heroines suffer again and again, whether in the bed-sit rooms of London, on the streets of Paris, or while shuttling across European borders, highlights their cultural and economic dispossession and their exclusion from full membership in the human communities that surround them. They are what one critic has called "border-walkers" along the boundary between the middle and lower classes, whose ethical difficulty is posed as both intimate and global.[98] Yet the marginal status of these characters is tied in many ways to their corporeal and geographical identities, much as we might say Rhys's was bound to her status as a white Creole woman from the Caribbean. They do not work but subsist off their bodies as models, chorus girls, and lovers of men with money. They suffer cold, hunger, and the pain of abortion or childbirth and are classed by the marks that race, gender, and geographical position leave on their bodies. Thus, in Rhys's fiction the ethical challenge of accounting for oneself to others intersects with the social and political limitations imposed by geography and located, embodied experience.

Though she is most celebrated for her late novel *Wide Sargasso Sea*, which takes place partly on the island of Jamaica, Rhys wrote the majority of her work in the late 1920s and 1930s while living in Paris, London, and elsewhere in Europe, and most of her fiction is set in these locations. Yet even in her early European writing, the problem of self-definition for her heroines is tied to Rhys's own status as a white Creole from Dominica. She was born in 1890 to a family that had deep roots on her mother's side in the white planter society in Dominica and to the identity known as "Creole" to mark its distinction from the newly arrived, still British, white population. Many critics have pointed to the legacy of ambivalence in Rhys's work that arises from this particular Creole past (although generally by reference to *Wide Sargasso Sea*).[99] Judith Raiskin describes the white Creole identity as perpetually split between European and Caribbean identities. "Rhys," she says, "examines in her fiction the influence each culture exerts on the other, and the fluidity of racial and cultural roles."[100] In the context of *Wide Sargasso Sea*, Benita Parry also argues for the importance of Rhys's split identity and her "representation of a Creole culture that is dependent on both [English imperialist and black Jamaican identities] yet singular."[101]

Rhys's own sense of her nationality or belonging is, however, difficult to determine. "I don't belong to anywhere but I get very worked up about the West Indies," she once said.[102] In her early stories, Rhys seems to shun West Indian themes and settings, developing an abbreviated style of writing and a disdain for description that makes the characters appear to drift in the modern metropolis. This perhaps explains why her mentor, Ford Madox Ford, who published her first stories in the *Transatlantic Review* and encouraged her writing career, claimed that "Rhys's business was with passion, hardship, emotions: 'The locality in which these things are endured is immaterial.'" On the other hand, as Veronica Gregg points out, Ford claims that "Rhys's position as a colonial contributes to her ability to represent the 'underdog' and makes her acutely critical of divisions inherent in European social structures."[103] Thus Ford identifies the complexity of Rhys's Creole, colonial identity, which neither proclaims its loyalty to an original space nor leaves that space fully behind. The published fragments from her diary make a similar point. In these fragments Rhys meditates on the "irritation, harsh, gritty" that she feels about "England and the English . . . their hypocrisy, their self-satisfaction, their bloody, bloody sense of humour." She remembers learning that "most English people kept knives under their tongues to stab me." At the same time she is caught in the colonial subject's conundrum, forced to acknowledge that, "all the books you read are English."[104] In other words, Rhys's deep ambivalence about her connection to both Dominica and England influenced her writing and thinking from the beginning of her career.

Still, it is clear that geographical location does matter for Rhys, especially as it brings to the fore questions of the interrelationship between metropolis and colonial outpost and between normative white European and racialized Creole or black identities. If we understand it as the science of human-landscape relations rather than some more static effort to map the spatial determinants of identity, geography can provide a means to understand the interactions between the social and physical world:

- The study of place seeks to describe and understand not only the location of the physical features of the Earth, but also the processes, systems, and interrelationships that create or influence those features.
- The study of space seeks to explore the relationships between places and patterns of activity arising from the use people make of the physical settings where they live and work.[105]

Geography can also be seen to supply the context for bodily experience of the world because aspects such as climate, topography and land use impinge on physical sensation and because other geographical factors such as urbanization, population growth, and changing notions of space evolve in concert with social and political development. A particular geographical landscape thus becomes linked to the human identities, communities, and social activities that take place in or around it; shifts in geography always have both corporeal and social implications. Further, as David Harvey has eloquently argued, the way we conceive of our relationship to space, place, and time inevitably intertwines with our concerns about social justice. Justice becomes a situated concept, bound to our material location even as "social constructions of space and time operate with the full force of objective facts."[106] This means that our conception of our relationship to space, place, and time often takes on a quasi-objective, determinative value that undergirds our understanding of our social roles and the potential for human justice that emerges out of them. The quasi objectivity of geographical determination is, of course, of particular significance in the context of colonialism, where the vagaries of location generate specific coordinates of identity along with their inscription in specific regimes of justice. In particular, for Rhys as a white Creole from Dominica, born into a family on the economic decline, the split between her presumed and actual status in the colony creates what seems to be an almost impossible identity. At the same time, her poverty and geographical place of birth locate her, as though by objective standards of measure, as a subaltern outsider vis-à-vis the metropole.

Rhys's vacillation between the geography of the West Indies and that of England thus implies more than her difficulty choosing landscapes or allegiances. Geographical identity implies the determination of her corporeal existence in specific relation to a place, population, and history. In *Voyage in the Dark*, Rhys grapples with this seeming geographical determinism by forcing the West Indies and England together in a strikingly unusual and original manner. In a 1959 letter, Rhys wrote, "There are two places for me. Paris . . . and Dominica . . . both of these places or the thought of them make me want to write . . . the West Indies started knocking at my heart. So—'Voyage in the Dark.'" In an earlier letter Rhys claimed that in *Voyage in the Dark* she was trying to present the character's past in the West Indies as vividly as the present (in Britain) and to show them "side by side."[107] By bifurcating the novel's landscape in this way and creating a new hybrid location, Rhys attempts to circumvent the privileging distinction between them and to deny the quasi-objective power of British metropolitan geography to exert dominion over colonial spaces and identities.

The descriptions of Dominica thus become fully realized only as they are seen as strangely interfolded into the British landscape lived by Anna Morgan as she begins her downward spiral to death.[108] What might seem to be signs of Anna's growing madness become, in the context of this narrative, indications of the reality of the colonial topography she still inhabits even as she lives in Britain, yet Anna can find no rational model that can help her unite the two places.[109] The first page begins with a confusion of landscape and climate: "Sometimes I would shut my eyes and pretend that the heat of the fire, or the bed-clothes drawn around me, was sun-heat; or I would pretend that I was standing outside the house at home looking down Market Street to the Bay. When there was a breeze the sea was millions of spangles; and on still days it was purple."[110] This same kind of climate or landscape confusion appears throughout the novel. Since England is almost always associated with cold in *Voyage* (as in all Rhys's work), when Anna becomes feverish her thoughts are instantly transported back to Dominica and to her home life there (31). Flowers at Savernake Forest remind her of flowers in the Caribbean, and a dreamlike state makes her unable to make sense of their differences. Colors, smells, even bends in the road can trigger a connection to her past home. The road to Constance Estates, Dominica, which she vividly remembers, is like none of the roads she has traveled since, yet its memory is triggered by thoughts of English travel and comes to stand in for her entire life's journey: "That's how the road to Constance is. . . . It was as long as a life sometimes" (151). It is as though Anna expects to zigzag around another bend in an English lane and encounter this road and the fragmenting experiences of her life will suddenly coalesce.

The novel raises the complexity of geography as both topographical and locational, having the power to situate and contextualize human communities within shared experiences of physical place. It is also deeply racialized, containing within it assumptions about populations, their living habits, and their social development. Indeed, the entire novel may be seen as a challenge to notions of geographical objectivity and an extended rumination on the inadequacy of the reference book description of Dominica: "Lying between 15° 10' and 15° 40' N. and 61° 14' and 61° 30' W. A goodly island and something highland, but all overgrown with wood" (17). Conceptions of centrality or marginality here do not follow the latitude and longitude lines increasingly made rational by the new science of geography in the first decades of the twentieth century. Nor do racialized identities stay attached to the specific groups or the particular geographical situations they were meant to describe. That Anna as a young girl wishes she could have been born into a black Dominican identity, with its seemingly more rooted traditions and culture, implies not only her acceptance of a sentimentalized, imperialist notion of black experiences in the colonies but also an understanding of her unmapped position as a Creole who is West Indian but not black and, as such, to white English eyes, without any acknowledged identity or location at all. As Peter Kalliney puts it, "Anna's affiliation with blackness . . . serve[s] as a marker of disaffection, becoming a way to describe her own status within the class and gender hierarchies endemic to metropolitan culture."[111] Her effort to claim an identity stands as a sign of its own impossibility. If Homi Bhabha has famously described racial appropriation and mimicry within the colonial context as the instantiation of the rule "not quite/not white," here Rhys extends the problematic of the "not quite" to both black *and* Creole white.[112] Without denying the privileged location of the white Creole within the Caribbean context, Rhys shows how the physical dislocation of her Creole heroine makes her all the more subject to geographical laws of race and exclusion.

Yet when Anna repeatedly tells her lover, Walter, "I'm a real West Indian . . . I'm the fifth generation on my mother's side," she tries to establish "West Indian" as a positive category of difference tied to a specific and racialized (white) identity and a determining cultural context (55). With this claim she is attempting to begin her own account of herself within a clearly marked colonial position and to situate herself as possessing that identity in relation to Walter and other English people. As Susan Stanford Friedman has argued, contrary to their quasi-objective status, geographical identities and the hierarchies of power connected to them are always constructed relationally and shift according to contexts and vantage points.[113] Thus in evoking her own genealogy and insisting on her life story, Anna attempts to create a category of relationship that separates her from the general British underclass and opens up the possibility of a higher position of power vis-à-vis Walter.

As part of this process the novel foregrounds its own structure of address in Anna's attempts to account for her life. The novel opens in medias res and gestures back to a time before its own beginning: "It was as if a curtain had fallen, hiding everything I had ever known. It was almost like being born again" (7). As Butler points out, an account of a self is always missing its own beginning: "I am always recuperating, reconstructing, and I am left to fictionalize and fabulate origins I cannot know. In the making of the story, I create myself in new form."[114] But Rhys's novels, I would add, make clear that this dispossession from one's own story is not simply a matter of the structure of address or the process of fabulation but also a function of our inscription into ongoing social and political discourses that predate, define, and extend beyond us. Her heroines are bound by those discourses to gesture again and again back to the time before their own birth rather than forward to a narratable future. While *Three Guineas* also opens in medias res ("Three years is a long time to leave a letter unanswered") and argues by reference to the past, it remains focused on the potential, difficult as it may be, for an alternate future where the story might change and where a different process of justice might emerge. In that sense, we might recognize a certain utopian optimism in Woolf's work, born from her metropolitan status and her faith, however tested, in the better future of social relations. Surely Woof's Society of Outsiders represents this impulse. Rhys's *Voyage in the Dark*, by contrast, makes no attempt to develop our faith in Anna's future. Her narrative seems always and inevitably to spiral back toward the constraints of her past, pointing out the hazards of her disenfranchisement and refusing any future that might arise out of its social matrix.

Anna's effort to generate her own story out of the reconstruction of the Creole identity in England is doomed before it begins, its politics a matter of Rhys's refusal to accede to a fantasy of self-determination, equal social relations, or an easy postcolonial justice. Walter cannot understand Anna's concern or perceive the Creole as a category of identity, bodily or otherwise. He is amused by the depth of Anna's worry about her identity, as though he not only can't see her exoticism as a real difference but also can't imagine why she would have use for an identity at all. Anna tries to tell him more about her past and of her frequently spoken desire to be black (which to her implies more authentically Dominican). In Mary Lou Emery's words, "Anna creates her own image of herself . . . she clings to this disjointed self even though others—lovers, relatives, acquaintances—reduce her status to a one-dimensional inferiority and insignificance."[115] But Walter's response elides any positive difference in her identity or its location and disparages her attempt at self-definition: "Everybody thinks the place where he was born is lovely" (55). Unlike her stepmother, or the schoolgirls, who in not only racial but geographical confusion, call Anna the "Hottentot," Walter is not shocked by the notion that she might wish to be black; for him, in her generalized, colonial exoticism and her sexual availability, it is almost as though she already is.

Further, that "Hottentot" was a specific term meant to apply to Khoikhoi women from South Africa enters not at all into the fact that the girls use the word for Anna. The epithet, in the white imagination, clearly implies hypersexuality of the sort attributed to Sara Baartman, who was labeled the "Hottentot Venus" and displayed, studied, and paraded around Europe in the early nineteenth century. The comment is thus proleptic; Anna in her youth is neither black nor sexualized. But in her abusive relationships with Walter and other men and her entrapment in Europe, Anna comes more and more to resemble the Hottentot Venus. The geographical and historical irony that attaches blackness to Caribbean, not African identity here becomes even more pronounced by the connection of blackness to the imprisoned and abused white woman. Geographical markers of difference tied to a specific time and place are thus destroyed, along with their potential for resistance to discourses of power. Instead, reified and restrictive identities cut loose from their cultural contexts can be imposed on subaltern bodies without distinction. The play of identities, and in particular racialized, female identities, in Rhys's novel thus demonstrates the extent to which colonialism breaks down the fluid interrelationships among geographical locations, subjectivities, and communities. Rhys's dislocated geography marks not only her desire as colonial subject to move from periphery to center without losing her located identity but also her challenge to a discursive regime that both ties her to the past and offers her no future.

The power of colonial geography to fix identities while at the same time denying their specificity also conditions the efforts at self-definition and self-description in Rhys's other work from the 1920s and 1930s. Like Anna in *Voyage in the Dark*, her heroines in *Good Morning, Midnight* and early stories such as "Vienne" are defined by others through the places they've been, the clothes they wear, or how often they change hotels. They seem unable to separate the situations they inhabit (complete with their social expectations) from their own self-accounts and become easily defined by the bodily identities into which they are thrust. At the same time, Rhys's plots often hinge on the disjuncture between these static or even retrogressive identities and the day-to-day experience of the characters, much as *Voyage in the Dark* revolves around the extent to which Anna is or is not a Hottentot. In *Good Morning, Midnight*, for example, characters are often identified only by their nationality and the effort of the heroine to understand them in that light. An American, a Russian, a Turk, and an odd assortment of French and English people are often categorized by simple reference to national stereotypes. But the main character, like Anna in *Voyage in the Dark*, exists in a sort of limbo, having become French on her marriage to a Frenchman but still obviously not French to the Parisians around her. Her hat "shouts 'Anglaise'" though she is no more at home in London than in Paris, as we learn from the fragmented passages of the novel that shuttle back and forth between countries and time periods.[116] She calls herself Sasha but offers in the first few pages that this is a name she has made up (12). As characters from her past come in and out of the novel, the narrative us no word to sum her up and no explanation about where she has come from. She gives birth to a baby who quickly dies, but she never becomes the type we would call a "mother."[117] Like many of Rhys's heroines, she accepts money and food from men in exchange for companionship, but we cannot really call her a prostitute. In terms of her social identity, then, "Sasha" does not really exist. For example, in the final section of the novel, "Sasha" encounters a gigolo who awakens in her the most direct feelings we have seen throughout the novel, yet we know that despite the intimacy of their encounter, he will only treat her according to their roles. We are therefore not surprised when he takes most of her small stash of money. Because she is not rich, she cannot be a gigolo's client; though she really cares for him, she cannot be his lover. So, in the end, she is his mark.

Rhys's heroines often encounter this sort of constriction of identity through the experience of poverty and the sexual possession of their bodies. Their poverty makes them quite literally streetwalkers, roaming Paris or London to distract themselves from their hunger or to scare up someone to buy them a drink. In *Good Morning, Midnight* Sasha is constantly on the move, and the narrative wanders with her, progressing in a sort of spatial strategy without direction or logic, bound to her attempt to distract herself from her situation. "What about the programme for this afternoon?" she says, "That's the thing—to have a plan and stick to it. First one thing and then another, and it'll all be over before you know where you are" (52–53).

Poverty also marks itself directly on the bodies of these women, who sometimes go days without eating or sit in the cold because they cannot afford the heat. The use of their bodies in a form of prostitution, then, is a corporeal sign of their overdetermined and omnipresent abjection. At the same time, prostitution functions in Rhys's novels as a form of women's work, inseparable from the heroines' other jobs as models, receptionists, and chorus girls. If Woolf in her "Middlebrow" essay wonders what it must feel like "being a dressmaker . . . being a cook, being a prostitute"—in other words, what it would be like to inhabit the world of working women—Rhys's narratives immerse us in the consequences of work that is literally embodied female. As models, chorus girls and prostitutes, or lovers of men with money, the heroines of Rhys's novels must trade on the exchange value of their bodies as a means to subsistence and in the process become both workers and commodities.

This commodification of women's bodies creates a dynamic in Rhys's work that skews the reciprocity necessary for ethical intimacy. For example, in Rhys's first novel, *Quartet*, Marya Zelli, whose husband is in jail, accepts aid from a couple named the Heidlers. In what appears to be a simple desire to help, they supply her with a place to stay when she is homeless and destitute. Quickly we discover that both Mr. Heidler and his wife, Lois, expect Marya to become his lover. The three are locked in a game of possession in which the only desire that gets satiated is Heidler's and the only one whose life is at stake is Marya. In other words, the relationships among the characters in *Quartet* revolve around the commodification of Marya's body, which becomes defined by its tendency to circulate. Heidler justifies his attempts to possess Marya by defining her as "that sort." Marya tries to resist Heidler's determination of her identity saying, "You don't know anything about me. . . . You can't lay down the law about me because you don't know anything." Yet Heidler's power in this novel is enough to make a reality out his pronouncement. Marya succumbs to his overtures and becomes the woman who can be "got" almost by virtue of his having willed her to be so. "He was forcing her to be nothing but the little woman who lived in the Hôtel du Bosphore for the express purpose of being made love to. A *petite femme*." Much like Anna in *Voyage*, Marya is not only commodified but remade into the entrapped, sexualized body on display, resembling in more ways than one the Hottentot Venus.[118]

The novel thus inscribes the matter of identity and of accounting for oneself to others within the fraught discourses of embodied existence and commodified possession. For Rhys's characters, it seems, the possibility of self-narration is always already constrained by the geographies of colonialism, race, and sexuality, which challenge the basis for ethical identity and relationship. As Delia Caparoso Konzett puts it, "Rhys's work . . . questions and dismantles the traditional foundations of morality and humanity built on the illusions of rightful ownership. . . . Sartre's existential principle of being for oneself (*l'être pour soi*) is dismissed by Rhys as part of the bourgeois sense of agency of which her uprooted characters have been deprived."[119] Rhys's early narratives pose the difficulty of being in-and-for-oneself for a heroine subjugated by her race, sex, or colonial position. Self-sufficient subjectivity becomes a privilege of the dominant position or, at least, contingent on access to a noncommodified existence. Then, we might further argue, since being-toward-the-other always involves risking the self, this subjectivity is also immediately put in jeopardy. Indeed, for Levinas, all ethics begins from this risking of the self; even "sensibility," he writes, "is exposedness to the other" or vulnerability.[120] But from a subjugated, commodified position, is it possible to "risk" one's self? Or does the risk loom too large, putting in jeopardy the subject's very viability? These are the crucial questions posed by Rhys's work. For Rhys's heroines, the profound vulnerability of the self within the gendered discourses of poverty and colonialism is perpetual and disabling, interrupting not only the coherence of their lives but also their ethical potential and futurity. The potential for ethical relation in *Voyage in the Dark*, *Good Morning, Midnight*, and *Quartet* succumbs to the experiences of dislocation and isolation of Rhys's heroines, whose subaltern identities determine both what they can say about themselves and who will listen. Heider's claim to know that Marya is "that sort" stands as an already-foreclosed response to the ethical question, "Who are you?" and to the problem of identity within Rhys's fiction.

Yet this conundrum is precisely the point. Rhys's work returns us to the matters of narration and structure of address as possible sites for both ethics and politics, but from a different direction. Whereas Woolf's *Three Guineas* generated the gap as a potential break from history, a hiatus in which the documentary impulse of war journalism might be questioned and the ongoing violence of war and patriarchy might be resisted, Rhys's novels describe narrative interruption as subject to history and perilous to the self. Yet the encounter between narrative ethics and the discourses of race, gender, and location in Rhys's novels from the 1920s and 1930s also points beyond this self-disintegration. Calling to us from their bed-sit rooms or from the back corners of cafes, Rhys's heroines push us to see not only the ethical difficulty posed by their experiences of cultural and economic dislocation but also the political implications of their disenfranchisement. Though these heroines cannot wrest control of their lives and bodies from the forces of dispossession and commodification, Rhys's novels nonetheless foreground their ethical and political claims. The disrupted trajectories of Rhys's characters point to the foreclosed future of colonial history, thus signaling for us as readers the impasse of empire. Read alongside Woolf's work, Rhys's novels mark the intimate scene of ethics as a site where colonial power relations are played out and where the gaps between incommensurable experiences emerge out of an imperialist history. If Woolf found it difficult to leap into the lives of the cook, the dressmaker, and the prostitute, Rhys not only inhabits those lives and maps their fraught colonial geographies but also forces us to recognize the challenge they pose to dominant narrative trajectories and the grounds of social and political relations. Thus, the limit of ethics in Rhys's fiction marks instead the beginning of its politics. In their fragmented and interrupted structure, built upon the difficult question, "Who are you?" and their invocation of complex colonial geographies, Rhys's novels mark the fraught path between intimate ethics and global politics while refusing to reproduce a future with little opportunity for justice.

TWO | Comparative Colonialisms
Joyce, Anand, and the Question of Engagement

> The fact is that around 1910 a certain space was shattered.
> It was the space of common sense, of knowledge (savoir), of
> social practice, of political power, a space thitherto enshrined in
> everyday discourse.
> —Henri Lefebvre, *The Production of Space*

> To open the dialectic between cosmopolitanism and geography
> is immediately to see that there can be no universality without
> particularity and vice versa.
> —David Harvey, "Cosmopolitanism and the Banality of Geographical
>   Evils"

> The presuppostion is that I live together not only with others
> but also with my self, and that this togetherness, as it were, has
> precedence over all others.
> —Hannah Arendt, *Responsibility and Judgment*

In his collection of essays, *Conversations in Bloomsbury*, the celebrated Indian writer Mulk Raj Anand, whose *Untouchable* I discussed in the introduction, described the beginnings of his novelistic craft. When he was a university student in England, Joyce's *Portrait of the Artist as a Young Man* spoke to him across the divide of culture and nurtured his desire to write: I "recognized myself in the hero of the *Portrait*."[1] In *Portrait* Joyce presented not only Stephen Dedalus's inner world, compelling to Anand in its own right, but also, importantly, a version of what was taking place within Anand himself. Comparing Joyce to his mentor, the Islamic poet Iqbal, and his poetic cycle *Secrets of the Self*, Anand preferred to follow Joyce, claiming him as a kindred spirit and model, if not strictly a compatriot. He decided that "the portrait is a good model for me, if I want to stage the recovery of self . . . in my novel" and resolved to begin that novel almost immediately. Anand secretly determined to pattern himself after Joyce, taking specific instruction not merely from Joyce's mode of narration and his representation of self-development but also from his rejection of religion and mysticism, his use of sound to transmit extralinguistic meaning in prose, and his complex cosmopolitan perspective.[2] From this moment he began his effort to forge a new English-language tradition in fiction for India.

What sense do we make of Anand's remarks about Joyce? How does his use of the Irish writer as a model and an inspiration help us understand both the politically engaged fiction that he will write about India's disenfranchised and the political contexts of Joyce's work? What does a transnational model of reading that connects the two writers across the distance separating Ireland from India have to tell us about the intersection of modernist narrative and political action? This chapter will address these questions by examining the complex correspondences that link Joyce's *Portrait* and *Ulysses* to Anand's early novels *Untouchable* and *Coolie*, written in the 1930s. In this comparison, I will argue, we can see the influence of important elements of Joyce's style on Anand's work, such as his insistence on material reality rather than what Anand calls "religious illusionism," his use of limited perspective and focalization as a means to representing and critiquing *Bildung*, and his emphasis on sound as a marker for both the uncontrollability of language and its locatedness. But even more important, we can see the way these elements are transformed and put to new uses within the literary, historical, geographical, and political contexts of Anand's work. Through this process of transformative recreation, Anand's modernism links back to Joyce's work, resituating it within a broader postcolonial geography and refocusing the way we read its politics. For example, the geographical impulses that make the material texture of the city crucial to Stephen's wanderings through *Portrait* and that create a cartographic *Ulysses*—famously, the only map of Dublin necessary in case of catastrophe—find their counterparts in Anand's attention to the particular Indian locations of his fiction and his development of a complex, rooted cosmopolitanism that in turn extends our understanding of Joyce's own. Modernist geography inexorably links these two writers, despite their distance in time and space, and helps to show the continuum of political commitment that undergirds transnational modernism. In another way, the challenge to liberal notions of the citizen as a universalized, representative man that is nascent in Joyce's *Portrait of the Artist* becomes more pronounced in Anand's novels about disenfranchised Indians. Anand's work disrupts the political assumptions that accompany the bildungsroman tradition, refocuses our attention on Joycean models of the citizen-subject, and brings to the fore the modernist critique of liberal notions of the universal, "representative man" that also motivates Joyce's work.

Thus, I suggest that Anand's use of Joycean techniques to trace the life of a displaced, wandering coolie or to show the untouchable Bakha in the context of his village streets highlights the political implications of Joyce's fiction even as it underscores Anand's own complexly rooted, cosmopolitan commitment. That Anand became a follower of Gandhi and embarked upon a long career as a social activist and writer of engagé fiction even as he remained a follower of Joyce demonstrates not only the link between Joyce's experimental prose and the socially committed novels of Anand but also the continuum of political engagement that inhabits transnational modernism. Indeed, the connection asks us to rework and redefine our understanding of engaged writing, allowing it to emerge as a central mode of many worldwide modernisms, made more visible by the transnational optic. Sartre long ago claimed that "art loses nothing by being committed. On the contrary ... the always new requirements of the social and the metaphysical involve the artist in finding a new language and new techniques."[3] Yet in practice, experimental fiction has often been described as separate from overtly committed writing, with modernism being distinguished from the more directly political work often dubbed "thirties literature."[4] Further, political readings of modernism often restrict their purview to local contexts, classifying transnational or cosmopolitan concerns as separate and secondary. Reading Joyce and Anand together works against both kinds of separation, asking us to consider stylistic experimentation as a component of a political commitment that is both geographically situated and transnationally engaged.

Further, if Anand, as displaced colonial subject, finds Joyce's phrase "I go to forge in the smithy of my soul the uncreated conscience of my race"[5] (and this is the specific passage he cites) meaningful for his own political situation in India, then we must also see Anand's use of that phrase as important for understanding Joyce. The phrase resounds for Anand because it connects the development of self with the creation of its community, thus generating a potential connection between his desire to "stage the recovery of self in a novel" and his increasing sense of responsibility toward India's dispossessed. Anand's work will focus on heroes who are so thwarted in their development that they often die in childhood and whose caste and colonial status prevents them from aspiring to civic citizenship as the "free individual subjects" of liberalism and the classic bildungsroman.[6] On the other hand, the trajectories of Anand's heroes bind them to the local geography and inscribe them into a range of surrounding communities and discourses whose shared languages display the potentially disruptive power of hybrid speech. Anand's novels thus not only challenge the notion of the exemplary or representative man at the center of the bildungsroman tradition but also build a narrative politics out of what I call, following Hannah Arendt, "enlarged thinking"—that is, a political mentality cognizant of the perspectives and voices of others and derived from within the web of stories in which we are situated.[7] In Joyce's *Portrait*, too, the breakdown of narrative self-certainty and play with multiple perspectives can be read as a challenge to the politics of the traditional bildungsroman and to its politics. Joyce's use of a focalized perspective, his construction of Stephen as embedded within a variety of discourses and his play with the performative uses of language all challenge the viability of the model of the singular, autonomous man. The heteroglossia and multiplication of perspectives in Joyce's work resist reincorporation into the unified, national language that is at the heart of the bildungsroman tradition and invite enlarged thinking into the place of political community.

The connection between the two authors also provides us with a new way into the ongoing discussion of colonial textuality from a crucial transnational perspective. Clearly, the question is not simply a unilateral matter of influence—though Joyce surely influenced Anand. Rather, this encounter highlights the multidirectional flow of global literature and culture, where streams of discourse move not just from metropolis to colony, or even from colony back to metropolis, but also, as in this example, from colony to metropolis to another colony and back again. As Elleke Boehmer points out, "Oppositional, nationalist, proto-nationalist, and anti-colonialist movements learn from one another as well as drawing from their own internal political and cultural resources or the political culture of their oppressors. Looked at from this perspective, anti-colonial nationalism emerges as an allusive, cross-cultural, intertextual, or interdisciplinary phenomenon."[8] Though this allusiveness or intertextuality is most often noted in a much later, postindependence group of writers, I will claim that we can already see similar correspondences in the contact between Joyce and Anand. Critics have pointed out that early-twentieth-century Indian writers felt connected to the Irish struggle. Irish writers, such as Yeats and the theosophist James Cousins, also turned to Indian writing as source material for spiritual and formal exploration.[9] By the early years of the twentieth century, political writers in Ireland had begun writing about the commonalities between British colonial rule in Ireland and in India.[10]

But what I want to argue here goes beyond remarking upon influences or commonalities. Discussing connections between the colonies and the metropolis, Boehmer remarks,

> Merely tracing correspondences ... can appear to leave too much, as it were, to coincidence. In that the new colonial writers themselves represented dissent and difference from source, their contribution can perhaps be interpreted in a stronger sense. Can they be seen as forming a constitutive part of the modernist movement rather than as being merely its symptom, or sympathetic effect?[11]

The "correspondence" between Joyce and Anand moves beyond coincidence and demonstrates Anand's position as a constitutive part of modernism, thus helping to realign modernism along global lines. Placing Anand in this way also forces us to reconsider Joyce's writing within the context of Anand's direct political engagement, which was perceived as so dangerous in pre-Independence India that his first three novels were banned there.[12] The later writer thus shifts our perspective on the earlier one, placing him in new global contexts and highlighting political implications of his writing that otherwise remain half-hidden. When we read Joyce and Anand together, what emerges is a complex textual exchange that highlights the geographical specificity of their colonial critiques; the challenges their work poses to conceptions of a representative, ethical subject; and the real political engagement, extended and made more overt in Anand's work, of their modernist narrative modes.

Geographical Joyce

John Joyce once said of his son James, "If that fellow was dropped in the middle of the Sahara, he'd sit, be God, and make a map of it."[13] While this statement may come as no real surprise to Joyce scholars, its significance as commentary about the profound geographical impulses of Joyce's work merit further exploration. Joyce's efforts to locate his narratives by specific reference to markers of landscape and climate, while at the same time mapping Dublin in its geopolitical history, participate in the broader development of modernist geographical ideas in the early twentieth century and demonstrate the extent to which geography functions as a crucial vehicle for understanding narrative engagement with the sociopolitical spaces of modernity, as we have also seen in Jean Rhy's work. Further, examining Joyce in the context of early-twentieth-century geography helps illuminate the nature and limitations of Joyce's nationalism and places his work more firmly within a specific history of transnational thinking. This geographical history, while not directly engaged in empire building or in resistance to it, nonetheless provides a new perspective for understanding Joyce's confrontation with Ireland's colonial status even while it carries implications for understanding his work within a global postcolonial framework.

Geographical theory has moved the spatiality of texts to the forefront, asking us to consider place or location, along with history or genealogy, as crucial to literary study and pointing out the extent to which geographical concerns undergird the social and political commitments of the novel.[14] The geographer David Harvey reminds us:

> Novels ... are "possible worlds." As such, they can inspire the imagination. They have influenced conceptions and imaginaries of the city and affected material processes of urbanization.... Literary works ... permeate thought in ... subtle ways, helping to create a climate of opinion or some "consensus of the imagination" in which certain kinds of political-economic action suddenly seem both possible and desirable.[15]

In other words, as we have seen in relation to Jean Rhys, novels not only respond to changing geographical conditions and record those conditions within their pages but also, by way of both content and form, generate geographical sensibilities and the social and political activities that surround them. If narrative fiction may be said to have any connection to action in the world, this kind of geographical creativity is a primary vehicle. Further, if, as Harvey suggests, novels influence the material processes of urbanization and modernization more generally, they do so by positing an alternative though related realm where these forces may be examined, imagined, and played out in ways that may be dramatically different from existing conditions or that highlight the material forces of change. In this "as if" realm, to use Paul Ricoeur's term, fiction turns away from the absolute referencing or mirroring of the world and toward an effort "to *redescribe* reality," which has social and political repercussions.[16] Thus, the power of the novel to redescribe a particular geographical location or to participate, by way of this redescription, in its historical development becomes crucial to the novel's potential for political engagement.

It therefore bears stopping to examine the implications of this connection between geography and fiction and its use in highlighting the potential for narrative action in the world. In "The Cartographic Imagination: Balzac in Paris," Harvey discusses Balzac's geographical sensibility in a way that is also valuable for understanding Joyce's. Harvey treats Balzac's engagement with Paris as a geographical enterprise that participates in the history of geography as a field while taking part in the development of Paris as the sociohistorical locus of an impending modernity. As has long been remarked, Balzac, like Joyce, created so detailed a portrait of his city that scholars have called it maplike.[17] Harvey, however, goes further and claims that Balzac's encounter with Paris is more active and generative: "Balzac . . . sets out to observe, map, interpret, dissect, and understand [Paris] . . . Balzac actively constructs a map of the city's terrain and evokes its living qualities. . . . It is through his cartographic method that he establishes his power within and over the city."[18] In actively mapping the city through his fiction, Balzac not only makes it legible to us in a new way but also shapes our imaginative understanding of its potential development.

Of course, maps are always selective, concealing as they reveal and focusing attention on particular areas while distorting others. Balzac shows us Paris in the process of being transformed into Benjamin's "capital of the nineteenth century" or into the site of modernity that both Baudelaire and Flaubert would variously imagine it to be. In focusing on the city's economic transformation into the locus of "compulsive capital accumulation and the commodification of everything, including pleasure, status, and power," Harvey argues, "Balzac's cartography constitutes an attempt to intervene in and resist that process." Thus, the active work of mapping at the level of narrative both recognizes and intervenes in the social and historical contexts of city life. There is, as Harvey points out, "something subversive" in it.[19]

Much of what Harvey says about Balzac's mapmaking might easily be applied to Joyce. His cartographic eye renders Dublin visible as a modern city, the "Hibernian metropolis" where such commodities as "Plumtree's Potted Meat" circulate along with the characters who desire them and where the geographical litany of the Dublin United Tramway Company official's bawling out the stops is interrupted by the "clanging ringing" of the tram passing by.[20] Joyce's narrative maps of Dublin, while seemingly exhaustive in their scope and famously meticulous in their detail, focus on the street-level dailiness of middle-class life—the butcher shops and pharmacies, the newspaper office and pubs. Harbors and strands become the sites of reflection and encounter; few characters, except Eveline's departing Frank, work the boats for a living. Women labor as laundresses and landladies, but the backbreaking physicality of Dublin as a working city goes largely absent from Joyce's books. The famous wanderings of Stephen and Bloom, who circle about the city only to meet each other by chance at nightfall, like the travels of the characters in *La comédie humaine*, document their shared inhabitance of a common path through the gritty streets of Dublin but also point to the vast maze of routes and places that do not see their feet.

Nonetheless, the geographical contexts for Balzac's Paris are different from those of Joyce's Dublin (as they are from the Indian locations in Anand's *Coolie*). Modernizing Paris in the early nineteenth century is a place of forward movement and positivistic energy, ripe for grand transformation on the order of Haussmann's midcentury rebuilding. The *embourgoisement* of Balzac's city has not yet given rise to the lassitude that will characterize Frederic's experience of Paris as recorded in Flaubert's *Sentimental Education*. Indeed, geographical tracts of the period tend toward the optimistic and expansive, marshalling the developing scientific methods of exploration and cartography to capacious effort to understand the world through maps. For example, Alexander von Humboldt's magnum opus, *Cosmos*, which began to appear in 1845 around the time of the *La comédie humaine*, was committed to the notion of the unity of the world cosmos, the interconnections of its peoples, and a vision of the "earth as a inseparable organic whole," with man as one element in a vast, global natural history, a crucial part of the earth's natural balance rather than its focus.[21] Modernity as it emerges in midcentury Paris, then, comes into being not only under the sign of sprawling commodity capitalism and the development of the bourgeoisie that Balzac maps so well but also within the positivist geography of organic human development and the interaction of populations within an expansive sense of space.

But the geographical contexts for Joyce's work are more explicitly national or imperial, with geopolitical connotations different from those of the nineteenth century. While Balzac's geographical sensibility helped to situate the historical and social development of bourgeois Paris within the positivist, expansive impulse of the geographers of the time, Joyce's writing maps modernizing Dublin within the political contexts of twentieth-century geographical thought and the tension between regional and national horizons. Geography developed as a discipline in the late nineteenth century as the push toward exploration and mapping of new territories accelerated. National geographical societies were founded, which sponsored expeditions into unmapped terrain and journeys of scientific discovery while also buttressing statist claims, imperial conquest, and colonial occupation.[22] Geographers participated in the expeditions of discovery and possession in such regions as Alaska, Antarctica, and Africa, and they accompanied the building of the transcontinental railroad across the American frontier, extending and solidifying U.S. hegemony in the West. The work of these missions in the service of both science and state was never a secret. As Harvey points out, "The Renaissance tradition of geography as everything understood as space, of *Cosmos*, got squeezed out. It was forced to buckle down, administer empire, map and plan land uses and territorial rights, and gather and analyse useful data for purposes of business and state administration."[23] The use of exploration and cartography in the service of the imperial nation-state system has a long legacy; in the twentieth century, geopolitical arguments based on cartographic claims were crucial on all sides during both world wars.

In the early twentieth century, this statist geography became more complex than it had been in the age of exploration. Attention shifted away from simple mapping toward a new emphasis on the observable relationships between people and land in a variety of regions and the multiple ways in which the two could be shown to interact over time.[24] Halford John Mackinder, the most celebrated British geographer, defined geography in 1887 as "the science whose main function is to trace the interaction of man in society and so much of his environment as varies locally." But while these new ways of defining the discipline emphasize their focus on human-landscape relations over time and the interconnection between the physical and the social or political characteristics of human communities, they remained enmeshed within a national political horizon and still often operated in service of the state and its imperial aspirations. So MacKinder describes the "many causes [that] conspire to maintain the greatness of London" as a metropolis, its historical development in response to its physical setting, and points out the geographical routes for the conquest of India. In his final defense of the discipline, MacKinder writes, "I believe that . . . a geography can be mapped out which shall satisfy at once the practical requirements of the statesman and the merchant, the theoretical requirements of the historian and scientist, and the intellectual requirements of the teacher."[25] Clearly, he has no intention of leaving "the purposes of business and state administration behind."

MacKinder argued that because the age of exploration had come to an end and all the world's surface had been mapped, the world had become a "closed system," in which all actions have worldwide repercussions.[26] In the twentieth century he developed the influential notion of the "world island," which links the interrelated histories of Europe and Asia to their geopolitical power:

> Whether we think of the physical, economic, military, or political interconnection of things on the surface of the globe, we are now for the first time presented with a closed system. The known does not fade any longer through the half-known into the unknown; there is no longer elasticity of political expansion in lands beyond the Pale. . . . Every deed of humanity will henceforth be echoed and reechoed in like manner round the world.[27]

MacKinder claims that the clash of state powers can no longer be understood by reference to a single territory and that the balance of power will depend on the control of what he calls the central "world island"—that is, the joint continent of Europe, Asia, and Africa, the center of which he considers the "geographical pivot of history." Though he does not say so, the essay implies that efforts to dominate this world island through state expansion and imperialism will be crucial to twentieth-century geopolitics.

While compelling in its ability to transcend geographical nationalism and to connect the development of empire to geographical forces, this geopolitical model also encourages the view of the Eurasian "world island" as the "center" and all other regions as the periphery, and it is one of the sources for the twentieth-century center/periphery model.[28] Crucially, the periphery comes into play only when it has a strategic impact on the struggles for control over the center. Further, MacKinder's model assumes that each national region on the map corresponds to a particular "people," and he does not hesitate to refer to the English as a "race" whose differentiation may be followed as it encounters different environments.[29] It is clear that the new twentieth-century geopolitics was bound to claims for the geographical necessity of empire and the marginalization of the periphery, as well as assumptions about the physical causality of race.

But Paul Vidal de la Blache, the most significant French geographer at the turn of the century, steers clear of Mackinder's geopolitical aims and counters racial thinking by advocating a model that has been called geographical "possibilism" and that I will term "modernist geography."³⁰ Rather than explore the implications of geographical systems for national identities or state power, Vidal looks to regions or "*pays*" as his primary unit of inquiry and discusses the interrelationship between humans and the earth they live on. In this way, Vidal's modernist geography focuses on environment not as a simple determinant (as it might have been in the nineteenth century) but rather as providing a set of possibilities that humans turn to their own uses, thus helping to create their own habitat over the long term. This is the crucial distinction of the French school, which became important not only for the development of French and American geography but also for the historians Lucian Febvre and Fernand Braudel.³¹ Vidalian geographical possibilism argued for the continuing connection between history and geography as disciplines and their divergence from models of biological determinism.

Vidal's understanding of the unity of the earth as the broad habitat for human activity also recaptures some of the globalism of Humboldt's earlier thinking and builds toward an almost cosmopolitan vision. Conceiving of the earth as a whole "whose parts are coordinated," Vidal sought to describe the environment as a "composite, capable of grouping and holding together heterogeneous beings in mutual vital relationships."³² Large regions and even the entire globe might come to function as one "world island" rather than being divided into MacKinder's central and peripheral regions vying with each other for geopolitical advantage. Unlike the nineteenth-century positivist geographers, Vidal emphasized that we cannot know the base, determining geographical conditions of human development since years of historical life and of human-landscape adaptation intervene.

Through Vidal's work, geographical and human history taken together become the study of influence, adaptation, and effect, rather than evidence for a clear predictive causality. This aspect of twentieth-century geographical thought will be crucial to what I call modernist geography, that is, geography as bidirectional, long-term, and relational, involving not only geographical causes of human development but also human effects on geography over the *longue durée* and often over large regions. Human adaptations to geography, seen over time, do not resolve into homogenous racial groupings. Vidal explains that "when an attempt is made . . . to discover the elements of the population, not only of a large region but even of a small one, lack of homogeneity is found to be the rule almost without exception."³³ Adaptation is an ongoing process of coalescence and blending that makes the description of "races" nearly impossible and that belies any simple or static description of locally identified groups.

Thus, I want to argue that Joyce's references to landscape, climate, population, and the map of Dublin demand to be situated within the history of geographical thought in the twentieth century and, in particular, the trends toward a cosmopolitan modernist geography exemplified to a certain extent by MacKinder but even more so by Vidal de la Blache. Like Balzac almost a century before, Joyce not only locates his events and characters on the map of the city but also shows us Dublin as it is in the process of being transformed by modernity and the geographical processes of human-landscape interaction. If for Balzac the process of mapping intervenes in the social and historical contexts of city life in order to show us the development of bourgeois France in the context of an interconnected organic earth, Joyce's geographical intervention focuses on the extents and limits of geopolitical frameworks for understanding space, the participation of Ireland in a broader region or world system, and the notion of possibilism rather than racialized determinism as a means of understanding cosmopolitan human community. Most important, especially in the context of this chapter, Joyce's geography highlights the complexity of his relationship to both nationality and cosmopolitanism, which will also connect him to Anand's writing about India. As Harvey claims in "Cosmopolitanism and the Banality of Geographical Evils," geography is not only the terrain on which the tension between nationality and cosmopolitanism is played out, it is essential to the very nature of those terms within Western thought.[34]

At first glance, however, it seems that, despite its cartographic qualities and its constant reference to location, Joyce's work is little occupied with the broad questions of landscape, the development of human populations over time, or MacKinder's kind of geopolitics. Indeed, natural Ireland makes few appearances in Joyce's work, entering, for example, in "The Dead" as what seems to be an imagined place of liberation in the west, what Seamus Deane calls, "a phantasmal place," which, in contradistinction to Dublin itself, appears to belong to premodernity.[35] Critical work on Joyce by Nolan, Duffy, Cheng, and Valente, to name a few, frequently raises the issue of Joyce's ambiguous relationship to Irish nationalism and empire, but when it turns to the specific geography evoked in the texts often treats them as "imaginative appropriations of space" or in terms of their evocation of an imagined national community.[36] But the west country is nonetheless "a geographical reality as well as a symbolic region" in *Dubliners* just as the concatenation of east and west in *Ulysses* forces a complex interrelationship between the Greek past and the Irish present, which Michael Seidel has termed "epic geography."[37] For Joyce, treating what Vidal calls the "unity of the earth," means rediscovering the relationship between these geographical spaces and any renewed historical or political identity that might emerge.

This way of understanding the crucial shift in geography at the turn of the century also opens up an alternate way of reading the much-analyzed ending of "The Dead." If Gabriel recognizes his need to "go west" and reconnect with the Irish national past, however fraught, then the beginning of snow that softly blankets all of Ireland at the end of the story shows his new openness to physical, rural Ireland and all that it symbolizes for Miss Ivors. On the other hand, this passage is clear in its insistence that Gabriel witnesses a particular kind of snowfall: "Snow was general *all* over Ireland. It was falling on every part of the dark central plain, on the treeless hills, falling softly upon the bog of Allen and, farther westward, softly falling into the dark mutinous Shannon waves."[38] It is not often that snow falls over all of Ireland and unites it in a single climate. This climactic unification is crucial for Gabriel because it means that his going west neither demands that he collude with empire (note the reference to the "mutinous waves") nor requires him to leave Dublin—or modernity and the continent—behind. In fact, one could argue that within the contexts of the bidirectional flow of influences in modernist geography, quite the reverse is true. Both possible implications—that he must leave his country behind and escape to the continent and Miss Ivor's false assumption that "his country" must lie discoverable in the west—succumb to this new geography, which is neither assimilative nor isolationist and which challenges facile assumptions about the source of human races or populations in separable terrains, regions, or soils. The opposition between the west as "authentic" Ireland and "inauthentic" Dublin is undermined, even as the physical boundaries between them are effaced. By recognizing with the geographers that the force of climate can serve to unify the region rather than separate the rural west from metropolitan Dublin and that the human-landscape relations create time and space as an intertwined matrix that undergirds human history and social life, Gabriel lays claim to an "inauthentic" notion of belonging that has its sources in modernist geography.[39]

It is clear that this geography not only challenges the claim to authenticity in the landscape of the west but also dismantles the distinction between national and cosmopolitan identities that seems to fuel Miss Ivor's criticism of Gabriel. As I have elsewhere argued, cosmopolitanism need not exclude local habits of loyalty or belonging; a world citizen may also carry ties to local communities or affiliations. Indeed, the history of European cosmopolitanism, from Kant forward, grapples constantly with the recognition that loyalties are often shared between the local and the global.[40] As Vincent Cheng reminds us, "If culture is both local and global . . . any nationalism worthy of the name would have to give space to the global contexts and cultures in which *it* operates."[41] Further, the snowy end of "The Dead" blankets not only the boundary between Dublin and the west, the metropolis and the natal soil, but also that between Ireland and its regional neighbors.[42] The snow that seems to be such a strong national symbol at the end of the story turns out to harbor its own cosmopolitan tendencies, upending the common reading that sends Gabriel back toward the Celtic nation.[43] The conventional meaning of the word "island" thus meets the geographical sense of the world *as* island, creating a regional model of human-landscape interaction that undermines the national claim to determinative, geographical status.

References in *Ulysses* extend the role of this new modernist geography, further undermining the simple determinative power of the narrative of location. For example, the phrase the "homerule sun rising up in the northwest" appears in both the "Calypso" and "Lestrygonians" chapters of *Ulysses*, where it is attributed by Bloom to Arthur Griffith, the founder of Sinn Fein (47, 124). It is usually glossed as a reference to the emblem of *The Freeman's Journal*, showing a sun rising behind the bank of Ireland on College Green. The motto, "Ireland a Nation," ran below this image. Weldon Thornton remarks that the confused geography of the image showing a sun rising in the west expresses Griffith's disdain for the journal, "which he felt was only pseudonationalistic."[44] Indeed, we can hear any number of pseudonationalisms here. Though Bloom quotes him with appreciation, Griffith himself may be mocked since the passage continues, "Ikey touch that: homerule rising up in the northwest." Why Griffith's commentary on the journal would be connected to Jewishness ("ikey") is hard to fathom, but calling Griffith "ikey" certainly puts the purity of nationhood itself in question. On the other hand, the Celtic nationalism of Sinn Fein leaves little room for Irish Jews. An "ikey" presence in the context of homerule signals both adulteration and resistance to a pure version of nationalism.[45] Since the Jews themselves hail from and represent the east throughout the novel (as does Bloom), the phrase "homerule sun rising up in the northwest" may also represent the nationalists' attempt to turn away from the "inauthentic" Irishness of those from the east. Certainly, the phrase itself and Bloom's appreciation of it endorses a certain inauthenticity.

Critics have long pointed out the concatenation of east and west, past and present, in the construction of space in *Ulysses*. Especially when we consider the intersection between Joyce's work and Anand's, this impulse in *Ulysses* highlights the importance of geography as the intersection of matters of space and temporality and emphasizes its implications for reading *Ulysses* within a postcolonial or transnational framework, traveling forward in time as well as back to the epic past. The novel represents the "layering of Irish and Mediterranean spaces,"[46] which gives sense to the Joycean phrase "Jewgreek is greekjew" (*Ulysses*, 411), to Bloom's musings about Turkish farmland (49–50), and to Stephen's constant reference to both Greece and Italy. This layering defines what Seidel calls epic geography, "which depends upon the principle of extension of the old or the familiar. Time extends space."[47] The novel's layering of east and west not only connects Ireland to an epic past but also seems to construct it as heir to a heroic history, which becomes part of its claim to nationhood and independence.

But given the regional contexts of early-twentieth-century cultural geography and its focus on the *longue durée* of human-landscape relationships, we might instead recognize this time/space layering as an integral part of bidirectional modernist geography and its challenge to the temporalities of the nation-state. The novel's construction of space as always adulterated or combined undermines any purely geographical nationalism as well as any teleological development of national history. Joyce's insistence that the past and present interconnect in the construction of current identities—what has sometimes been referred to as his cyclical view of history[48]—relies on an ongoing, bidirectional, and relational construction of human space that draws on the human history of global migrations and movements. His "jewgreek is greekjew" emphasizes an almost Vidalian understanding that lack of homogeneity is the rule rather than the exception for human populations seen in regional perspective. Further, his concatenation of east and west, past and present, refuses the "center and periphery" model that serves to situate the peripheral east in a different, retrogressive temporality. In this way the geography of *Ulysses* defies the imperialist construction of the colony, whether Ireland or India, as the site of cultural and political underdevelopment and the characterization of its modernity as belated. For Joyce as for Anand, this alternative geographical logic becomes important to a postcolonial critique.

When Stephen walks over Sandymount Strand, pondering the significance of the beach and the history of invasion it has witnessed, which links an imperialist past with the space of the present, we clearly see the geopolitical implications of this kind of geographical thinking. As critics have long pointed out, in both *A Portrait of the Artist* and *Ulysses* Stephen stands for the principle of wandering, becoming what Cheryl Herr has called a "a wanderer in a maze . . . an initiate traversing a labyrinth, . . . a metro-colonial moving through territory that both alienates and attracts."[49] In *Portrait* Stephen's childhood walks with his father and uncle Charles propel him back toward the Dublin mountains, Irish politics, and the "legends of their own family" that occupy his elders (64). Later in the novel, however, Stephen's wanderings through the streets of Dublin mark his lack of connection to any one place that might connect him to home, family, or nation and the fear he ultimately expresses toward "the country roads" of Ireland (210). The wandering that becomes endemic to the text maps this trajectory and inscribes Stephen's passage from dutiful inheritor of Irish family legends to exiled chronicler of a cosmopolitan nationalism.

On the strand in *Ulysses*, the same principle holds. Thinking of his own past, Stephen's thoughts turn to the characterization of Ireland as "isle of saints" and sages, a popular comment that, as Joyce puts it in his essay of the same name, "goes back to the most ancient times, when the island was a true focus of sanctity and intellect, spreading throughout the continent a culture and a vitalizing energy."[50] The beach would then represent historical Irish openness to the sea, to travel, and to dissemination of knowledge (an aspect especially appealing to Stephen and to Joyce). In this light, the landscape represents both an influence on the Irish character and its constant connection to other regions, other islands, and the world. On the same page, however, reference to the crackling of what Stephen calls "human shells" underfoot (*Ulysses*, 34) and later "bones for my steppingstones" makes clear that the "sands and stones. Heavy of the past" (37), under the watchful eye of the Martello tower, are heavy with the history of loss of life in conquest. The strand's material is composed of the crushed Irish, its landscape inseparable from its human history and the geopolitics of imperialism. From the perspective of MacKinder, this beach would play a pivotal role in describing Ireland's vulnerability to conquest and its strategic place in regional struggles for power. From a postcolonial perspective, the beach becomes like the west in "The Dead," doubly cathected as the site of both resistance and defeat.

Further, as Emer Nolan points out, the episode on the strand also contributes to the complicated notion of race and its relation to geography in Joyce's writings. Stephen "believes himself to be involved in this history of his ancestors not merely imaginatively, but . . . by means of his blood-inheritance: . . . 'their blood is in me, their lusts my waves' (*Ulysses*, 38)."[51] Yet the subtle sarcasm of the passage undermines its function as a moment of conventional race affiliation. The passage refers with seeming seriousness to Viking invasions and the effort of Malachy to repel them in A.D. 980: "Galleys of the Lochlanns ran here to beach, in quest of prey . . . Dane Vikings, torcs of tomahawks aglitter on their breasts when Malachi wore the collar of gold" (*Ulysses*, 37–38). But "Malachi wore the collar of gold" is a stock phrase from a popular song called "Erin Remember," based on a poem by Thomas Moore. This song expresses the nostalgic view of history that Joyce's writings so often refute and exhorts the Irish to remember their days of glory "ere her faithless sons betrayed her."[52] It is not the sort of song that we can imagine either Stephen or Joyce singing, and it makes a mockery of Stephen's reengagement with national heroism.[53]

Stephen may comment that he shares his blood with the "horde of jerkined dwarfs, my people," whom he imagines having descended on the beach to fight for Ireland, but his description of them exaggerates their oddity and undermines his identification with them. Stephen's notion of his connection to these ancestors fits within a Vidalian perspective, which requires us to see geography as bidirectional rather than a simple, one-way determination of human populations by their physical circumstances. Stephen must move back into the past as though he himself were one of the ancient Irish ("I moved among them on the frozen Liffey" [38]) rather than presume his heritage as their blood-based descendent. Conquest changes Ireland's geography irrevocably, and what Stephen is able to understand of his racial identity is dependent on the long history of human-landscape interaction made manifest on the beach. As Joyce put it in "Ireland, Island of Saint and Sages," "Nationality . . . must find its reason for being rooted in something that surpasses and transcends and informs changing things like blood and the human word."[54] What we might call Stephen's "race" or even his nationality, then, is not determined by a simple one-to-one correspondence between what a landscape provides and what a people become, as earlier geographers (and even some later ones) would have argued, but rather must be understood as an ongoing amalgamative force that disrupts simple determinism because it focuses on interrelationship, mutual influence between landscape and human life, and the concatenation of space and time. Despite its evocation of a quasi-racial matrix of identity, Stephen's encounter with the fraught geography of the strand serves to undermine any sense that location determines national character.

If for Stephen it is the strand that brings him into contact with the transnational encounters of geography, for Bloom it is the water. Much has been said about Bloom's symbolic connection to water throughout *Ulysses*, from his bath in the morning to his hand washing at the end of his journey. But beyond its epic importance, water clearly connects Bloom to island life and to the global oceanic and climactic systems that surround it. For example, in the Ithaca chapter, as Bloom turns on the faucet to fill his kettle, we learn the complex trajectory of the water as it flows from the Roundwood reservoir in county Wicklow to Dublin: "What then did Bloom, waterlover . . . admire?" the text asks. Answer: "Its universality . . . its vastness in the ocean of Mercator's projection . . . its preponderance of 3 to 1 over the dry land of the globe, its indisputable hegemony . . . its persevering penetrativeness . . . its metamorphoses as vapour, mist, cloud, rain, sleet, snow, hail . . . its ubiquity" (549). Remarkable for its depth of geographical knowledge and detail, this passage also records the geography of water as a global phenomenon that submerges distinctions between landmasses, between center and periphery, and between human histories. The geographic force of water effects the "slow erosion of peninsulas and islands" even as its "alluvial deposits" generate new ones (549). The "continental lakecontained streams" merge into the "confluent oceanflowing rivers with their tributaries and transoceanic currents," connecting the waters of county Wicklow to the currents of the gulfstream (549). Like the snow falling over all of Ireland in "The Dead," the water that flows from the world into Bloom's faucet demonstrates the shaping and aggregating power of geography and the universality of such forces as "vapour, mist, cloud, rain, sleet, snow."

Declan Kiberd has said that "the problem of the Irish was not so much rootlessness as the fact that they had roots in too many different places at once."[55] For Joyce, Irish civilization was "a vast fabric, in which the most diverse elements are mingled."[56] The geographical sensibility that Joyce inscribed into his work and that surfaces in the maplike texture of the pages of *Ulysses*, the spatial wandering of both *Portrait* and *Ulysses*, the constant reference to matters of location and climate, and the emphasis on a sort of geographical "possibilism" as the basis for national affiliation all help us see the implications of this claim. Building on the same kinds of insights that led early-twentieth-century geographers to stress the unity of global terrestrial phenomena, the dominance of broad regional rather than national features of landscape, and the ongoing interaction between diverse human populations and their environments over the long term, Joyce's work develops a profound modernist geography that gestures beyond the local/global dichotomy. Joyce's geography resists simplified notions of racial identity and nationalism and works toward a cosmopolitan sensibility that draws on the geographical notions of regional interconnection; it also undermines the geopolitics of center and periphery so crucial to European imperialism. Thus, Joyce's fiction not only shapes our understanding of Irish geography and intercedes in its sociohistorical development, as Harvey would claim, but also intervenes directly in the geopolitical "problem of the Irish" and the matter of its coloniality. The geographical Joyce is a postcolonial Joyce, and his texts intervene in the temporal-spatial construction of Ireland as territory, island, and nation while also marking its ambiguous geopolitical status in the world. Indeed, as Harvey tells us, "there is something subversive in it."

Anand's Cosmopolitan Roots

In the work of Mulk Raj Anand, geography works in similar ways to link matters of national space to questions of colonial status, cosmopolitanism, and justice. Writing, like Joyce, from a variety of places throughout his long career, Anand locates his fiction in the cities and villages of his home country, where the daily existence of his lower-caste, impoverished heroes highlights their inscription within the discourses of caste and coloniality. Doubly positioned in the space/time of their Indian locations, these heroes are bound to the material world that surrounds them and placed into social and economic roles that derive from the past but are reinforced by the contemporary situation of imperialism. The life of Bhaka, the untouchable, which I have discussed in the introduction, is inseparable from the physical space of his village, where the objects and colors in the maze of streets catch him up a riot of desire.[57] At the same time, the crowds jostling around him on those streets raise the threat of contact with caste Hindus and the paradox posed by Bakha's status: untouchable yet, in the crowded village streets, destined to be touched. Thus wandering in Anand's work adds a dimension of danger missing (or less salient) in Joyce's novels. The labyrinth of daily life entraps Bakha in a space not only of commodified desire and the restrictions of historically determined identities but also of hunger, fear, and the potential for harm from bodily contact.

In Anand's second novel, *Coolie*, Munoo's journey—from the rural Punjab to the northern factories of Daulatpur, the southern shantytowns of Bombay, and then back to the Punjab not far from where he began—forms the texture of the protagonist's passage toward adulthood and his concomitant encounter with India. In the final chapters of the novel, the sight of the northern mountains near Simla arouses in Munoo a "feeling which he always used to have in his childhood, the urge to say how very fecund God was when He created the huge mountains and the vast sheets of waters which were the rivers." But this notion of God becomes ironic when Munoo notices the "coolies and hillmen trudging up to Simla, borne down beneath the sacks of foodstuffs on their backs."[58] For Anand as for Joyce, geography becomes the space where past and present identities collide and where the materiality of daily life enters the conversation about nationality and imperialism. Yet for Anand, perhaps more than for Joyce, the narrative encounter with this terrain, with the impoverished and restricted lives of his ordinary heroes, and with the matters of nationality and cosmopolitanism leads toward political action and resistance. In building a new tradition in fiction for India that draws its inspiration from Joyce even as it responds to the rhetorical exigences of its Indian heroes and locations, Anand crafts a cosmopolitan Indian modernism that engages directly with matters of caste, poverty, national identity, and colonial status. It thus demonstrates the continuum of political engagement that underlies transnational modernism and carries implications for reading both Anand and Joyce.

Anand was born in Peshawar in 1905 to the family of a civil servant, and distinguished himself as a teenager by his studiousness; his voluminous reading in Urdu, Persian, and English; and his interest in poetry, which he began writing at an early age as a disciple of the poet Iqbal. In the heady period after 1918, Anand was swept up in the growing rebellion in the Punjab and began a long life of political activism. He was arrested and caned in Amritsar for innocently breaking curfew during the Jallianwalla Bagh Massacre of 1919.[59] He was again arrested in 1924 for political activism in Lahore. Anand later traveled to London, where he studied philosophy at the University of London while also attending lectures by luminaries such as G. E. Moore and C. D. Broad. His connections within the London literary world brought him into the living rooms of Leonard and Virginia Woolf and into contact with E. M. Forster, T. S. Eliot, and most of the figures of literary Bloomsbury, though he became increasingly uncomfortable in that milieu. He experienced the 1926 general strike in London as a watershed event that revealed the similarities between British workers and the untouchables in India. As he put it, "Not only were the British imperious and strong-minded in the colonies, but [they] also could suppress their own working people."[60] He began to read widely in socialism and to explore the problem of the Indian underclasses under British colonial rule. But his long and illustrious career as a writer of fiction began in 1922, when he first read Joyce, devouring both *Portrait of the Artist* and *Ulysses* and discovering in them a new vocation as a writer. In patterning himself after Joyce and vowing to become the "uncreated conscience" of his race, I will argue, Anand picked up the mantle of experimental modernism, recreated it for the Indian context, and used it to elaborate a complex, rooted cosmopolitanism that would intervene directly in the problem of Indian justice.[61]

Untouchable (written between 1928 and 1932) is Anand's first novel and the one most often discussed in connection with his early literary influences. An apocryphal story claims that Gandhi himself edited the manuscript that Anand brought, half written, with him from London, cutting out excess language and insisting that its hero become less of "a Bloomsbury intellectual." Though there is no extant manuscript and no proof of the story, the assumed trajectory of Anand's early career still rests on this tale, guiding critics to comment on Anand's return to India as a "decisive shift," a return to authenticity, and an embrace of social realism.[62] Yet *Untouchable* reflects "a boggling variety of other styles, modes, and lexicons," many of which owe recognizable debts to European narrative modes."[63] Bakha's self-awareness forms the core of the novel, allowing us to view the material circumstances of his restricted life through his perceptive but limited eyes, and from time to time in interior monologue highlighting Bakha's "unique sensitiveness as against the people of the upper caste who thought that merely touching him is a degradation."[64] In the published novel Bakha could in no way be termed a "Bloomsbury intellectual"; indeed, critics generally describe him as "naïve." Yet the novel's day-in-the-life structure references both *Mrs. Dalloway* and *Ulysses*, which we know Anand read and recommended to his friends, as well as

Joyce's emphasis on material existence. The novel's triumph derives from the combination of narration focalized through the complexity of Bakha's inner thoughts and emotions, which are often granted guiding power over the narration, and "prose [that] subtly picks up the dense corporeality and tactility of Bakha's existence."[65]

Yet as I've pointed out, this brilliant novel, called the first work to take up the outcaste as hero and an early entry in what has come to be called *dalit* ("the oppressed" or untouchable) literature, also develops its distinct mode directly in response to the harsh realities and contradictions of modernizing India in the early twentieth century.[66] In this sense, I'd like to claim, *Untouchable* underscores the importance of conceiving of modernism as a mode of writing that arises in many forms, guises, and locations in concert with the social, political, and aesthetic developments of modernity, and that generates new and complexly rooted cosmopolitanisms. Anand's concern throughout his career with growing mechanization and the consolidation of industrial capital, with changing patterns of domesticity and the growth of cities, with increased focus on the individual psyche amid growing recognition of the political constraints on his or her freedom in the modern world, and with the political disenfranchisement of the impoverished and the colonized—that is, his engagement with the problematic of modernity within a particular Indian situation—arises out of both local and global influences.[67] Thus it is important not only to see modernism as part of a flow of global literature and culture that connects colony to colony, bringing Anand into contact with Joyce, but also to see how local versions of modernism in their geographical specificity alter the ongoing global conversation. Anand's combination of political engagement and experimental modernism helps us see Joyce's texts in new light, reading them, for example, within the context of postcolonial Indian linguistic hybridity or debates about caste.[68] If Elleke Boehmer invites us to see colonial writers "as forming a constitutive part of the modernist movement rather than as being merely its symptom, or sympathetic effect,"[69] Anand's writing, as we see it in *Untouchable*, *Coolie*, and many of his later works, becomes such a constitutive force by generating new forms and categories of modern writing that respond to and refigure Joyce and also shift and extend the shapes, geographies, and political commitments of modernism writ large.

The problem in reading *Untouchable* as a modernist text lies in knowing how to look. If we search for the recognizable elements of European modernist technique, such as a beginning in medias res, play with chronology, or heavy use of interior monologue or stream of consciousness, we will be disappointed. There are only two short passages of interior monologue at the end of this third-person narrative (though we can imagine that there may have been more before Gandhi advised Anand to cut the "Bloomsbury" out). Bakha's day begins at dawn and unfolds in chronological order with few interruptions of sequence. The description of street scenes that punctuate the novel as Bakha performs his work cleaning latrines and gutters, scavenging food for his family, or playing hockey with the other boys who serve the British regiment bears little resemblance to the cinematic technique of *Mrs. Dalloway*. In fact, the most striking stylistic characteristic of this novel may be the variety of styles and modes, from romance to patriotic monologue to psychological analysis, that periodically erupt through its ostensibly realist surface.[70]

Still, we can claim *Untouchable* as modernist by virtue of its insistence on the human, material world as the sphere of activity, its restriction to a day-in-the-life format, its focus on the consciousness of a poor sweeper boy, and its many other formal and political challenges to expectations for Indian writing. In his lecture "Roots and Flowers," Anand points out the many ways that he sought to create *Untouchable* as distinctly modern within an Indian context, acknowledging that he "imbibed the lessons of style and construction of the contemporary novel" from Joyce and set out to focus his novel, like Joyce's, on "the transformation, by the imagination, of human beings through their conflicts in a given time space continuum." Anand calls himself an "advance guard writer" who uses "timebound moments of heightened awareness, symbolic of all time" to bridge the gulf between the traditional Indian "recitalist" narrative and the new modern novel."[71] His new novel would thus be self-consciously and importantly "timebound" and would focus on the "work-a-day world of [his] hero-anti-hero," as seen through his dreams, reminiscences, and stream of consciousness, and would depict him as a "real man of real flesh and blood" complete with all his contradictions. Still, Anand makes clear that this new modernist novel remains deeply Indian: "I do not think, as against the chauvinists, that the influence exerted by European technique has made [the] Indian novelists less Indian. The richness of content, the ideas and the actions of our struggle to be human, to remain alive and grow, in our Gandhian time, keeps them unmistakably Indian."[72] *Untouchable* marks the emergence of this particular Indian version of modernism, uniting social and political struggle with a renewed technique.

The matter of touch, clearly a key aspect of a novel called *Untouchable*, provides another way to recognize Anand's modernism. The novel revolves around the literal principle of untouchability, our understanding of the term, and the viability of such a concept. Toward the beginning of the novel, Bakha, caught up in the joy of having been able to purchase some sweets, accidentally bumps against the sleeve of a caste Hindu. Defiled by Bakha's touch, this man berates him while a crowd gathers and surrounds Bakha, who can not push his way through for fear of defiling others. Eventually, the defiled man slaps him hard enough to knock Bakha's turban off his head and his candy into the dust. This inauspicious event sets the tone for the day, in which Bakha will suffer several accidents and moments of abuse. The novel delights in narrating the physical sensations of its hero and the material world around him; it is as though the narration revels in what it is supposed to revile and as though the outcaste who may not be touched has a special relation with sensory experience. Indeed, Bakha is almost glorious as he displays his prowess in cleaning the latrines in the morning: "A soft smile lingered on his lips . . . and he slowly slipped into a song. . . . And he went forward, with eager step, from job to job, a marvel of movement dancing through his work" (17). During the street scene, his pleasure in the taste of the candy is palpable: "His mouth was watering. . . . The taste of the warm and sweet syrup was satisfying and delightful" (46).

Yet when the fateful collision occurs, it goes unrecorded in the narrative. We are as surprised as Bakha to hear the man yell, "'Keep to the side of the road. . . . Do you know you have touched me and defiled me!" (46), or perhaps more so, since we have been falsely lulled into expecting reliable, omniscient narration. The gap here stands as a sign that this narrative will be subjective and partial and also marks a disruption in experience or sensation that parallels Bakha's own: "Bakha stood amazed, embarrassed. He was deaf and dumb. His senses were paralyzed" (46). Thus, the novel plays with the irony of the touch, which cannot be felt by readers because it is absent from the narration nor felt by Bakha because his senses are paralyzed at the moment, but which, within the world of the novel, has the capacity to threaten and defile. The novel pushes the notion of "untouchability" to its utmost meaning—not just the touch that defiles but also the touch that cannot exist—and inscribes this extreme meaning into the novel's key scene. It also bonds the reader to Bakha, the hero, in the common experience of the sudden violence of this event. This unnarrated, impossible touch sets the stage for all the further action of the novel and for the reader's relationship with its hero. Its omission from the page and existence in a world beyond narrative experience demonstrates the degree to which Anand's exploration of the principle of untouchability becomes a crucial component of his innovative narrative technique.

This is precisely where we can also read the connection between modernism and Anand's rooted cosmopolitanism. For *Untouchable*'s success surely lies in its intensely local attention to Bakha's material situation and in the connection it draws between his geographical situation and India's encounter with social and political modernity. E. M. Forster claims in his preface that "*Untouchable* could only have been written by an Indian" because the novel never succumbs to a sentimental or orientalizing perspective on the sweeper community or to the moralizing gaze of an outside reformer.[73] The plight of the outcaste in *Untouchable* cannot be assimilated to a European notion of alienation or exile: Bakha's body is marked from birth as not to be touched, and he cannot erase this stigma by assuming a different mentality or willing himself back into society.[74]

On the other hand, Anand makes clear that his experiences in Europe and his discovery of European class politics help form his understanding of the untouchables. If he realizes after the general strike in 1926 that British colonialism was connected to a pervasive system of class oppression, he also acknowledges that the stigma of untouchability in India is more pervasive and permanent. In an interview he commented that in Europe "the sweeper, after having done the sweeping of the road, [was] now dressed in a suit, and nobody [asked] him if he [was] an untouchable or a touchable."[75] *Untouchable* presents the particular situation of the outcaste Indian, who cannot change his fate by changing his shirt. In its focus on Bakha's encounters with other Indians and his interactions with the environment that surrounds him, the novel locates its hero within an Indian discourse about untouchability as a problematic of Indian modernity. At the same time, by the final section, the novel widens its purview, asking us to understand Bakha's situation as connected to other struggles across the world and part of a complex cosmopolitan politics. The poet who speaks of the flush toilet in the final pages also speaks of the paradoxes of India's connection to the world: "Gandhi may be wrong in wanting to shut India off from the rest of the world . . . because as things are that can't be done. But even in that regard he is right. For it is not India's fault that it is poor" (151). Ultimately, as he walks to his home after hearing these speeches, Bakha is able to connect the two positions, resolving to speak to his family of both Gandhi's inspiring words and about the possibility of a future without latrines. By dreaming both of Gandhian Swadeshi and of a machine-age future connecting India with the world, Bakha thus resolves, at least for the moment, the paradox of Indian modernity.

Speaking later about the genesis of the novel in India, Anand echoes this paradox and casts it in geographical terms. If "there was no self-conscious novelist who was not influenced" by the efforts of European novelists, still, the emerging writers of India were inspired by the Gandhian revolution. The task of the young generation of writers was to develop Indian fiction out of the two continents at once:

> The English writing intelligentsia of India was . . . a kind of bridge trying to span, symbolically, the two worlds of the Ganga and the Thames through the novel. . . . Their roots lay in the local landscapes of North and South India. But they seem, along with quite a few others to have done something which is not generally admitted—to have brought some roots from abroad.[76]

Thus Anand describes a perspective as "rooted" both in the local landscape and in the European world. Though Anand is less explicit in his use of geographical principles than Joyce, the concatenation of east and west, center and periphery, described in this passage shares something with the geography of *Ulysses*. The combined rivers of the Thames and Ganges and the layered worlds that surround them become the fertile terrain for Indian writing in English and for the new located tradition that will emerge. If modernist geography posits the essential question of space as a matter of ongoing, bidirectional "relation" rather than cartographic fact and begins from the premise of a closed world system in which an event in one corner is always echoed around the globe, then Anand's writing in the 1930s also arises out of a modernist geographic sensibility, which contributes to a rooted cosmopolitanism.

But it is also important to note Anand's refusal of a simplified internationalism or the erasure of differences between the Indian and British contexts. The Ganges and the Thames remain specific geographical locations, much as are the land- and streetscapes of *Untouchable* and *Coolie*. Anand makes clear that "the novels of Indian English writers are primarily part of Indian writing and not English literature" and are tied to its literary history "from the forest books downwards." In

Roots and Flowers Anand discusses Joyce's streams of consciousness that "flow ... into the river of the novel" and the "ocean of memories" in *Finnegan's Wake*.⁷⁷ But rather than picture a day along the Liffey, as does Joyce, Anand creates his day-in-the-life story on the banks of a brook "once with crystal-clear water, now soiled by the dirt and filth of the public latrines ... the absence of a drainage system had, through the rains of various seasons, made of the quarter a marsh which gave out the most offensive stink" (9). Unlike the shaping and aggregating power of Bloom's free-flowing Irish waterways, Munoo's river stagnates and stinks, overwhelming its banks with the detritus of human existence cut off from the purifying forces of the global water system. Munoo's almost picaresque journey across the length of India in *Coolie* creates what we might call a geographical atlas of India, complete with discussion of resources, climate, and terrain as seen from the specific perspective of Indian poverty rather than from Joyce's mostly middle-class gaze.

Further, if Balzac's impulse to mapping both indicates and intervenes in the early-nineteenth-century development of commodity capitalism in the metropolis. as Harvey points out, then Anand's Indian geographies show the development of capitalism in colonial economies and systems of labor that have both local and global consequences. *Coolie*, as its name implies, revolves around the principle of human labor within the Indian colonial context. Munoo is employed in a British-owned cotton factory whose roofs are described as "undulat[ing] like low hilltops to the peak points of conic chimneys" (191), linking the Bombay landscape irrevocably to the geography of industrial capitalism. He ends his life in the personal service of an Anglo-Indian memsahib, with whom he reexperiences "the twinkling lights on the hillside" of his home province from within the traces of a rickshaw (309). Anand's Indian geographies also show the inverse of the middle-class commodity fetishism that grew along with the novel in nineteenth- and early-twentieth-century Europe. Both Bakha and Munoo are filled with desire at the sights and smells of the objects to be bought in bazaars and shops, yet these necessary items of human sustenance and pleasure are inaccessible to Anand's desperately poor heroes, unlike Plumtree's Potted Meat in *Ulysses*. The problem of modernity as Anand explores it is therefore not the ubiquity of the disembodied object world and the triumph of exchange-value capitalism as we might understand it in the European context, but rather the inaccessibility of objects of real, material use-value and the obstacle this poses to any possibility of Indian justice.

Thus we must read Anand's commentary on his combined European and Indian roots as an expansion of the possibilities of locatedness rather than an escape from it. As Harvey puts it, "Some form of geographical knowledge is presumed in every form of cosmopolitanism," and the specificity of that knowledge is what makes possible a liberatory process.[78] Anand's modernism thus becomes a multifaceted mode, one that grows out of his encounter with European experiments in the novel and European social movements, as well as his literary and political participation in Indian modernity. In *Untouchable*, *Coolie*, and other, later works, Anand helps us understand the importance of what we might call a "rooted cosmopolitanism" not only for making sense of his literary career but also for our understanding of the modes, locations, and politics of modernism.[79]

Anand's version of this rooted cosmopolitanism emerges clearly in many essays he wrote after 1940. In particular, "The World I Hope For" (1943), part of a series broadcast by the BBC Eastern Service that placed Anand alongside George Orwell and others, describes his understanding of world citizenship, its rejection of domination by "any particular race, religion, party, group, or vested interest," and its connection to social, economic, and political freedom:

> I hope for a world in which men and women can enjoy real freedom (social, economic, political, intellectual, and emotional freedom) in common with other citizens of the world. . . . I hope for a world in which states voluntarily abdicate some of their unlimited power, and pool their economic, military, and political resources for world federation.[80]

This perspective owes much to Kant's vision of a cosmopolitan federation as a specific antidote to the rule of despots and the "barbaric freedom of established states."[81] Kant's essay "Perpetual Peace" elaborates this notion as the grounds for international law and government that will make standing armies unnecessary.[82] But Anand's insistence on social welfare and economic equality as one of the bases of world citizenship shifts the Kantian ideal toward more specific engagement with justice and the everyday concerns of poverty, social inequality, and colonization. He argues that the connection of the Thames and the Ganges and the development of what I would call "as if" justice would come not from "rounded philosophical judgments" but from portrayal of the "work-a-day worlds" of ordinary men and women in the sphere of global human relations.[83]

For Anand, the issue goes beyond simply taking pleasure in other people and places or taking "an interest in civilizations, their arguments, their errors, their achievements . . . because . . . it will help us get used to one another" and build toward peace, as K. Anthony Appiah puts it.[84] Anand uses cosmopolitanism as a framework to examine the paradoxes of capitalist imperialism and to combat the violence of conquest and factionalism within India. In his essay "The Search for National Identity in India," he describes the pattern of conquest and religious conflict that occupies much of Indian history, as well as its lingering desire for unity.[85] For Anand India's crucial heritage is one of multiple cultures and religions that mingle, not always happily, to form Indian culture. "In spite of all the cultural conflicts, there has always been the residuum of all the cultures, surviving, generation after generation. This has left an ethos which is recognizable in every Indian, whatever his race, religion, or colour. The paradox is as relevant today as it was in the past."[86] This ethos, Anand hopes, will enable India to overcome colonialism without turning its back on Europe. He often remarked on his mother's syncretic religious life, which incorporated Sikh prayers into a mostly Hindu practice, remembering "the mandala of Gods . . . on which stood images of Guru Nanak, Krishna, Aga Kahn, Yessuh Messiah and a snake engraved on metal."[87] For Anand, this type of cultural and religious syncretism, which borrows rituals from one practice and employs them in another or transports words from one cultural context to another, provides a model for both postcolonial Indian identity and for modernist literature. It rejects the search for pure cultural authenticity as the basis for a unitary nationalism even as it extends the multiple roots of twentieth-century Indian life, pushing toward a postcolonial future that draws from the conquests and paradoxes of the past. At the same time, it argues against the development of a purely national literary tradition, building instead a rooted, cosmopolitan modernism that, in its cultural syncretism and formal iconoclasm, also stays true to Anand's vision of the legacy of Indian cultural history.

Anand, Joyce, and the Question of the Representative Man

Anand's complex cosmopolitanism also seeps into the narrative level of his texts. By creating his new novel for India around the lives and voices of untouchables and coolies and making them neither symbols of an emerging unitary nationalism nor representative of a universal position, Anand foregrounds their challenge to caste and cultural fixities and to the expectations for character in the Indian narrative tradition. In recognizing *Portrait of the Artist* as a model for "the recovery of self . . . in my novel,"[88] Anand connects Joyce's modernist bildungsroman with his own attempt to depict the "emergence [of the anti-hero] from the anonymous mass into the quick of his individual life" and to highlight his claim to justice. Instead of the open-ended and timeless form of the traditional Indian "recitalist" narrative, which focuses on the will of the gods as the source of events and couches its moral lesson in terms of dharma, Anand's Indian "advance guard" novel would be "time-bound" and centered on the ordinary hero's "experience of this world, in the here and the now . . . not governed by the Absolutes of religious belief."[89] It would seek to capture the syncretic cultural and linguistic life of India through play with what Anand called the sound-sense of words, and at the same time it would re-create the coolie hero as the possessor of this powerful aspect of language.[90] In this way Anand's novels, like Joyce's *Portrait*, both embrace and rework the expectations of the bildungsroman within the geographical and political spaces of colonial modernity, employing experimental narrative techniques to challenge the genre's expectations for character and self-development and to shift the liberal, political model of the universal representative man that lies at its core.

First, by recasting the generic boundaries of the bildungsroman, both Anand and Joyce question the genre's assumptions about the emergence of the self within national-historical contexts. To be sure, critical perspectives on the bildungsroman differ in how they understand the genre and the way it positions its hero in relationship to his nation. According to Marc Redfield, the paradoxical status of the bildungsroman ensures that it both "drives in the direction of the universal" and remains integrally connected to notions of "formation and cultivation" within a given historical and cultural situation.[91] So for Franco Moretti in his classic study of the genre, "the *Bildungsroman* had always held fast to the notion that the *biography of a young individual was the most meaningful viewpoint for the understanding and the evaluation of history*."[92] The hero of the eighteenth-century European bildungsroman comes of age within the framework of national-historical time, in and through which he emerges as an individual, reaching his ideal in unity with the state.[93] In Jed Esty's words, "The classic genealogy of *Bildung* begins with Goethe, Schiller, Lessing and Herder. This lineage establishes the genre's roots in a burgeoning nationalism based on an ideal of organic culture whose temporality and harmony could be reflected in the developing personality at the core of the *Bildungsroman*."[94] This accounts in part for Hegel's reading of the bildungsroman as an inherently conservative genre, emphasizing the socialization of the hero back into his society as a consequence of his self-development rather than any more libratory push toward continual individuation. For Bakhtin, the hero of the bildungsroman "emerges *along with the world* and he reflects the historical emergence of the world itself. He is no longer within an epoch, but on the border between two epochs, at the transition point from one to the other. This transition is accomplished in him and through him."[95] While novels in the bildungsroman tradition from the twentieth century may not reflect the same faith in this epochal transition as do those from the eighteenth, the question of transition remains paramount, as does the coincidence of the hero's emergence with that of his country or milieu.[96]

Yet—and in many ways this is simply the reverse side of the same coin—this model of the novel of development is intimately tied to a sense of universalizable subjectivity and the notion of the hero as an exemplary, universal, or representative man."[97] Even Bakhtin, who makes Goethe's historicity and attention to location a key point in his discussion of the bildungsroman, focuses on the notion of the emergence of the hero as "a new unprecedented human being" who has significance for the "historical future" writ large.[98] For Moretti the ultimate goal of the bildungsroman is the final synthesis of self and normative world into the "free individual of liberalism," the universal model of subjectivity and political citizenship that undergirds much European political theory from the Enlightenment onward. This seems to be the choice: either *Bildung* tied to romantic identification with and reincorporation into the nation-state or *Bildung* as the assumption of an exemplary, universal status, the representative man who "transcends political, racial and class differences."[99]

But it is not so clear that the twentieth-century bildungsroman, including *Portrait* (sometimes described as the genre's twentieth-century apotheosis), successfully accomplishes even the primary goal of advancing self-development.[100] As Jed Esty puts it, the modernist bildungsroman often has a surprisingly antiteleological shape. Whether Woolf's Rachel Vinrace, who, like Munoo in *Coolie*, dies before she can reach maturity, or Wilde's Dorian Grey, who becomes caught in the time warp of endless youth (and we might certainly include Stephen Dedalus in that group), characters in the modernist bildungsroman often subvert what seems to be the most salient component of the genre—development—even as the novels cling to the genre's language, structure, process of characterization, and ethical claims. Further, Esty also points out that in the antiteleological bildungsroman, what often disrupts the development of the protagonists is a colonial plot or setting.[101] For Anand, whose entire oeuvre emerges out of the colonial context, it seems that there is no possibility of traditional *Bildung*; his heroes cannot even dream of development. Doubly disenfranchised by India's colonial status and their underclass identities, both Bakha and Munoo emerge almost in spite of their national story rather than along with it. The intrusion of the imperial or colonial situation into the tradition serves to interrupt not only the hero's development but also the temporal-spatial model of the nation that corresponds to it. For Joyce and Anand, recasting the matter of *Bildung* becomes part of their broad reengagement with colonial geopolitics, national belonging, and cosmopolitan identity.

A transnational perspective focused on the geopolitics of empire and colonialism forcibly readjusts our understanding of the modernist bildungsroman. Whereas critics looking from within only the European tradition might debate the success or failure of the twentieth-century bildungsroman, from a transnational viewpoint we might recognize concerns shared and made more overt in the work of Anand and others, and this in turn help us to reread the European texts. If *Portrait* leaves Stephen at what critics have seen as a moment well before maturity (and we may disagree about how mature he is even as he enters *Ulysses*), *Coolie* cuts its hero down in his midteens. Without claiming that Anand supplants, completes, or corrects Joyce, I would suggest that *Coolie* teaches us a lesson about how to read *Portrait*. The imbrication of nation and biography in a bildungsroman set in a colony struggling for its independence ensures that the biography cannot go far. The demands of the bildungsroman tradition for a hero who emerges along with the epochal transition of the world around him are necessarily thwarted. The politics of the bildungsroman in this place and time must be one of disruption, disillusionment, and dislocation, even as we begin to glimpse the possibility of another kind of story. Thus, reading Anand into the body of modernism rather than as its appendage, mirror, or mime means that the heroism of a coolie who suffers every conceivable setback on his road to maturity, even while becoming a spokesman for a grassroots movement of rebellion before his death at a young age, ought be seen as the model of modernist engagement with the consequences of enlightenment historicism and the bildungsroman.

Further, in both *Portrait* and *Coolie*, I would argue, the main characters are presented as neither "free individual subjects of liberalism" nor isolated heroes who become reincorporated into national life. Breon Mitchell claims that in *Portrait* the concrete separation of the hero from society, as in the earlier bildungsroman genre, gives way to "unbridgeable spiritual distance."[102] Yet we see in Stephen's interior musings, his interaction with others, and his focalization of the narrative the constant appearance of other voices and concerns, which always surround his moments of isolation or distance and interrupt his reverie. Munoo in *Coolie* is even more contained within a communal discursive world, but one that keeps shifting as his social context changes so that he can neither be separate nor, because of his class, his hill background, and his growing political awareness, become incorporated into the social world around him. Because both of these characters are implicated within multivocal, socially constructed identities and within various hierarchies of discursive power that are often treated ironically, they can neither be absorbed in nor escape the social realm and so can not accomplish the traditional project of *Bildung*. The formal innovations that create these novels as focalized yet intensely heteroglossic narratives also transform the social and political projects of the bildungsroman.

I want to turn, then, to the ways that *Coolie* and *Portrait* raise these political questions about the status of the exemplary, representative man of liberal thought. In *Coolie* we see Munoo forced out of his home in a hill village and sent to find his way in almost picaresque fashion through a number of menial jobs in an extraordinary series of locations throughout India. While working as a servant for a bank official, in a pickle factory, in a cotton mill, or as a rickshaw boy before his death at fifteen from consumption, Munoo encounters the entire social fabric of India. He is befriended in unexpected places: among other servants, coolies, and cotton-mill workers but also in the house of the pickle factory's owner and in the home of an emancipated Anglo-Indian woman.[103] Yet the brilliance of the novel lies not only in the material detail of the various trials that Munoo is made to face but even more so in the way that Anand captures Munoo's internal life and his struggle to respond to the discourses and power hierarchies that surround him.

While the style of the novel contains few of Joyce's moments of fixed internal focus, it is focalized in much the same way, with a third-person perspective that is limited to what Munoo can know and understand and that develops over the course of the novel as Munoo grows up, much as does the perspective in *Portrait*. Munoo's lack of experience in the opening chapters, while not quite on the order of Stephen Dedalus's, is strikingly represented in a tone both limited in perspective and deeply ironic. This ironic perspective begins the critique of the bildungsroman in both novels. For example, in an early scene that takes place in the house where his uncle leaves him to work as a servant, Munoo suffers constant reprimand because he has no idea of the rules of proper conduct for servants and no one bothers to tell him. When the lady of the house turns on the gramophone, Munoo wanders in from the kitchen, dripping utensils in hand. "He felt emboldened. He wanted to hear the music, to see and touch the singing machine . . . 'how lucky I am, he thought, that there is a wonder machine in the house where I have come to serve'" (29). Munoo's naïveté guides the narrative here, which can only hint at what he doesn't understand. He gets carried away by the music and begins to dance around on all fours like a monkey, and Munoo is completely unaware that he is fulfilling the expectation of the lady of the house, who has been calling him a monkey all along. A few pages later, the same dynamic of subservience is played out between the householder and his boss at the Bank of India, aptly named Mr. England, whom he has invited to tea. The household does its utmost to impress the Englishman, who recoils in disgust at their food and can't wait to leave. By the end of the scene, however, it is he who has been called "monkey-faced" (55) by the highly educated Indian doctor who lives there. The ironic stance of the narrative is such that only the reader is aware of the many levels operating here; for Munoo, our eyes and ears, the visit of the Englishman is all spectacle. This scene highlights the layering of irony in the novel, which, like the rest of Anand's work, is too often simplified by being called "social chronicle."[104]

This scene also recalls, however, several episodes in *Portrait* in which the combination of a radically focalized perspective and a variety of competing discourses and power relationships serve to introduce irony into the serious subject of *Bildung* in a manner that critiques and revises the tradition. The scene in which Stephen is asked, "Do you kiss your mother?" by the older fellows at school operates in much the same way as the scene in *Coolie*, highlighting a naïve subject caught between multiple layers of discourse. As Trevor Williams puts it, "The scene illustrates the crossover from linguistic innocence" to a situation "in which words become charged with meaning depending upon one's position in the social group. The struggle for dominance, for the right to provide 'the right answer' is here engaged."[105] In this short scene, the power relationships are similar to those in *Coolie*: Stephen, not knowing the codes of conduct among the schoolboys, presents himself as eager and direct, which gets him into trouble. He quickly answers "yes" when asked if he kisses his mother at night, reverses his answer, then succumbs to confusion not just about what the "right" answer is but about the very meaning of the word "kiss." The fact that he asks, "What did it mean to kiss?" (11) indicates that he is outside the discourse of sexuality employed by the bigger boys. They exert power by withholding this level of meaning from him. Yet we as readers know he is caught in an oedipal struggle here and that the language of sexuality will become a crucial element in his development. Further, the power hierarchies at play here, while not overtly a matter of colonial status, are significant and part of the broad structure of authority surrounding Stephen—the boys are in positions of authority over him because they withhold the social and metaphorical meanings of kissing from him. The rules of the "schoolboy fraternity" are "more open than the virtually unnoticed recruitment into the ideology of church and state ... [yet] at the level of language the interpenetration is so complete as to seem natural."[106] The episode thus revolves around Stephen's becoming socialized into the male values of the school, which in turn are imbued with the languages of church and state. We can read this moment, and Stephen's inability to choose one answer or another, as the beginning of his trajectory toward exile.

Beyond that, however, we can see that the specific terms of the choice make less difference than Stephen's instruction in the vagaries of the performative and his inscription into discursive systems of power. Stephen is not in control of the way his performance is coded. Whatever words Stephen uttered would be "wrong," and even worse is his vacillation from one to the other. What is required of Stephen at the moment is not an assertion of his meaning-making ability in language but the reverse—his disavowal of the power to make meaning and his performance, with his answer, of his subservience to the other boys. Thus, the semiotic imperative, as it were, of the episode is not within the specifically linguistic realm. Like Munoo, who is unaware of what it means, socially, to play a monkey, Stephen doesn't know what social meaning attaches to the verbal performance of a kiss or how to respond to a question whose answer is always already known. In both novels, the withholding of this social level of meaning making by those in authority is made a crucial component of the hero's coming of age and his insertion into the surrounding discursive systems and power hierarchies. This withholding of access to meaning is inscribed into the text not only at the thematic level but also by way of its refusal of narrative omniscience, which places Stephen's (and Munoo's) confusion at the center of the scene, and by its constantly expanding ironies, which multiply the text's refusals until we can no longer sustain a heroic version of self-development.

Much later in the novel, Stephen's discussions with the dean of studies foreground his inability to control the social meaning of his words, despite his stunning verbal pyrotechnics. As many critics have pointed out, this episode raises the question of coloniality most directly in the novel.[107] Critics have amply discussed the complexity of the interchange about the word "tundish" between Stephen and the dean of studies. But the passage immediately preceding that, where Stephen discusses John Henry Newman's use of the word "detain" and confuses the dean is equally interesting. Stephen here seems to be the one in control of multiple levels of language, running verbal circles around the dean and aware that he is attempting to exert power. Stephen highlights Newman's particular use of "detain," which Newman takes from the version of Ecclesiasticus used as an antiphon in catholic services and which carries an unusually positive connotation of the word that implies being celebrated or embraced rather than hindered.[108] Stephen refers to this as the use of the word according to the "literary tradition" rather than the "tradition of the marketplace" and quotes the use of "detain" in the phrase "I hope I am not detaining you" (164). But the dean misses Stephen's point on two levels, answering "not at all," according to the "marketplace" use of the word, and missing Stephen's "literary" reference to Newman completely. In this short passage we can thus see Stephen not only lay claim to the literary tradition for himself but also demonstrate that the dean exists outside it, in the common world of the marketplace.

In this short section of *Portrait* Joyce also invokes Newman by mirroring the form of the antiphon, thus inscribing Stephen's claim to the literary tradition into the narrative. An antiphon (from "*antiphonen*" sounding against, responsive sound, singing opposite, alternate chant) is a liturgical chant that involves interplay between voices and serves to highlight underlying meanings in the psalm to which it responds.[109] The intercut dialogue between Stephen and the dean functions much like this kind of "alternate chant":

> The use of the term in the marketplace is quite different. *I hope I am not detaining you.*
> —Not in the least, said the dean politely.

>   —No, no, said Stephen, smiling, I mean . . .
>   —Yes, yes: I see, said the dean quickly, I quite catch the point: *detain*.
>
>   (164)

The emphasis here, unlike in a standard antiphon, seems not to be on the particular meaning of a verse or speech but on the absence of meaning in the conversation made salient by the confusion over the word "detain." Or what emerges in this scene is Stephen's recognition of the dean's inadequacies and his own better command of the tradition. Thus, a form that is meant to highlight deep spiritual meanings in psalms, dissolves into empty repetition ("No, no. . . . Yes, yes") and wordplay that highlights the barrenness of what the dean can offer Stephen. Still, any power gained by this wordplay is fleeting, as the tundish scene makes clear. In both episodes Stephen must offer his knowledge and linguistic ability for the use of the (less gifted) dean, which reinforces his subservience even as he resists internally. There is nothing he can say that will prevent this enactment of power in this scene. Thus the profound lesson in coloniality here is not just about possession of the literary tradition or the power to control language ("it is his before it is mine") but, beyond that, the notion that among the colonized, real-world discursive authority trumps language play, no matter how adept.

The problem of the hero's inability to transcend his linguistic embeddedness or to retain his authority in and through the language that surrounds him is also crucial to the beginning and end of *Portrait*. The subject's emergence into the world in the bildungsroman presupposes his eventual coincidence with worldly aims and ideals; his ability to rise as the representative man rests on the assumption of a commonality of values, extended and made overt through the language of the novel. But the radical repositioning of language in Joyce's text reverses this assumption. Stephen is unable to exert personal control over the social meaning of the language he uses, and his development begins and ends with a riot of heteroglossia that both inscribes him into a range of social discourses and also explodes the possibility of a unified common language at the level of the text. If, as David Lloyd has made clear, the autonomous, representative subject at the heart of the traditional bildungsroman belongs to the dominant literary tradition, this disruptive, "uncommon" language, and the refusal of Joyce's novel to render up an alternative, unified position from which to decode the text, positions it closer to what Lloyd calls the "minor": "a literature that remain[s] in an oppositional relationship to the canon and the state."[110]

Portrait's opening pages quickly demonstrate this attitude: "Once upon a time and a very good time it was there was a moocow coming down along the road." Whose voice are we hearing? How is it presented to us? Whether understood as a direct transcription of the father's voice telling the young Stephen a story, the story told in indirect discourse through the main narrator's perspective, or a recasting of an oft-told story in young Stephen's voice, we can see that Stephen's voice at this moment is inseparable from his father's. And narrative perspectives continue to merge: "His father told him that story; his father looked at him through a glass; he had a hairy face" (6). We are also being told this story by a narrative voice focalized through Stephen and must struggle as he does to distinguish self from other, son from father refracted through the glass, as if through a Lacanian specular image turned outward. We know from John Joyce's letter to his son (31 January 1931) that this was a story Joyce heard from his father, and we also know that it was a version of an Irish myth (225n5.13). By beginning Stephen Dedalus's story of development with this tale, Joyce inserts him into a narrative matrix that immediately widens from the specific and personal (Simon Dedalus speaking to Stephen) to the cultural and mythic, yet he does not establish the authority of that myth as a guide to making meaning. Stephen does not begin his journey in full and autonomous possession of his Irish cultural genealogy (which, in any case, is adulterated from the start), nor are we as readers granted enough access to the story and its pasts to be able to use it as a guide. Given that the status of the founding mythologies of Irish culture is precisely what is at stake in Ireland's resistance to colonial rule, this moment also begins the novel's constant engagement with the anticolonial struggle and the pitfalls of national consciousness, made more salient by its saturation of all levels of the text.

I read this same overdetermined social embeddedness in the use of language at the end of the novel, where Stephen's diary represents the collapse of the appearance of narrative unity into the assemblage of its parts and voices. Within the space of five pages we read quotations from Blake and Yeats; references to Dante, Shakespeare, and the Bible; transcriptions of conversations with Davin, Cranly, and others; and moments where Stephen appears to be speaking to himself. "O, give it up old chap! Sleep it off!" he tells himself, voicing what many readers also wish they could tell Stephen in his final moment of self-aggrandizement. At no other time in the novel is it so apparent that Stephen's narrative is a conversation of many voices, dialogic in the most profound meaning of the term and often contradictory. If Stephen says to Cranly that he does not fear to be alone (208), he demonstrates a near addiction to conversation. His claim to "silence, exile, and cunning" is of course spoken aloud, and his talk of exile is fraught with the potential (and the knowledge, once we have begun *Ulysses*) that it will be impermanent. These dialogic and deeply ironized final sections make very clear that the narrative does not support Stephen's belief that he can retreat into a personal aesthetics or into a way of understanding his place in the world separate from those around him. Even his famous comment, "I go to forge in the smithy of my soul the uncreated conscience of my race" (214), which held so much significance for Anand, is undermined by the deep irony of this final section. In that sense, the text's extreme heteroglossia works against the consolidation of the hero's development and his potential for reconciliation with his social world. The end of *Portrait* is neither a moment of triumph or maturation of the individual hero nor a conservative moment of his reincorporation back into society but rather the explosion of the conventional bildungsroman along with its enforcement of liberal subjectivity, its reliance on a common, unified perspective, and its assumption that language provides a transparent means for the expression of *Bildung*.

What replaces the "fusion of the liberal subject" here is not another version of the universalizable, exemplary man but a social subjectivity formed by something like "enlarged thinking," which moves us from an isolated individualized perspective to one that always takes place among the voices of others, within a particular community, and by reference to specific political and rhetorical exigences.[111] Enlarged thinking counters the notion of a punctual self, able to "remake himself by methodical and disciplined action . . . and [able] to take an instrumental stance to one's properties, desires," and communal obligations."[112] It makes the self coextensive with the company it keeps and its politics subject to the range of rhetorical situations and discursive positions that surround it. For Arendt even the solitary self exists in a sort of community with itself, which in turn connects to the political world of the collectivity and its politics. "The presupposition is that I live together not only with others but also with my self, and that this togetherness, as it were, has precedence over all others."[113] And as we have seen, for Arendt togetherness, no matter how small or how fleeting, always invokes the polity and our responsibility to act within it. Togetherness forms the very basis for our political existence.

Arendt foregrounds this notion of the company we keep, or the community we join, as one created by the human stories, real or fictional, that come into our minds when we think and by the virtual dialogue we carry out with our imagined company.[114] Narrative becomes crucial not only as the domain of action—the web of stories that responds to the question of identity in the world—but also as the means for moving from this "enlarged" way of thinking to a potentially active political engagement with others. In the first instance, judging requires an imaginative effort to understand the positions of others or to fleetingly inhabit their perspectives. This is the basis of enlarged thinking, and it builds on Kant's understanding of the common ground of the *sensus communis*. But in contradistinction to Kant (and to Rawlsian political theory), Arendt emphasizes the intersubjective nature of that imaginative act, its cognizance of the differences among those it imagines, and its refusal of a singular universal perspective. "We can say that the more people's positions I can make present in my thought and hence take into account in my judgment, the more representative it will be. The validity of such judgments would be neither objective and universal nor subjective . . . but intersubjective or representative."[115] In other words, Arendt elaborates a new version of the representative man as one who inhabits a number of subject positions and discourses at once without subsuming them into a common identity or language or becoming blind to their differences. Enlarged thinking works to create a plural space for ethical and political action in the world while a politics based on intersubjectivity ensures that the representative never becomes the universalized, exemplary "one." And since this intersubjective act of imagination occurs through dialogue, speech, and narration, literature becomes not only the source for lives and stories but also the crucial site of our engagement with those stories and the ground for potential political action.

Arendt's linked conceptions of enlarged thinking and engagement hold profound implications for understanding the potential for political commitment in fiction and the situation of the representative man or hero who emerges from it. Many of the formal innovations in *Portrait*, and especially its play with multiple perspectives and discourses, might in this light be read as its entrance into politics, where the question of just how self and community are implicated in each other overrides the possibility of Stephen's self-mastery in language or his reincorporation into his social world. Further, politics here becomes clearly a narrative matter, and the breakdown of narrative self-certainty and coherence also connotes the breakdown of the notion of the singular, exemplary man with his aspirations to universality. Joyce's experimentation with focalized perspective, the problem of language as at once a form of social control and its undoing, and the matter of Stephen as decentered subject all ask us to think politically about Stephen's relationship to the many communities that surround him and to revise our notions about both the conservative force of *Bildung* and the moral power of the singular, autonomous man. The modernist heteroglossia and multiplication of perspectives in *Portrait* undermine the notion of a unified, common language and open out toward the promise of enlarged thinking and politics.

The same dynamic is even more obviously the case in *Coolie* for Munoo, who never has the potential to aspire to universality or self-completeness, whose failure to mature as in a proper bildungsroman is even more starkly drawn than in *Portrait*, and whose position outside the conventional category of the representative man is more absolute. Anand's very title makes clear (as in the earlier novel *Untouchable*) that Munoo will remain part of a class of people within a particular place and time, rather than an epochal, exemplary figure. Once again, we can see political engagement in its critique of the bildungsroman tradition because we know that the colonial power hierarchies and discourses surrounding Munoo prevent him not only from progress toward individuation but also from the possibility of civic citizenship. But that he nonetheless commands our attention and compassion and eventually rises in the climax of the novel to direct political engagement as a member of a worker's action, also means that the novel has proposed an alternate logic of politics and selfhood, one based in non-universalized, situated subjectivity and enlarged thinking, which we can also use for reading Joyce.

The matter of the uncontrollability of words and the impossibility of restricting their meaning even within the power hierarchies that surround them plays a crucial role in this alternative political logic for both Joyce and Anand. It moves them toward the oppositional language position that Lloyd associates with the "minor" and, even more important, places them once more outside the universalized archetypal experience, which Lloyd claims "both legitimates and transmits the ethnocentric ideology of imperialism."[116] By undermining the power of a unified common language yet highlighting the potential of language to function extra-semiotically, beyond its role in discursive systems of authority, Joyce and Anand also open the possibility for resistance at the level of the text. Certainly, it is clear that in these novels language itself often escapes limitation to singular systems of meaning and to operate extra-semiotically or by reference to patterns of hybridity that exceed the bounds of codified languages. This is what Derrick Attridge, echoing Derrida, has identified in the Joycean context as "the remainder, that aspect of language's functioning, which in spite of its necessity is often repressed from our consciousness." There are many moments in *Portrait* where nonsense or repetition or rhythm and melody emerge.[117] From the "tra, la la" on the first page through "apologize put out his eyes" and the repetition of "stephaneforus" later in the novel, the musicality of pure syllables surrounds Stephen, existing outside his efforts to control the meaning of his words but also often outside the performances of power on display in the "do you kiss your mother?" episode. Sound often takes the place of semiotics as the focus of language use, with the result that another level of play complicates the social terrain the heroes must traverse. This is not in and of itself oppositional. Clearly, avant-garde language can serve any number of political positions, and the shattering of linguistic coherence does not necessarily shake a regime. Still, the multiplication of discursive positions, the generation of hybrid uses of language, and the emphasis on extra-semiotic modes of meaning making can disrupt the illusion of a singular, authoritative language, along with the teleological history of a unitary, national community, even while creating space for "minor" voices, alternative patterns of *Bildung*, and new political geographies.

This kind of language use is precisely what Anand responds to in pointing to the musicality of Joyce's language as an important element that connects the writers and a crucial aspect of his new Indian novel. As he puts it, "The sound of the words dictating sense" in Joyce's writing was like his "mother's mumbo-jumbo prayers," which combined elements from several different religious traditions and languages in the syncretic fashion that was so significant for Anand.[118] He comments that he loved listening to his mother's Sikh prayers even though they were in a language he did not understand because he could take pleasure in the sound of the words and their importance for his mother without worrying about their meaning. So when the first three paragraphs of *Coolie* each begin with the repeated utterance its hero's name, "Munoo ohe Munooa oh Mundo" (7), turned into a musical mantra—much like the schoolboys' shouts of "stephaneforus" in *Portrait*, we know that we are being asked to attend to the "remainder," to the level of language use that escapes semiotics and the control of the user and that has the potential to confuse or resist conventional discursive authority and disrupt the normative languages of the *sensus communis*.

These kinds of moments appear regularly throughout *Coolie*—more frequently, indeed, than in *Portrait*. Sometimes it is in the form of a cry of fear or surprise uttered by Munoo as he is accosted or derided; other times it is in the form of a string of abuse ("ohe you seducer of your daughter!" [143]; "you illegally begotten . . . you son of a pig" [154]) that is not meant to be interpreted literally. Still other times it is the rhythmic repetition of syllables or sounds that add extra dimension to the connotative power of speech. These are cosmopolitan moments in the text, when languages and contexts merge (much as they did in Anand's mother's syncretic prayers), bringing Hindi into contact with English, or cultural expressions from one region into the space of another while performing a linguistic concatenation not altogether different from the layering of east and west in *Ulysses*. When Munoo stumbles onto a train bound for Bombay the name of the city reverberates with the power of suggestion, its sound promising a paradise unlike anything Munoo has known. "'Bombay, Bom-Bom-Bombay!' the word seemed to strike like the pendulum of the Town Hall in his brain . . . as if the reverberations of the note had conjured up all the elements of his life in a deep echo" (159). When he arrives and sees the poor sleeping on the streets he realizes that "this place is no different" from the northern cities he has left. But the miraculous sounds of the city echo all he has known and desired and are at odds with "the queer din of forty odd lingos" in the bazaar. The electric light of the shops reduces the goods to a riot of colors "vermillion, scarlet, yellow and green, which shone now garishly, now dazzlingly, upon Munoo's eyes" (180). Thus the associative sound sense of the musical word "Bombay" combines with the din of the streets and the defamiliarized scene to create and extend the profound dislocation Munoo experiences in the southern city.

This use of language becomes more directly political, however, in the climactic scene when the Bombay factory workers are put on short wages and determine to strike. They gather near union headquarters, waiting and listening.

> The babble of many tongues whispering, half in fear, half in expectation, rose in waves. The loud words of an official . . . shrilled aloft as a kite or a crow flying in a zigzag curve across the sky. A phrase like 'down with wage cuts' . . . poised itself like a songbird . . . the

fluctuating voice of the myriads of men becoming the one pointed symbol of their poverty and wretchedness.

(256)

The voice of the coolies, in no matter what language, takes on symbolic power beyond the meaning of their uttered phrase, linking myriads of men in fear and expectation. Their collective speech becomes both a sign of their abjection and an act of protest against it. Later, the union leader Sauda exhorts the crowd, which calls back "Shabash! Shabash! Sauda Sahib! [Bravo! Bravo! Sir Sauda!]" (260), taking on force through its appropriation of a hybrid public language outside conventional systems of discursive power. This speech is in many ways the climax of the novel and one of its most moving moments, as we sense the potential for collective action among the disenfranchised crowds and see Munoo rise to real engagement. The shared call and response creates a community among the workers, however fleeting, that takes on real political force. Despite the fact that the authorities successfully break up the strike by pitting Hindus against Muslims, this performance of language here unites the coolies as possessors of the remainder—play, the power of language that can exceed the bounds of authority, and layers of meaning not glimpsed by the coolies' British and Indian overlords.[119] Their shared language is neither the possession of the British nor any "original" language of Hindu authenticity, and despite their many tongues, it creates them as a community that acts politically.

The unusual quality of language in Anand's fiction has also been marked as crucial to the development of Indian writing in English and its representation of India's linguistic diversity. In the 1930s and 1940s, debates raged about what kind of language should be used to represent Indian experience. Critics take R. K. Narayan to task, for example, for using English almost exclusively, especially when at times his English seems either stilted or impoverished.[120] Others defend the unusual syntax or vocabulary in Narayan's work as an effort at representing Tamil speech patterns within an English-language narrative.[121] Anand, in those moments of nonliteral meaning making, sound sense, and emergence of the remainder, also takes a significant step toward the incorporation of local languages and habits of speech into English-language writing. At times he attempts to translate Hindi and Punjabi phrases into English; at other moments what emerges is a representation of the sound of that language in English, without concern for its absolute intelligibility, highlighting what Ben Conisbee

Baer calls, referring to *Untouchable*, the "lack of fit between the various levels of street Hindi or Punjabi and English."[122] As Anand puts it,

> I found, while writing spontaneously, that I was always translating dialogue from the original Punjabi into English. The way in which my mother said something in the dialect of Central Punjab could not have been expressed in any other way except in an almost literal translation, which might carry over the sound and sense of the original speech.[123]

At other times Anand will mix the two languages, putting snippets of English within a Hindi phrase or vice versa. He incorporates new coinages without apology, arguing in his essay "Pigeon-Indian: Some Notes on Indian Writing in English" that the real everyday use of a combined language, whether it is transparent in meaning or not, ought to be represented in the fiction that emerges out of India.[124]

Anand's resistance to verbal transparency and his synthesis of languages often engenders critical responses that try to reinforce the values of verisimilitude and reinscribe them within a national frame. Critics note that "although awkward," Anand's novels "are pioneering in their attempt to render into English the exuberant dialects of Northern India."[125] On the other hand, I would argue that reading Anand from a transnational perspective, in light of his own notion of rooted cosmopolitanism and also in connection to Joyce, makes clear the inadequacy of describing these quasi-Hindi, quasi-English moments in Anand purely in terms of verisimilitude. However important they may be to the development of a new vernacular in India, they are equally crucial as moments of syncretism, disruption, and play. If the new "pigeon English" of the coolie or the untouchable cannot be assimilated into either the standard English of empire or the Hindi of a caste-conscious India, then it contains the possibility of new cosmopolitan linguistic geographies. This neither/nor language provides the moment of potential power for those shut out of conventional hierarchies since it creates its own system of signification and its own linguistic communities. This language use also points the way out of Stephen's conundrum regarding the dean's use of the words "detain" and "tundish," for a newly developed syncretic language can never be called "his before it is mine," nor will it always succumb to the possessor of power over the marketplace tradition.

Thus, this use of language—of style, if you will—carries heavy political and social weight. It belies the truism that engaged writing lacks interest in stylistics and that political novels tend toward stripped-down realism. It also connects the political dimension of our understanding of style in both *Coolie* and *Portrait* to the critique of the geographies of empire so crucial to both Joyce and Anand. What escapes control in Anand's novel is Munoo, his name, what he stands for, the coolie, the orphan nation, just as Stephen escapes his definition not only by family, religion, and Ireland but also within the rubric of the autonomous, representative man. If we see Anand's *Coolie* as definitely and dramatically an anticolonial novel because it musters the forces of a revised model of *Bildung* to the side of an orphaned laborer, because it insists on material reality and not the mystical or religious realm as the scene of self-development and enlarged thinking, and because it presents the many layers of discourse within a highly focalized novel as still leaving an empowering linguistic remainder, then we might also read those elements, which Anand saw and admired in Joyce's *Portrait*, as important to political struggle. Reading Joyce and Anand together from a transnational, comparative perspective helps make a case for Anand's work as a constitutive part of transnational modernism, one that brings the imbrication of modernist experimentation and politics to the center of the conversation and reorients our notions of modernism toward the political engagement that helps motivate it. Reading Joyce and Anand together also forces us to see the correspondences that, like the concatenation of east and west in *Ulysses* or the layering of spaces and languages in Anand's work, undermine the geopolitics of empire. We are thus encouraged to look beyond the words in *Portrait*—"I go to forge in the smithy of my soul . . ."—to see a political struggle for discursive authority that brings Stephen, Munoo, and us as readers into the realm of enlarged thinking and political engagement.

Part II

Modernism in the Zenana | THREE
The Domestic Spaces of Sorabji, Hussain, and Ishvani

> Indian women did not begin to write novels until the
> independence of India.
> —Anita Desai, "Indian Women Writers"

> As we encounter more and more writers from the Indian
> subcontinent . . . we must guard against any facile
> tendencies to elide or erase the intricate histories
> that these narratives chronicle.
> —Sangeeta Ray, *En-gendering India*

Near the end of the celebrated Indian novel *Kamala*, written between 1889 and 1894 by Krupabai Satthianadhan, the eponymous protagonist, a young Hindu woman who has suffered the death of her beloved father, the disdain of her husband, and the loss of the man she loves, leaves home with her infant daughter. In pity, her husband offers her money, which she declines while telling him he will never see her again. She wanders, distraught and nearly suicidal, until a glimpse of the heavens filled with stars calls her back to a life of community service and charitable work. The narrator tells us, "It may seem strange that such an experience as this should have been felt by an ignorant Hindu girl. But . . . Kamala was different from other Hindu girls . . . she had herself learnt to feel and think."[1] By feeling and thinking for herself, Kamala separates herself from her traditional domestic identity, not only leaving her husband but also discovering the potential solace of independence and work. She endures hardship, the death of her child, and later that of her husband, ending her days as a widow driven to acts of charity. Her decision not to remarry and to devote herself to good deeds has been described by many critics as a retreat into the husband worship ("*pativrata*") of a traditional Indian wife. But, I would argue, it also gestures beyond this paradigm, toward the possibility of a transfigured domestic sphere, with room for expanded female independence and agency.[2] Kamala seems poised on the threshold of a domestic modernity but cannot yet see what lies ahead.[3]

This tension between the traditional zenana (or women's sphere of the home) and a potentially reconfigured, modern female space becomes a dominant concern for the many Indian women writers who were developing an English-language narrative tradition between 1900 and 1947. Yet despite the enormous recent increase in critical writing on Indian literature, little attention has been paid to these writers. Their work is often hard to obtain or out of print.[4] The classic text on Indian writing in English, which treats all women novelists together in one chapter, remarks that "it is . . . only after the second world war that women novelists of quality have begun enriching Indian fiction in English."[5] Again and again, critics discuss the "big three" of the late-colonial period: Mulk Raj Anand, R. K. Narayan, and Raja Rao—while the writings of Iqbalunnisa Hussain, once referred to as "the Jane Austen of India" are unavailable.[6] It is thus surprising to discover that the apparent lacuna in the history of women's writing does not in fact exist and that women were key players in the development of Indian writing in English in the twentieth century. Their novels and autobiographical accounts exhibit extraordinary range and candor about the situation of women in late-colonial India and tackle head-on the problematic of a modernizing domestic sphere.[7]

Writers such as Cornelia Sorabji, Iqbalunnisa Hussain, and G. Ishvani, whose work I will raise in this chapter, describe ordinary heroines, both Muslim and Hindu, in and out of purdah, who struggle like Kamala with the restrictions of traditional roles even while desiring to remain within their domestic and social spheres. In many of their novels, home becomes a modernizing, contested space that women begin to shape in ways that diverge from tradition, creating more permeable boundaries between public and private while demonstrating the important links between domesticity and the life of the nation. Their fiction often exhibits a surprising range of options for women, following its heroines on paths of education and self-development that challenge simple assumptions that women in India during this period were mired in tradition, entrapped by purdah, and not yet modern enough to be writing sophisticated fiction. In fact, many of the narratives written by Indian women in the late-colonial period engage in complex ways with the conventions of narrative fiction and autobiography, developing an intersecting critique of gender and genre that seeks to realign women's social and political identities while opening a space for an alternative narrative modernism. In the narratives of Sorabji, Hussain, and Ishvani, the challenges of India's colonial status, its changing economy, and its modernizing roles for men, women, and families give rise to hybrid genres, poised between autobiography and fiction, as well as to forms of bildungsroman where the protagonist is multiple and the journey of discovery takes place behind the purdah screen. These narratives foreground displacement and dislocation even inside the threshold of the zenana and make domesticity a vehicle for engagement with postcoloniality and the public sphere. The modernism these texts create is figured by liminal zones and thresholds where acts of discovery, representation, display, and narration, create and transform an often hidden but ever-emerging domestic world.

These pivotal texts also ask us to reconsider the role of women in the development of Indian modernity and to recognize the powerful ethical and political engagement their texts evidence. Ideas of nationality and culture in India during the period of colonialization and early independence often depict a feminized and domesticated nation brought under scrutiny within the masculine sphere of public discourse and reform. The historian Antoinette Burton points out that "twentieth-century feminists reappropriated the discourses of house and home that had been seized on by male Indian nationalists since the nineteenth century, linking domesticity expressly to their own reform agendas in ways that both consolidated that 'traditional' idiom and refigured it as a new subject of public political discourse."[8] Commentary by a wide range of public voices in the period characterized India as feminine, connected to the home and to an idealized past, while the role of public women was often sanctioned by their concern for domestic affairs. For example, Sarojini Naidu, president of the Indian National Congress in 1925, invokes the age-old characterization of Mother India (*Bharat Mata*), arguing that her goal is "to restore India to her true position as supreme mistress in her own home ... and to try to set [her] mother's house in order."[9] She thus casts her progressive politics within existing discourses that demand the restoration of a feminine domestic space and equate that restoration with nation building. Her argument for the franchise remains couched in the terms of "separate goals, separate destinies."[10] In 1927, the American Katherine Mayo's infamous and polarizing book, *Mother India*, called up a similar paradigm in order to force public debate on the issue of child marriage and the treatment of women.[11] By focusing on dramatic stories of young girls brutalized by older husbands or forced into early procreation, Mayo launched an exaggerated, ethnocentric, and sensationalist argument against Indian self-rule. Women's bodies and domestic spaces served in the period not only as the source for nostalgia about an idealized past but also as the locus of debate about India's political future.[12]

This fraught discursive terrain, which makes the struggle over ideals of women's roles and domesticity central to India's postcolonial modernity, also lies beneath narratives by Sorabji, Hussain, and Ishvani (among others), connecting them irrevocably to the political debates of the period. By focusing on the complexity of life in the zenana, these narratives challenge the paired notions positing that the political contest for India primarily concerns the control of public space and that India must turn its back on the domestic sphere, which is too easily denigrated and connected to the past. According to the historian Mrinalini Sinha, civil society in colonial India revolved around regional, religious, and cultural communities in which women served as a sort of "inner essence," whose status was zealously guarded because it was unregulated by colonial law, providing a realm of autonomy.[13] In the early twentieth century, however, the development of political nationalism and the intense debate surrounding *Mother India* challenged the civic status of these communities and "brought the 'inner' domain of the community . . . within the purview of the intervention of the state." Reform movements in the late 1920s and early 1930s placed women at the heart of discussions surrounding such legislation as the Child Marriage Restraint Bill and united them, if only contingently, as a political constituency. This moment in the development of political nationalism thus "provided public legitimacy . . . for an alternative construction of women . . . as paradigmatic citizen-subjects of a nation-state-in-the-making."[14] But the paradigm of the female citizen-subject could not exist without a posited interconnection between the social life of the domestic sphere and the public life of the nation. It required women to be seen as capable of agency and depended on the rhetorical reconstruction of the zenana as both domestic and political.

Writers like Sorabji, Hussain, and Ishvani participate in this political "moment" by generating just such a rhetorical reconstruction of the zenana. In fact, I will argue, Sorabji takes up this problematic well before the Mayo controversy while Hussain and others extend it beyond the period of its ascendency in the rhetoric of public politics. Their texts resist the easy slide from idealized woman to idealized nation or the too simple transition from denigrated child bride to educated modern wife common among the reformers and generate a complex discourse surrounding domestic life. By placing domestic servants and secluded women at the center of their narratives, Sorabji, Hussain, and Ishvani rework the thresholds between public and private, modern and traditional, creating the zenana as a complex space in which questions of ethical agency become intertwined with matters of personal authority and where relationships among women in a shared kitchen carry implications for their status in the emerging nation. Their narratives suggest that women need not leave the zenana to raise concerns of national import and that their emerging modernity develops by way of their participation in traditional sites and rhetorical practices.

These narratives thus offer a discursive proving ground for an alternative modernism bound to the social and political positions of women and the emergence of the modern citizen-subject in late-colonial India.[15] Their complex negotiations of boundaries and thresholds, their rhetorical reconstruction of female identities and spaces, and their constant engagement with the discourses surrounding public and private roles all mark their narrative mode as inseparable from the tensions and contradictions of the modernizing domestic sphere in India and crucial to its emergence. Yet critics have long missed the narrative complexity of these female-authored texts, and at times have denigrated them for their departures from a more seamless realism. These texts show some of the formal hallmarks we have long associated with European modernism: textual merging of fact and fiction; play with external and internal realities; disruptions of time and order of emplotment; attempts at new narrative perspectives (though to be sure, little use of fixed internal focus); and focus on the everyday life of ordinary figures.[16] Yet in the foreword to Hussain's *Purdah and Polygamy*, for example, Sir Ramalinga Reddy apologizes that "here and there the structure and the idiom may strike the English ear as strange, outlandish."[17] On the contrary, I would claim, these strange or outlandish moments in this and other female-authored narratives mark the places where these complex political and discursive concerns disrupt the text's surface and foreground its modernism.

But the challenge of these texts in the Indian context goes beyond simply identifying the experimental elements they share with European modernisms and their importance to global modernism. These texts intervene in the development of Indian narrative tradition by resituating domesticity and recasting its rhetorical modes. For example, whereas in earlier Indian writing the zenana was usually represented by outsiders, in the narratives I will discuss, the denizens of the home contribute their voices or guide the narration as someone privileged to enter behind the purdah screen. The texts perform a complex ethical negotiation, inviting us into an evolving domestic space while guarding against its presentation as problem or spectacle. At the same time, these texts rarely assign a privileged truth value to the women of the zenana, often undermining their narrative authority or foregrounding the matter of who speaks and to whom. Thus, the narratives that emerge present a view of zenana life not as a reified object of ethnography but rather as a complex and evolving discursive problematic. When they multiply subject positions or narrate the same event from different perspectives, these texts are not mimicking modernist formal devices imported from afar but participating in the rhetorical re-creation of Indian domestic life and the construction of a twentieth-century Anglo-Indian tradition in fiction. Further, by troubling the distinctions between autobiography and fiction, often violating what has been called the autobiographical pact,[18] these narratives by Indian women bring the problematic of domestic modernity, with its troubled distinctions and hybrid locations, into conversation with the matter of genre. Hovering on the threshold between fact and fiction, even as they describe and redescribe the contested spaces of the zenana, these narratives challenge our expectations for narrative fiction even as they generate an alternative modernism for India.

As we begin to read modernism and modernity in more worldwide locations and into the development of literary traditions outside of European temporalities, our understanding of modernist modes and periods will necessarily shift. In the context of India in the early twentieth century, it seems crucial to allow texts to cast their own versions of modernism in response to the specific forces of economic, social, and political change and in concert with the rhetorical reconstruction of community and nation. R. K. Narayan once said, "We are all experimentalists," implying that the process of developing the English novel in India forced every writer to hazard the possibility of a new literary language and new Indian-Anglo forms.[19] At the same time, another critic claims that "political consciousness flows in the very life-blood of Indo-Anglian fiction . . . political consciousness as the very staple of fiction."[20] The narratives explored in this chapter reveal both of these properties. Modernist narrative, as Indian women writers came to invent it, responds aesthetically to changing social structures, economies, interpersonal relations, and ethical obligations. It inscribes anxieties about subjectivity and voice into its play with the border between autobiography and fiction and concern about changes in social and political life into its experimentations with chronology and emplotment. In these ways, I argue, little-known narratives from late-colonial India such as Cornelia Sorabji's *Love and Life Behind the Purdah*, Iqbalunnisa Hussain's *Purdah and Polygamy*, and G. Ishvani's *Girl in Bombay* show us not only the ethical and political dimensions of women's domestic modernity but also the experimental possibilities for our understanding of what transnational modernism can be and do.

Uncloaked Lives: Cornelia Sorabji's Revealing Narratives

In the opening chapter of her 1934 autobiography, Cornelia Sorabji, the first Indian woman to pass the British bachelor of civil law exam (1892), longtime advocate for women in purdah, and gifted writer of fiction inspired by those for whom she advocated, writes:

> The gospel of Work she [her mother] got very securely into our minds at home from the very earliest years. We were in the world to serve others. . . . And all self-discipline, however trivial, was to this end and was glorified thereby. I remember, for instance, when I was eight years old, realizing for myself that I was the slave of a story, and deliberately practising shutting down the book when I had got to the most exciting part.[21]

She here writes of the way that a story can lay claim to our attention and emotions and the powerlessness a young child can feel in the face of this claim. Her mother enjoins her to learn the self-discipline appropriate to her class status and to her upbringing; she practices shutting the book in order to control her appetites and behavior. Force of will allows Sorabji to resist the pull of the book, and she touts this as a moment of growing self-control and discipline.

Yet we may also read this passage in another way. "I was the slave of a story," she says, as though the story were separate from the book held in her hands and had a claim on her that might outlast the moment of reading. The rhetorical situation of reading, in which the implied author enjoins the reader to espouse a position vis-à-vis the text or the text itself makes demands upon the ethos of the reader, can seem coercive, especially to a young child. Taught to value self-discipline and self-reliance, this situation disturbs Sorabji. She feels herself enslaved and resists that position by the only means at her disposal.

But the experience also seems to evoke in her a connection to the problem of personal enslavement, which will have resonance later in her life as she takes up the cause of women who are imprisoned in their households. In using the word "slave" Sorabji locates her moment of ecstatic reading within a broader context where the matter of slavery or servitude has real and daily significance. This little girl, growing up in a well-off and well-connected Parsee family in India, surrounded by servants, yet directed by family expectations to find her own way "to serve others," understands full well the meaning of that directive.[22] From a young age she felt compelled to put her intelligence to direct and practical use and to exploit it to help Indians of various castes and religions, though often with a degree of condescension formed by her elite upbringing. The use of the word "slave" also has resonance because of Sorabji's commitment as an adult lawyer to the legal representation of women who were otherwise not able to defend themselves in personal matters and her long-term interest in the life stories of disenfranchised women and children, whom she will sometimes describe as near slavery. A writer from a young age, she was drawn to the stories of the household servants and their acquaintances and of the women living in purdah, or *purdanashin*, to whom she ultimately devoted her professional life. *Sun Babies*, her collection of stories published in 1904, showcases vignettes in the lives of the servants of a household, many of whom are young children. In this collection and in the contemporaneous *Love and Life Behind the Purdah* (1901), the narrative impetus is to focus on those who serve and are often overlooked, to grant them individuality and voice by telling their particular tales, often with focus on their own storytelling, and, in so doing, to press their ethical claims upon us as readers.

As with other narratives I will take up, the stories in *Sun Babies* rest on the dividing line between fact and fiction and seem deliberately to confound the question of genre. They are narrated in the first person, and the narrator is sometimes addressed as "Miss Sahib," someone who might be Sorabji or perhaps any interested female observer.[23] And yet there are no other external markers that would indicate an autobiographical context for these stories, which are crafted with a narrative force that asks us to read them as fully fashioned "stories." Sorabji's narrative voice is active, and it reshapes and recasts even those stories she purports to be simply transcribing.[24] Though the ostensible mode is fiction, she pushes for the illusion of verisimilitude, with a first-person narrating voice that claims to "encounter" these characters yet engages with them in a manner beyond simple ethnography. Rather than suffering from such generic vagueness, however, these stories become all the more compelling as semifiction and help us to read Sorabji as occupied with more than the presentation of local color or the search for native "information" that is often ascribed to her.[25] By combining the aura of authenticity usually reserved for documentary or autobiographical texts with the rhetorical complexity of narrative fiction, I would argue, these tales resist the objectifying gaze that Sorabji is sometimes accused of using and look forward toward a complex and self-reflective, modernist stance. We can see Sorabji, at the turn of the century, troubling the discursive certainty that inhabits works like Satthianadhan's *Kamala* by focusing our attention on the domestic and generic thresholds of the text.

This work not only worries the distinction between fact and fiction but also employs the liminal zone between the two as a place of ethical encounter and an engagement with modernity. In other words, Sorabji's narratives create a rhetorical situation where narrator and reader are asked to approach the characters while shifting their understanding of those characters and their location within a changing India.[26] Like the ethical folds in Woolf's writing, the generic thresholds in Sorabji's work invite us into an ethical encounter with the text across irremediable gaps of knowledge and experience. The quasi-fictive stance of these stories delimits a space of encounter where each character is both in the world and *as if* in the world, real and unreal at once. In this way, though she writes only a few years afterward, Sorabji's stories inscribe the emerging problematic of modernity at the level of the text in a way that Satthianadhan's *Kamala* does not. They foreground the matter of accounting for oneself in narrative, which we have seen also to preoccupy Woolf and Rhys and inscribe into the story itself the issue of the narrator's development as a knowing ethical subject. Paul Ricoeur has argued that the ethical dimension of the self grows not only out of an encounter with otherness but also in the further step that requires self-reflexivity, the perception of oneself *as* an other—a process that inheres in and requires narrative. Further, questions of self-reflexivity and narration always verge on the matter of action—"who speaks?" is closely related to "who acts?"; "the self" and "action" are reciprocally constituted.[27] The subject/narrator of Sorabji's stories is often thrust into such self-reflection, revising her view of her own self-knowledge or her ability to comprehend even as she recounts her tales about others. She constructs the possibility of acting ethically toward her subjects while exploring the problem of "who speaks." Thus, I would argue, the generic complexity in these stories and, indeed, in much of Sorabji's writing, not only solicits an ethical response from readers toward its subject matter but furthers the process of ethical self-reflection at the level of narration, engendering a modernist reencounter with discursive authority.

The evocation of autobiography also points to the ways that Sorabji's stories challenge the autobiographical pact. Autobiography as a genre relies on the notion of a "pact," a set of shared assumptions between implied readers and implied author. This pact concerns the proposition that the text is presenting "truth" about a subject's life story. This need not imply that an autobiography actually rests on referentiality or is constructed out of a faithful transcription of external reality but rather that the "pact" names the self-referential function of the autobiographical narrative. As Philippe Lejeune puts it, "Telling the truth about the self, constituting the self as complete subject—it is a fantasy. In spite of the fact that autobiography is impossible, this in no way prevents it from existing."[28] Autobiography is a collaborative act even when accomplished by one person; that person is always multiple and self-referential when writing. Autobiographical faithfulness becomes a matter of being truthful about the process of self-reflection in narrative and can occur even when the narrative itself is fictive.

But the movement to ethics in Sorabji's quasi-autobiographical stories revises this pact significantly. The narrative situation declines to demarcate the subject of the autobiography or the terms of the collaboration between narrator and reader, and it often sidesteps the problem of self-referentiality by turning the text over to its characters. The call to action comes not from a positing of the self as another, as per Ricoeur, but more often, it seems, from engaging the reader in moving toward the other, whose story becomes significant for revising the self. This sort of autobiography mobilizes the potential ethics of the rhetorical situation more strenuously. Rather than the implied author and reader becoming complicit in a shared assumption about an autobiographical "truth," the reader is enjoined to share the narrator's ethical response to the characters and situation being narrated, and thereby to understand the narrator herself.

We thus come back to the matter of being enslaved to a narrative. Does Sorabji envision her narrators or her readers as the slaves of the stories she tells? Certainly, the narrator appears at times to do the bidding of her subject matter rather than the other way around. In both *Sun Babies* and *Love and Life Behind the Purdah*, the narrator of the stories describes herself again and again as forced to revise her perspective, particularly toward her lower-class or secluded female characters; to accord them voice and agency; and to demonstrate her indebtedness to them. To varying extents in the stories in these two volumes we hear the narrator comment on how the character has called the story into being or has so drawn her that she is compelled to write. In *Sun Babies*, the stories most often begin with a sort of condescending bemusement about the character in question: a boy who pretends to manliness, the son of a night watchman who has pretensions about the protection he offers, an old *khansamah*, or head of the kitchen, who is hired in part because he is "irresistibly picturesque" (a drawing is included).[29] Yet as each story progresses this character invariably commands a kind of attention that limits the possibility of stereotyping and compels the narrator to engage directly with him or her. Often the development of the story shows the narrator to have underestimated the main characters—the "picturesque" breaks through the surface and shows its contours; the servants display the ability to shape their own fates. Even more important, the narrator often must shift perspectives as the tale progresses, as though the process of writing and discovery has effected a change. She is often unable to sustain the dichotomy between narrating voice and narrated subject matter, between knowledgeable memsahib and illiterate servant, and thus between self-referential (autobiographical) subject and character who is other.

For example, the story "Fleetfoot," in which we encounter the *khansamah*, begins with the narrator's initiation into the art of housekeeping by this picturesque old man. He instructs her to keep daily accounts and tells her each evening what she is to write down: such and such amount for a good hen, so much for the greens for dinner, and so on. "'Has the Presence written it all as I say? It must be written,'" he tells her, and she complies with amusement. Eventually he insists that she travel into the marketplace to see for herself the prices for the food he has been buying. When she arrives there with a local boy to do her bargaining for her, she discovers that the *khansamah's* prices have been dramatically inflated. She confronts him with this apparent thievery, only to have him acknowledge the discrepancy: "'Yes!' he said, 'the prices were not *one word*, theirs and mine . . . did not the Presence command me to teach her the way of keeping house? This is the very beginning of the teaching, that one should never write down what is told one. Ai! Miss Sahibji, but *never*" (60). The *khansamah* then exhibits an old book, filled with his own accounts, and promises that the extra she has been paying for food has all along been transferred into the household's coal account (61). The narrator acknowledges that she underestimated this man on many fronts—his complexity, his awareness of her assumptions about him, and even his literacy. She becomes educated into the process of bargaining in the marketplace, which according to the *khansamah* is the definition of "good housekeeping." She learns to understand the threshold of the house as a marker for the imbrication of the marketplace and domestic economies (both verbal and otherwise) rather than as a boundary. She must also revise her understanding of her own position as narrative authority into one dependent upon the complex calculus of the *khansamah*'s discourse.

Thus, not only is this episode a lesson in the need to acknowledge the *khansamah* as wiser and more complex than he seemed, but it also clearly presents a domestic pedagogy of writing. The narrator must not simply write what she is told; she must learn to distrust the verbatim account and its reliance on an everyday transparency of meaning in language and to discover another way of hearing what is communicated. When the prices "are not one *word*, theirs and mine" yet are nonetheless accurate, words become signifiers for a relationship of understanding rather than of any direct or objective truth. Narration becomes more than simple transcription. It relies on the narrator's relationships with those speaking and their claims on each other, as well as her understanding of both domestic practices and market economies. The story describes its own conditions of creation, specifies the way it must be told, and prescribes its mode of reception as part of the reciprocal logic of the domestic sphere. The narrator's imperative, in this sense, is the obverse of being a slave to a book as a reader; the act of narrating ethically constrains both readers and narrators.

The questions of servitude, domestic logic, and narrative self-sufficiency emerge even more clearly in the story "My Master's Slave," the first in *Sun Babies*. In this story a young boy named Pagal ("crazy" in both Bengali and Hindi)[30] arrives at the door of a well-to-do householder and takes his place among the many supplicants who come to bargain or beg favor. The householder, usually referred to as "the Presence," deals with these figures disdainfully: "seldom was eastern potentate more autocratic or more loved for his autocracy" (2). The boy, who looks to be seven years old, is described as "a thing smaller than usual" waiting in front of the house (2), and is referred to with the pronoun "it." We are hardly surprised that the gardener tries to answer for him since we expect him to have no more capacity for language than any other object in the courtyard. But the boy discloses his subjecthood: "'Presence, I am a man-child. While years were yet few, my mother turned me adrift to earn my living. . . . Now that my years are many, I would do the work of a man" (3). The force of the story seems to revolve around the comedy of a "crazy," homeless seven-year-old insisting upon his manliness.

But if we attend to this story carefully, the claim to manliness is not so very comic. On its surface, the story requires us to accept the condition of this child, who must maneuver for a job, place to sleep, and spot in which to cook, as unremarkable. The *chaprassis* (official messengers or servants at the doorway) accuse him of being a "*badzat* [bad one]" (4). But the boy persists in his intention to become the personal servant of the householder and will not deal with the usual intermediaries. This hubris in a homeless waif strikes all concerned as inappropriate; the Presence must suppress a smile at his behavior. After he is offered the employment he desires, the narrative focuses on some of the humorous ways in which this homeless waif acts officiously, refusing to take an important message for another, intercepting visitors and judging the worthiness of their business with the Presence. To the Presence, he says, "Command me," while to all others he is willfully independent. As the narrator puts it, "To the Protector of the homeless, Pagal, was a dog in devotion and loyalty; to the outside world, a fiend" (9). His claim to manliness seems to overstep not only his age and his background but also his position in this supremely hierarchical world.

Yet this story also works to question the assumptions of servant behavior and status as well as the conditions of domestic servitude by playing with narrative authority. Pagal, the crazy "thing" on the pathway at the opening of the story, gives way to a boy with a name, position, and, importantly, a narrative voice. The story ends by assigning him the status of storyteller: "One more only of his sayings will here be recorded. He spoke in a parable to his old enemy, the khidmtagar [butler]: 'the owl and the hen waited together for the morning. . . . The light is of use to me,' said the hen, 'but of what use is it to you?'" (21). The boy who has been caring for himself and cooking his own meals from the age of five and who has been ingenious in securing a home and position for himself in the household of an important local figure exhibits an autonomy not seen among many of the other characters. He also becomes a narrator in his own right by the end of the story as a framer of sayings and parables. In this guise he not only interprets his own actions but also shapes the way that he is seen to fit into the household hierarchy. His relationship with the *khidmatgar* (butler) for example, would normally be subservient, with no way to challenge the *khidmatgar*'s interpretation of his role in the household. Yet in the parable of the owl and hen, Pagal casts himself as the one able to make use of the light. In creating roles for himself and the *khidmatgar*, he constructs himself as voice of authority and the *khidmatgar* as the receiver of wisdom. Narrative here conveys interpretive power, which serves to adjust the hierarchy of the servants' world. It also reconstructs the ethical relationship between Pagal and his interlocutors, including the narrator, who must henceforth respond to the mutual claims placed on them through narration.

The narrative of "My Master's Slave" thus puts in question not only the specific status of Pagal, who moves from object to subject, derided child to wise man, and from the focus of narration to one who can speak in his own parables, but also asks us to challenge our understanding of the meaning of domestic servitude, when such a one bows in obeisance to the man only known through such epithets as "the Presence" and "Protector of the Homeless." Indeed, the title phrase, "my master's slave" might by the end almost be reversed, as we see Pagal in his full glory, examining the claims of those who have come to petition the householder and acting almost as the Presence himself, turning unworthies away.

We might then ask the question, if a narrative can enslave someone, as Sorabji originally claimed, can it also liberate? When we come to see Pagal transformed from object to narrating subject, besting his enemy the *khidmatgar* and rising to become a hero of sorts, we are tempted to answer "yes," at least within the realm of the tale. The question becomes even more salient as we move into the stories for which Sorabji is most celebrated, those of the *purdahnashin*. When Sorabji narrates the stories of those whom she considers to be imprisoned in the zenana, both because of the force of the male world around them and their own unwillingness to break through the boundaries of their enclosures, she seems to assign her narratives the power to redress this servitude. In her other, more autobiographical writing, Sorabji argues that public politics cannot address the problems of secluded women in India, whose limitations she sees as derived in part from their own ignorance and isolation. Yet she seems to imply that uncloaking the lives of the *purdahnashin* and narrating their stories might prompt change within the zenana and provide the best route to reform. Without identifying with either the secluded women or the radical reformers who would transform the domestic world by legislation, Sorabji's early *purdahnashin* stories constantly return to the question of modernity, its effect on women, and the necessity of narrating the story of a modernizing domestic sphere from within the zenana. The modernist force of her narrative technique, then, lies in its construction of a mediating perspective on the threshold, neither dedicated insider nor outside authority, able both to present and to comment upon the previously untold stories of the *purdahnashin*.

Sorabji began these stories when she returned in 1894 from studies in Oxford and London. Having passed the BCL, she was nonetheless refused a regular law degree and prevented from joining the bar in either England or India.[31] She returned home and accepted an invitation from the maharajah of Baroda to write a report on education. At this point she was called to represent women living in purdah before the courts. By 1904, she had campaigned to be officially recognized by the government as a woman zenana official to the Court of Wards, where women are offered legal protection. In 1907 she was granted a full-time government salary to do this work in Bengal.[32]

This career trajectory is impressive in its own right.[33] It shows an extraordinary dedication to the representation of women and to the possibilities of the legal system, as well as an assumption that the situation of women in seclusion is akin to imprisonment. Sorabji writes about a client in 1914: "The lady still to some extent a prisoner—wants me to make every effort to take on her case. She lives in a house rented by her husband . . . I hear her tale of woe."[34] Sorabji's career also demonstrates her belief in the power of the existing imperial government to respond to reasoned argument and demonstrated need. She remarks again and again in her private papers about the respect that Indians owe to the British and records dismay at the riots that emerge after 1919, commenting on her sadness "that India should be misrepresented in this way by the rebels. Where we know how law-abiding are the real people of India."[35]

Her position in these early years owes more to the tradition of the "bountiful lady" than to any deep camaraderie with the mostly Hindi women she counseled. Her papers often express a disdain for traditional Hindu society and for the women who often endorsed their own enclosure. Yet her effort to give voice to secluded and powerless women, both through narrative and in court appearances, belies any critical tendency to dismiss her outright. Her intelligence, diligence, and social status put the lie to the stereotype that Sonita Sarker calls "Asian women as the oppressed constituency of the empire" (271) and mark her as more than a duped or submissive subject.

Further, it is clear that Sorabji's self-presentation, even within the pages of her more overtly autobiographical works such as *India Recalled*, as well as her unpublished essays collected at the British Library,[36] can not be taken simply as a transparent representation of her views. These overtly autobiographical narratives, I would argue, are as much concerned with refusing the assumption of transparent referentiality and worrying the boundary between fact and fiction as were the earlier stories. They are also intensely strategic, designed to represent and "translate" India for a British audience. In fact, these texts exhibit a marked difference in tone from her letters and private papers, which after 1919 become increasingly open to the idea of Indian independence while her published work did not. *India Recalled*, written in England for an audience of British sponsors, whose interests she acknowledges periodically in the narrative, remains staunchly pro-British and opposed to Gandhi's movement. "Poor Gandhi!" she writes,

> His truths were built upon deceptions, his loyalties upon verbiage.... His latest cry, the removal of 'untouchability' as a social service endeavor has, however, undone him. The Outcastes or *Harijans* ... themselves point out to him that they are not hungering and thirsting after righteousness in the company of their betters; but after bread and water and the means of preserving their mortal bodies.[37]

This is reformer's talk, practical in the extreme, which admits only that untouchables are poor and must be helped. Gandhi's campaign to rename the untouchables and to allow them entrance into temples is painted as a disruptive and counterproductive legislative "stunt." Sorabji, I would argue, is seeking to convince her expected British audience that she is a subject capable of heightened thought and the self-reflection necessary for autobiography. Here, indeed, the pact between reader and author may be seen as socially motivated and collaborative rather than in any sense based in "fact."

However, in her occasional talks Sorabji demonstrates her fierce commitment to a version of Indian women's history that contradicts claims that Indian women lack the desire for equality. In "Tea-Time Talks" (1937), she elaborates on the various histories of Indian women from different religious traditions, emphasizing that a middle ground must be sought between the resistance to any change among observant Hindus and the too quick modernization of the theosophists:

> The unchanging East has changed rapidly through the last century in all particulars. . . . To racial cleavage must be added difference consequent upon the pace, severally, at which we travel. The masses are still held fast in the second century, in superstitious and hampering custom. The small advance battalion may be described as in the twenty-second century, so quickly do they move. Between, the Progressives, are helped forward chiefly by political propaganda. While we honour the vanguard, we must not forget the rear; and that our strength lies in evening the pace.[38]

Not so hidden here is Sorabji's animosity toward the retrogressive forces of religion; less obvious is her jab at the stereotype of the "unchanging East." Even in this talk, aimed at English ladies interested in enlightenment at teatime, she makes clear that Indian women can neither be simplified nor held hostage to orientalist ideas of a static India. History intervenes as the harbinger of modernity, carrying with it concern with speed, uneven development, and disequilibrium. If the country races too fast ahead, Sorabji worries, women may find themselves entirely displaced, lost in the temporal-spatial gap between progressive politics and the superstitions of the second century. The ethical problem of women's domestic "imprisonment" requires us to "even the pace" of historical and political modernity and narrative becomes the locus for just such an effort.

In this sense, through her autobiographical and political writing, Sorabji constructs herself as an ethical intermediary within the system of empire and a mediating force in the development of Indian modernity. Amenable to both British and Indian perspectives, she belongs fully to neither. She can speak with the Hindi and Muslim women and represent them "directly" because she is Indian, but because she is a Parsee, well to do, and educated in the West, she is not subsumed within the idealized category of "Indian woman." She plays down her narratives as a casual affair yet at times betrays the concerted efforts behind her self-creation. On her youthful return from England she writes, "I sailed back, then, for India, . . . determined to find a way of helping those who I claimed as my portion: but as hopelessly without a programme of action as I had been when I left for England. I had a kind of—was it Faith, or Instinct?—that, if I were destined to help, a way would open, . . . provided that I took every reasonable opportunity that came along" (46). Sorabji's autobiographical works position her as a liminal figure, mediating between the zenana and the wider world, between the British and India, as between the traditional past and the modernizing present. Indeed, her ability to cross thresholds in many directions and her insistence on the importance of hybrid, multiethnic, and multilingual positions creates her as a modernist subject even as she resists the push toward India's postcolonial status. Her narratives become part of her plan of action, enacting the ethical role of the intermediary for the zenana while helping to open it toward the modern public realm of law and politics.

In the stories collected in *Love and Life Behind the Purdah* the notion of the intermediary is also key, both as a trope and as a figure for the way in which Sorabji's tales function within the broader context of modernizing India. Over and over again in these stories and the accounts that flesh out *India Calling* and *India Recalled*, Sorabji or her narrator places herself in the position of intermediary between two parties in a conflict or between a woman and the external world, often representing the modern legal apparatus to the secluded woman, and vice versa.[39] The narrator gains access to the secluded woman and gains her confidence in order to confirm her identity, ascertain her position, and represent it to society. She thus secures the woman within the modern framework of civic identity—there can be no doubt about who and where she is. The further task is to transform this female civic identity into a postcolonial citizen-subject, no longer under the arbitrary rule of the male head of household or considered a ward of the state, able to take on the role that, as we have seen, was so crucial to reformers of the time. The narrator as intermediary and the narration itself (as stand-in for Sorabji's testimony at the Court of Wards) become the means toward such modern citizenship for Indian women and therefore participate in recasting the rhetoric of domestic and political spheres. In *India Recalled* Sorabji describes a case where the woman who needed to testify was in seclusion. When Sorabji goes to visit she is refused entry behind the purdah screen and told she must speak to the woman without seeing her. Sorabji persists, whereupon it becomes clear that the woman is in another house entirely. Had she acquiesced to the blind meeting she would have taken false testimony from an unknown person. In telling this story, Sorabji insists on the principle of knowability through narration—that what she can see with her own eyes as the truth will become known through the intervention of writing. Without it, like the purdah woman beneath her burka, the truth would remain cloaked, and justice could not be done. The narrator creates a pact with her readers that enlists them with her in uncloaking the "truth" of the *purdanashin* and her claim to full civic citizenship, thereby also ensuring their recognition of her narrative authority.

The stories in *Love and Life Behind the Purdah* employ this trope of the intermediary but increasingly test the transparency of narrative authority. In this sense it is possible to trace Sorabji's increasing skepticism about the distinctions between life inside and outside the zenana and the authority of the narrative intermediary. In "Behind the Purdah," we follow a Western doctor treating women in an Indian rajah's zenana mainly through her letters to a friend in London. The doctor interprets her clients and "translates" their behavior into terms the Londoner can understand, yet this understanding, as the story makes clear, is increasingly suspect. This story exhibits an unusual complexity of narrative perspective that not only shifts from second to third person, and moves into the epistolary form, but also becomes unreliable and self-undermining by the end.[40] The opening paragraphs are written from a second-person perspective, as the narrator leads us on a journey inside the zenana. At the outset we are told, "There was time for a regular series of impressions to lounge through your unoccupied mind . . . the more abject you felt, the more likely was it that you would appreciate their pinchbeck glories." The second-person perspective forces a sort of queasiness here, creating us as abject and setting the scene for a story of discomfit, poisoning, and elder neglect. The directed journey continues: "Before you look further, you should note the way the men [on the verandahs] work. 'Tis non-Western; topsy-turvy; the needle pulled away from you . . . instead of vice versa. . . . The manipulation of that mass of glittering gold and silver becomes fascinating—But . . . Miss Rebecca Yeastman, the lady-doctor, through whose sun-spectacles we have been looking, is summoned to the *darbar*-room." We learn the name of our guide and understand why she is looking through Western eyes at the tailors, but the narrative accomplishes our connection to her by fiat, leaving us no room to maneuver or to propose our own response to the scene. Further, the narrative circles around the basic matter of plot: who has called this British lady doctor to the zenana, and why? The narrative claims that Dr. Rebecca Yeastman is "self-possessed and brisk"; "she was a thoroughly good creature, every faculty of her; of that you were certain." But here again, the reader is enjoined to a position not yet sustained by the story, as though the narrator cannot allow us to form our own opinions or think through the evidence.[41]

This structured and almost coercive narrative opening is mirrored at the level of the plot as we penetrate deeper into the palace. A strange trajectory into the anteroom, where the doctor becomes aware of hidden eyes assessing her worth, dissolves into a labyrinthine passage into the heart of the women's quarter, "through . . . dark, intentionally devious passages" and "into a room large and square, with windows too high for purposes of outlook, and closely barred against all use as ventilation" (72–73). In this mysterious place the doctor immediately sees and diagnoses the Rani, who is lying beautifully clothed on a bed, in no apparent distress as simply "bilious." This diagnosis is rejected, and the doctor is informed that the Rani is instead the victim of poisoning. The supposed poisoner, the mother-in-law, is hauled before a magistrate and exiled from her home despite the doctor's protests. Thus, the story revolves around the power of those looking into the zenana to know what they are seeing and to control the narrative construction of that truth. The narrative's assumption seems to be that the Western-trained doctor will bring her rational gaze to bear on the mysterious inner world of the palace and promulgate the truth. However, the palace inhabitants, coded as "intentionally devious" like the zenana they inhabit, also gain power over the narrative by structuring the doctor's visit. They trick her into examining the food for poison and are able to lodge a complaint against the mother-in-law on the basis of this planted evidence. The doctor's powers of observation and her attempts to tell a different story about the Rani count for nothing. The story thus seems to endorse an orientalist reading of the inscrutability of the zenana and the irrationality of its practices.

However, as though underscoring the insignificance of Dr. Yeastman's ability to control her own story, at this point the narrative shifts abruptly, accomplishing what we might recognize as a modernist break with unified narration. This break serves to undermine the authority of the story's original perspective and to question the rhetorical position forced on the reader in the previous pages. The second section of the story begins in England, in the room of a student doctor, Miss Marion Mainwaring. She reads "sheets of closely written foreign paper, and you—you creep behind her and look over her shoulder" (76). The story takes an epistolary form, from this moment until the final paragraph, quoting from letters between Dr. Yeastman and Miss Mainwaring, her friend, that describe the exile and eventual death of the old Rani at the hands of her household. From a narrative that insisted on scripting its readers' every response, we move to one that gives little narrative guidance beyond the insistence that we read.

"Can't you see it all?" the final letter proclaims, yet we are at least two steps removed from being able to see the action, located as we are behind the shoulder of Marion Mainwaring, as she reads.

The consequences of this narrative shift are to transmit to us as readers the sense of manipulation that Dr. Yeastman experiences at the hands of the household and to underscore the degree to which the zenana works according to its own logic rather than by direct observation or scientific rationality. We are left in the hands of the British observer, who seems to function much in the tourist-ethnographer role that the historian Antoinette Burton has also ascribed to Sorabji. The result for Western readers might be to endorse an orientalist mistrust of the cultural habits of the East and a patronizing disparagement of the women in the zenana, who plot and scheme against their own family members. Yet, as we have seen, Sorabji's occasional writings resist such an orientalist perspective. Further, I would argue, the accusatory second person combined with the epistolary structure and break with seamless narration in this story all work against this orientalism. Like Woolf in *Three Guineas*, "Behind the Purdah" uses narrative interruption and an epistolary frame to challenge the assumption of consensus implied by narrative realism and to ask the difficult question, "Who are you?" of the narrator. Here, we as readers are interpellated as accomplices of the narration ("you"!). In the epistolary sections, we know nothing other than what the doctor writes to her friend, yet we must fill in the gaps between letters and the logic of the plot ourselves. If the narrative casts an orientalist gaze, it is by necessity our gaze, and we are per force swept into its limited perspective.

Thus we are also implicated along with the doctor, who did not notice when the Thakrani ("lady"—here, "mother of the Rajah") was removed from the house. Moved to a location in England, distracted by the narrative, which has insisted we focus our attention elsewhere, and convinced by the line "can't you see it all?" we have presumed the narrative's transparency and verisimilitude. In fact, it is the very principle of complete and rational narration, seemingly endorsed by its first section, which has been called into question in this story. Rather than simply presenting an orientalist critique of the inherently irrational Indian household, "Behind the Purdah" suggests that not only is the zenana irrational but so are we—along with the doctor and the narrative itself. That is, trust in narrative authority has been undermined in this story, along with the idea of an omniscient Western(ized) narrator, and the possibility of a rational approach to the vagaries of zenana life. The narrative undoes our generic expectations in order to unravel our assumptions about Indian domestic life.

This is not to say that Cornelia Sorabji was not committed to the power of rationality to accomplish reform in India. Yet in this story the experiences of a modernizing world, where Anglo women doctors enter the zenana and courts use scientific tests to decide the fate of a *thakrani*, beget only a fragmented story with no settled perspective and no recourse to an absolute truth. Narrative becomes the site of the conflicting perspectives about women living in seclusion. If, as I have claimed, the construction of a modern citizen-subject in India in this period depends upon the discursive realignment of domesticity and female voice, then Sorabji's narrative uncertainties participate directly in this process.

Further, the function of the intermediary, which Sorabji served for *purdanashin* who needed representation and which she inscribes into her texts as the narrator's role, also becomes a vehicle for engagement with modernity and modernization and the increasing permeability of the domestic sphere. If, as Antoinette Burton describes it, Sorabji was aware that modernity was "pressing up against the very walls of the zenana,"[42] then her effort to represent that world as intermediary must be seen as an aesthetic response from the threshold of modernity, not simply the attempt to represent the archaic *purdanashin* to a world leaving them behind. Sorabji's writing presents a struggle to develop a form of narrative mediation that can account for their experience on the edge of modernity. It seems to accept, as a premise, that what one is told may not explain the truth and that, in the Khansamah's words, "one should never write down what is told one." In the end it suggests that despite pacts of varying kinds that make ethical claims on narrators and readers, narratives, whether autobiographical or fictional, cannot present a truth about which we can reach consensus, however provisional. We are asked to face the text and the world it presents to us in terms of the claims they place upon us yet without taking them at "face value," as it were. At the same time, I would argue, this ironic or distrustful narrative stance cannot be reduced to a simplified orientalist politics where the mysterious zenana world is coded as unchanging, unfathomable, and dangerous. Because Sorabji persists in creating narratives that ask not only how the zenana can be represented but also, importantly, who will represent it and from which threshold, she resists even as she evokes the simplified tale of zenana life. There can be no better description of the complicated problem of engagement in modernist writing or of the complex ethical challenge twentieth-century narrative can propose than this paradoxical situation of ironic or suspicious responsibility to a social world.

Coming of Age in Seclusion; Or, Purdah and the Modern Girl

If Cornelia Sorabji's narratives stand on the threshold of the zenana, serving the role of intermediary, other writings by women from the late-colonial period plunge us more directly into that domestic world, both Hindu and Muslim. While the number of reformers, male and female, casting their eye on domestic life in India was already large by the end of the nineteenth century,[43] the narratives that treat the zenana from within, taking up secluded young women as heroines, grew in number in the 1930s and 1940s. Because more women became educated and were able to leave the domestic sphere in this period, more fiction writers emerged with direct experience of life behind the purdah screen. Writers like Iqbalunnisa Hussain and G. Ishvani participate in the development of a subgenre of coming-of-age narratives where the heroine often travels no further than to her husband's compound, her personal challenges may come from within the family unit rather than from without, and the matter of growing independence requires negotiation with the strict surveillance of enclosure. At the end of the nineteenth century, in Krupabai Satthianadhan's *Kamala*, the heroine faced an all-or-nothing choice between proper widowhood or seeming exile. In *At Home in the World* (first published in 1915), Rabindranath Tagore presents, in Sangeeta Ray's words, "a kind of female Bildungsroman that . . . provides no resolution to the various conflicts elaborated in its pages." In the end, its heroine is castigated for having failed to "reconcile tradition with modernity."[44] In Sorabji's writings from earlier in the century, as this chapter has claimed, Indian women's identification with domestic life is tacitly accepted, requiring an intermediary to bring her into the realm of civic life.

On the other hand, in novels like those by Hussain, Ishvani, and Kamala Sathianadhan, written in the early 1940s, the domestic world takes center stage not only as the location of conflict over modernization but also as one of its generative forces. These novels foreground the matter of space, and in particular domestic space, as the crucial matrix not only of female coming of age but also of India's impending modernity. If not quite "laborator[ies] for social experimentation" as were the private homes of British modernists such as Virginia Woolf, the domestic spaces for these late-colonial Indian women writers held the possibility of new arrangements of family life with profound social and political implications.[45] As in Virginia Woolf's work, recasting the rhetorical structure of domestic identity and power demands the concomitant expansion of notions of narrative structure and revision of the conventions surrounding plot, action, and narrative voice. In novels like Hussain's *Purdah and Polygamy*, Ishvani's *Girl in Bombay*, and Kamala Sathianadhan's *Detective Janaki*, the matter of purdah is no longer beyond reproach, nor is a modernized female identity inconceivable within the home. These narratives refuse the absolute dichotomy of home and world even as they negotiate strategies of female development in and around the constant surveillance of the domestic compound. They therefore resist reformers' efforts to reinscribe the idealized model of Mother India into the twentieth-century zenana, while narrating their heroines' movement from a position subject to direct surveillance to one in possession of her own gaze as active citizen.

Much of the discourse surrounding the modernization of Indian domestic life in the first decades of the twentieth century rests on the assumption that modernity is being foisted on Indian households from outside and must either be resisted as a force for imperialism or embraced as a means around it. Gandhi employs the traditional, rural home as a sign of India and a place for resistance and Swadeshi (self-sufficiency) or *swaraj* (self-rule). He rejects modernity as imposed from without, linked to European values, and unnecessary, even as he encourages women to take up civic life and join the public movement.[46] Others, like Tagore, ultimately reject Gandhi's version of Swadeshi because of what they see as the limits of nationalism, arguing that Indians should "set [their] house in order"[47] through social work, education, and domestic reform rather through nationalism. Modernization here is double edged, promising education, progress, and global connection while often seen as Westernized, dangerously violent, and spiritually disruptive. The home in these arguments becomes the space for resistance to modernity's discontents. At the same time, reform organizations, especially around the *Mother India* event, voiced renewed interest in domestic efforts to modernize India by reducing child marriage, extending female education, and developing women's roles in social work. While the household and women's roles within it are crucial to these reforms, they become the proving ground for ideals about the public good and Indian modernity writ large rather than the place where an indigenous modernity comes into being. On the other hand, in the narratives I will consider here, the domestic world takes center stage as the location of conflict over modernization and as one of its generating forces. These novels foreground the matter of space, especially domestic space, as the crucial matrix not only of female coming of age but also of India's impending modernity.

Girls and their development, then, come to the fore in the narratives by women from the 1930s and 1940s in a different way than in earlier Indian fiction in English or in the writing by the most celebrated late-colonial writers Anand, Narayan, and Rao. Like their predecessors, the heroines of Hussain's *Purdah and Polygamy*, Ishvani's *Girl in Bombay*, and Kamala Sathianadhan's *Detective Janaki* seem caught in a never-ending effort to adjust themselves to the expectations of those around them, and they constantly battle with the restrictions of early marriage, religious obligations, or expectations for their conduct as wives and daughters, which are perpetuated and enforced in the domestic spaces of household life. Yet within and sometimes against these confines these narratives present heroines who develop and expand their experiences of the world, exhibit agency in the conduct of their own lives, and ultimately refigure the relationships of the household so as to construct a position of active subjectivity rather than remaining the object of the policing gaze. While they may choose to live their lives primarily within the zenana, it becomes a more permeable place, subject to changing economic demands on the household but also linked to the public life of the nation.

Beyond that, these texts ask us to reexamine our assumptions about women's experience of coming of age in the early twentieth century and to revise, once again (though in a different way than in the novels of Joyce and Anand), our expectations of a narrative of development. If the classic bildungsroman takes a hero, separates him from his family, and subjects him to a series of trials and tribulations along his journey to maturity, these novels place the struggle toward development within the home (and often within purdah), rarely isolate their heroines, and often end with an ambiguous compromise between the individuation desired by the protagonist and the intersubjectivity of female life within the zenana. Marriage in these narratives is always in question though sometimes refused, and education becomes a continuing process of acculturation and revision rather than a stage to pass through. Further, if we classify these texts as a sort of bildungsroman, then the questions they pose become even more interesting. How do we mark maturity for a woman in purdah who is expected to marry young? What measure of success do we accord to the woman who refuses an arranged marriage and flees the country? How do we account for narratives that merge fiction and autobiography, as so many of these Indian texts do?

Yet what is perhaps most striking in these narratives of female coming of age is the extent to which these heroines develop and transform their own life stories as well as the possibilities for narrating subjectivity within community. On the one hand, critics of the British female bildungsroman, such as Susan Fraiman and Lorna Ellis, grapple with the perception that many British novels in this subgenre seem to doom their heroines to failure. Girls in the female bildungsroman often seem to lead static or retrogressive lives in the face of societal restrictions, though, as Ellis makes clear, they often "construct themselves as subjects by manipulating the signs of their objectification."[48] Those who come of age as members of minority populations or, as Jed Esty has pointed out, in colonized situations, are often described in a sort of opposite trajectory, where development is not only stifled but reversed.[49] On the other hand, the narratives examined here, taken collectively, challenge these expectations by showing their heroines as self-reflective ethical subjects, able, as Ricoeur makes clear, to link narration to action, flirt with new paradigms, and often, if not always, revise the specific demands of Indian domestic households. In developing multiple points of view as the basis for female agency, as in the polygamous household of the novel *Purdah and Polygamy*, or constructing the heroine as the subject rather than the object of the policing gaze, as in the female detective novel *Detective Janaki*, these narratives offer a model of the female novel of development that not only revises the expectations that have emerged from a Euro-focused canon but also helps imagine new life trajectories for women within the modern Indian context.

One of the most striking narratives of its period, Iqbalunnisa Hussain's *Purdah and Polygamy: Life in an Indian Muslim Household* (1944), now sadly out of print, seems most obviously to respond to the tradition of the English novel. Compared by one commentator to a novel by Jane Austen, Hussain's book introduces us to the compound of a modernizing Muslim household, which conveys much about its inhabitants, just as the description of Mansfield Park or Pemberley in Austen's novels introduces crucial information about characters and relationships. The house itself, "an imposing building, standing in the heart of a city," "commanded respect and awe," and it holds clues to the family within—it is "peculiar . . . like its inhabitants." On the other hand, by the third sentence we also learn that "its high blind walls made a stranger take it for an unguarded jail, and literally it was so for its women folk."[50] If the inhabitants are to be understood by reference to the physical structure of the compound, then by the third sentence of this novel we know that the place is not benign and that the women within are prisoners. The awe-inspiring view from the outside belies the constrained and supervised view from within, and the novel fluctuates regularly between the two.

The quick passage from one perspective to the other in this opening paragraph also highlights the novel's sophisticated use of irony, employed much as in Anand's *Coolie*, as a means of critique. That is, while on its surface *Purdah and Polygamy* presents a dispassionate description of the family that inhabits this compound, through use of free indirect style to represent the characters' points of view; through allusion to outmoded, extreme, or ill-conceived habits of education and religious expression; and through occasional overt criticism by the narrator, the narrative constantly undermines the practices of this household. The comparison to Jane Austen in this sense is apt; Hussain, like Austen, presents her social commentary under what appears to be the realist surface of a novel of domestic life. The opening line of chapter 5, "It is a well known fact that man is superior to woman in every respect" (49), makes explicit reference to the opening line of *Pride and Prejudice*. Yet the narrator of Hussain's *Purdah and Polygamy* is more bold in her condemnation of the world of her characters, alluding to the "plight" of the women in this compound (1). The plot of the novel, as it unfolds, makes clear that these characters will not redeem themselves or overcome their limiting situation. Though we may come to feel sympathy for its heroine, Nazni, there is little in her to admire at the outset and still less by the end of the novel, when we learn that after her mother-in-law's death she will perpetuate the polygamous household system and the power structure that has formed her. The 1944 foreword to this novel points out that Hussain "deals with the ordinary, the familiar, not with the romantic and heroic" yet castigates her for the "fervour of a moral and social purpose which sometimes leads her to didactic outpourings." On the other hand, we can see in this novel an extraordinary attempt to narrate what the author of the foreword calls "social purpose" by way of an "unsparingly ironic" tone.[51] Under the narrator's unflinching gaze, the men and women of the compound are seen as deeply limited. Their way of life, along with its understanding of Islam, its insistence on purdah, and its unreflective espousal of polygamy, is placed under indictment, and the only possibility of an ethical or just situation must emerge through the ironic undermining of the unified narrative perspective and the multiple points of view that develop by the end.

At the same time, *Purdah and Polygamy* shares with the work of other English-language writers of the period, such as Anand, Narayan and Rao, concern with the everyday lives of nonelite people and with their connection to the broad contexts of late-colonial Indian politics. We are accustomed to remark of European modernism that it breaks conventions in its championing of the everyday and its interest in ordinary heroes. Modernist writing in late-colonial India is perhaps even more direct in its connection of interest in the everyday to public politics. If for Raja Rao the village of Kanthapura in his novel provides the setting for the emergence of Gandhian political virtues, and the ordinary women and men there become the vehicles for a powerful wave of public activism, for Hussain the domestic sphere might have potential to be the location for activism on behalf of women and for changes in the everyday private lives of Muslim families. The novel focuses around the power relationships within the zenana and the importance of such domestic affairs as marriage agreements, sleeping arrangements, kitchen chores, and child care, making clear that these are serious and complex affairs that determine the lives of women. In placing women's daily conflicts in the kitchen and their efforts at empowerment at the center of the novel, she invites an implicit juxtaposition with the many public struggles for education, economic self-sufficiency, and self-rule that surrounded the writing and publication of this novel.

Still, the narrator's modernist, ironic tone functions to undermine any inclination to cast these women as potential models for Mother India or to mark the zenana as the center of nostalgia for traditional Indian life. The novel resists espousing traditional domesticity as a virtue and the home as the bastion of resistance to modernity in part because Hussain depicts the Muslim home in this novel as only barely affected by modernization. If, as Burton claims, in this period the kitchen becomes the site for a contest over modernization, in the kitchen of the compound in *Purdah and Polygamy* the contest has barely begun. The kitchen in this novel functions as the central place of surveillance, where wives must be present, visible, and subject to the controlling gaze of the mother-in-law. Despite the possibilities it holds for female-centered, communal awareness, the shared and central kitchen, as in the rest of the sequestered female quarters of the compound, remains the place of most resistance to modernization or change.

Indeed, this gap reflects the late emergence of modern roles for women within Muslim households in India. As a contemporary, Sakinatul Fatima Wazir Hasan, writes in a 1938 symposium paper:

> Just as in the field of education so in the political and social sphere of our national life the part played by Muslim women has been very small. Among the upper and middle classes purdah is still the rule, and orthodoxy which seems to have found its last resort amongst the Muslims of India, is firmly entrenched. There is no other Muslim country in the world where in social matters like the purdah, marriage, and status of women generally, so much dull-witted reaction prevails as in India.[52]

Though in the 1930s and 1940s more and more Muslim women were leaving purdah behind, "the custom continued to be so widely practised that when Hussain wrote her novel in the 1940s she could depict every single one of her middle-class female characters in a strict state of purdah."[53] As the novel makes clear, the Muslim woman living in strict purdah in India in the 1930s and 1940s remains "entrenched" in her compound and her traditional roles, even as possibilities for her future are emerging in the external world. Victoria Rosner has persuasively argued that for British modernism the spaces of private life were a "generative site."[54] So, too, is it for these Indian narratives of the late-colonial period. But as we have seen in Sorabji's narratives, the zenana functions as the borderland between tradition and a modernizing future, and its cultural work remains caught between the often contradictory expectations for each.

For example, the household in *Purdah and Polygamy* is from the outset torn between traditional values and new attitudes toward money, which are shifting the expectations for domestic life in the period. The house belongs to a man named Umar, a landlord who has increased his holdings and wealth through careful living. He abstains from polygamy, we are told, so that he can economize, and his attitude toward his wife and two children seems also deeply connected to his cautious attitude toward money. "He knew full well that women being unreasonable creatures could not be trusted in money matters. He himself bought all that was necessary for the house. [His wife] needed no money because she never went out of the four walls of the house" (2). Here, the link between avarice and the containment of women in the zenana is clearly drawn. If Umar makes it understood that his wife's duty is to serve her husband by cooking all of his food, the result, as the narrator points out, is that he can employ fewer servants. What we might expect to be matters of deep belief or adherence to tradition are immediately tied to worldly, commercial, and ultimately prurient values of the acquisition, expansion, and preservation of individual wealth—values that Umar struggles to pass on to his profligate son, Kabeer. Importantly, these values are also in opposition to a different set of commercial principles—that of the bourgeois marketplace. Zuhra needs no money because she does not participate in the buying and selling of goods and must rely on her husband and other male relatives to furnish her household with necessary items. In the years after Umar's death, which takes place in the second chapter, this system begins to unravel. Kabeer has no respect for the accumulation of land as wealth and patrimony and seeks only to maximize his income or make profits from selling off property. This more modern, bourgeois perspective on wealth is quickly at odds with the tradition of a stable, well-insulated, and well-supported zenana, and it subjects the household to pressure that it ultimately cannot support.

The Muslim religious setting of the novel is equally undermined in the opening chapter. Kabeer is unwilling to apply himself to his studies at madrasa, and his parents routinely allow him to stay home or otherwise escape study. His mother, Zuhra, "did not believe in the child's going to school every day. She was of the opinion that there was not much to learn" (8). Indeed, the family's approach to Islam is a ritualized one characterized by a collection of habits and rules rather than an examined spirituality or belief. When Umar is dying from cancer he invokes Islam in his decision to be content with his fate and not call in a doctor, but the narrative makes clear that this is a decision based as much in his characteristic avarice as his spiritual acceptance of death. If the family goes to great lengths to follow Muslim ritual and to bury him with great circumstance (and expense), we ought not read it as a sign of the purity of their devotion or piety. Rather, as Umar's sister suggests, they "'do everything very grandly to keep up his name and fame'" (12).

Hussain's biography and political writings serve as intertexts to expand and elucidate her understanding of Islam and her critique of both purdah and polygamy. Hussain was herself raised in strict purdah, married at fifteen, and had several children before becoming the first woman graduate of the Mahrani College in Mysore in 1930. She studied further in England and became deeply involved in the education of Muslim girls and women, founding an Urdu girls' middle school and a teachers' association for Muslim women when she returned to India. Although the record of her life has been mostly erased, we know that in 1935 she traveled to the International Women's Congress in Istanbul, spoke on education in London and in Mysore, and became a member of the All India Women's Congress, one of the most important national women's organizations of the late-colonial period.[55] She published her lectures along with other articles, which she wrote for newspapers like the *Deccan Times* and the *Eastern Times*, in a 1940 collection entitled *Changing India: A Muslim Woman Speaks*. That volume includes essays on the difference between the principles of Islam and the practices of Mohammedanism, on the position of women in Islam, and the differences between Muslims and Hindus, as well as position pieces discussing the obstacles that purdah presents to social progress, the effect of early marriage on Indians, and the idea that "There Is No Polygamy in Islam." She reserves her harshest words for the overly ritualized practices of what she called Mohammedanism, which differs from Islam in that it does not adhere to scriptural tenets and "lays fixed religious dogmas and sets a rigid spiritual truth." These dogmas form the basis of the practice of both rigid purdah and polygamy, for which she finds no support in the spiritual texts. As the writer of the foreword to *Changing India* puts it, "Her main objective has been to release the women of India and particularly the women of the Indian Muslim world from the state of ignorance and quiescent resignation which false tradition has imposed on them."[56] Thus, when the first chapter of *Purdah and Polygamy* raises the issue of the kind of religious practice present in Umar's home and the family's lack of concern for spiritual education, it is to alert us to the problems inherent in this kind of Muslim household and to the falsity that Hussain believes undergirds it.

Throughout *Changing India* Hussain also emphasizes the connection between family and nation by playing on the enduring trope of "moral mother" as the force for growth and development within the household. This connection works in two directions at once: Hussain looks backward to the foundations of Islam to discover that "in spiritual and temporal matters Islam gives equal rights and respect to womanhood" (8) and forward to the future because "it is the woman who educates and trains the child. It is she who guides a man in his emotional, moral, and social activities" (8). Thus, as many before Hussain argued, woman represents the potential development of both citizenry and nation and the crossroads of past and future. "The elevation of the family or the nation is possible only when woman is treated equal to man and given an equal share in the service of her nation and the land. Surely the recognition of her worth is indispensable for the formation of a strong nation for otherwise it will remain incomplete" (9). The notion the nation's strong "formation" is crucial here since Hussain describes many of the ills of present-day India in bodily terms, blaming the physical degeneration of the Muslim populace in part on the personal deformation caused by purdah among its women. "Seclusion has undermined the health of Muslim women.... Purdah with illiteracy and ignorance has cramped their personalities" (47).[57] This argument echoes some of the reformers' language surrounding the *Mother India* event within a specifically Muslim context. The Muslim woman's body signals the potential for futurity for both family and nation and must be protected from the ravishes of immoderate seclusion. The community's response to the challenges of modernity revolves around the corporeal and psychic health of its women, who must be liberated in order to be whole.

Interestingly, Hussain's collection of essays presents a marked contrast to another anthology published in the previous year (1939) by Raja Rao and Iqbal Singh, also called *Changing India*. Whether Hussain had read this anthology or purposefully repeated its title makes little difference.[58] These two collections speak to each other necessarily. Both take up "changing India" in its two senses—by describing changes already taking place in late colonial India and furthering those changes through political and social action. In Rao and Singh's version, however, the matter emerges as a deeply historical process of evolution toward the goal of a modern independent India. "It is our belief," they write, "that this evolution has not been haphazard, but consistent and logical."[59] They define three periods in the process set in motion by encounter with the Western world: first, "bewildered admiration"; second, "hostility and resistance"; and, finally, what they call the contemporary "correct perspective" (9). The collection includes many of the preeminent thinkers of the previous hundred years, from Raja Rammohun Roy through Tagore, Ghose, Gandhi, Iqbal, and Nehru. Published in England by Allen and Unwin, it is clear that the audience for the volume is British and its focus is Indian attitudes toward the West.

Still, the contrast with Hussain's book is striking. Hussain looks to Islamic history and practices in order to diagnose (and solve) the problems of her age, focusing on the issues of family life, poverty, physical health, and liberty within India. Rao and Singh's collection gathers philosophical commentary on the idea of India, notions of god and humanity, conflicts between East and West, *swaraj*, and empire. Women are hardly mentioned in the whole anthology, and poverty emerges as a subject only for a discourse on the importance of education. Bodies, male or female, are absent; the effects of early marriage, multiple childbirth, or seclusion on general health do not warrant commentary; and purdah and polygamy are barely discussed. Rao and Singh's volume makes clear that even in 1939 women's bodies and concerns may be easily excised from the conversation about India's historical and political modernity.

Within the novel *Purdah and Polygamy*, however, the problems of women's domestic spaces, their status, and their bodies are intricately interwoven and tied to the question of familial progress and modernization. It is clear that a successful wife is defined by a body that will submit to supervision, domestic service, and strict enclosure while retaining its strength and beauty. The matter of polygamy in this novel represents the quest for such a woman/body and stands as commentary about the futility of such a search, especially in the modern era, when matters of religion, commerce, and domestic economy are shifting. After Umar's death, his widow Zuhra moves quickly to marry her son, Kabeer. A suitable wealthy girl is chosen, and Kabeer, who has not been consulted, becomes obsessed with her beauty: "He was worried about her physical beauty. The question of temperament never struck him." (31). His new wife, Nazni, is a beauty who is described as "looking like Venus" (560), yet marriage has a clear bodily effect on her. As is the custom, as a new bride in her husband's home she must restrain herself physically, making her presence in the home negligible. "She was not expected to open her eyes in her husband's house for five weeks and not to talk for about two months.... She was not expected to eat more than a morsel" (48). In fact, this physical self-abnegation becomes permanent as Nazni almost immediately becomes ill in pregnancy, retreats to her parents' house, gives birth, and is diagnosed with heart disease. The narrative makes clear that her illness is in part a physical response to her marriage and her enclosure in Kabeer's family compound: "She felt better in her mother's house. As soon as she returned home her illness reappeared" (64). But her mother-in-law, who has counted on her new daughter to be present in the kitchen on a daily basis and to take on the cooking, is full of disdain. Once Nazni has removed herself from the kitchen and the compound and shown her body to a male doctor, she considers Nazni an unsuitable wife and immediately plans Kabeer's second marriage.[60]

Because Nazni's body is unruly in so many ways, she is cast off as Kabeer's primary wife.

Kabeer marries a second wife, Munira, a lower-caste girl whose family has conspired to hide her ugliness from her prospective mother-in-law. Nazni is described as "small, thin and delicate" (64), but Munira is "dark, with deep-pock marks, and her upper teeth projected prominently" (70). As Zuhra tells her, "You have neither beauty nor wealth. . . . Your only weapons are your strength and spirit" (73). From the moment she arrives she is constantly on the move, cleaning, cooking, and serving Kabeer and Zuhra, which ingratiates her to her mother-in-law, if not to her husband. Though she manages to seduce him once, carefully closing her lips over her protruding teeth as she smiles, he disdains her, referring to her as an "ape" and "the negress" (100–101). Zuhra rejoices in having a daughter-in-law who obeys her meekly and works "vigorously" (99), but Kabeer responds to her color, her looks, and her energy as animalistic and unbefitting of his wife. While it is clear that Munira fits the servile role of wife better than Nazni and that her body is better able to sustain the rigors of becoming a mother, continuing to cook and care for her husband even as her pregnancy progresses, her darkness and lack of beauty nonetheless mark her as unfit. Ironically, neither woman embodies what a "wife" is meant to be in this household. As the narrative makes clear, the expectations of women to be both able housekeepers and frail tremulous creatures, vigorous and yet contained, companionable and yet willingly servile, are contradictory and impossible to fulfill. The commentary on polygamy in this novel results from Kabeer's endless quest to find the embodiment of a wife who doesn't exist. In this way, *Purdah and Polygamy* creates a more obvious and explicit counter-bildungsroman than such British novels as *Jane Eyre* and *Villette*.

Further, if Munira has been "brought in by the back door"(113), as Nazni's father describes it, the narrative is clear that she will never leave. Nazni's well-off and modernizing family allows her to move back and forth between households and go to the women's section of the cinema, though she remains in purdah. Munira's poverty, lack of education, and lack of recourse to a powerful natal family force her to remain in the inner spaces of Kabeer's compound for the rest of the novel, almost inseparable from them. When she is confined to her room in childbirth, her polluted status should prevent her from immediately going back into the kitchen, but she cannot stay away long. In fact, the family's growing reliance on Munira's presence in the kitchen creates a source of power and contentment for her, further underscoring the paradox that the wife most suited to the servile role nonetheless is scorned, treated like an untouchable,[61] and referred to by Kabeer as "the servant."

The inner rooms of the compound and the kitchen become contested territory as a third wife is added to the polygamous household and rooms are shifted among the women. The architecture of private life thus plays a role in the possibilities for development among the compound's inhabitants and its confrontation with the modern idea of private spaces. The supervision of behavior within the communal enclosed spaces becomes paramount since, as a sign of his escape from his mother's control, Kabeer moves out of the house and into his offices. Zuhra, his mother, changes her quarters so she can observe and control the compound with almost panopticon-like discipline but, despite her constant watching and peeking though keyholes, she is unable to retain full control. Kabeer's third wife, Mahgbool, a beautiful and wealthy girl whose independence and education mark her as a modern woman, is immediately granted her own private space and leads an active life within her quarters, singing, embroidering, writing, and reading, as well as entertaining her male cousin, who comes almost daily to visit. If Mahgbool describes her passage from her father's house to her husband's compound as that from a "semi-prison to a real one" (191), the supervisory function of the prison is put under pressure by her arrival.

Mahgbool is figured as the counterpoint to Munira since she is active and vigorous. But she is described in terms that liken her to a man, rather than a servant, and so cannot fulfill the role of ideal wife.

> She was an institution in herself. Her mastery over the Urdu language had made her crazy after papers, magazines, romance and poetry. . . . She was a good organizer and an economical manager of the house. . . . Her father often said that she was as a son to him, his secretary and his right hand. She was active and hated to while away her time. . . . Everything she did was self-learnt.
>
> (189)

Unlike the other women in the household, Mahgbool benefits from the modern monetary economy and from Kabeer's willingness to sell off his patrimony for ready cash. Because she receives pocket money she is able to purchase food instead of cooking it in the kitchen (thus removing herself from identification with that space), and this further defines her as modern, masculinized, and connected to the bourgeois economy that the household rejects for its women. As Munira puts it, when hearing of Mahgbool's bank account, "How disgraceful! Then all the men know your name. It is only bad women's names come to the notice of men" (197). Mahgbool not only does not recoil at the idea of her name being known; she spends her money on the publication of a collection of her own poetry with her name attached, which she hopes will make the family fortune (242), thus underscoring both her usurpation of masculine roles and her connection to the modern economy.

Mahgbool is further marked as an unsuitable wife when her body is scarred in a kitchen accident. She spills boiling water on her hands and feet, at once damaging her beauty and marking her body as not only unsuitable in the kitchen but also unsuitable as a love object. Zuhra sees Kabeer sneak expensive medicines to her, recognizes Mahgbool as a body she can not control through her vigilance, and uses her knowledge to reassert her authority over her son, renew her surveillance of the inner compound, and reestablish codes of gendered conduct. Telling Kabeer that "in this house everything is upside down. A world of fuss is made over a scar" (221), she also accuses him of becoming feminized. "Yes that is the only thing left for you now. Shave your moustache, put on her dress and become her nurse" (222). By the time Mahgbool's wounds have healed, the potential of her modernity to smash the complacency of the zenana and disrupt the gendered roles of the entire household has been both revealed and contained, and she is ostracized almost into nonexistence.

The remaining chapters of the book succumb to a disorder of both plot and structure that mirrors the disorder of this household. The book races quickly through Kabeer's fourth marriage to a poor tenant girl, whom he tries to hide from his mother's gaze, and through a prolonged digression involving his son's adulteries. When the son is attacked by an orthodox group made aware of his loose behavior, he tries to escape by shouting "I am not a Muslim" (289), bringing full circle the novel's emphasis on the absence of scriptural Islam or, indeed, any real belief system in this household. Even the son's quickly arranged marriage can not reinstate traditional order in this compound or promise that in the years after the deaths of Kabeer and Zuhra and the departure of Mahgbool, which occur in the final pages, anything like a calm complacency will return. Though the narrative sums up the action in the last two sentences, telling us that Nazni gains Zuhra's "coveted position" as supervisor over her two remaining co-wives, the continuity of this family as an intact and functioning traditional household has been shattered.

But the signs of narrative "disorder"—interruption of order, acceleration of temporal progress, shifts in point of view, gaps in knowledge—that grow in the final chapters of this novel are also present earlier in the narrative and demonstrate the challenge of this important text. The reader is sometimes dropped suddenly, through free indirect style, into the minds and voice of a character, and between chapters the narrative goes back in time and starts forward again from a different perspective. These moments demonstrate experimental technique meant to disrupt the calm surface of a mimetic narrative, just as the increasingly unregulated activities in the household belie the calm exterior of its enclosure walls. Between chapters 8 and 9, for example, when Nazni's family first learns of Kabeer's second marriage, the perspective shifts: "Nazni's family thought about the remarriage very differently from Kabeer's people" (112). The narrative drops back in time, before the events that take place at the end of the previous chapter, and then moves forward again in Nazni's parents' household, as though the disynchronous perspectives demand a similarly disynchronous time frame. Nazni's brother embraces a modernized perspective on women's roles, defends Nazni's "rights" (116), and considers it a "blessing to make a woman independent and strong" (115), arguing that she should not be forced to return to the zenana. The novel employs this structural innovation in order to highlight the conflict between modernity, with its language of civic identity and citizenship, and a false attachment to the residual formation of polygamous Islam.

At several other points, *Purdah and Polygamy* jumps from one perspective to another, quickly elides time, or unapologetically presents gaps in knowledge or in causality. From the moments when Zuhra's perspective on marriage invades the narration ("Why do people bring daughters-in-law if not to have real and well-earned comfort?" [50]), to the dispute over Nazni's trip to the cinema, where the narration skips abruptly back and forth from Kabeer's conversation with his mother to his discussion of this conversation with Nazni (62), to the elision of the years before the final episodes, the novel often departs dramatically from the realism evoked by its connection to Austen. These vagaries elicit an apology from the author of the foreword, who attributes them to Hussain's lack of knowledge of the language (4). Yet her *Changing India*, written several years before *Purdah and*

Polygamy, exhibits an extraordinary fluency of expression in English, making it unlikely that the novel's disruptions are the result of her inabilities. Rather, I would argue, they show us the reverse—Hussain's competence in English allows her to use word choice, narrative structure, emplotment, and experimentation with narrative perspective as vehicles for her critique of zenana life. If modernity creeps into the novel through the byways—Kabeer's shift in attitude about money, Nazni's mobility, Maghbool's authorship and financial independence, the changing architecture and use of the rooms in the compound, and the final disruption of the calm surface of zenana life—then it also invades the style and structure of the novel, making it vastly different, in the end, from a Muslim remake of *Pride and Prejudice*.

At the same time, these disruptions of formal unity and use of multiple perspectives combine with the novel's trenchant critique of polygamy to undermine the dogma of the traditional bildungsroman in a manner that connects it to the modernist critiques of Joyce, Woolf, and Anand, among others. If the opening of the novel makes clear that the heroines will be expected to experience their coming of age within the confines of the household, obviating the possibility of any outward journey of discovery, the rest of the novel works to disrupt expectations of singular self-development. The problem cuts both ways: the demands of the polygamous household make it impossible for any single woman to rise to the status of ideal wife, therefore creating an expectation that a community will replace the individual as the female "heroine" of the novel. At the same time, the novel constantly undermines any attempt to recuperate the individual woman as the locus of self-knowledge or the synthesis of Islam with modernity; Maghbool's utter failure and abrupt departure from the household is a clear case in point. The novel presents an alternative, communal female perspective arising from within the household, behind the purdah screen, but nevertheless not within the purview of the strict "Mohammedanism" that Hussain so condemned. By multiplying perspectives and shifting among the women, *Purdah and Polygamy* raises the possibility that a changing order within the household, where strict surveillance and reliance on men is replaced by female interaction and independence, might lead to development and empowerment for its women. If, after the death of both Kabeer and his mother at the end of the novel, Nazni "inherits" the position as head of the zenana, she is seen as constrained and mediated by the other female voices around her in a way that her mother-in-law was not. Thus, the novel's ironic narrative stance, its multiplication of perspectives, its disruption of emplotment, and its ultimate disorder give rise to a modernist challenge to ideas of individual female development that not only puts in question prevalent assumptions in the late-colonial period about women's domestic situation and role in political life but also challenges our understanding of the allegiances, voices, and modes of transnational modernism.

The Domestic and the Political

Two years after *Purdah and Polygamy* was published, a smaller volume by a writer named only as "Ishvani" appeared in London. *Girl in Bombay* purports to be a true-to-life memoir, put together by the author to fulfill her need to reminisce about the past. "To burden one's friends and acquaintances with long memories of the past would hardly be fair. It was better to write about them. . . . But I will try to be as accurate as possible in setting down my own memories."[62] What follows is surely fictionalized, written like a first-person novel, complete with dialogue and detailed description. The narration develops location, plot, and characters in a tightly structured manner and enlists the reader in concern for the young girl at its center. Thus, like Sorabji's narratives of the previous decades, *Girl in Bombay* uses the borderline between fiction and autobiography as a site for play with the conventions for writing a woman's life under circumstances of modernity.

By claiming to be a first-person autobiography, Ishvani's *Girl in Bombay* also explores the borders of the autobiographical pact, as did Sorabji. If we take these narratives collectively, we can see that they not only challenge the generic distinctions between fiction and autobiography but develop an alternative Indian tradition that straddles both genres and an emerging modernism that rests on this kind of generic confusion. Leigh Gilmore notes that women's autobiographies often resist easy definition within the standard laws of autobiography. She argues that they "are not so much autobiograph*ies* as autobiograph*ics*, those changing elements of the contradictory discourses and practices of truth and identity which represent the subject of autobiography" cross-culturally.[63] But as the Indian case makes clear, genre develops in situ. As "culturally active media," to borrow a phrase from Spivak, autobiographical narratives not only respond to generic traditions but also engage specifically with local expectations for narrative and life story while performing culturally significant work.[64] If we take the narrative innovation among Indian women writers seriously—as seriously as, for example, that accorded Raja Rao, whose novels are often discussed as inaugurating a particularly Indian mode of fiction linked to mythology and epic—then we will discover a set of texts that combine autobiographics, documentary realism, and fiction to create quasi-public texts out of mostly private lives, thereby developing a culturally located, experimental women's modernism.

In *Girl in Bombay* the protagonist comes of age in a liberal Koja Shia household in Bombay that does not observe purdah and whose members travel widely. She is permitted to go to school and participate fully in the life of her community, and under these circumstances she grows happily towards maturity. After her mother's death, however, her father remarries, and her stepmother imposes traditional restrictions, claiming that "education was a lot of ridiculous nonsense and that the only destiny girls were capable of fulfilling was marriage" (64). When the possibility of marrying a seemingly modern man arises, Ishvani rushes at the chance to leave her stepmother's home. However, after beginning what seems to be an open, modern marriage with a man she likes and respects and who has insisted on getting to know her before their marriage, she is forced into purdah by his mother and grandmother. She is isolated from the outside world and from the social and political engagement that was part of her upbringing, and she retreats to the solace of stories and dreams. Finally, she summons her courage to leave her husband and his family, eventually divorcing him and sailing off to enter university in England. The book's foreword tells us that the author had done the same.

The matter of religious conflict, even beyond the question of purdah, motivates the narrative of *Girl in Bombay*, as it does many of the texts from the 1940s. Here, the narrator is forced by her husband to renounce her family's particular heritage and join the followers of the Aga Khan.[65] In other novels of the period, such as Mumtaz Shah Nawaz's *A Heart Divided*, the conflict is between Muslim and Hindu neighbors in the growing inevitability of a divided India. In both cases, the question of religious identity serves multiple roles, standing as a sign of the heroine's independence as well as her ability to retain her own beliefs and her agency. In *Girl in Bombay*, Ishvani's forced renunciation of her particular Koja sect marks the climax of the novel, prompting the heroine's decision to leave her husband and her country while signaling her simultaneous social disenfranchisement and personal independence. In this sense, religion becomes a crucial component to the way we read these novels as examples of a modernist female bildungsroman or as autobiographics. Development is never a self-willed process nor a sequence of maneuvers by a self-complete, intact subject seeking to find her way in the world; it is always undertaken within the context of a religious community or structure of belief. Even when, as in *Girl in Bombay*, the heroine finally departs on a journey of development, she leaves her natal community only by necessity. Like Maghbool in *Purdah and Polygamy*, she renounces the model of marriage foisted upon her but does not relinquish her religious heritage.

But the question of religion also clearly carries direct political weight, particularly in Muslim narratives of the period. Growing divisions between Muslims and Hindus in Indian communities, as well as political conflicts between the Muslim League and the Congress Party in the period after the 1935 Government of India Act, complicate the role of Muslim affiliation within these narratives. In the 1940 Lahore Resolution, the Muslim League officially called for the establishment of Pakistan, pointing to "religious, cultural, economic, political, administrative" differences that needed protection.[66] Yet in *Girl in Bombay*, Ishvani belongs to a group of Kojas who represent a modernizing impulse within Islam and do not fear connections with Indians of other religions.[67] As Ishvani puts it, "Though we were Muslims, our household was composed of a conglomerate of other religions" (14). And despite the Muslim affiliation of the family in this quasi autobiography, all are staunch followers of Gandhi.

Even beyond the question of religious affiliation and loyalty, the action of *Girl in Bombay* unites the domestic and the political directly. For example, the time of Ishvani's betrothal coincides with the period in 1921 when Gandhi issues a call for "hartal" (closing all shops and businesses) in response to the prince of Wales's elaborate tour of India. The narrative skips back and forth between the preparations for the wedding and discussion of the political movement for home rule. "In our house the chief topic of conversation, aside from the preparations for my marriage, was Gandhiji's programme for civil disobedience" (115). The narrative also swings back and forth between discussion of a love letter from Ishvani's fiancé and a prolonged discussion of Gandhi's movement, thus asking the reader to connect the home and "home-rule" while highlighting the thwarted modernity of Ishvani's authoritarian marriage.

In chapter 11, Ishvani's husband asks her to enter the Aga Khan community in obedience to the request of his elders. The following day, Ishvani leaves her mother-in-law's house to visit her sisters in the hope of escaping this request. What she encounters instead is the political texture of everyday life and the inescapable connection between her household problems and the problems faced by India. A general strike in response to the Amritsar massacre has been called, making it unsafe to be about town, but Ishvani is not aware of it because she has been secluded in the zenana. Ishvani's husband must come rescue her from her sister's house, and they have a hair-raising ride back to his family's home, where she is once again kept in ignorance about the events of the world and forced to acquiesce to the exigencies of tradition. This episode presents the deep irony that the protagonist's isolation and forced ignorance cause her to leave the zenana on the only day of the year when she will indeed be unsafe. The narrative pushes not only toward greater freedom and education for women and the modernization of religious practice but also, and importantly, toward recognition that the politics of the nation are deeply imbricated with the politics of the home. The notion of Mother India is complicated and reformed in this narrative, and its connection to a traditional domesticity, separate from the realm of politics and protected from the conflict of religion, is rejected. In this narrative the home that is disconnected from politics is a dangerous one, and the secluded girl is, because of her ignorance and dependency, a drag on the nation.

Independence still comes with a price for Ishvani. With the support of her sister and uncle she is also able to divorce her husband and arrive in England unencumbered. What becomes of her thereafter is beyond the scope of the narrative, which is focused on her domestic plight and escape. But another novel of the period, *Detective Janaki* (1944), by Kamala Sathianadhan, narrates a yet more capacious version of women's domestic life in late-colonial India.[68] The long-time editor of the *Indian Ladies Magazine*, Kamala Sathianadhan also wrote *Stories of Indian Christian Life* with her husband and was the subject of a biography, *Portrait of an Indian Woman*, by her daughter, Padmini Sengupta (1956).[69] In *Detective Janaki*, her only novel, the usual trajectory of female coming of age is compressed and upended. The heroine refuses her arranged marriage within the first twenty pages, finds a husband by answering an advertisement in the newspaper, develops a happy married life in her own household, and continues to work for pay. Thus, the moment of defiance, where she accuses her stepmother of trying to marry her for pecuniary purposes, becomes the beginning of a life's journey of development, not its end, and the rejection of the traditional marriage economy marks the moment when the heroine becomes not only a civic citizen, able to make marriage and living arrangements on her own behalf, but also a participant in the modern social economy.

Detective Janaki also straddles genres and regimes of surveillance. It combines the domestic and the detective novel, creating a heroine who works in her home ("Janaki looked forward very much to her own home, where she intended questing for detective work"), and takes on a profession that requires her to practice domestic surveillance (she not only watches couples and families from hiding places along roadsides and in the village but sometimes secrets herself inside their homes or spies through windows).[70] That, with her husband's help, she develops a thriving business, solving many cases by the end of the book, makes clear that the novel means to establish her as a model of a working woman who is able to become successful by upending the economy of surveillance. At the same time, the narrative focuses on the increasing marital happiness between Janaki and her husband, presenting female identity in its modernity both inside and outside the home.

The domestic aspect of the novel is further emphasized by the nature of the cases that Janaki takes on. The advertisement that she inserts in the paper reads: "Women, who have domestic problems to be solved, or who have become involved in troublesome affairs, will find a friendly helper in an Indian woman-detective, who has set herself to work of this kind" (44). Her cases usually concern dispute or subterfuge between husbands and wives and often involve problems of jealousy within households. Often the case involves Janaki in looking through windows into houses or otherwise intruding into domestic spaces. On one occasion she works like Sorabji to help question women living in purdah yet ends up being imprisoned in the zenana and barely escapes. Generally speaking, however, as a liminal figure, Janaki moves in and out of domestic spaces among all the castes in her village and brings private matters of marital love and treatment of children out into the open even while helping to police matters of social order and domestic justice. Thus her modernized female subjectivity serves both domestic and public roles even as it puts at risk the divisions between the two.

Other political issues enter the novel obliquely, making clear that the readjustment of female subjectivity and domesticity also carries implications for broad notions of social justice within a modernizing India. Janaki engages in social work among the slum households and rescues a young girl destined to become a temple slave. Janaki's husband, Seshan, also plays a role as a member of a gang of thieves who has stolen from the rich and given to the poor, Robin Hood–style. Written during the great Bengal famine of 1943, this novel mobilizes against the kind of indifference among governmental groups both local and imperial that has been blamed for the severity of the famine. And yet there are no national politics here—no mention of Gandhi or even of women's political organizations, no explicit stands on partition or on the matters of purdah and polygamy. Nor, in the end, do either Janaki or her husband become involved in any social movement beyond their village. The national politics of this novel lie waiting beneath its domestic surface, like one of the secrets hidden by the figures in Janaki's cases, waiting to be detected and examined.

Indian fiction has politics in its blood. Critics have also long remarked that the movements for independence helped fuel the development of English narrative in the late-colonial period. But women's writing has been largely left out of that account. Whether because it seemed only nascent, out of synch with modernist temporalities, and seemingly sentimental or tradition-bound or because its preoccupation with domestic spaces made it look apolitical and unconcerned with public issues, Indian women's narratives in English from the late-colonial period have been largely ignored and certainly left out of the account of the development of modernism and modernity in India. On the other hand, *Detective Janaki*, *Girl in Bombay*, *Purdah and Polygamy*, and the narratives of Cornelia Sorabji, along with other writing of the period, make clear the complexity of women's response to public and private ideologies, their engagement with the concerns of impending modernity, and their use of narrative innovation as the site of engagement with regimes of gender and domesticity. Far from serving merely as the antecedents to the great flowering of postindependence Indian writing, or as adjuncts to the canonical (male) writers of the 1930s, these women writers were creating innovative and stylistically complex narratives that inaugurated new modes of living and organizing domesticity. In that sense the narrative experiments of Sorabji, Hussain, Ishvani, Sathianadhan, and others serve as narrative interventions in Indian modernity, generating discursive models of the new female citizen-subject even as they recast the rhetoric of the domestic sphere. As key texts of Indian modernism, these narratives push toward a deeper accounting of the intersecting discourses surrounding public and domestic life in late-colonial India and the combined critique of genre and gender roles so crucial to Indian modernity. In the end, then, these long-overlooked narratives invite us not only to glimpse modernism in all its complexity in the zenana but also to recognize its importance to our understanding of modernist modes and commitments worldwide.

FOUR | Commitment and the Scene of War
Max Aub and Spanish Civil War Writing

> Works of art are after-images or replicas of empirical life.
> —Adorno, *Aesthetic Theory*

> The future must be understood not as the preordained, or as the constrained. In order for there to be politics and ethics now, in order for there to be history and reflection on the past, the future must be open.
> —Elizabeth Grosz, *Time Travels*

> Truth was indeed the first casualty of the Spanish Civil War.
> —Antony Beevor, *The Battle for Spain*

"It is not easy to convey the nightmare atmosphere of that time,"[1] George Orwell wrote of the period in 1937 when the course of the Spanish Civil War became more grim and political repression from the left in Barcelona complicated the differentiation of right and wrong for both sides. But despite the nightmarish conditions and the difficulty in getting the story correct, writers were drawn to the Spanish Civil War in great numbers, churning out narratives, poems, and newspaper dispatches with astonishing regularity from the outbreak of war in 1936 until well into the postwar period.[2] For English-language readers, the extraordinary success of Ernest Hemingway's *For Whom the Bell Tolls*, which sold half a million copies in the first six months and almost won a Pulitzer Prize,[3] the many other accounts from writer-volunteers, and the widespread admiration for the Lincoln Brigade, whose stories have been told in several powerful histories,[4] have made the heroic tale of the international volunteer and his distanced yet committed perspective on the Spanish struggle a staple of Spanish Civil War lore.

Yet the preponderance of writing about the Spanish Civil War comes from Spain (or Spaniards in exile) and is written in Spanish. In *The Novel of the Spanish Civil War*, Gareth Thomas documents at least 124 full-fledged war novels published in Spanish in the years between 1936 and 1966 (when prior censorship was removed in Spain), and many more beyond that date, the majority of which have never been translated into English. In these novels, whether of the left or right, the figures of the stereotypically heroic Spanish peasant or of the valiant international brigadier struggling with lack of supplies and poor weaponry—stock figures in the English-language works—are replaced by a more complex portrait of the Spanish people forced to make hard choices in a time of personal and political struggle and by an awareness of the ethical complexity of total warfare, when brutality exists on all sides and can seem inescapable. Though few generalizations can be drawn about these many works, which emerge out of both Nationalist and Republican camps and take on an immense variety of forms and styles, it is clear that Spanish-language Civil War narratives place the struggle directly within the context of Spanish literary and political history, connect it to ongoing commentary in Spain about the nature and status of experimental writing, and often develop new narrative strategies in response to the complexity of perspectives and the chaotic, shifting political positions that emerge over the course of the war.

At the same time, the marginalization of Spanish writers chronicling the war that took place on their own soil also speaks more broadly to the matter of modernism and the way that it was canonized in the twentieth century. The model of literary modernism, which, one might say, began with the Leavises and continued through such key texts as Bradbury and Macfarlane's *Modernism: 1890–1930* and beyond, highlighted particular kinds of experimental prose (stream of consciousness, fragmentation) and particular perspectives (the crisis of subjectivity, political disillusionment) predominantly within the Anglo-American, French, and German traditions. This critical tradition created what Anthony Geist and José Monleón call "an extremely distorted canon that stubbornly excludes the Hispanic production."[5] Even recent studies, such as Peter Nicholls's *Modernisms*, Peter Conrad's *Modern Times, Modern Places*, and David Bradshaw's *Concise Companion to Modernism*, spend no more than a page or so considering Spain (though the two-volume work edited by Liska and Eysteinsson contains an excellent "case-study" of Catalan modernism).[6] But, in the words of Mary Lee Bretz, "while some characteristics attributed . . . to international modernism mirror traits that have . . . been ascribed to Spanish cultural production of the period, others bear only a tangential relationship or differ considerably."[7] As I have argued throughout this book, if we restrict our gaze to a specific set of texts, formal attributes, or series of attitudes, we risk ignoring the various shapes and guises of modernism as it arises in response to aesthetic, social, historical, and rhetorical demands in a variety of locations. Further, dominant models of European modernism not only rely on common forms and perspectives but also trace a common developmental history from symbolism through futurism and Dada and on into a "high modernism" that emerges between the world wars. Spain has a literary history that complicates this trajectory, especially since it did not participate in either world war. While futurism and Dada were immensely influential, some critics argue that modernism properly begins earlier in Spain, in the literary experimentation of the generation of 1898.[8] Many from this generation, such as Antonio Machado, Miguel de Unamuno, and Pío Baroja, continued writing through the 1920s and into the 1930s and preside over the dramatic evolution of Spanish modernism in the early twentieth century.

But during the first decades of the twentieth century a strong wave of Spanish modernism arose in connection with the artistic centers of Paris and London.[9] Practitioners of symbolism, Dada, and surrealism moved back and forth between Barcelona and Paris, helping to develop a burgeoning Catalan and Spanish avant-garde and bringing vanguardist ideas and practices from the peninsula into contact with artists and writers elsewhere in Europe.[10] Many of the most celebrated modernist artists and writers in Europe in the 1920s and 1930s, such as Pablo Picasso, Salvador Dalí, and Luis Buñuel, emerged out of this nexus in Spain, though they are rarely discussed in relation to it.[11] After the founding of his *Revista de Occidente* in 1923, which circulated widely both in Spain and abroad, Ortega y Gasset's modernist theories about art and literature also became immensely influential. But the fact that Spain and Catalonia, especially the cities of Madrid and Barcelona, were hotbeds of artistic innovation throughout the pre–Civil War period disappears from most critical histories of modernism.

The legacy of this repression persists in current critical ignorance outside of Spain about the range of Spanish writing in the twentieth century. Pascale Casanova's *The World Republic of Letters* turns to Spain as an example of an isolated national literature, stagnant and seemingly disconnected from the international sphere. Casanova cites Juan Benet, who came of age as a writer in 1950s Spain, cut off from the most innovative aspects of his country's literary heritage, who claims that "all the writers between 1900 and 1970, every last one of them, wrote in the manner of the generation of 1898, a naturalism adapted to the Spanish style. . . . This was a literature that was already ruined; it already belonged to the past before it was written." On this evidence Casanova claims that Benet "single-handedly revolutionized the Spanish novel."[12] Yet the vibrancy of the avant-garde in the pre–Civil War period, which continues after 1939 among writers in exile, is clear. The exiled Spanish writer in the Americas ultimately comes to inhabit a position much like the colonial writer attempting to participate in the literary debates and conversations of the metropolis. Erased from public consciousness in Spain, unknown in literary capitals like Paris, exiled writers seem to have the wrong language, the wrong approach, or the wrong purpose. Spanish Civil War writers become the silenced voices of Spain's double defeat, censored, ostracized from continental literary movements and cast into the diaspora, often having to move to Mexico and other postcolonial spaces in order to be heard at all in the metropolis.

This chapter will seek to help redress this marginalization by treating Spanish writing on the Civil War as part of the broad development of European narrative innovation before midcentury. By looking at the phenomenon of Civil War writing within the context of modernism and examining the continuity between experimental narrative and war writing, this chapter challenges the assumption that choosing sides dooms narrative to that "ruined naturalism" Benet so decries. In response to the situation of total war, where commonplace distinctions between the home front and battlefront disintegrate and where the patterns of everyday life in the besieged areas become completely disrupted, the very effort at verisimilitude in fiction often leads writers and artists beyond the boundaries of conventional realism or naturalism. The ethical imperative to bear witness and assume responsibility for others in the face of extreme violence and social disorder produces fiction that often verges on the encyclopedic. It records, displays, and documents events, situations, and relationships among characters caught up in the struggle and demands that its readers acknowledge their claims on our attention. For some writers the effort at a politically committed hyper-verisimilitude—or what Max Aub will later call "transcendental realism"—also produces fiction that inscribes the war's chaos, disruption of temporal order, and challenge to social and familial relationships within the narrative proper.[13] These narratives develop particular modernist strategies to respond to the extraordinary events of the world's first total war, while at the same time displaying their partisanship.

In the case of Max Aub, one of the most significant novelists on the Spanish Civil War, who began writing in the 1920s but completed his mature work in exile after the war, the abandonment of narrative omniscience, disruption of plot order, and adoption of a labyrinthine narrative structure instantiate resistance to a totalizing perspective that not only coincides with Aub's Republican sympathies but also undermines Nationalist representations of the war that emphasize order, vigor, and battlefront power. This chapter will begin by examining the Spanish modernism developed by Aub's magisterial novel cycle, *El laberinto mágico* (*The Magic Labyrinth*), in which experimental style, irony, and detachment participate in the task of bearing witness and imagining justice. Yet the danger in such a partisan use of narrative, modernist or not, as George Orwell has claimed and I discuss in chapter 1 in relation to Woolf's *Three Guineas*, is that it runs the risk of succumbing to propaganda. If political narrative works to persuade by manipulating perspectives and guiding responses, what separates it from the overt use of print and other media to generate partisan support? By examining Orwell's celebrated memoir *Homage to Catalonia* alongside multimedia responses to the war, including Spanish propaganda posters, the film *The Spanish Earth*, which was narrated by Ernest Hemingway, and the collaboration between Aub and André Malraux on the film of *L'espoir: Sierra de Teruel* (*Man's Hope*), the second section of this chapter will explore the liminal zone between partisanship and propaganda across a variety of media and perspectives. For Aub, Orwell, and others responding to the war, irony, play with verisimilitude, and modernist narrative experimentalism can perform the important political role of resisting and confounding propaganda even while blurring the boundaries between reportage and commitment, whether in print or the visual media of poster art, photography, or film.

Rear-Guard Perspectives: Aub's Civil War Labyrinth

Aub's work, and in particular his six-novel Civil War cycle, *El laberinto mágico*, which is at once a tour de force of narrative innovation and a moving chronicle of Spain during wartime, puts the lie to any rigid division between the avant-garde activity of the 1920s and Civil War writing. His postwar writing demonstrates the power of a certain sort of hyper- or transcendental realism and political engagement to push narrative innovation forward, and the possibility of bringing modernist styles and perspectives into synchrony with the task of bearing witness. If we say that the interpenetration of battlefront and home front, the failure of technology to save lives or end conflicts, and the shock of total war, are among the key experiences of modernity, then the Spanish Civil War inflicts that experience of modernity on all who are touched by it.[14] Aub's responses to the Civil War, like those of many other Spanish writers, are modernist first of all because he accepts the imperative of responding aesthetically to that experience in a manner that calls for new forms and styles. Second, we may call Aub's war writing modernist because it embraces formal experiments in narrative structure, temporal order, and perspective even as he marries this structure to a mode he calls "transcendental" or "new" realism. Further, Aub's war novels, like the best other writing on the war, invest narrative with a capacity to bear witness while questioning political pieties and resisting the lure of propaganda. His *Laberinto mágico* demonstrates the extent to which the moral and political exigencies of war reporting, even when addressed retrospectively, can propel and sustain the political engagement of avant-garde writing.

Aub and Spanish Civil War Writing

The vibrant critical tradition among Spanish-language critics often divides war literature into that written at the height of the struggle and that produced in retrospect, years afterward. Clearly, Ramón Sender's *Contraataque* (1937) (*The War in Spain*),[15] produced directly and quickly from frontline experiences and with the express purpose of trying to convince the democratic world to intervene in Spain, is different in almost every way from a multivolume work written over the course of decades, like José María Gironella's trilogy of novels *Los cipreses creen en Dios* (1953), *Un millón de muertos* (1961), and *Ha estallado la paz* (1966) (*The Cypresses Believe in God, One Million Dead*, and *Peace Has Broken Out*), which treats the war from longer historical perspective. If Sender calls his *Contraataque* "recuerdos, escritos velozmente, sin propósitos de composición literaria [memories, written quickly, without the intention of composing literature],"[16] it is nonetheless a war narrative, complete with characters, plot, and action at the battlefront. Its lack of retrospect, historical context, or well-developed relationships among the characters all might be termed typical of the narrative produced quickly during the course of the war.

At the opposite end of the spectrum, both in terms of politics and of narrative, Gironella's work consciously sets out to counter this approach, adopting a longer historical viewpoint and insisting on a perspective that accommodates both sides of the struggle. Gironella famously claimed to have read 1,000 books in preparation for writing.[17] The first volume in the trilogy, Gironella's best-selling 1,000-page novel, *Los cipreses creen en Dios*, covers the five tempestuous years of the Republic, before the war; only in the second 1,000-page installment, *Un millón de muertos*, do we reach the war itself. As he puts it, "My plan has been to give a panoramic view of what our struggle was and what it meant; to try to strike a balance by canceling out one happening with another, and to synchronize the situations on the two sides."[18] *Un million de muertos* has been called the first postwar novel to depict atrocities on both sides of the conflict. Though Gironella fought alongside the Nationalists during the war and it is rumored that "Franco [because he was] portrayed heroically—personally authorized" the publication of the novel, in this retrospective narrative Gironella avoids succumbing to propaganda by presenting a sweeping perspective across political camps.[19]

Yet the rigid division of Civil War narratives into contemporaneous and retrospective can also keep us from seeing continuities and dialogues between and among these writings, which are crucial for understanding Aub's work. If Sender (among others) writes at first with more reportorial and admittedly propagandistic purposes and later more dispassionately, "objectively," or historically about the war, that does not necessarily mean his later work is uninterested in reporting the war accurately or lacks commitment to a political perspective.[20] In Gironella's work, impartiality is an explicit value, and one made possible only with the benefit of temporal and physical distance from the war: "How was I to strike a balance . . . ? Only by seeking the perspective given by time and space, by painfully facing the facts." Yet personal experience and subjectivity nonetheless insert themselves into the novel: "The task of informing myself . . . became plagued with difficulties as prickly as sea urchins. Frequently my personal experience has proved to be so much dunnage, for memory is a mirror that gives me back distorted and spectral images once the facts are isolated from the complex that produced them." Writing from exile, from a temporal distance of fifteen years, and with the benefit of having lived in both Nationalist and Republican Spain, Gironella is plagued by the possibility that reality, seen through the haunted mirror of memory, would become not only distorted but completely "atrophied."[21]

Though his political allegiances lie clearly with the Republicans, this kind of mixture of motivations and commitments also characterizes the writing of Max Aub. Largely unknown to Anglophone readers, Aub's oeuvre includes nine plays, a number of poems, several collections of short stories, and at least ten novels. He collaborated with André Malraux by writing the screenplay for the film version of the Civil War novel *L'espoir* and later in exile assisted Luis Buñuel in the making of his celebrated film about Mexico, *Los olvidados* (*The Forgotten Ones*). In his postwar career in Mexico he became successful as a writer of screen- and teleplays and as a literary critic, novelist, and professor. Aub has been called "by far the most important literary chronicler of the Spanish Civil War," but astoundingly enough, *El laberinto mágico*, which is a spectacular and wide-ranging attempt to chronicle the war's effect on ordinary people, is only just beginning to appear in English.[22] With dozens of characters interconnected in a myriad of ways, the novels often threaten to spin out of control—or succumb to the merely encyclopedic. Yet the narrative power by which we are compelled through these truly labyrinthine novels resides more in their accuracy of detail, strength of characterization, and complexity of situation than the sheer abundance of textual material. The novels work on the most direct level as reportage, and on the most abstract, as meditation on humanity and the situation of total war. Taking place primarily on the home rather than the battlefront, Aub's novel innovates in its insistence that the war might be chronicled without long battle scenes, description of weaponry, or detail of the hardship of the front. Instead, he chronicles the chaos in ordinary life and the challenge to social relationships posed by total war.

Most significantly, *El laberinto mágico* marries the experimentalism of prewar Spanish avant-garde writing to the realism of the war narrative, incorporating shifts of time and perspective, nonlinear, labyrinthine structures, and even at times the use of fantasy. This combination, which speaks to the ongoing tradition of Spanish avant-gardism as well as the possibility of nonpolemical war writing, helps Aub, much like Woolf, marshal narrative innovation to the critique of war, thus avoiding the monologic, scripted responses demanded by propaganda. As we have seen in chapter 1, propaganda in its many guises is one of the most widely circulating cultural products to emerge from the Spanish Civil War. On both sides of the struggle, the hallmark of the propaganda image or pamphlet is the manipulation of perspective in a manner that encourages an emotional, unmodified response to the subject matter—precisely what Woolf resists in her play with the photographs in *Three Guineas*. And like Woolf's use of a modified structure of address, the complexity of perspective in Aub's narrative counters propaganda's simplified representation of a larger-than-life conflict that can only be read heroically. In its refusal of both the graphic scenes of battle horror and the construction of larger-than-life heroes and its depiction of the chaos of war rather than the unity of either side, Aub's six-novel cycle replaces the epic war tale with a modernist version of the Civil War as a labyrinthine struggle played out on city streets among ordinary people. The imagination of a potential justice that emerges from this enormous work becomes predicated on a negotiated and provisional communal solidarity played out across complex personal loyalties and disputed battle lines, and this countermands the political catchphrases and directed responses of the propaganda machine.

Spain and Spanish cultural production has rarely been discussed as part of the broader European development of modernism, despite the key place of Spanish artists, filmmakers, and writers in the history of modernism. As Jordana Mendelson puts it, because "the chronology of Spanish modernity and its contours are different from the rest of Europe during the early twentieth century . . . Spain's story is often marginalized from the grand narratives that explain the logic of cultural modernism between the wars. However Spain suffered its own political crises . . . [which places] Spain firmly within the conditions and conflicts of modernization."[23] The disastrous war with the United States in 1898, which resulted in the loss of Cuba, occasioned much of the kind of collective despair, reevaluation of nation and empire, and exploration of social roles and subjectivity that emerged in the aftermath of World War I elsewhere in Europe.[24] But Spain's literary avant-garde clearly developed along its own lines and in conjunction with the demands of its particular history of nation building, revolution, and civil war, as well as in ongoing relationship to avant-garde movements elsewhere in Europe. Though the modernism we can remark in Spain bears signs of its connection to surrealism and Dada, this Paris-focused avant-gardism mixed with the home-grown literary experimentalism of Unamuno, Baroja, and others, giving rise in the late 1910s and 1920s to such avant-garde movements as "ultraism," "creationism," and, more generally, "vanguardism."[25] We can thus read the developments of Spanish avant-garde writing in the mid-twentieth century as aesthetic responses to a particular modernity that also speak profoundly about the nodes of interconnection among varieties of transnational modernism.

By Spanish scholarly tradition, writers are generally divided into schools and generations (1898, 1914, 1925, or 1927), few of which span the period from pre– to post–Civil War. In Spain, criticism regarding writers of the influential generation of 1927 usually stops at the beginning of open conflict in 1936, when many histories mark the beginning of a new generation.[26] Other studies of modernism or vanguardism often focus on the 1910s and 1920s, ending at the beginning of the conflict, despite the fact that many of the lives and careers of key writers span the period.[27] Yet when we look beyond the generational model and past the categories that also divide exiled writers from those who remained in Spain, we can see broad continuities across the range of twentieth-century Spanish experimental writing. Born out of the defeat of 1898 and transformed by the political history of the second Republic and the total warfare of the civil conflict, Spanish modernism emerges as a new mode of experimental writing, released from the nostalgia that characterizes the generation of 1898, and, by means of the war, more closely tied to politics than was the generation of 1927.

Max Aub's life and work also speak directly to the interconnection among generations in Spain, the intense sense of belonging that characterizes Spanish writing of the period, and the productive nexus between the Spanish avant-garde and broader European modernisms. As a writer of both the pre- and postwar periods who composed in Spain as well as in exile in France and Mexico, Aub defies easy classification. He was born Max Aub Mohrenwitz in Paris in 1903 to a French Jewish mother and a German father who was a prosperous businessman. When war broke out in 1914, Aub's father was caught in Spain and, realizing that his German background would make him unwelcome in France, remained in Valencia and brought his family to join him. Once Aub had finished his basic schooling, he joined his father's business, traveling with him throughout Spain and on his own in Europe. It is in this period that his lifelong identification with the country developed, despite his foreign birth, the fact that Spanish was not his native language (and he always spoke it with a French accent), and his eventual exile to Mexico. As Francisco Longoria puts it, "Aub *escogío* ser español [Aub *chose* to be Spanish],"[28] and he became a Spanish citizen in 1924. He was cosmopolitan in the deepest sense of the word; like many of the writers I have discussed in this book, he was both rooted locally and at home in the world.

Aub began writing short prose pieces, poems, and theater sketches as an amateur before leaving school, and he subscribed to all the major literary magazines in French, German, and Spanish, including *La Nouvelle Revue Française* and *España*. When Ortega y Gasset, one of the cofounders of *España*, struck out on his own and began publishing *La Revista de Occidente*, quickly the premier vehicle for Spanish vanguardism, Aub came immediately under its influence and soon began publishing in its pages.[29] Aub can thus be said to have come of age with the development of literary vanguardism in Spain and to have the imprimatur of Ortega, its ostensible literary doyen. Indeed, his earliest narrative works, *Geografía* (1929), *Fábula verde* (1933), and *Luis Álvarez Petreña* (1934) have many of the stylistic trademarks of the modernism Ortega described as "la literatura deshumanizada [dehumanized literature]."[30]

Ortega's ideas about modern literature as expressed in his *Ideas sobre la novela* (Ideas about the novel) and *La deshumanización del arte* (*The Dehumanization of Art*) left a long legacy among the writers of the 1920s and are crucial to any discussion of modernism in Spain. Although no specific style is associated with Orteguan vanguardism, many of the texts attributed to the movement, and published in and around *La Revista de Occidente*, by the *Revista*'s press, and in the collection of books called Nova Novorum follow the principles set forth by Ortega in these two essays. The long historical process of "dehumanization" severs art from the responsibility of direct engagement with the human world and emphasizes the "disinterested enjoyment of the aesthetic object as a fiction."[31] Because it is based on a subjective reality, in which there can be no absolute truth and where multiple realities can coexist at once, Ortega's "new art," like other varieties of modernism in Europe, becomes flexible and fluid in terms of its relationship to the world:

> One and the same reality may split up into many diverse realities when it is beheld from different points of view.... Any preference can be founded on caprice only. All these realities are equivalent, each being authentic for its corresponding point of view.... Thus we arrive at a conception of reality that is by no means absolute.[32]

Since belief in any given reality is a question of caprice, dehumanized art will avoid the expectation of realism or the representation of any particular narrative as the transparent depiction of life. As one critic puts it, "Ortega's real argument is simply that the nineteenth century's tendency to confuse life with art, and therefore to assign to the latter the function of representing reality, was an aberration from which artists in the twentieth century have happily recovered ... the dehumanization in question means little more than the greatly reduced importance on narrative and description in literature."[33] In another essay, Ortega also argues that art should focus our attention on aesthetics: "La obra de arte viva más de su forma que de su material [the work of art lives more in its form than in its material]."[34] This is not to say that Ortega's dehumanized art is completely divorced from its social and historical situation. In his 1928 *Revolt of the Masses*, for example, Ortega turns explicitly to social theory, discussing the danger of anti-intellectualism and going so far as to equate fascism with barbarism.[35]

Aub, in the 1920s, embraced the Orteguan focus on form, irony, farce, and the rejection of classic realism. His *Geografía* (published in 1927 in *La Revista de Occidente*) is a retelling of the Phedre story primarily through dreams while *Fábula verde* has been called "una extraña combinación de fantasía, simbolismo y misterio [a strange combination of fantasy, symbolism, and mystery]."[36] Yet for members of Aub's generation, young in 1925, this practice of dehumanized art leaves their growing political interests and commitments without significant means of expression. While *Fábula verde*, as a tale of existential despair and recovery, might be said to have social significance, it is without direct ties to the surrounding social or political world. As one critic puts it, this mode of art makes the writers around Aub "levantar una barrera artificial que separa, de una parte, sus preocupaciones e ideales sociopolíticos, y de otra, sus actividades artísticas [raise an artificial barrier that separates, on the one side, sociopolitical preoccupations and ideals and, on the other, artistic activities]."[37] In 1925 Aub wrote a poem that clearly expresses conflict over this separation of art from social concerns:

Habremos de dejar pasar
por la corriente de la vida,
sin preocuparnos para nada,
. . . .
¿Tenemos derecho, poeta?

[We will have to let pass by
the current of life
without being involved in anything,
. . . .
Do we have the right, poet?][38]

By 1928 Aub became a socialist and joined the Partido Socialista Obrero Español. He became increasingly involved in left-leaning politics and began to publish essays in leftist journals as well as continuing to write plays and narratives. In 1933, a year of increasing tensions between the left and right, he traveled to Russia to see socialist theater firsthand.[39] By 1936, and the victory of the popular front, he was in charge of the socialist newspaper *Verdad*. Aub edited this newspaper as the pressure on the failing government increased and the violence between left and right escalated in 1936, and he stayed on into 1937, after Franco's attack and the beginning of the war. He was still composing poetry and other short works throughout the 1930s even as he took on more public responsibilities, serving as a key member of the Alianza de Intelectuales Antifascistas par la Defensa de la Cultura (Alliance of Antifascist Intellectuals for the Defense of Culture) and becoming deputy commissioner of the Spanish pavilion at the Paris World's Fair and part of the delegation that commissioned Picasso's *Guernica* to hang in it.[40] The increasing demands of these commitments and Aub's continued questioning of the roles and purposes of poetry led him to challenge the wall between politics and art and to begin the transformation of Orteguan vanguardism into a new engaged writing.

Transcendental Realism and the Problem of Engagement

In the early 1930s Aub began to develop a narrative mode he would later call "transcendental realism,"[41] which marries vanguardist experimental narrative with a socially and politically engaged realism. That is to say, he raised the issue of representation of the world and the writer's responsibility to his time and place, without relinquishing Orteguan ideas about multiple realities and the impossibility of transparent mimesis. In addition, Aub's new narrative style retained his interest in the sounds and shapes of language, the power of metaphor, and the expansion of literary forms. The full development of transcendental realism as a mature style occupied the rest of Aub's career, yet it emerged in the mid-1930s, pushing away the notion of experimental narrative as "dehumanized" and replacing it with a new mode that responds to the human demands of time and place and the political commitments they bring with them. We can understand this mode, I would argue, as a significant variety of literary modernism that also bears connections to the later development of magical and hyper-realism, particularly in Latin America.

In 1945, from his exile in Mexico (after having spent from 1939 through 1942 in concentration camps in France and Algeria), Aub elaborated on this new mode in his "Discurso de la novela española contemporánea" (Discourse on the contemporary Spanish novel). He comments on the inability of the French schools of writing from the early years of the century to remain influential outside of Paris and describes the end of the kind of Orteguan "style for style's sake" approach to narrative. In its place he identifies what he calls a "new realism," one that profits from the philosophical and linguistic experiments of the intervening years and that never seeks to erase the trace of its writing.

> Todo parece predecir el éxito de un realismo que un crítico mexicano, adjetivó trascendente, a mi juicio con acierto . . . por hecho de ser un arte llamado a traspasar y penetrar en un público cada vez más amplio. Realismo en la forma pero sin desear la nulificación del escritor como pudo acontecer en los tiempos del naturalismo. Subjetivismo y objetividad parecen ser las directrices internas y externas de la nueva novelística. . . . Se han acercado al ambiente no con afán de describirlo, sino de comprenderlo y emitir juicio, y esta es la diferencia fundamental con el naturalismo pasado: el escritor, ateniéndose a la realidad, *toma partido*.

> [Everything seems to predict the success of a realism that a Mexican critic described as transcendental, correctly, to my mind . . . for the sake of being an art called to go beyond and penetrate each time an ever wider public. Realism in form but without desiring the nullification of the writer as happened in the age of naturalism. Subjectivity and objectivity appear to be the internal and external principles of the new novel. . . . They have approached life not with eagerness to describe it but with the desire to comprehend it and deliver justice, and this is the fundamental difference from the naturalism of the past: the writer, attending to reality, *takes part*.][42]

"Transcendental realism" thus begins with the scene of writing and carries as its hallmarks a combination of subjectivity of perspective and objectivity of focus on the surrounding world. It places no priority on description for its own sake and instead privileges comprehension. It not only acknowledges the role of the author/narrator, and never tries to banish him from the text, but also asks for his participation and demands that he become a part of the narrative and, by implication, also part of the world around him. By emphasizing the words "*toma partido*"—which may be translated as "takes part," "works for something," or "takes up sides"—at the end of this passage, Aub also emphasizes the more literal meaning of the word "*partido*," which is the Spanish term for a political party and has the same roots as "partisanship." In other words, he implies that the writer of transcendental realism takes a partisan rather than a dispassionate perspective on reality and uses his writing to take up sides. Aub's *Laberinto mágico*, which he began in 1939 and continued to write while imprisoned in France and afterward in exile in Mexico, becomes an example of that principle.

Aub's "transcendental realism" shares with the work of modernist writers like Woolf a focus on the importance of presenting "reality" as filtered through subjectivity into narrative rather than an attempt at dispassionate objectivity. In *El laberinto mágico*, Aub introduces a myriad of characters and situations, but rarely with extensive description of them or the things around them. As he puts it, "Creo que el valor del hombre está en la relación de él y las cosas, y no en él y en las cosas. Es decir, que lo único que cuenta para mí, es la síntesis [I believe that the value of man is in the relation between him and things, and not in him and in things. That is to say that the only thing that counts for me is synthesis]."[43] Aub presents this synthesis through the reactions of characters to their surroundings rather than direct description of those surroundings, and he pushes the reader into experiencing the particularly chaotic world of Civil War Spain by way of narrative inscription of that experience. Time accelerates and decelerates, places are often indeterminate, dialogue is freely intercut and interrupted, and the plots of the six novels in the cycle become more and more labyrinthine. Like Faulkner, whom he admired, Aub interweaves historical events and personages into his novels but privileges their position in a local, human drama rather than their world-historical roles. Transcendental realism, in Aub's work is thus far removed from the realism of Tolstoy or Galdós, to whom he acknowledges his debt,[44] and is aligned in significant ways with other twentieth-century modernisms. Like the work of Woolf, Anand, and other writers I take up in this book, *El laberinto mágico* presents an imaginative realm of "as if" that transcends the everyday reality of the world even as it is committed to redescribing it. If the labyrinthine structure of the six-novel cycle constantly puts in question the possibility of a viable future for

Spain and for its inhabitants, Aub nonetheless imagines in these novels the potential for a creative opposition in which the meaning created among human beings as they work and live is not interrupted by random violence or the force of an authoritarian regime. The volumes skirt a fine line between the ethical clarity of their reportage, honest as it is in chronicling violence and defeat, and the political impulse to point toward an alternative, "as if" future where personal community survives as a source of justice even in an increasingly chaotic public sphere.

In the opening of *Campo abierto*, the second novel of the sequence,[45] Aub creates transcendental realism out of fragments of lives placed under the pressure of total war. The characters of the many vignettes appear without warning or introduction, and we often catch them in the middle of dramatic, life-threatening situations. Who these characters might be, where they are, even what they look like seems beside the point. For example, the novel begins with a section titled "Gabriel Rojas," which plunges us immediately into the presence of Gabriel and his wife, who is about to give birth:

¿Como te encuentras?
Gabriel Rojas se despatarra ante su mujer, las manos en la cintura.
Angela contesta cerrando los ojos:—Bien.
—¿Quieres que vaya a buscar al médico?
—No.

(13)

[How are you?
Gabriel Rojas sprawls in front of his wife, his hands on his waist.
Angela answers, closing her eyes:—Good.
—Do you want me to go for the doctor?
—No.]

As the baby arrives, Gabriel rushes out for the doctor only to be told he has already started for their apartment. Relieved, Gabriel begins to return home, thinking about his new daughter and unaware that the first battles of the war are raging on the street. Within minutes, however, he is caught in the crossfire and killed. The narrative presents Gabriel's death dispassionately, without added description or pathos. We are told that he is not aware of the "rintintin" in the street (18–19), and we share his ignorance, unable to see the development of the fighting. All that occurs happens without explanation, "Un ruido seco, un golpe. Negro [A sharp noise, a blow. Black]" (19). In this manner Aub introduces us to the beginning of the Civil War in the chaos, constant anxiety, and indiscriminate violence of total war, and he does so in a mode of pared down, subjective "realism" that can be true to those experiences.

At the same time, the novel's first page, like many of the chapter headings in its third part, begins with an inscription of the date: 24 July 1936. This marks the novel as situated during the first battles of the war (which started in Morocco on 17 July and twenty-four hours later on the mainland of Spain).[46] Though we can not be sure what city we are in (probably Valencia), and the battles do not enter directly into the action of most of the early vignettes, which take place primarily indoors and among a small set of civilian characters, Aub here demonstrates the interweaving of history and fiction that is crucial to *El laberinto mágico*.

The volume ends on 7 November 1936, the eve of the crucial battle for Madrid and the day when, expecting defeat, the Republican government moved from Madrid to Valencia. Because the Republican forces were unexpectedly able to hold off the better-supplied and trained Nationalists, the historic battle for Madrid demonstrated the potential power of the Republican coalition government when united with a determined populace. Key moments from the street fighting invade the novel's third section, and characters who had seemed distant from the war or disconnected from one another appear on the scene together, along with historical figures, all fighting, fleeing, or struggling in some way. Like the citizens of Madrid, the characters of this novel find themselves swept into the fight no matter what their personal inclinations.

That Aub places *Campo abierto* in this epochal period and thrusts his characters into the midst of such a key battle demonstrates the degree to which his transcendental realism marries reportage with narrative imagination in responding to the situation of total war. It also marks the importance of rearguard perspectives to the novel, which rarely ventures to the front and insists on counting the everyday experiences of violence and trauma as crucial aspects of the experience of war. By plunging his characters into the fighting in the city, Aub also plunges them into the anxiety and temporal disorder of total war. If, as Paul Saint-Amour has argued, the effect of total war is not only the death and devastation of civilians and entire cities but also the dread of being trapped in the next battle or the next bombing, then Aub's *Laberinto* is from beginning to end a saga of total war.⁴⁷ The sense of ominous anticipation, of what Saint-Amour calls a "pre-traumatic stress," pervades the cycle's many volumes even though, because of the intensely focalized third-person perspective, which seems almost without peripheral vision, neither the characters nor the reader ever gain enough information to know what to expect. In *Campo abierto*, as the battle for Madrid looms, the characters remark on the empty streets around the Prado and on the flight of the locals: "No comprenden el porqué, pero se sienten en peligro inminente de caer en manos del enemigo [They don't understand why, but they feel themselves to be in imminent danger of falling into the hands of the enemy]" (294). Out of nowhere a column of unarmed civilians, trying to march like soldiers, appears, but they look more like prisoners than soldiers. In the proleptic mode of the total-war novel, the narration tells us, "Van a morir; pero no, como tal piensen, en duelo con el enemigo, sino huidos, en manada, segados por las ametralladoras, contra un enorme paredón, o allí arriba, en la Plaza de Toros . . . Y ahora sí, le entra el miedo, a borbotones, como no lo tuvo nunca en campo abierto [They are going to die; but not, as they think, in a duel with the enemy, but fleeing, in a pack, cut down by machine guns, against an enormous wall, or there above, in the Plaza de Toros. . . . And now, yes, fear gushes in, as it never had in the open field {or countryside}]" (295). The temporal disruption of the battle is described in anticipation rather than in retrospect here, and the traumatic effect of the fear that "gushes" like a war wound before it happens creates the war as something that exists just around every corner and in the imaginations of every citizen, even before the fighting begins.

Written between 1939 and 1968, each of the six novels in *El Laberinto* takes place in a different key moment, from before the war through the immediate postwar period, but the first three volumes bear a special relationship to the material that they portray. That is, Aub composed them soon after the events depicted and while Spain and its future were still being contested. These volumes thus play the role not only of fiction but also of direct political opposition.⁴⁸ The protagonist of the first volume, Rafael, an antihero of sorts, becomes caught up with the Falange in the early days of the uprising in Barcelona. At first, he participates because they pay him and because he finds their work exciting and cannot understand why one side is better or worse than the other. By the end of the book, however, he has found community among the Republican fighters on the barricades. Increasingly, as the cycle goes on, the specter of warfare seems tied to the thrust of the fascists into Barcelona, into Madrid, toward Valencia.

Aub's chaotic assemblage of characters, his temporal disruptions, and his tendency to allow the intensely focalized narration to jump from one character to another without warning all serve as a counteracting force, displaying collective difference from the Nationalist putsch and from the misguided leadership on both sides. In its broadest outlines, the novel cycle creates what we might call a decentered, quasi-anarchist community that generates resistance by foregrounding its refusal of simple sloganeering and governance by violence.

Further, the three first novels in the cycle were written partially out of Aub's experience of Vichy French concentration camps in the years 1939 through 1942.[49] Thus, they may be read not only as Aub's response to total war and to the partisan perspective demanded by his transcendental realism but also as a literary response to politically motivated incarceration. Though he had begun *Campo cerrado* before the end of the war, the later novels emerge from fragments scribbled down in the camps in France and Algeria or on the way to Mexico:

> Me detienen, en Francia, por comunista—no lo he sido nunca por la vieja raigambre liberal. . . . Ese tiempo dura cerca de tres años, llevo en mi equipaje los versos de Quevedo y un diccionario: las notas y los recuerdos que acumulé necesitarían cien años de vida para convertirse en libros.
>
> [The held me in France as a Communist—which I never have been because of my old liberal roots. . . . This period lasted almost three years. I carried in my luggage the verses of Quevedo and a dictionary: the notes and the memories that I accumulated would require a lifetime of a hundred years to transform into books.][50]

The splintered sensibility and the quality of disconnection in *El laberinto* reflect not only the chaos of war and opposition to fascist militarism but also the dual experiences of incarceration and exile. Readers have sometimes criticized Aub's novels for their lack of internal psychology; rather than take up something like a Woolfian tunneling process, they proceed almost metonymically, skipping from character to character in a series of loose links that together construct a tenuous community. This quality may in the end be the legacy of Aub's forced dissociation from Spain and the disillusionment of the years spent in the camps. The presiding metaphor of the "labyrinth," much discussed in the critical literature on the novel,[51] invokes a notion of entrapment that seems clearly tied to his years of imprisonment, but Aub also applies it to the Spanish situation writ large. As Michael Ugarte puts it, as the novel cycle progresses, "the passageways of the labyrinth multiply, making an escape (exile) impossible.... The constant presence of the labyrinth as a device renders the historical progression of the war (as well as the novels themselves) an illusion."[52] Indeed, the notion of unified forward progress, whether temporal or political, succumbs quickly to the experimental structure and ironic tone of Aub's novel.

Indeed, even while these novels demonstrate their Republican sympathies, they are more intensely focused on the ethical (and narrative) problems of entrapment, total war, and failed history, which challenge easy faith in Enlightenment models of personal liberty or in rational discourse as the basis for a viable politics. Historians of the prewar period note both its chaos and its failed potential. The popular front of 1935 seemed to offer the promise of a united coalition against fascism; in reality, it marked the ascendancy of the Soviet-backed communists at the expense of the anarchists (CNT) and independent Marxists (POUM). Groups on the left, including the Republican government in Barcelona, privileged their consolidation of power over the interests of everyday citizens and, under pressure of war, took action to restrict the strength the unions and the workers they represented. Aub's novels explore the problem of ethics in a situation where individuals use one another for personal and political ends and where violence rather than communication becomes the key mode of social expression.[53] They ask how we can posit politics when we can assume neither the potential for historical progress nor the efficacy of human action and when the specter of violent death is always right around the corner. How do we generate political activity when the basis for solidarity in party politics is bankrupt and the future appears only as the proleptic glimpse of the violence to come? If we agree that politics must rely on events or human activity to generate relationships, must understand some community or polity as the locus of ideas of rights and justice, and must presume a future toward which any acts or propositions gesture, then these novels emerge at the very limit of politics. In fact, some critics have argued that Aub's novels, especially the early volumes of the *El laberinto*, use the war to present a negative view of human capacity.[54] Yet I would argue that by forcing his characters into the labyrinth of the Civil War and refusing to assume the continued progress of Spanish history, Aub allows his work to enact the difficult search for ethics even where no ethics seems possible and to conceive of a potential politics that, under threat of total war, requires an effort of the imagination to manifest.

The first volume in the cycle, *Campo cerrado* (*Field of Honour*), which moves with its main character through the prewar period and ends with the historic first fighting in Barcelona, is a case in point. Unlike the other novels, *Cerrado* follows one character, Rafael Serrador, from childhood until the beginning of his participation as a young man in the early street fighting. Rafael has few redeeming qualities. His upbringing leaves him isolated from others, unresponsive, and passive. His sexual initiation, in which a woman living in the house where he works simply crawls into his bed and makes use of him, presages the way that fascist and anarchist groups will later manipulate him and his passivity in response to their actions. He moves through the events of his life, which increasingly correspond with world-historical events in prewar Barcelona, as though there was no reason to act. Like Merseult in Camus's later novel *The Stranger*, to which *Campo cerrado* has sometimes been compared, Rafael's single dramatic act involves murder—he throws a prostitute, whom he believes has betrayed one of his friends, into the sea. He commits this murder as though in a daze, without purpose or self-justification. Only afterward does the narrative shift, breaking into a rare descriptive passage about the city and the sea, in which the elements take on the emotions not experienced by Rafael. "El día nace subrepticiamente . . . la noche recula de miedo, se escurre y oculta. La luz es cobarde y no viene de cara [The day is born surreptitiously . . . the night recoils in fear, slithers away and hides. The light is timid and hides its face as it advances]."[55] Rafael falls onto his bed and sleeps while the narrative, switching from third to first person, recounts his nightmares, in which the dead sing, revealing their seaweed tongues, and the sea displays snakes and other dangers: "Mi mano está fría, transparente y muerta. . . . No me bañaré nunca más en el mar [My hand is cold, transparent and numb. . . . I shall never go swimming in the sea again]" (79; 87). But in the next chapter Rafael resumes his life as usual. He is never arrested for the crime, and though the incident will reappear periodically in his mind, often evoked by a simple mention of the woman's name, Matilde, it does not again become the cause of existential doubt or personal transformation.

On the other hand, when the chaos of 1934 breaks into the novel in the following chapter, Rafael is pushed into more dramatic self-questioning. Rather than simply place his characters into the unfolding political drama, Aub works references to the events into many levels of the narrative. The narrator reminds the reader of the date or of a significant event in political history, and, like the reappearance of the prime minister's car in *Mrs. Dalloway* or the references to Irish songs in *Ulysses*, the detail connects the text with a broader world. After Matilde's death we learn that we are in the period surrounding 6 October 1934, when Lluis Companys proclaimed the independence of the Catalan State though he was quickly removed, the movement suppressed, and many citizens jailed. If the conversation in the novel surrounds the relative benefits of socialism versus anarchism, and Rafael begins to question his beliefs, it is because the streets are full of protest and many among his acquaintance are being imprisoned. Aub does not describe the streets or the conflict. Companys is barely mentioned in this chapter. Yet through its characters and structure, the novel engages deeply with the question of independence and of personal and political liberty. As Rafael puts it, "Yo . . . tengo cierto repugnancia en aceptar moldes que otros hayan forjado como continente de mi pensimiento. Hay algo que se me levanta adentro [I . . . feel sick at having to accept moulds that other people have shaped as containers for my thought. Something rises up inside me]" (86; 95). Clearly, Rafael's sense of entrapment, the impossibility of action, and the necessity of doing what can't be done is also an inscription of the politicohistorical exigencies of the first week in October 1934. The "something" that is rising within him mirrors the impulse toward liberty that is rising in the streets, yet the movement is put down.

The complexity of this novel is displayed in Aub's unwillingness to grant Rafael an easy epiphany or to argue that personal freedom leads to political justice. In this sense, Aub insists upon a model of political action that acknowledges the limitations of individual human choices and the necessity of human community, responsibility to others, and everyday human interconnection. In a letter to a friend written in 1949 and reprinted in *Hablo como hombre*, Aub suggests his distance from existential philosophy and from writers like Kierkegaard, Unamuno, and Sartre, on just such grounds:

> El existencialismo . . . es un 'positivismo de lo subjetivo' . . . y les leva a un nihilismo, a una negación de toda vida futura. . . . El entrañarse en el ser—en su propio ser—les hace creerse el centro del mundo, de un mundo perdido, pero ombligo al fin y al cabo, sin darese cuenta de su transcendencia humana, no por eso menor transcendente.
>
> [Existentialism . . . is a "positivism of the subjective" . . . and takes them toward nihilism, the negation of all future life. . . . The search for the heart of being—of one's own being—makes them create it as

the center of the world, of a lost world, but at the center, when all's said and done, without becoming aware of its human transcendence, which is not less transcendent because of that fact.][56]

For Aub, this immersion in existential subjectivity leads to nihilism about the future and to impotence. But Aub posits generosity as essential to human life and being among others as central to the human condition: "No hay duda que, al darse cuenta del mundo que le rodea, el hombre toma posición. No hay vuelta de hoja, ni manera de huir. . . . Estamos dentro [There is no doubt that, upon becoming aware of the world that surrounds him, man takes his position. There's no doubt about it or any way to escape. . . . We are in the middle]."[57] Aub presumes solidarity or community as the basis of the human condition, from which our potential for human activity, art, and political action arises.

Rafael's search for personal meaning leads nowhere. He gets caught up with the growing Falange movement without making any conscious choice. He listens to the protofascist diatribes of the nationalist Luis Salomar with barely a word for or against. When asked if he would like to make some money painting Falangist symbols on the walls of the city at night, his response is "Qué más da [What the hell]" (121; 137). Rafael also gets seduced by an illusion of community, believing that he belongs to the Falange even though many of his friends are anarchists or communists. Only after having gone through arms training among the fascists, and on the eve of battle, does he discover that he has no fascist values. The novel seems to suggest that this is a man who, at least until the end, is unable to believe.

Yet if we read closely, between the fascist diatribes or the defenses of communism, in the small lines of dialogue that emerge as Rafael's often interrupted utterances, we can detect another sensibility emerging, one that begins to replace the illusory community of the Falange with the potential polity of the street. When he first encounters the fascists, Rafael asks Salomar if those are the men who are going to save Spain. Salomar replies that he is not interested in men, only in ideas and history (105–6; 120). Rafael asks, "And the poor?" to which Salomar can only respond that for them there are no rich and poor people, only an empire and its history (106; 121). In the chapters that follow, this question about the poor or another about the lives of workers appears as a recurring litany for Rafael. When Salomar lauds the fact that the youth have turned to politics, Rafael replies that only the rich ones have changed: "Los obreros están donde estaban [The workers are where they were before]" (124; 141). Though his questions are brief and his speech inconsequential amid the cacophony of voices in *Campo cerrado*, their repetition marks his growing concern for pragmatic justice and the beginning of an alternative to the rhetoric of both political groups. Rafael rejects the abstraction of the People or the Nation and reminds the intellectuals around him that ideas do not put bread on the tables of the poor.

If he remains without a viable form of political action other than violence and continues to claim that he believes in nothing (153; 178), it is because of the paucity of vision among those of both left and right and because the community they have offered has been illusory. The final section of *Camp cerrado* takes place in Barcelona on the night of 18 July 1936, the day after the military uprising begins in Morocco, spreads across the country, and threatens Barcelona. When the workers and anarchists took to the streets that night, they were refused arms by Companys, the head of the Catalan Generalitat, despite his knowledge of the generals' uprising elsewhere in Spain and the clear evidence of plans for a similar rising in Barcelona.[58] The Republican government resisted arming the workers and empowering the labor unions and CNT for fear that they would use the arms against the government. In response, the CNT called for a general strike, captured a ship full of weapons, and distributed them among the unions. The streets filled with anarchist fighters, who for a time were able to take over the city by convincing the Civil Guard, sent out to contain them and recapture the weapons, to join the struggle instead.

The events in Barcelona, which form the culmination of this volume, make clear that solidarity arises out of resistance to totalizing political organizations, whether of the right or left, and that the real triumph of this moment in Barcelona is the creation of a pragmatic political force out of the ethical imperative to community among the people. The call to action is a call that comes from the street, and it mobilizes individuals like Rafael to act, despite the threat both of aerial bombardment from the fascists and opposition from Republican forces. Buenaventura Durruti, the CNT leader, confronted the officers sent to take back the rifles, asking them to disobey. "Civilize yourself by making common cause with the people," he told them.[59] Indeed, Rafael's decision in *Campo cerrado* to join with the anarchists becomes just such a civilizing decision. Rather than follow the directives of the fascists who have recruited him, he answers the call of the workers rising in the streets:

> Por primera vez, Rafael López Serrador se ve desde fuera. Y se siente hombre ... La soledad era mi propio sentimiento. He vivido en mis adentros, pensando que el mundo era una discontinuidad de cercas ajenas. Y estos hombres están ahí, juntos, movidos por un mismo sentimiento, sintiéndose hombres. ... Y, lentamente, con cuidado, Serrador alarga la mano.
>
> (178)

> For the first time, Rafael López Serrador sees himself from the outside. And he feels like a man. ... My loneliness was my own feelings. I've lived inside myself, thinking that the world was a tangle of alien fences. And these men are here, together, moved by one single feeling, feeling themselves to be men. ... And, slowly, carefully, Serrador stretches out his hand.
>
> (209–10)

Though he dies at the end of *Campo cerrado*, Rafael's newly awakened concern for the realities of life among ordinary people and for everyday, pragmatic notions of liberty rather than the abstract ideas of both the communists and the fascists, connects ethical community to political action and becomes one of the guideposts of the remainder of *El laberinto mágico*.

A constellation of metaphors surrounding Rafael also connect him to Spain and to the Spanish people's struggle, thus extending the implications of his transition from brutish and isolated individual to politically active comrade. This struggle is everywhere linked to the ethical question of what distinguishes the human from the animal and to the singular nature of the human being. The book opens with a much-celebrated description of the running of the "toro de fuego"—"fire bull"—in Rafael's village, in which Aub begins his reappropriation of stock Spanish imagery and its connection to the mythical labyrinth. In the dead of night a bull has its head covered and its horns set on fire and is released in the center of town. As the villagers taunt it and test their courage by approaching it, the bull tries again and again to escape. But all it can do is circle the plaza: "Ronda el toro su forzado circuito" ["The bull goes around his enforced circuit" (15; 8). In Ugarte's words, we can see here an image of the "republic ... set loose in the labyrinth of Spain."[60] The metaphor returns later when the people rising up in the streets of Barcelona are described as having "lenguas de fuego [tongues of fire]" (177; 208). Rafael's senses awaken: "Por primero vez veo vivir gente en movimiento: murriendo, en las astas del toro ... esta que era mío sólo, sentimiento, es ahora una cosa externa que liga al uno con el otro [For the first time I see people living in movement: dying on the horns of the bull.... This thing that was mine alone, feeling, is now an external thing which links one to another]" (177; 209). [177]. Rafael reproaches himself for having been inhuman ("¡Qué animal, qué tonto animal he sido! [What an animal, what a stupid brute I've been]" [178; 209–10]) even as he discovers the sense of fraternity tied to the commonality of bodily or sense experience, physicality, and nonverbal communication.

On the barricades at the end of the novel, this sense of common bodily experience becomes the source for a social polity. As he is asked to help build, Rafael remarks, "Empujar, cargar, llevar, moverse, hace fuerza: eso es vivir [Push, load, pull, carry, move, force: that's living]" (192; 226). Though Logorio points to this passage as the moment when Rafael finds himself,[61] what is more important is his commonality with others on the street. This moment in the text, in its emphasis on verbs, physicality, and nonlinguistic modes of communication, is clearly echoed in other passages, providing some of the most lyrical language of the novel. The people of Barcelona are what matter at the end of the novel, not the individual development or epiphanies of this particular hero. As Thomas puts it, "His heroism is a centripetal force which draws in other characters despite themselves."[62] Politics becomes contingent on action that creates community, and not the other way around.

In tying this sort of being-toward-the-other to political action, Aub points toward a politics that doesn't rely on abstractions about the nation, generalizations about the people, or the construction of a hero who reaches greatness through self-understanding. He rejects the model of much of the writing of the generation of 1898, which often used nostalgia for the Spain of previous eras as a basis for renewal of the "people." In addition, as Thomas points out, "Aub adopts a position diametrically opposed to the Falangist authors and their Nietzschean hero" by creating a hero who is unconscious of himself and of his reason for being but not of his connection to the struggle.[63] Like Rafael, the novel aligns itself with the Republicans in the end, but not by joining the suspect ideology of the popular front or by answering a unilateral call to duty. Rather than ask us to choose among the various ideologies elaborated at length in the novel or believe in Rafael's heroic potential, Aub suggests that politics will arise out of recognition of the demands that others make on us, our inability to create fully human identities in isolation, and the importance of the bodily world and action as the source of human power. This must be the corrective to Rafael's earlier "what the hell," his inability to convert his concern for the poor into a personal morality, and his passivity in the face of the demands of others. The novel cycle's insistence on an open, dialogic structure, in which characters appear and disappear (both within individual volumes and from book to book), episodes follow no determinate order, and no single voice dominates the perspective, undermines any temptation on the part of readers to impose a driving purpose on the novel or to assimilate it to the agenda of any particular party. Yet the novels insist again and again on the importance of collective action, at the barricades in Barcelona, in the streets of Madrid, and among the characters, who find themselves embattled in many different ways as the war rages on. In other words, though it refuses the political verities of parties of the right and left and rejects the trajectory of a heroic war novel, *El laberinto* nonetheless posits the potential for revolutionary justice, born of the actions of a community of ethical individuals and antiauthoritarian politics. If the hope of justice implies being able to imagine the future of human possibility accessible to all, the narrative pathway toward that future need not be straight. In the fragmented, labyrinthine pages of *El laberinto mágico*, Aub uses transcendental realism to illuminate the difficult and circuitous path of the people of Spain towards an alternate, imagined future.

"Everyone Writes as a Partisan": Irony, Propaganda, and Cinematic Engagement

The problem of how to write a "true" response to modern warfare also generates a tension between documentary reporting and propaganda surrounding the Civil War, in both English and Spanish. Hemingway famously argued that the events of the war were so important that "if a writer has participated in them his obligation is to write them truly rather than assume the presumption of altering them with invention."[64] Nonetheless, his novel *For Whom the Bell Tolls* has often been attacked for its lack of verisimilitude. Hemingway's hero, Robert Jordan, adventures behind the lines with a band of local guerillas in a manner that rings patently false to most critics with knowledge of the war and seems to reinforce a notion of rural Spain as the source of a sort of premodern, nostalgic truth that is also common in propaganda from the war. The action bears little resemblance to any wartime events, and Jordan is unrecognizable as a member of the international brigades, while his broken and famously bad Spanish makes his profession as a Spanish instructor unbelievable. One explanation for the divergence between Hemingway's statement on war writing and his actual practice is that he participated little in the war, yet unlike Aub, he attempted to write about the front. The critic Allen Josephs suggests another explanation: "His invented story allowed Hemingway to write about the war and about Spain, his own version of Spain, without writing about the otherwise inescapable political dimension of that conflict. To avoid the politics of the war ... Hemingway invented his own war."[65] Thus the conundrum of war writing: To tell the truth one must eschew political propaganda and attempt to write truthfully what one has witnessed, even if distasteful. Yet sometimes, as in the Spanish Civil War, the truth is inescapably political and subject to manipulation, and avoiding that fact often leads to fantasy, illusion, and propaganda.

On the other end of the spectrum, Orwell's *Homage to Catalonia* is nothing if not an attempt to be true to his experiences in Spain, though not necessarily to any objective, universal understanding of the war. The memoir reads like an ironic travelogue, recounting Orwell's journey to Spain, enlistment in the militia, training, fighting, injury, treatment, and departure. Told from a self-critical first-person perspective, *Homage to Catalonia* creates Orwell's voice as seemingly honest and transparent, displaying his weaknesses and illusions and admitting his failures of understanding. "I had come to Spain with some notion of writing newspaper articles but I joined the militia almost immediately, because at that time and in that atmosphere it seemed the only conceivable thing to do.... There was much in it that I did not understand, in some ways I did not even like it, but I recognized it immediately as a state of affairs worth fighting for."[66] Yet at the end of this compelling memoir, after we have come to trust the narrative's voice as sympathetic and straight-talking, Orwell shatters the illusion of verisimilitude: "I believe that on such an issue as this no one is or can be completely truthful. It is difficult to be certain about anything except what you have seen with your own eyes, and consciously or unconsciously everyone writes as a partisan ... beware of my partisanship.... And beware of exactly the same things when you read any other book on this period of the Spanish war" (231). If Orwell does not "write [events] truly," this narrative, and all war writing, must be seen as tainted, inescapably partisan, and therefore, according to Orwell, suspect.

Thus, even as his ironic, self-undermining narrative offers us a personal response to the war (if not quite the extended engagement of Aub's *Laberinto magico*), Orwell raises the problem of war writing and its relationship to propaganda. As Dougherty and Janowitz have defined it, propaganda in the context of war is the "planned dissemination of news, information, special arguments, and appeals designed to influence the beliefs, thoughts, and actions of a specific group."[67] Propaganda was a prime mode of aesthetic engagement with the war in Spain, and it is evident in the expansive and innovative use of narrative text, graphic art, and cinema, often in combination with one another, that emerged in the war years. In order to influence the public response to the war, these multimedia texts play with the manipulation of perspective, the problem of verisimilitude, and the connection between aesthetics and political action, all of which are clearly tied to broader questions of modernist narrative as well as to Orwell's statement about war writing. Mark Wollaeger has claimed that modernism and propaganda come of age together in the first decades of the twentieth century and occupy a shared terrain.[68] If the problem for the war writer is to acknowledge that the truth is inherently transformed by the process of being crafted, narrated, and put to a purpose and that, as Orwell claims, partisanship is inescapable, then war writing may always verge on propaganda, even when it foregrounds its status as reporting.

At the same time, modernism's position in what Wollaeger calls a "liminal space" between two extremes highlights the political valence of key modernist claims about narrative unreliability.[69] Modernist rejection of transparent verisimilitude can lead to its embracing not only heightened subjectivity but also the persuasive power of invective, as is the case with a writer like Céline, or the manipulation of commercial desire, as can be seen at times in Joyce or John Dos Passos. As Susan Rubin Suleiman argues, the proliferation of perspectives in a narrative does not make it immune to the emotional claims and blinkered vision that characterize propaganda.[70] If propaganda is "communication of ideas designed to persuade people to think and behave in a desired way," which always benefits those doing the persuading, then the highly subjective, focalized perspective of a modernist narrative that seeks to change points of view or promote specific behavior may be seen as propaganda.[71]

This is not to claim that all modernism is propaganda or, pace Wollaeger, that the two modes necessarily overlap. In this section I explore the impulse to propaganda and its limits in the narrative texts, graphic art, and cinema that emerged in response to the Spanish Civil War. There is no avoiding the partisanship of a subjective point of view and the fact that it may participate in hidden regimes of influence, whatever their purposes. Modernist narratives may escape obvious didacticism but manipulate readers through, rather than in spite of, their nonlinear structure or their rejection of omniscience. Clearly, the situation of total war in Spain, which blurred the boundaries between home front and battlefront, civilian and soldier, also pushed partisanship into all arenas of aesthetic response, making even the journalist on the street a participant-observer. I will argue, however, that the high degree of self-reflection, ironic detachment, and openness of form that characterizes much modernist narrative may militate against the effects of propaganda, just as does Woolf's challenge to the epistolary structure of address. Suleiman claims that the ideological or propagandistic novel is essentially teleological, because it wants to impose a single response as the outcome of the text; monologic, because this outcome is not subject to debate; and authoritarian, because the reader is presumed to agree already with the position of the narrative, is enjoined to participate, or is otherwise constrained or "programmed" in his response. If this is the case, then modernist narratives that challenge these modes by being antiteleological, dialogic, and open to a variety of readings, even when they clearly espouse political positions, might escape the extremes of propaganda.[72] By offering the possibility of multiple perspectives, refusing to determine or restrict the reader's gaze, or taking up self-reflective, distanced, or ironic stances, modernist narratives are less easily employed for propagandistic purposes. So, I would argue, when Orwell calls our attention to his partisanship, he breaks some of its hold on our attention and our emotions. By examining multimedia efforts to represent the war by Orwell, Hemingway, Joris Ivens, and André Malraux, I explore the tension between political engagement and propaganda in text, graphic image, and film and trace not only the liminal zone between propaganda and engaged war narratives but also how modernism steps in between them.

Homage to Catalonia has been called one of the best books written on the Spanish Civil War in any language.[73] It achieves that status for many readers because it refuses omniscience, the idea of coverage, or the possibility of objectivity while also eschewing fantasy. Part cautionary tale, part travel narrative, *Homage to Catalonia* seems to proceed from the perspective of a voyager offering his "impressions" and making light of their political implications. The narrative unfolds like many traveler's tales, taking us from the moment of Orwell's fresh-faced arrival in Spain to his clandestine departure under threat of arrest. In between we follow his trajectory through unfamiliar lands and situations, his encounters with local citizens and with military leaders from abroad, and his passage through several stages of appreciation for and disappointment with the people of Spain. At the same time, as Orwell warns us, the partisanship of the narrative prevents us from reading it as pure reportage or an attempt at complete war coverage. In fact, as many commentators have remarked, Orwell saw only a small corner of the war in Catalonia for a few short months in 1937 and therefore had only a partial understanding of the extraordinarily complex political event.[74] The book's strength must rather lie in its refusal of the illusion of coverage and its play with the possibilities of taking a travel narrative to war.

Dislocation is the precondition of any travel narrative, even one that also bears the marks of reportage and political commentary directed at those back home. The traveler must bring habits and language from home in order to help the reader see the strangeness of the unfamiliar scenery while asking the reader to acknowledge his commonality with the narrator in marking the foreign as such. On the other hand, cultural theorists from Clifford Geertz to James Clifford and Mary Louise Pratt have made clear the impossibility of separating the safely familiar from the exoticized time/place of the strange.[75] At the end of the twentieth century Clifford could write, "One no longer leaves home confident of finding something radically new, another time or space ... the familiar turns up at the ends of the earth"; at midcentury, though, that very familiarity, when found abroad, often disrupted not only expectations of otherness but also the political stances predicated on the distinctions between home and away.[76]

Orwell's narrative revolves around this problematic and employs it in order to disrupt our expectations about his engagement with Spain and to challenge the political verities that accompany them. Rather than a heroic tale of his service in the International Brigades or playing on the preexisting sympathies of the Republican supporters at home, *Homage to Catalonia* asks us to acknowledge the complexity of the home/away, us/them, familiar/strange, hero/ordinary man dichotomies. For example, Orwell begins his narrative by describing his brief encounter with an illiterate Italian militiaman having difficulty reading a map of Spain, with whom he discovers a fleeting yet profound connection. "Something in his face deeply moved me. It was the face of a man who would commit murder and throw away his life for a friend—the kind of face you would expect in an Anarchist, though as likely as not he was a Communist" (3). Given that Orwell's sympathies lie with the anarchists and that his readership was likely to be anticommunist, this throwaway comment indicates that Spain has confounded Orwell's (and his readers') expectations. The narration continues, "Queer the affection you can feel for a stranger! It was as though his spirit and mine had momentarily succeeded in bridging the gulf of language and tradition and meeting in utter intimacy ... I also knew that to retain my first impression of him I must not see him again; and needless to say I never did see him again. One was always making contacts of that kind in Spain" (3–4). The episode stands in metonymically for the whole of Orwell's several months in Spain. The strangeness of finding commonality with an Italian communist prefigures the reversal at the end of the memoir, when Orwell and other supporters of the POUM are forced to flee the new communist-backed Republican government. The entire narrative, then, becomes predicated on the process of double dislocation that takes place when the foreign becomes intimate, the intimate foreign, and political verities are upended. In grounding his ironic antipolemic in this process of dislocation and reversal, Orwell also undermines its potential use as propaganda for any political agenda.

Orwell's embrace of the unfamiliar, of habits of mind described as particularly Spanish, and of the principles of anarchism also provides the means for reassessing his British heritage and British political complacency. When he arrives back in England, Orwell remarks on the isolation of rural life and its ability to hold onto the past:

> Southern England, probably the sleekest landscape in the world. It is difficult when you pass that way ... to believe that anything is really happening anywhere. Earthquakes in Japan, famines in China, revolutions in Mexico? Don't worry, the milk will be on your doorstep tomorrow morning. . . . Down here it was still the England I had known in my childhood.
>
> (231)

That his British readers might still be living this untouched life, safe from earthquakes, famines, and revolutions, becomes the impossibly strange reality of Orwell's return. In the end, *Homage to Catalonia* seems bent on disrupting the complacency of home and on making sure that the faith in the promise of milk in the morning, in life proceeding as it always has, will no longer absolve the British of the political exigency of understanding "what is really happening" in other places.

Thus, in a profound sense, in its narrative stance, its structure, and the stories it recounts as well as those it leaves out, *Homage to Catalonia* is partisan, just as it warns us. It insists on the connection between politics and aesthetics, yet, I would argue, it never becomes pure propaganda because it works by dislocation and dissociation rather than by direct statement and presents its political statements even as it warns us against believing in them. In his later essay "Why I Write," Orwell says, "What I have most wanted to do throughout the past ten years is to make political writing into an art. My starting point is always a feeling of partisanship, a sense of injustice . . . I write it because there is some lie that I want to expose, some fact to which I want to draw attention, and my initial concern is to get a hearing." The thirties "debunked art for art's sake," he writes in "The Frontiers of Art and Propaganda," and "reminded us that every work of art has a meaning and a purpose . . . that our aesthetic judgments are always colored by our prejudices and beliefs." But Orwell states that "propaganda lurks in every book" and never claims to write as an objective observer.[77] It is also clear that Orwell hoped that *Homage to Catalonia* would function in some ways as propaganda: to present a case through the use of intellect as well as emotion, to exhort its readers to take up a position, and to make the opposing perspective (complacency about the war) seem inconceivable. From this perspective, *Homage to Catalonia* occupies the borderland between the partisan and the didactic, risking the label of propaganda in order to reflect its thoroughgoing engagement.

Mobilizing Propaganda

It is important to remember that the word "propaganda" has not always been pejorative and that its meaning shifted during the 1920s and 1930s in both Europe and the United States. Until World War I the most common meaning of the term concerned Catholic efforts to propagate the faith.[78] While the *Encyclopedia Britannica* contains no entry for "propaganda" in its 1911 thirteenth edition, by the post–World War I fourteenth edition (1929), it appears with its twentieth-century meaning. The British inaugurated the calculated use of misleading information to support a political cause, which became associated with the word "propaganda," during the First World War.

When they circulated rumors that the Germans had filmed the sinking of the *Lusitania* or had crucified a Canadian soldier, misinformation became not just a weapon of war against the enemy (as it often had been) but also a tactic used to heighten emotion and rally the people to the cause.[79] The British also pioneered the use of film in war reporting, by 1917 producing films highlighting the British war effort.[80] In the United States, Woodrow Wilson hired the journalist Walter Lippman and the psychologist Edward Bernays to create "scientific" propaganda designed to sway the American public to the British cause. But by the 1920s and 1930s, as the governmental use of propaganda became public knowledge, several studies emerged that condemned its use, some calling it a "greater evil in war-time than the actual loss of life."[81]

Propaganda is one of the crucial cultural products to emerge from the Spanish Civil War, both in Spain and abroad. Well before the war, both the governments of Miguel Primo de Rivera and of the Second Republic had active propaganda agencies that published all manner of materials, from nation-building tourist guides to pro-Republic posters and broadsides, as well as pamphlets about modern farming methods. These materials were not all overtly designed to sway opinion on a specific topic but often worked to generate public sentiment toward nation building. At the onset of the Civil War, the mechanisms that produced such materials were quickly harnessed to the varied purposes of war propaganda. In the major cities held by the Republicans, Madrid, Barcelona, and Valencia, and in San Sebastián, where the majority of Francoist publications originated, the production of printed materials—whether broadsides, magazines, special stamps, or post cards—continued at a brisk pace. One study counts 454 serial publications with propagandistic purposes in the Republican zone between 1936 and 1939. Another study of all serial publications in the Francoist zone includes 961 items.[82] Jordana Mendelson estimates that the total number of serial publications in Spain during the war years was as high as 2,000. As she puts it, "Multiply this number by the individual issues edited of each title, and one gains an appreciation for the ubiquity and importance of artists' participation in the creation of thousands of highly visible, widely circulating, and far reaching publications."[83] Of course, not all of these were explicitly engaged in war work or political commentary, yet, as Mendelson makes clear in her study of these periodicals, "magazines published during war are not neutral objects" and the distance between explicit political propaganda and general-interest periodicals was increasingly small.[84]

Many of the general-interest illustrated magazines edited by the trade unions, such as *Artes Gráficas, Moments,* and *Mi Revista,* carried discussions of propaganda or the role of art and artists in time of war alongside more entertainment-oriented fare.

Official propaganda efforts during the period of the Popular Front Government in Spain (1936–37) can be seen clearly in the posters created by the Ministerio de Propaganda in Madrid, the Ministry of State (Ministerio de Estado de la República Española), and the official tourist office (Patronato Nacional de Turismo), among other groups. Some have such straightforward comments as "La República crea, el fascismo destruye [the Republic creates, fascism destroys]" appended to an image of a worker constructing a dam and power lines (fig. 4.1) or "Para salvar el arte de España hay que aplastar el Fascismo [to save the art of Spain we have to crush fascism]" printed over the image of a crumbling old wall on a poster from the tourist bureau (fig. 4.2).

Other propaganda pieces feature much more dramatic exhortations to action, such as a poster dominated by a blood-spattered map of Spain with a knife stuck into the region of Asturias, which pleads with the people: "Ayuda, albergüe y amparo a las familias evacuadas [help, house, and protect the evacuated families]" (fig. 4.3). In general, Republican Civil War posters seek to construct a story about the Republic as the protector of the Spanish people and patrimony that directly counters fascist claims and mobilizes the nationalist emotions of the populace. Even the Red Aid posters employ bloody images of *"miseria," "destrucción," "persecución,"* and *"muerte"* along with documentary photographs in the service of an antifascist message: "Esto es el Fascismo! [This is Fascism!]" (fig. 4.4). This example, like many of the most dramatic propaganda posters, employs the documentary "evidence" of the photograph and the assumption of its truth value to propagate a one-sided agenda. The "reality" of the Spain it depicts is seemingly indisputable; the political position seems to follow as a matter of course.

Many Republican propaganda posters mobilize dramatic images of women and children in danger, women weeping, or dead children. It is important to recognize the way that they highlight the need to protect the women and children of Spain and to underscore, contrary to Francoist claims, the commitment of the Republic to the Spanish family. While many of the posters contain violent and bloody scenes, dead children appear more frequently than any other image, which helps generate the "scripted emotional response" that defines propaganda and that so preoccupied Virginia Woolf. While viewers might

Figure 4.1. A Republican propaganda poster from the Spanish Civil War: "The Republic creates, fascism destroys." *Source*: Spanish Civil War poster collection, POS-SP. CIV. WAR-A01, no. 6. Library of Congress, LC-USZC4-7330.

Figure 4.2. A Republican tourist office poster from the Spanish Civil War: "In order to save the art of Spain, it is necessary to crush fascism." Madrid, Patronato Nacional del Turismo. *Source*: Spanish Civil War poster collection, POS-SP. CIV. WAR-.S66, no. 1. Library of Congress, LC-USZC4-7436.

Figure 4.3. A propaganda poster from the Spanish Civil War, responding to the bombing of Asturias: "Asturias!—Valencians! Help, shelter and aid the evacuated families of the heroes of the North." José Calandín, Valencia: Socorro Rojo Internacional, Comité Provincial Valencia. *Source*: Spanish Civil War poster collection, POS-SP. CIV. WAR-.C20, no. 1. Library of Congress, LC-USZC4-7522.

respond in a variety of ways to pictures of Spanish art under threat, the clear and present danger to innocent civilians posed by the German bombers shown in these posters generates a more univocal and predictable response. Depictions of the threat posed by the German planes to both the cultural patrimony and the national progeny also formulate the matter of the war in terms of continuity of culture and nation versus the disruption of a violent and mechanized modernity. Thus, the intersection of propaganda and modernism is here made more complicated by a specific antimodern thrust on the Republican side (which has its counterpart in the acknowledged antimodernism of the Falange). Where modernity means the generation of new agricultural and labor practices, Republican propaganda offers its support; when it brings the populace under threat from powerful and wide-ranging weapons of destruction, piloted by a mercenary soldiery from abroad, propaganda must generate opposition.

The Falange and Francoists, for their part, used a more regular and sometimes uniform perspective in their propaganda and poster art,

Figure 4.4. An antifascist propaganda poster from the Spanish Civil War: "This Is Fascism." Antonio López Padial, Socorro Rojo Internacional. *Source*: Spanish Civil War poster collection, POS-SP. CIV. WAR-.P11, no. 1. Library of Congress, LC-USZC4-7531.

which is less likely to use photographs, more likely to show masculine images, and also given to mobilizing antimodernist sentiment. Slogans on these posters emphasize unity against a common enemy, usually depicted as a male communist, and show the fascists as liberators, unifiers, or rescuers. (One of the most striking of these posters shows a huge hand clutching men representing leaders among the left, proclaiming "¡¡España ya eres libre!! [Spain, now you are free!!]" (fig. 4.5).

Magazines from the Falange perspective, like *Flecha*, an illustrated paper for children published in San Sebastián (1937–38); *Cauces*, a literary magazine published in Cádiz (1936–37); *Fotos*, touted in 1939 as the most popular magazine in Spain; or *Vértice*, the "Revista Nacional de Falange Española Tradicionalista [national magazine of the traditional Spanish Falange]," which continued publishing until 1946,[85] despite their differences, tended to present fewer photographic images of battle horror on their covers, more scenes of traditional Spanish family and farm life, and, predictably, more views of Franco in heroic poses. Nonetheless, the fascist propaganda was inspired by the same impulse as that from the Republican side: to disseminate a particular view of the reality of Spanish life, to build identification between the viewer and the nation in peril, as depicted in dramatic images, and to create a direct connection between the threats depicted and the need for a particular response.

As we have seen, international audiences were the focus of much of the propaganda effort, as the Republicans and fascists competed for international opinion and financial support. The Falangist *Vértice*, though written in Spanish, contained summaries in French, German, Italian, and English.[86] Many of the Republican posters were issued in multiple versions in French, English, and Spanish. Virginia Woolf alludes to the packets of photographs that "the Spanish Government sends . . . with patient pertinacity about twice a week" in her classic antiwar essay, *Three Guineas*.[87] The task of the propagandist became that of representing to the world not only what was happening at the moment in Spain but also what was to happen in the future, both in Spain and abroad. Thus the play between the past and the future, the preservation of cultural patrimony and the projection of a would-be future Spain, becomes the key dynamic of many of the pieces of propaganda on the right and on the left. These propaganda materials display a teleological focus and monologuism that aligns them with the *roman à these* and other authoritarian narratives. On the left, it is no surprise that the tourist bureau was at the forefront of the poster campaign or involved in attempts to display the real threat of the

Figure 4.5. A Falange propaganda poster from the Spanish Civil War: "Spain, now you are free!" Falange Española. Jefatura Nacional de Prensa y Propaganda. Sección Mural. *Source:* Spanish Civil War poster collection, POS-SP. CIV.WAR-.F3447, no. 3. Library of Congress, LC-USZC4-7362.

Figure 4.6. A Falange propaganda poster from the Spanish Civil War: "To speak of Falange is to name Spain." Falange Española. Jefatura Nacional de Prensa y Propaganda. Sección Mural. *Source*: Spanish Civil War poster collection, POS-SP. CIV. WAR -. F3447, no. 4. Library of Congress, LC-USZC4-7358.

Figure 4.7. A Republican propaganda poster from the Spanish Civil War, in English. Junta Delegada de Defensa de Madrid, Ministerio de Propaganda. *Source*: Spanish Civil War poster collection, POS-SP. CIV. WAR-.S64, no. 1. Library of Congress, LC-USZC4-7446.

fascist carpet-bombing attacks to heritage sites in Spain. One poster from the Ministerio de Propaganda, produced in English, Spanish, and French, shows a photograph of a mother and child in a broken doorway, planes flying overhead. The caption, "What are you doing to prevent this?" is directed both to the destruction of the building or to the bombing of women and children (figure 4.7). Other images directed at the international community seemed to depict the most famous Spanish artists, such as Goya and Velázquez, as under attack and clearly sought to make clear that anyone who ignored the appeals of the Republic was condemning them to disappear.

Common images also link the Republic to the world by praising the International Brigade volunteers or depicting the fascists as invaders. Like some of the magazines, the Republican posters printed in several languages were clearly meant to convince the people of Great Britain, and France that the war against fascism would soon come to their turf. The poster I discussed in relation to Woolf in chapter 1 is a striking example. It shows a dead young girl and planes massed overhead and is captioned, "If you tolerate this, your children will be next!" (see fig. 1.5). Of course, the documentary photographer cannot capture images of British citizens under an attack that is yet to come, but the selection of a generic child without discernibly Spanish clothing and the composition of this poster, with the image of the child blown up to dominate the page, all lend "veracity" to the claim that British children will be next (a French version of the same poster was also produced). In other examples, the use of photomontage, increasingly popular as a technique for constructing these images, helps to extend and generalize the message by creating the presumption that the horror depicted is neither unique nor temporally bound. The function of propaganda, then, becomes a version of prophecy. The role of the image is not only to document, confront, and persuade the viewer but also to show two paths to the future and the necessity of choosing one of them. While the political valence of generating a particular future is clear, the ethical implications of controlling and directing the viewer toward that end are not.

At the same time, one of the most distinctive features of the war and the propaganda that represents it, as we have seen in Aub's work, is the transition from clearly delineated boundaries between home front and battlefront to the situation of total war. The Republican posters showing dead children under the threat of German planes play on the fact that carpet bombing made no distinctions between soldiers and noncombatants, and the common image of city streets under bombardment—most often the streets of Madrid, which underwent an extended siege in November and December 1936—underscores the daily, personal threat of air raids. When the posters ask, then, "What Are You Doing to Prevent This?" of their English audiences, or promise, "If you tolerate this, your children will be next!" they refer not only to the inevitability of the fascist threat to the people of Great Britain but also to the coming scene of total war. The specter of bombing raids over London, a harbinger of World War II, is evoked by these images, along with the implication that safeguarding women, children, and the home front, as was still possible during World War I in Britain, would be impossible. In other words, the war propaganda brought into question the tranquil distance from Spain of a rural England where, in Orwell's words, "the milk [would] be on [the] doorstep tomorrow morning." It is no wonder that for many, such as Virginia Woolf, these images sent from the Spanish government were deeply unsettling.

By 1937 plans had begun for the Spanish Pavilion at the Paris World Fair, which was meant to act, like the posters, to show the world what was happening in Spain, to galvanize opinion around the Republican cause, and to prompt the French, British, and Americans to drop their policy of nonintervention. In other words, it functioned in many ways as a propaganda installation, hoping to create the viewer's future actions even as it guided his or her experience in the pavilion. Much has been written on the Spanish Pavilion and its ultimate failure to change world opinion or generate new political policy, which I will not attempt to repeat here. In many ways, the late opening of Spain's offering (it opened weeks after the other buildings) was symptomatic—it simply was too late to reverse the damage that had already been done by the unwillingness of Britain, France, and the United States to intervene. Critical focus on Picasso's *Guernica*, first displayed at the pavilion, and its deployment as propaganda has distracted from analysis of other work there, but the debate about its value in both aesthetic and political terms raises the key question of the pavilion as a whole (which is not unlike the one with which Orwell was grappling): To what extent can a partisan work of art that intends to manipulate the viewer's thoughts and actions also permit the free range of response necessary to apprehend a work of art and respond ethically to it?

Amid the work by Picasso, Miró, and Calder on view at the Spanish Pavilion was another example of engaged art, the film *The Spanish Earth* by the Dutch filmmaker Joris Ivens (narrated by Ernest

Hemingway). A collaborative effort among Ivens and a group of American writers and filmmakers (including John Dos Passos, Archibald MacLeish, Lillian Hellman, and Dorothy Parker) designed to document the events in Spain and to enlist support for the Republic, the film had been shot between March and May 1937, in the village of Fuentedueña, on the Madrid-Valencia road, and in Madrid. It was completed and released just in time for the opening of the Spanish Pavilion in June of that year.[88] *The Spanish Earth* was originally planned as a scripted film that would narrate the history of small-town Spain from its situation under the monarchy into the present day of the war, highlighting the attachment of the people to the land and the important land-reform efforts of the Republic. However, once on site in Spain, in the midst of the escalating war, Ivens scrapped his plan and constructed an entirely different film. What emerged is regarded as a masterwork of documentary technique, a film in which a constructed narrative about the fortunes of a small-town family in the throes of war is combined with formal footage of the effort to irrigate the fields of Fuentedueña, as well as documentary images of the war, filmed with a hand-held camera. The film contains an uncredited speech by Dolores Ibárruri, better known as "La Pasionaria," one of the most rousing of Republican partisans, famous for her slogan "no pasarán! [they shall not pass!]." The narrative commentary, originally to be scripted by Dos Passos, was ultimately written and read by Ernest Hemingway.

The Spanish Earth attempts to develop individual characters in Fuentedueña and in the later scenes in Madrid in order to accomplish what Ivens later called "personalization"—the effort to make documentary content immediate and accessible by focusing on individual figures.[89] The filmmakers staged scenes in Feuntedueña almost as though they were on a set, re-creating the efforts of the villagers to take back land that had been held by the aristocracy and make it agriculturally viable through irrigation, and setting up a fictional narrative about the departure to the front of a young man named Julian.[90] Once in Madrid, closer to the fighting, however, such staged scenes became impossible, in both technical and personal terms. The film scholar Thomas Waugh uses a line from the narration of *The Spanish Earth* to sum up the problem of staging scenes in the documentary: "men can not act before the camera in the presence of death."[91] On the technical side, it became impossible to use the heavy, immobile equipment standard on studio sets. In Madrid the crew followed a communist-affiliated regiment, shooting the battle taking place around them "from the point of view of both its defenders in the front line suburbs and the air raid shelters within the city itself . . . the battle material . . . has a style whose spontaneity contrasts with the orderly, lyrical mise-en-scène of Feuntedueña."[92] There was no possibility of structuring this material except in the editing room; in the end, the unscripted events of the battles in the streets disrupt the narrative effort at "personalization" and dominate the style of much of the film.[93]

Thus the formal requirements of documentary filming intercede in what begins as a more purely propagandistic project. The sentimental story of the development of Feuntedueña under the Republic coincides with stock accounts of the agrarian roots of the Spanish nation that were employed in the propaganda of both right and left in the lead-up to the war and that also had resonance abroad. The creation of a family that loses a son to the war builds from common tropes about the family's place in the community and the solidarity of the rural people, which the film ties to the Republican cause by intercutting images of bread coming out of the oven stamped with the initials of the CNT (Confederación Nacional del Trabajo), or pictures of the young men learning to be soldiers in the arid fields. Yet in the handheld scenes, Spain becomes a more nuanced and more modern place. Images of machine guns bring the film into the twentieth century, and the streets of Madrid bustle with dangerous energy as the cuts of the film speed up. By the time we arrive at the political rally and La Pasionaria's speech in the transitional middle of the film, the univocal, scripted narrative has been modified and expanded. If the speech makes clear that this will be the film's telos—the rousing to activism on the part of the Republic of all those listening, both at the filmed rally and, through the film's agency, in other times and places—the restricted viewpoint of propaganda has been expanded by the multiplication of viewing perspectives and angles, which undermine the dominance of the unilinear narrative story shot from an unwavering, omniscient perspective.

In his essays on the nature of documentary filmmaking, and on *The Spanish Earth* in particular, Ivens discusses committed art and propaganda and elaborates on his decision to construct the film with a strong point of view. Documentary film was still developing as a genre in the 1930s; as Ivens points out, there were few ready venues for distribution of *The Spanish Earth* in the United States.[94] *The Spanish Earth*, a half-fictional, half-documentary work, further confounded expectations of genre.[95] Though the film was not part of any organized propaganda campaign, either in Spain or in the United States, it emerged out of Ivens's discovery that newsreel footage coming out of Spain during the war had mostly been shot from the Nationalist perspective.[96] *The Spanish Earth* was meant to rectify this absence and from the start was committed to a Republican point of view. Further, Ivens makes clear that in the documentary form he developed in *The Spanish Earth* and other films from the 1930s, he purposefully challenged the notion of documentary objectivity:

> In both the United States and in England, there were demands for more "objectivity." I was often asked, why hadn't we gone to the other side, too, and made an objective film. My only answer was that a documentary film maker has to have an opinion on such vital issues as fascism and anti-fascism . . . if his work is to have any dramatic or emotional or art value.
>
> (136)

The difference between a mere newsreel and a documentary that might make claims to art status thus hinges, for Ivens, on point of view. Further, Ivens claims that subjectivity makes a documentary more persuasive in its presentation of the truth than a more objective film would be:

> I was surprised to find that many people automatically assumed that any *documentary* film would inevitably be *objective*. . . . Do we demand objectivity in the evidence presented at a trial? No, the only demand is that each piece of evidence be as full a subjective, truthful, honest presentation of the witness's attitude as an oath on the Bible can produce from him.
>
> (137)

For Ivens, the reconstruction of events in the village or the creation of fictional story lines in *The Spanish Earth* helps to produce a more truthful picture of the conditions in Spain under Franco's assault.[97]

But in a 1939 essay called "Documentary: Subjectivity and Montage," Ivens rejects the negative connotation of propaganda and the insistence that truth and propaganda are necessarily at odds. By accepting the propaganda label for his film, he recasts the very idea of propaganda and extends it to all art that "takes sides." "We were immediately labeled as propaganda, and in a way, I accept that label . . . I say the same thing is true of a lot of artists. Take Rembrandt . . .

take Breughel." Yet in the same essay Ivens also offers a more explicit example of what he considers "straight propaganda": "When we show the German coming down . . . I knew that there would be people who would not understand those long German words, so I held the scene a little longer, to get them annoyed, and then I had the commentator say 'I can't read German, either.' In other words, I think you sometimes have to anticipate the feelings of your audience."[98] The step beyond committed documentary with a clear point of view rests on the deliberate manipulation of audience emotion through words and images, with the intent to motivate them to act.

It bears stopping for a moment to consider places in the film where image and commentary work together to create an almost inescapable emotional response on the part of the viewer. The moment where the writing in German remains untranslated follows a series of images of a bombing attack on Madrid and on Feunteduéña. Because in both its rural and its urban scenes, the film focuses on the faces of people, the shots of the faces of young boys in the streets of Madrid—looking "for bits of shell fragments as they once gathered hailstones"—just before they are shelled, create a personal connection for us to the losses among the Republicans, not unlike those generated by the propaganda posters. After zooming in on their dead bodies the film cuts to Feunteduéña, where children are calling out, warning of an air raid. We see the planes silhouetted in the sky against the pastoral landscape with which we are familiar from the first reel of the film while the commentary tells us, "Before, death came when you were old and sick, but now it comes to all this village. High in the sky in shining silver it comes to all who have no place to run, no place to hide."[99] By showing us shattered doorways and maimed children under an image of the Nazi aircraft, this scene generates a distinction between the innocent, pastoral Spanish people, for whom the sequence of life and death has been disrupted, and the ruthless, mechanized German bombers, whose unknown and untranslatable speech marks them as supremely foreign to the values of the local people. The two long, mostly silent scenes of the bombing attacks in Madrid and Feunteduéña, where the film reaches its highest emotional pitch, culminate in the deeply ironic tone of the comment "I can't read German either," while the camera zeros in much more quickly on the identifying tags of a dead German pilot. The film presses the conclusion that Spanish children are worthy of individualization while German pilots are not. Even the more sympathetic treatment of a group of dead Italian mercenaries in the next shot, where the camera lingers for a moment on a face, comes nowhere near the level of emotion and personalization granted to the scenes in Feuntedueña.

The intercutting of images in combination with apt but sparse commentary at the end of the film makes similar use of the connection between the Republicans' fight and the heritage of Spanish life on the land, that has been the main conceit of the film. As the people of Madrid repel Franco's forces from the road to Madrid, the villagers in Feuntedueña complete their irrigation ditch. The final scenes show military vehicles and cars speeding by as Hemingway comments, "The bridge is ours. The road is saved." The scene switches immediately to the opening of the sluice into the irrigation ditch and the flow of water to the fields to grow more food. The film has made a connection not only between the need for food and the Republic's ability to continue the fight for Madrid but also between the ancient values of the Spanish people, represented by the effort to improve the land of Feuntedueña, and the fight of the modern Republic. The intercutting of the final images—road, irrigation ditch, road, ditch—connects the old lifestyle of the pastoral scene, which was dominated by shots of donkeys and rudimentary tools at the opening of the film, to the modernity represented by the stream of vehicles over the bridge. Rather than leave modernity to the Germans, flying over in their silver planes, Ivens insists that the Republicans (and, by implication, the true Spanish peasants) can also become modern. Thus the film mobilizes stereotypes of rural Spanish life, nostalgia for a premodern agricultural lifestyle, and the gaze of the travelogue even while assuaging worries that the Spanish people are not up to date enough to win the battle (or to justify foreign intervention). If total war threatens not only the streets but also the family life of the people of Madrid, the community spirit and resiliency of the Spanish people will rise to meet that threat with equivalent modern energy.

L'espoir: Sierra de Teruel, a lesser-known film from the same period, operates with similar emphasis on the values of rural Spain in the fight for the Republic, although with less technical agility. The film, begun on location in 1938, was finished in France, after the crew fled from Barcelona in the final days before it fell to Franco. A version of André Malraux's novel *L'espoir*, adapted for the screen by none other than Max Aub, it focuses on an episode from the novel involving the bombing of one of Franco's airfields, the downing of the fighter plane, and the dramatic rescue from a mountain top of the heroic crew, and it only occasionally widens its point of view. The film, like Malraux's novel, features an international brigade of former WWI pilots who offer their services to the Republican air force.[100] Yet by condensing and intercutting the air-war episodes with scenes in local villages among the loyal Republican peasants, *L'espoir: Sierra de Teruel* devotes less attention to the international pilots than does Malraux's novel. The staged scenes about the pilots, shot with professional actors on a sound stage, often appear static, but the images of the villages and the rural people who help rescue the pilots in the final scene bustle with interest and activity. While Malraux's novel has often been criticized as simple propaganda, these scenes in the film, infused with the faces and images of Spaniards, tell a more nuanced story of the battle of Teruel and accomplish something like the kind of "personalization" that Ivens endorses. The film succeeds almost in spite of its too simple plot, multiplying and prolonging the moments where we see and judge for ourselves and calling our attention to the daily struggles of the villagers rather than to the overdetermined heroism of the international volunteers.

The screenplay opens with the pilots as they develop plans for bombing a bridge and struggle with inadequate planes and explosives. Rather than depict the Madrid or Guadalajara missions from the novel, *L'espoir* focuses on the epic battle for Teruel, which became one of the Republic's last stands, but little in the opening scene of this sometimes-amateurish film orients us to these characters and their role in the war or the strategic context of the air raid that will dominate the film's action. For example, the film opens with discussion of a dead Italian pilot, but we learn nothing more about him or why he has joined the Republican air force. In a later episode, upon being given a leadership role in the brigade, a German pilot confesses that his "father is one of the fascist leaders in [his] country," but the film never explores the implication of this genealogy. Jean-François Lyotard, in his essay *Soundproof Room: Malraux's Anti-Aesthetics*, contends that because Malraux's work focuses on the "mise-en-scène of dramatic moments . . . The realist consistency of the characters is neglected: any oddity or tic is enough to identify them." The writing takes on the quality of a montage of repeated actions rather than a developing realist narrative, in order to highlight the repeated horror of the facts.[101] Thus we can understand the absence of narrative and character development in both novel and film to be a representation of the inexorable logic of war, which reduces individuality to a "tic" and diminishes the potential for development.

Lyotard also ties Malraux's work to his notion of the *différend*, claiming that in *L'espoir*, "the scenes of actual war . . . are not battle scenes in their proper order. The elliptical turn indicates a vague *différend* from which there is no exit."[102] The battle scene as *différend*—a site of discursive incommensurateness or dispute with no end—becomes a useful way to understand not only the intercut war scenes of Malraux's *L'espoir* but, perhaps even more so, the labyrinthine texts of Aub's novel as well as the hybrid product of the two writers, *L'espoir: Sierra de Teruel*.[103] The notion of battle as *différend* connects the inexorable quality of the Civil War to the film's lack of narrative development. By denying the pilots and their missions psychological depth, narrative development, and political context, the film highlights the repeatability of events and the conflicts that underlie them.

Further, the camera work of *L'espoir: Sierra de Teruel* ultimately belies its ostensible focus on the air brigade and highlights instead the vibrant heterogeneity of the people caught behind Nationalist lines. While the scenes among the pilots contain few camera angles and generally focus on two or three figures, once the film goes into the villages, it uses a larger variety of shots and wider angles of vision. We see the streets of the village as men run down them, watch as sniper's bullets make holes in a window screen, and watch the men and women of the town create homemade explosives. The effect of this expansion of viewpoint is to disrupt the film's efforts to fuse the viewer's gaze with the perspective of the director. The moments where the film makes possible other ways of viewing—when we see the sideways smile of a peasant as the camera passes by, when we take in the extent of the poverty in the villages, when we look away from the line of wounded pilots descending the mountain top at the end of the film to marvel at, instead, the sweeping scene of care and industry—mitigate against a univocal account and a fully scripted emotional response. As the film wears on, the expanding use of the mobile camera also brings with it some of the sensibility of Ivens's efforts at personalization. The Spanish people under siege, in all their visual and discursive heterogeneity, become the real subject matter of the film and its claim on our attention.

Yet the film treads a fine line between propaganda and engagement, between its unquestioning endorsement of the heroism of the pilots and its efforts to push us toward action on behalf of the villagers. If, as Orwell warned, we must be wary of the partisanship of the cultural products of the Civil War, we must also be alert to their ability to engage us ethically and politically. Aub's *Laberinto*, Orwell's *Homage*, Ivens's *Spanish Earth*, and Malraux and Aub's *Espoir: Sierra de Teruel* all present the conflicts of the war as open-ended disputes—*différends*, we might call them, whose outcome remains in play, no matter the end of the battle or the story. The specter of total war brings the rearguard perspectives that dominate these works into constant contact with the vicissitudes of battle and forces the matter of choosing sides, even when, as Orwell makes clear, neither camp has a monopoly on good behavior and there are no undisputed heroes. Modernity shows its face again and again—the bombs that drop into the street in *Campo abierto*, and even more ominously in *The Spanish Earth*; the effort to irrigate the Fuentedueña fields in that film; even the long reconnaissance flight of the pilots in *L'espoir: Sierra de Teruel* present the war as a battle of and for modern technology. Yet the possibilities of a modernizing society raise new options for community—on the Barcelona barricades as they appear at the end of *Campo cerrado* and between the illiterate villagers and the international pilots throughout *L'espoir: Sierra de Teruel*. In skirting the scripted response of univocal propaganda, these visual and literary narratives of the Spanish Civil War present an alternative means to an "as-if" future, one where multiple perspectives, labyrinthine plots, and open-ended disputes become sources rather than impediments for a new politics. If, as Adorno puts it, artworks are a sort of "afterimage" of the empirical world, offering back to reality what it can not countenance directly, and as Elizabeth Grosz has argued, justice depends on the possibility of imagining an open future, an always deferred moment just beyond our reach,[104] then perhaps Aub's labyrinthine narratives, Orwell's ironic memoir, and even the multimedia images of such films as *The Spanish Earth* and *L'espoir: Sierra de Teruel* are the aftereffects of war that nonetheless point the way to a future imagined justice.

Arising from the Cornlands | FIVE
The Working-Class Voices of Conroy and Le Sueur

> Even as the old movement is expiring, a new one is flickering into life and a new generation, equally brash, confident or angry will announce itself.
> —Daniel Aaron, *Writers on the Left*

> We champion the cause of the weak and defenseless, we combat the greed of industrial barons who are converting American laborers into abject serfs, we decry the intolerance that endeavors to abrogate the inherent rights of free speech and assembly . . . and inscribe on our banner: 'ART FOR HUMANITY'S SAKE.'
> —Manifesto of the Rebel Poets

> The body is not a thing it is a *situation*: it is our grasp on the world and sketch of our projects.
> —Simone de Beauvoir, *The Second Sex*

Agnes Smedley begins *Daughter of Earth*, her compelling and distinguished 1929 novel of working-class life, with a disclaimer: "What I have written is not a work of beauty, created that someone may spend an hour pleasantly; not a symphony to lift up the spirit, to release it from the dreariness of reality." She dwells on the details of the life she will depict and its connection to the despair and ugliness of poverty in the United States. "I belong to those who do not die for the sake of beauty. I belong to those who die from other causes—exhausted by poverty, victims of wealth and power, fighters in a great cause. . . . For we are of the earth."[1] Her novel seems predicated on its difference from the glitter of a jazz-age memoir, from the well-orchestrated coherence of an example of literary realism, and from the aestheticism of a modernist novel. To tell the story of those who live and die simply and in dreary poverty seems permanently and inexorably divorced from concern with literary form and, in Smedley's own terms, from the idea of the beautiful. The aesthetic itself seems to be exiled from this novel of a working woman's coming of age.

Nonetheless, this passage and the entire novel attest to Smedley's concern with craft and with the challenge of structuring a text to coincide with her working-class experience. Remembering a crazy quilt her mother once made, she writes, "I shall gather up these fragments of my life and make a crazy-quilt of them. Or a mosaic of interesting pattern—unity in diversity. This will be an adventure."[2] Despite her claim to be unconcerned with aesthetics, Smedley reaches for the "mosaic" metaphor to describe the quality of her narrative and its structuring principle. If the term "interesting" here replaces "beautiful," Smedley's text nonetheless reaches toward achieving "unity in diversity," building some sort of recognizable order out of a fragmented life, without erasing its crazy-quilt pattern.

Despite her protests, I would argue, Smedley's effort to create a new narrative in order to tell the fragmented story of a life of "the earth," of characters who struggle materially and die ugly deaths and whose speech can not be made to echo the elevated language of literary fiction, has affinities with the projects of modernist writers. Smedley, like the modernists, was seeking to represent the diversity of everyday experience within the confines of a redefined narrative structure and style and to use experimental form to elaborate a realm of "as if" that gestures toward an alternative politics. This is not to recast *Daughter of Earth* as an avant-garde text; Smedley's novel does not foreground technique or experimental form as do the works of Joyce, Woolf, Faulkner, and Dos Passos. At the same time, like those authors, she remakes the novel and our expectations of it by at once refusing many of the conventions of realism and pushing it toward greater fidelity to lived experience, everyday language, and the material conditions of modernity.[3] From this extradiegetic introduction, through the novel's rambling plot (which moves from the Missouri hills, through California, to finish up in New York City), to its extended treatment of the protagonist's political education in the last chapters, *Daughter of Earth* refuses to curtail its ambition or to force it into any conventional structure.[4] Equal parts semi-autobiographical memoir, coming-of-age story, extended muckraking reportage (complete with description of conditions within brothels and prisons), socialist political treatise, and, not least, narrative fiction, *Daughter of Earth* challenges our expectations on nearly every page. It makes clear that, contrary to most accounts, literary innovation in the United States in the 1920s and 1930s sometimes emerges from an apparently antiaesthetic stance.

As I argue in this chapter, the narrative strategies that allow many of the radical writers of the 1920s and 1930s to incorporate working-class voices, rhythms, and experiences into narrative fiction also resist a dominant, unified perspective that might silence those voices. Thus the restless, shifting narrative perspective of Jack Conroy's *The Disinherited* or the floating, collective voices of a group of women in Meridel Le Sueur's *The Girl* deserve recognition not only as aesthetic responses to the conditions of modernity in the United States, particularly for working-class people in and out of employment, but also as key aspects of the ways that the texts register resistance to those conditions. As Le Sueur puts it, "I didn't want these short novels to be published unless they would serve the purpose of illuminating the struggle between the dying class of the oppressor and the rising class of the oppressed. This is the crucial axis of our time, not merely an aesthetic."[5] For writers like Le Sueur and Conroy, who were deeply committed to agitation on behalf of the working class, the struggle becomes the link between form and content, driving their often unusual narratives—which include frequent departures from conventional realism in the form of fragmentation, dispersal of narrative authority, disruption of the division between fact and fiction, and incorporation of vernacular and folkways—but also undergirding their efforts to write the lives of the downtrodden out of oblivion. Their writing insists on what I will call, following Le Sueur, a narrative practice of "contact" that makes the specific, embodied experiences of working-class life in the Depression era central to their imaginative accounts and insists on their role in building resistance into narrative textuality.

In addition, these authors expand our understanding of radical writing in the 1920s and 1930s by elaborating a crucial link between the private lives of poor people and their public identities as workers, thereby also bringing the ethical dimension of those lives to bear on matters of public politics and justice. In narratives by Le Sueur and Conroy, for example, the suffering of women in domestic abuse or a son's painful loss of his father is interlinked with the difficulties the characters face obtaining and participating in wage labor in the Depression era, highlighting the complex relationship between the private and public spheres, whose separation was fiercely defended in public discourse of the time, and also insisting on the importance of the ethical relationships of private life to any political response to the plight of workers. Further, by allowing the private or intimate realm to color the public roles of its characters, novels like *The Disinherited* and *The Girl* demonstrate how domestic concerns become crucial to the development of the "worker" characters in working-class fiction, just as they are to the middle-class heroes of drawing-room fiction.

If novels by Jane Austen, for example, employ the domestic realm to highlight the intersection between personal morality and social codes of ethical behavior, these working class narratives use the extended treatment of characters' domestic lives to foreground their complex ethical values and relationships, as well as the frequent conflict between these private values and public expectations of workers. In novels like *The Disinherited* or *The Girl* personal obligations between and among workers; ethical bonds among family, friends, and neighbors; and community relationships among groups of women highlight patterns of values that contrast sharply with the sphere of work, where competition for employment, disregard for personal circumstances or needs, and hierarchical organizational structures hold sway. By emphasizing this conflict between private and public values, the sounds, forms, and interests of working-class fiction by writers like Conroy and Le Sueur harness narrative innovation to the critique of modern American working-class life while at the same time demonstrating the role of "contact" in moving between ethical obligations in the private realm and the possibilities of a future public justice.

Smedley's image of the mosaic also helps highlight the connection between modernist forms and practices and the working-class literature that emerged in the United States in the 1920s and 1930s. While scholars have long worked to resurrect the careers of leftist writers who were silenced during the 1950s and who, even now, remain less known than they might be, only a few in modernist studies have tried to bridge the gap between working-class literature and U.S. literary modernisms. In *Mosaic Modernism: Anarchism, Pragmatism, Culture*, David Kadlec argues that many of the innovative techniques of literary modernism—for example, its use of the mosaic or collage form, its often improvisatory quality, its attempt at direct presentation of the object in poetry, or the collapse of interior and exterior perspectives in narrative—have their roots in late-nineteenth- and early-twentieth-century anarchist, pragmatist, or generally "anti-foundationalist," political cultures.[6] His argument about the political valences of modernist form, which focuses on William Carlos Williams, James Joyce, Marianne Moore, and Zora Neale Hurston, thus also helps us recognize the modernism of Smedley's mosaic structure, and the heritage held in common by both working-class and modernist writers in the United States. Rita Barnard also argues that many American novels of the 1920s and 1930s are "deeply responsive to some of the quintessential features of social modernity and to the challenges they present to conventional fictional forms."[7] By focusing attention on their choice of language, she claims, these writers made the social realities of different American communities more visible and visceral. "For many American modernists it was precisely by attending to words, by revitalizing them and by placing them in new contexts that the novel could begin to do political work." Joseph Entin argues that "for many artists, modernism was a mode of social engagement rather than evasion, an aesthetic form in which socially committed writers and photographers registered the violence of class distinctions, racial discrimination, and industrial injury." And Michael Szalay claims that "new deal modernism" often "refused evaluative criteria external to itself," becoming more performative than conventionally aesthetic.[8] Still, writers considered "proletarian"[9] or attached to Marxist organizations like the John Reed clubs, are all too often considered to be followers of a communist literary line rather than independent and innovative writers making complex use of a variety of influences. The epithets "thirties literature" and "proletarian literature" still come with the assumption that political commitment imposes "social realism" and instrumental use of narrative and eliminates experimentation in form and content.[10]

This argument derives in part from the oft-repeated comment of Philip Rahv, editor of the *Partisan Review*, who claimed in 1939, as the *Review* was evolving away from its leftist roots, that proletarian literature was "the literature of a party disguised as the literature of a class."[11] Rahv's comment oversimplifies not only his own history of connection to left literature but also the diversity and range of working-class fiction in the period, which was not all under the direct sway of Communist Party directives. Even for authors like Smedley and Le Sueur, who were lifelong members of the party, communist ideas about the form and content of proletarian literature do not limit the possibilities of a text. While certainly some writers imbibed party doctrine sufficiently to insist on an arbitrary "formula of conversion" at the end of a novel or to impose "an externally derived doctrine upon the irreducibility and complexity of lived experience,"[12] just as many did not. For women, whose experiences were often excluded from descriptions of the proletariat, or for authors in regions like the rural Midwest, whose writing addressed concerns foreign to the literary center in New York, the one-size-fits-all description of a communist-directed working-class literature is even less apt.

On the contrary, I base this chapter on the premise that working-class literature in the 1920s and 1930s was a diverse body of work that responded to the challenge of the Depression with a variety of narrative forms and purposes and that despite its sometime rejection of modernism's perceived aestheticism, was committed to a complex narrative engagement with the problematics of modernity that bears many affinities with modernisms elsewhere, especially with that of the Harlem Renaissance.[13] I look at texts by writers outside the New York nexus, especially Jack Conroy and Meridel Le Sueur, examining their efforts to create narratives of social consciousness out of the everyday lives, habits, and verbal rhythms of women and men from the American Midwest. Outside the stream of proletarian fiction dominated by the New York press, which in the 1930s often promulgated Communist Party doctrines and silenced writers on the fringe, Conroy and Le Sueur formed their own literary communities and developed independent guidelines for literary work that would "break down [their] isolation, individually and regionally," and innovate both politically and stylistically.[14] Conroy's work insists on its episodic narrative structure, which creates "*skaz*," or sketches from "overheard" stories and interrupted autobiography, and then corrals those sketches into a communal tale of political disenfranchisement and burgeoning consciousness. Its almost anarchic structure models a worker's politics that is as decentered as Conroy's influential Radical Poets group. Le Sueur's writing highlights the ethical complexity of ordinary women's lives and challenges political pieties by experimenting with collective voice and blurring the boundaries between reportage and fiction. In *The Girl*, the suffering of female bodies in hard labor, hunger, childbirth, or partner abuse generates an iterative style that rejects the authority of a presiding narrator and emphasizes the "contact" between lived, embodied female experiences and the intimate ethics of narration.

These working-class narratives thus take us beyond the conventions of either narrative realism or a modernism characterized by interiority and aestheticism in order to allow orality, folk culture, and the materiality of everyday life, especially as it is displayed through the bodies of working women and men, to emerge as the locus of a politically engaged, experimental narrative tradition. Like the narratives of the Harlem Renaissance or by the Indian women writers I explored in chapter 3, the working-class narratives in question here often challenge the distinction between private ethics and public justice, generating an oppositional politics out of the gap between the worker's reality and the priorities of dominant public culture. The innovative forms and voices of working-class fiction make narrative central to their engagement with the problems of Depression-era life, even while demonstrating the power of a decentered, anti-foundationalist model of justice and political community.

Rebel Poet: Jack Conroy's Vernacular Modernism

When it is termed "proletarian fiction," fiction by and about working-class people often conjures up images of the factory floor or the cacophony of busy urban streets. It seethes with people, is covered with dirt, and is dominated by the harsh sounds of machines. As Daniel Aaron puts it, writing of Mike Gold's classic *Jews Without Money*, the book describes an "ill smelling world . . . of flies, bedbugs, litter, of saloons, whores, gangsters, swarming immigrants, and poor Jews suffocating in their rattletrap tenements."[15] The Lower East Side of Manhattan becomes the matrix for the development of the idea of proletarian fiction. In "Towards Proletarian Art," the 1921 essay that established the terminology in the United States, Gold writes, "All I know of life I learned in the tenement . . . I am not an individual; I am all that the tenement group poured into me." The art that he envisions emerges out of these kinds of experiences, which awaken solidarity with the masses and lead toward an active (and masculinist) revolutionary posture: "The masses of America have awakened. . . . Now at last they are prepared to put forth those huge-hewn poets. . . . The method of erecting this proletarian culture must be the revolutionary method—from the deepest depths upward."[16] In *Jews Without Money* the tenement also sets the stage for the establishment of the image of the worker "knee-high in rubbish and lint," laboring in the "gloom, in the stench" of the inferno-like factory.[17] While there are proletarian novels set in rural towns, these novels arise primarily around specific, watershed events involving factory work, like the 1929 textile workers' strike in Gastonia, North Carolina, rather than out of the texture of everyday life for the rural working classes.[18] Images of urban life and factory toil dominate our ideas about the genre so much that in the 1935 classic *Some Versions of Pastoral*, William Empson begins by defining proletarian art narrowly as "the propaganda of a factory-working class which feels its interests opposed to the factory owners.'"[19]

But if we turn away from the word "proletarian," attached to "literature" by Gold and others in the 1920s, "officially sanctioned by the C[ommunist] P[arty] USA," and debated as a term ever since,[20] toward a more capacious definition of working-class writing, then the priority on the urban, factory experience, and on the surrounding tenement life, need no longer hold sway. Even Empson recognizes the importance of this revision, discarding the narrow definition of proletarian literature almost as quickly as he introduces it, explaining that "the wider sense of the term includes such folk-literature as is by the people, for the people, and about the people." This is why, for Empson, proletarian literature has some suggestion of the pastoral about it and justifies its place at the beginning of *Some Versions of Pastoral*.[21] Adopting this wider sense of working-class literature as by, for, and about working-class people thus opens up the possibility of a pastoral setting and an agricultural or rural working-class literature, in addition to that based on the factory floor.

It also makes possible more subtle approaches to proletarian literature than does its definition as "propaganda" in the interests of the workers, or "literature as a weapon in the struggle for social, political, and economic justice," as current criticism sometimes puts it.[22] While the working-class fiction in question here certainly positions itself "for" workers and wades deeply into the struggle for their rights, it does not subscribe to an established approach to the cause, an instrumental purpose, or a specific aesthetic. In 1934 Philip Rahv defended proletarian writers against the propaganda charge, saying that "propagation of ideas, moods, and points of view is inherent in the very nature of art" and that the young proletarian poets are learning how to translate politics "into human terms" and tie it to the real conditions of life.[23] Just as we saw with Spanish Civil War writing, 1930s engagement with the struggle in the United States becomes crucial to the effort at representation and to the formal innovation of the texts. The power of novels like *The Disinherited* or *The Girl* comes from the deep imbrication of politics and narration, which renders the commitment of the text integral, unavoidable, and compelling.

The binary view of class and culture, pitting the industrial worker against the bourgeoisie, that arises from the definition of proletarian fiction as propaganda in the interests of the workers is also one of the reasons working-class women's writing has so often been left out of the account. Since working women's concerns and experiences seemed not to fit into the kind of proletarian frameworks or plots proposed by Gold, they were often deemed bourgeois.[24] Paula Rabinowitz points out that "by defining the proletariat as masculine," literary radicals "replace[d] women in the drawing room." "Radical women's writings" she claims, "de-form genre." They force us not only to revise our expectations of proletarian narratives to accommodate women's experiences but also to acknowledge the nexus of experiences and commitments that combine to generate the forms of radical writing.[25]

At the same time, a more capacious definition of working-class fiction also corrects the priority on New York and Chicago that is our legacy from Gold and the *Partisan Review* of the mid-1930s. From the time of Gold's founding of the journal *The New Masses* in 1926 through the early 1930s, as the Depression took hold, tales of the difficult and impoverished lives of American workers from all parts of the country, rural and urban, emerged in large numbers.[26] Indeed, by the early 1930s, there was a positive "vogue" for writing about the plight of workers, which was being developed out of experiences in the Missouri mines and the Midwest farm country, as well as from the factory floor or tenement hallway.[27] Journals like *Rebel Poet* (1931–32) and *The Anvil* (1933–35), both predecessors of *The Partisan Review* (1934–), as well as *Midwest* (1936–37), *Blast* (1933–?), *Frontier* (1920–1933), *Midland* (1915–1933), *The Left: A Quarterly Review of Radical and Experimental Art* (1931), and the later *New Anvil* (1939–40), presented a broad vision of the possible themes, forms, and locations of American working-class fiction while also interconnecting and promoting a community of writers in the Midwest.

Jack Conroy, cofounder of *Rebel Poet* (1931–32), *The Anvil* (1933–35), and *New Anvil* (1939–40); author of the acclaimed novel *The Disinherited* (1933); and winner of a Guggenheim award in 1935, was among the most prominent and influential working-class writers in the early 1930s and a crucial member of this Midwestern community. An uneducated son of a Missouri miner, who began his literary career by taking correspondence courses, Conroy at first became a key player in the literary sphere around Gold's *New Masses* at the end of the 1920s and the lynchpin among a rising group of Midwestern writers. Encouraged in his efforts by H. L. Mencken, Mike Gold, John Dos Passos, and Pascal Covici (who was later to edit *The Grapes of Wrath*), he rose to mainstream prominence on the strength of his 1933 novel, *The Disinherited*, which sold 2,700 copies and was translated into seven languages, only to fall into obscurity by the early 1940s. As Daniel Aaron puts it, "*The Disinherited* . . . brought Conroy into the literary limelight. He did not remain in it very long."[28] Sidelined in part by the editorial policies of Rahv and others and by the unwillingness of editors to embrace the kind of eclectic writing that he championed,

Conroy represents the crucial though often ignored Midwestern nexus of American working-class writing and the distinctive multi-vocal, mosaic modernism at its core.[29]

Though he was born in 1899, most critical discussion of Conroy picks him up in the early 1930s, when his role as author or editor put his name on mastheads and title pages. Yet having escaped the mines, worked among railroad machinists at the Wabash shops, completed correspondence courses instead of high school, and attended a year at the University of Missouri, by 1921 Conroy was already writing and building his extensive network of literary contacts. His writing career began with essays in the *Railway Carmen's Journal* and poems in such regional little magazines as *Pegasus*, *Northern Light*, and the *Spider*, where he had a brief stint as an editor in 1928.[30] As he put it in a later interview, "My memories of the Thirties are embedded in the literary underworld, that of the little magazines that were not based in New York City. Before my first novel was published, I was never farther East than Detroit, though I'd seen most of the West, Northwest, Midwest and South by way of boxcar."[31] In 1928 he moved to Toledo to work in an automobile factory, where he observed the lives of the factory workers who would people the fiction he soon began to write.

By the end of the 1920s, Conroy was already demonstrating the concern for working-class lives in all their variety as well as the fine ear for speech rhythms and vernaculars that would distinguish his work. In the factories he observed the racial tension that pitted black workers against white, and in 1929 he published a poem called "Dusky Answer" that demonstrates his early interest in the speech rhythms and "sociolects" of black and white workers and inaugurates his long-term effort to integrate black claims for justice into the movement for working-class rights as well as to promote and publish black writers.[32] Early in his career as an editor Conroy devoted an entire issue of *The Rebel Poet* to black writers, with an extended editorial that demanded an end to the "horrible injustice against the negro race" and also called upon "all negro poets and writers to join their ranks with ours in indicating and welcoming the crumbling of capitalist-imperialism."[33] Langston Hughes graces the pages of *The Anvil*, and Richard Wright's first publications in a national magazine appeared later in *The New Anvil*, as did one of Margaret Walker's first short stories. In 1935, Conroy won a Guggenheim fellowship to study and write about the migration of Southern factory workers to the North, "and inasmuch as Negroes predominated in these migrations," as he later put it, the project led him to an extended focus on black life.[34] In 1938 he joined the Illinois Writers Project in Chicago, where he worked alongside Nelson Algren, Studs Terkel, and Arna Bontemps, in the same office where Katherine Dunham and Richard Wright had recently occupied desks. With Bontemps, who sat "twenty feet away," he "began to compare notes on Negro Migrations within the United States." They extended their collaboration on the WPA project "The Negro in Illinois" into an important history of black migration, *They Seek a City*, and to decades of collaboration.[35]

Back in Ohio in 1928 he was also already building the rhizome-like networks of interrelationships among radical writers whose work he would promote to the *New Masses* or in H. L. Mencken's *American Mercury* and ultimately publish in his own literary journals.[36] The writers who emerged around him in Toledo and Detroit and also in Minneapolis and Chicago shared their concern with the difficult lives of the working class; they were, on the other hand, eclectic in their politics. While many eventually affiliated with the Communist Party, they were not doctrinaire in the way that many communists would become. Some, like Joe Kalar, were following in the iconoclastic tradition of the Wobblies. Others came from the long tradition of populist anarchism in the rural Midwest that would also give rise to Meridel Le Sueur. In 1928, with the editors Lucia and Ralph Cheney, Conroy formed a worldwide organization called the Radical Poets, and began publishing its newsletters and planning its first anthology, *Unrest*. As Douglas Wixson, Conroy's biographer, makes clear, "The Rebel Poets organization represented no single political agenda, movement, or artistic credo. . . . Joining the Rebel Poets were anarchists, liberals, Communists, Christian Socialists, Wobblies, populists." They sought to build a literary journal and a radical literary movement through the loose "rhizomatous" association of this eclectic group, rather than to create a system of correspondents or experts to digest the literary material or promulgate some specific editorial line.[37]

It was this decentered, nonhierarchical kind of network that made the group effective and created it as an alternative to the organized, layered power structure of the Communist Party and its journal *The New Masses*. *Rebel Poets* published a wide range of writers from a variety of political and literary perspectives, including Louis Ginsberg (Alan Ginsberg's father), Kenneth Fearing, Sherwood Anderson, and Langston Hughes, as well as a number of lesser-known black writers of the period. Its manifesto made clear the group's openness:

> Nothing but general sympathy with our aims is required of members. Affiliated with no political party . . . we champion the cause of the weak and defenseless, we combat the greed of industrial barons who are converting American laborers into abject serfs, we decry the intolerance that endeavors to abrogate the inherent rights of free speech and assembly . . . and inscribe on our banner: 'ART FOR HUMANITY'S SAKE'[38]

Though overshadowed from the start by Mike Gold's *New Masses*, with its powerful editorial perspective and clear communist affiliation, the Rebel Poets organization and the eponymous journal that emerged out of it in 1931 captured the anarchist-pragmatist sensibility of the Midwestern radicals and set the agenda for all of Conroy's future editorial work. The Rebel Poets group, and Conroy in particular, embraced the quasi-anarchist, anti-foundationalist approach to both politics and literature that also informed Conroy's editorial decisions and his own writing.

Nonetheless, the *Rebel Poets* ultimately became caught up in the ascendency of Soviet influence in American left politics and the development of the "cultural front."[39] The drift of the journal toward party affiliation disturbed Conroy, especially because it was the result of a directive from New York. In May 1932, the New York branch of the Rebel Poets organization met to affirm Soviet principles of art and to "polemicize the [*Rebel Poets*], turn it into a keen-edged axe in the proletarian struggle," under the leadership of Philip Rahv. The New York group sought out Communist Party support for the journal and tightened editorial control of its content, narrowing its acceptance policy and angering many contributors. When Rahv and the New York group demanded overarching authority to censor publications, Conroy moved to disband the editorial board instead.[40]

In 1932 the formation of the All Soviet Writers Union seemed to open up the realm of communist literary production beyond the party faithful and the strictures of Proltkult since all Soviet writers were encouraged to join. Walt Carmon, a friend of Conroy's who was in Moscow, described the scene: "General atmosphere wonderful. Since the C-O-R-R-E-C-T boys were landed on their tails in April, all writers including non-party are working more freely and everybody happy. Object: include all writers possible, criticize 'em but show that they are ours. None of this holier than thou goes and they mean it."[41] Though by 1934 the promulgation of Soviet realism would seriously restrict writers in the USSR, the All Soviet Writers Union appeared to Conroy and his friends to be a ratification of his policy of inclusion. Conroy wrote, "The comrades have cleaned house over there with their usual thoroness [sic], and the ideas I have been trying to inculcate in *The Rebel Poet*—sniped at both from the Left and the Right—will be dominant in radical literature from now on."[42] With this ideal in mind, and as a sort of vindication after the failure of *Rebel Poets* at the hands of the Rahv circle, he began publishing a new journal, *The Anvil*. As he later said, "The motto of the Anvil was, 'we prefer crude vigor to polished banality' . . . it published no criticism, thus keeping free from the ideological disputes, then raging among the New York Intelligentsia, particularly those who were looking at the world with Marx colored glasses."[43] In the creation of *The Anvil*, Conroy made clear the journal's eclectic, pragmatic intent: to "publish stories about American men and women who have been beaten downward or shaped upward on the powerful anvil of life in the U.S. today."[44]

The Anvil was soon to become one of the most significant little magazines of the left in the period, and it stayed true to its antifoundationalist, anarchist sensibilities and the decentered, rhizomatic structure of the Rebel Poets organization. It circulated widely in the United States and abroad, and not only in communist circles; by 1935, when it was swallowed up by the new *Partisan Review*, it boasted a print run of 5,000. Langston Hughes, Meridel Le Sueur, James Farrell, Michael Gold, Nelson Algren, and William Carlos Williams were among its contributors—writers who did not all share a political or literary perspective. For Farrell, Caldwell, Wright, and Algren, among less celebrated other writers, Conroy's work at *The Anvil* provided mentoring, encouragement, and publication at the beginning of a career or when other avenues were closed.[45] Most important, *The Anvil* placed no restrictions on its writers and their politics, maintained its editorial independence, and steered clear of theoretical debates by publishing only poetry and fiction, not "dialectical gymnastics."[46]

Writing in *The Anvil* often links the domestic and working lives of the poor. Conroy championed a lean, vernacular style that often uses the marks of orality to experiment with the possibilities of working-class narration and to elicit ethical response or insight from small moments of interpersonal connection or "contact"—experiences of confluence or synergy between people and their bodily or material circumstances that highlight their ethicopolitical situation. The stories present what Derek Attridge terms "a singular staging of otherness," which calls readers "not only to appropriate and interpret the work . . . but also to register its resistance and irreducibility."[47] The ethical power of a novel arises from the way that it refuses being made to function as a pure instrument of a moral message and—through its resistance to the transparency of language or the appearance of verisimilitude—challenges its readers' "preferences and preconceptions."[48] In other words, writing in *The Anvil* makes ethical claims on its readers by way of its confrontation with the received notions of proletarian fiction and its frequent refusal of smooth, univocal narration. The stories neither domesticate nor sensationalize the difficult situations they record nor smooth over the textual disruptions they present.

Though wide-ranging in style, the stories in *The Anvil* thus create their ethical challenge on the level of the text by employing narrative strategies that defamiliarize, break the expectation of a consensus point of view, or give voice to divergent sensibilities. They are not radically experimental in the conventional terms of modernism— they do not employ stream of consciousness, unreliable points of view, or fragmented chronologies. Yet their incorporation of intensely local perspectives, dialects, and slang; their adoption of subjective, involved, and sometimes multiple points of view; their incorporation of folklore and folkways; and their magnification of the narrative disruptions as occasioned by working-class life and speech all combine to challenge the expectations of consensus-based realism and its representation of social conditions in the United States. They establish an ethics of dissensus—or refusal of the dominant consensus—that revolves around a decentered, anti-foundationalist narrative authority and that disrupts dominant models of working-class life on both left and right.[49] In this sense they share much with Harlem Renaissance texts, which mount a broad critique of the expectations of literary realism by emphasizing folkways, oral cultures, and the process by which cultural and "linguistic outsiders" can disrupt social and narrative conventions.[50] Like those texts, I would argue, these stories should be termed "modernist" because they are examples of "vigorous and persistent attempts to multiply and disturb modes of representation," in relation to the ethical lives of working-class people and their material situations under the economic and social conditions of late modernity. Their experimentation with narrative voice and perspective works to challenge received ideas of the public and private lives of workers in the Depression-era United States even as it recenters our notion of modernism around a literary and political nexus.[51]

Several stories collected by Conroy and Curt Johnson in the *Anvil* anthology, *Writers in Revolt*, exemplify the way that this vernacular modernism engages the reader with the ethical singularity of workers' lives. Nelson Algren's short story "Within the City" is a finely crafted, first-person response to the sight of a "mulatto girl" dancing in a "dime burlesque" on State Street in Chicago. The story, much like Claude McKay's celebrated poem "The Harlem Dancer," attempts to bridge the gap between the solitary girl and the sympathetic viewer, who goes "each day" to watch but must be distinguished from the other "old men who lean forward in their seats": "This is a vast and terrible city, with small lights burning all in a row. Within their gleam the ragged men wait, the men from the farms that are mortgaged now and the men from the mines that long since closed down. The men wait in a row beneath the lamps, and the mulatto girl sways slowly." As the story progresses we move outward to imagine that the girl lives in one of the many rooms on State Street, "three flights up and two doors to the rear," without running water. "She walks up slowly, her hands on her hips, counting the steps as she walks. I think that when she reaches the top she pauses and thinks, I am alone in this city now, and all about me are the alone men." In emphasizing the aloneness of this woman and the other men, the narrator seems also to underscore his own isolation even as the effort of narration takes him beyond his own experience into hers. Thus, the narrative enacts an effort toward ethical encounter and recognition. The story uses the connective power of narrative to remedy the objectification of the mulatto dancer and to pierce the quiet space surrounding her. By the end of the story, Algren tells us, he "walked with the mulatto girl" and learned her history, thus completing the trajectory of the story from its solitary first line ("Everyday I go down to the dime burlesque") to its final culmination in political community ("one day . . . all the daughters of the poor will rise"). In four paragraphs, Algren's story moves from the isolation and quiet of the unknown and the unheard to the merging of voices in a political community by way of this encounter between the girl and the narrator. The narrator's leap into the life of the mulatto dancer and into an imagined account of her world of poverty and isolation, not unlike Woolf's attempts to inhabit the lives of others, creates an "as if" narrative with direct political consequences—a potential reality where political community and revolt seem not the possible result of a chance encounter in a bar but its inevitable future.[52]

Erskine Caldwell's "Daughter," cast in a third-person, omniscient voice and dominated by a melodramatic plot, appears more traditionally realistic yet ultimately revolves around a similar moment of "contact." The main action of the plot—a poor black sharecropper's shooting of his eight-year-old daughter—takes place before the story begins; the narrative focuses on the man's morning in jail and on the scene around him as the town learns the news and congregates there. Like many of Caldwell's heroes, the sharecropper, Jim, seems of limited intelligence and ability to communicate.[53] Urged by the townsmen to claim his daughter's shooting death was an accident, Jim clarifies: "'Was it an accident?' 'No,' Jim said, his fingers twisting the bars. 'I picked up the shotgun and done it.' . . . 'Daughter said she was hungry and I just couldn't stand it no longer. I just couldn't stand to hear her say it.'" This matter-of-fact statement—that Jim shot his daughter in the middle of the night because she had said that she was hungry once too often—is repeated several times in the next pages, while the townsmen pepper Jim with questions about why he didn't ask for help and comments like, "'It don't look right to kill a little girl like her.'" But the cause of the daughter's hunger becomes apparent: despite having farmed successfully for the year, Jim lost all of his shares to his landlord as payment for a mule that died, and was left with nothing with which to feed his family. Hearing this, the townspeople undergo a transformation; cries about Jim's poor treatment of his daughter become cries that the landlord acted unfairly. In the end, the crowd rallies to Jim's defense, pries the bars open, and releases him while the sheriff simply walks away. The gradual revelation of the story is the willingness of the town to process its own sort of justice, and to forgive, if not approve, Jim's killing of his daughter.[54]

The process of the narrative leads us to revaluate not only Jim's seeming stupidity but also his agency. Victimized by the sharecropping system and a ruthless landlord, the story suggests, the tenant farmer cannot be held accountable for the suffering that he causes. The narrative does not aspire to universal ethical principles or endorse the action of its protagonist. Rather, it suggests that in reaching common cause as they release Jim, the townspeople have developed an ethical understanding directly out of their shared experience that needs no abstract, principled explanation. It is clear that the landlord is at fault in this crime and that the official judicial perspective, which called on the sheriff to hold Jim, is inadequate to the complexity of justice and their everyday lives. By focusing on the speech of the men who question Jim and banter among themselves, the story creates an ethical community with its own categories of understanding, which develops in the narration into a direct challenge to conventional notions of political justice. In other words, by recording Jim's claim to ethical integrity and the developing consensus of the crowd, Caldwell's narrative bridges the gap between ethics and the political dimensions of these sharecroppers' lives. The use of the vernacular and the emphasis on Jim's location and working conditions as key to his predicament are not merely elements of local color but rather part and parcel of the narrative's effort to dislodge the universal-consensus point of view and to insist that we acknowledge the specific ethical and political challenge of the lives of the rural poor.

These two stories, and others like them that were published in the *Anvil* and other small Midwestern magazines, can also be discussed in terms of their development of an American proletarian version of the Russian genre of *skaz*, the "sketch." As it was developed by Soviet writers and critics after the revolution and codified by the formalist group of critics, the *skaz* form tends to minimize plot and to focus instead on narrative discourse, especially as it incorporates oral or folkloric forms. As Wixson points out, it was a form well suited to unschooled writers, who might incorporate their voice and experiences directly into the text.[55] And yet it is also clear that some of the *Anvil* writers took up this form in great seriousness, and in all its complexity, pushing it towards its implications for proletarian politics. As writer Joe Kalar put it in a letter to Conroy, "I had no conception of the potentiality of the sketch" until he began to use it in his stories about Minnesota miners and paper-mill workers.[56] *Skaz* need not be limited to the short sketch but could be incorporated as a segment of a longer work or mined for its connection to folk traditions and the vernacular. In the work of many of the *Anvil* writers, *skaz* provides an essential building block of a decentered, vernacular working-class modernism.

According to Eichenbaum, whose classic discussion of Gogol's "The Overcoat" codifies the term, the text that has elements of *skaz* will use a personal tone to develop an extended narrative out of an anecdote or series of anecdotes. It relies on the markers of orality, repeated words, particular idiomatic expressions, puns or metaphors, and "the actual elements of speech and verbalized emotions," to turn the series of anecdotes into a complex tale that often begs to be read aloud.[57] The power of this form for the *Anvil* writers came in its ability not only to capture the experiences and ethical understandings of working-class people but also to present it in their own voices and in a way that might mimic the power of conversation or public speech. The goal of the Rebel Poets had been to create a decentered, antifoundationalist community of radical writers around the world; *The*

Anvil continued this work in part by way of *skaz*—the promotion of a literary style that captured and reproduced the scene of meeting or community in all its vocal variety. Further, although *skaz* became an official component of approved Soviet literary style, the *Anvil* stories demonstrate its importance to the development of a proletarian political culture, even beyond Communist Party orthodoxy, in the United States.

Skaz is also important because it highlights the potential polyvocality of narration and encourages the emergence of multiple discursive positions within a single text and foregrounds their ethical and political claims. Mikhail Bakhtin, in *Problems of Dostoevsky's Poetics*, argues that this aspect of the *skaz* places it in the center of the development of the post-Dostoevskyian novel and its ethical engagement with otherness. As he puts it, Eichenbaum's analysis of *skaz* "completely fails to take into account the fact that in the majority of cases *skaz* is above all an orientation toward *someone else's speech*, and only then, as a consequence, toward oral speech." That is, the speech represented is often not the author's—it belongs to a storyteller-narrator or a character within the text and often represents a "low" or nonliterary perspective. "In most cases *skaz* is introduced precisely for the sake of *someone else's voice*, a voice socially distinct, carrying with it precisely those points of view and evaluations necessary to the author. What is introduced here, in fact, is a storyteller. . . . he belongs in most cases to the lower social strata, to the common people . . . and he brings with him oral speech."[58] Thus when *skaz* appears in the *Anvil* stories it carries a particular openness of form that disperses narrative authority among a multiplicity of voices and perspectives while placing us in contact with their material circumstances. The oral qualities of the texts become not just evidence that their authors were untutored or markers of their folkloric origins but ways in which the diverse perspectives, languages and ethical concerns of U.S. workers disrupt and reorient any narrative tendencies toward closure and generate a new version of U.S. working-class modernism.

The Disinherited

Conroy's own writing from the period, and in particular his celebrated novel *The Disinherited*, provides an example of the way that innovative use of *skaz*, polyvocality, and the vernacular reorient narrative in a constant movement toward "*someone else's voice*" and its demands for justice. Conroy's refusal to contain the novel within an autobiographical frame dominated by a unified perspective acknowledges both the impossibility of fully accounting for oneself to others in narrative and the vernacular power of a decentered community of workers within the specific political context of the 1930s. Though it has often been derided by critics, the episodic and multivoiced quality of *The Disinherited* links Conroy not only with this community of workers but also to the modernisms of Harlem Renaissance writers like Zora Neale Hurston and the more formally experimental work of Hart Crane. *The Disinherited* works to disrupt the sentimental, consensus view of the poor by asking readers to recognize the ethical singularity of the lives, voices, and situations of its working-class figures, and their concomitant claims for political justice, while creating a modernist narrative whose form and language puts us in contact with those claims.

On the one hand, growing up in fits and starts as Conroy was editing *The Anvil* and searching for ever-elusive steady employment, *The Disinherited* has a strong autobiographical component. It begins by chronicling the coming of age of a boy who, like Conroy himself, lives the hard life of a miner's son and then leaves town to make his fortune in a series of towns and factories. (Here it bears some resemblance to the almost picaresque journey of Munoo in Anand's *Coolie*, and to the downward spiral of Munoo's fortunes as he moves from job to job.) Readers of Conroy's early sketches for the book, including H. L. Mencken, one of Conroy's mentors, urged Conroy to make the book more coherent and cohesive as an autobiography.[59] Others, including the editor at his eventual publisher, Covici-Friede, insisted that the fragmented quality of the narrative be smoothed over and the markers of orality toned down—in other words, that it be transformed into a more conventional novel.[60] Yet in the final published version Conroy seems to have followed this advice only so far.[61] The episodic, incoherent quality of *The Disinherited* may be seen in part as a refusal of the closure customary to a more traditional autobiographical novel and an acknowledgment that what Adriana Caverero calls the "narratable self" is always enmeshed in relation, always addressing its narration to an interlocutor and listening to other voices.[62] Much like the Indian novels of the zenana that I have discussed in chapter 3, Conroy's novel seems to posit a multiple protagonist without succumbing to the reductive impulse to speak for a class in a single voice. *The Disinherited* is an hybrid novel that exhibits its generic idiosyncrasies at every turn, refusing to relinquish its multiple voices and mosaic structure. Whenever it looks to be assimilable into a particular recognizable narrative mode, it resists, turns another way, and forces us to reassess. Beginning like an autobiographical coming-of-age story, it proceeds into an adventure tale about a couple of young workingmen making their way in the world, and finishes as reportage about the consequences of the economic collapse and the rise of worker consciousness. All along it includes songs, poems, and overheard stories; merges local vernacular into the presiding narration; and at times gives over whole sections to the voice of a "comrade" back from an adventure or come down on his luck. It is a compendium of voices and tales, knit together as a series of sketches, and it insists on polyvocality, the vernacular, folkways, and diversity of perspective.

The novel revels in its display of voices, recording scribbles on boxcars, songs sung on the picket line, and travelers' tales. For example, when the protagonist, Larry, begins work as a boxcar repairman at the Wabash Shops, he collects the writings he discovers inside the cars. The narrative records the whole range of these writings, from notices about houses of prostitution (complete with phone numbers) to overused limericks to the "tags" of traveling hoboes "New York bound."[63] Sometimes the voices of the cars come from live men caught traveling inside, like a bum rescued from a freezer car, who shouts, "Holy Jesus! Holy Jesus!" over and over, his voice gradually gaining power as he thaws. For a moment this hobo's voice and his tale of survival inside the freezer take over the narrative, ending with his proclamation that he is now "hungry enough to eat a dead skunk, tail and all" (109). In a sense, the narrative is lent to this half-frozen bum for the duration of the episode—he becomes Bakhtin's storyteller, the other whose voice becomes the purpose of the narrative and a marker of its ethical orientation. Then, just as quickly, he is out of the book, sent off down the road with a gift of fifty cents for some supper. On the next page we hear the voice of the shop foreman, exhorting the men to work harder: "humpty diddy, and do your jawin' of a night" (110). Each episode in the novel carries its own characters, rhythms, and vernaculars, creating an almost "ethnographic" quality, yet the narrative rolls onward like a snowball, gathering more and more voices as it goes.[64]

This polyvocal narrative based on a collection of vernaculars helps generate the novel's anti-foundationalist politics and enables it to escape the didacticism that mars some of the proletarian fiction of the time. As Matthew Hart has claimed, "the vernacular . . . has a politically *representative* function in that it stands in for the otherwise unspeakable reality of social exclusion."[65] The complex community of voices in the narrative pushes us beyond any simple version of worker solidarity and toward a recognition of the diversity of backgrounds, languages, and interests that drive a political movement based in workers' experiences. Rather than succumb to the typical proletarian plot, where the path to class solidarity comes from the growing coincidence of the hero's interests with his fellows' or the evolution of a political vocation, this novel develops by speaking out in many ways at once. In the scene at the Wabash Shops, for example, immediately after the frozen bum's story, the men learn that a strike has been called. Once again the novel expands its collection of vernaculars, quoting strikers and scabs alike and recording their slang.[66] As the grievance committee chairman puts it, "If we took the ten per cent cut, next time it'd be twenty. So tomorrow we pull the pin" (110). The management advertises immediately for new workers, and the striking men, including Larry, take shifts policing the yards to keep out the scabs. New voices surface in the narration, representing the many characters drifting through the novel in search of work. A farmer boy is accosted and replies when questioned, "Ya dang right I come t'git a job in them shops. I seen the ads and the proposition looks good t'me. Criminentlies, I'm tard o' ol' farm work" (113). With a word from one of Larry's friends he is told to "jis ankle back the way you come" and, demoralized, goes on his way. In a sign that the moment has become more ominous, another bum who wanders by never gets to tell his tales and is interrogated and sent on his way. In the short period of the strike, the men become intent on defining the boundaries of their community in order to preserve their jobs, and the collection of narrative voices of the previous pages, it seems, becomes a means of documenting and containing the threat from outside.

At the same time, by listening to the farmer boy's voice; recording its rhythms, slangs, and habits; and responding in kind, the striking workers also expand their community and its potential power. On one level the novel seems to set the vernacular world against the educated bosses; the advertisement for scab labor, inserted almost as a separate document within the narration, appears in standard, though abbreviated, English while the represented speech of the strikers does not. Yet this is too simple. Attention is often called to the fact that Larry speaks in "big words like [he] had an education" (143), and at times he is given to musings worthy of a poet. When attributed specifically to Larry, the narration also sticks primarily to standard written English and the conventions of prose fiction; the many explicit signs of orality emerge primarily among other characters and voices. Yet there is no question that Larry stands with the strikers. He may be educated and a poet, but, the book makes clear, he is a rebel poet. The community of workers defines itself here not simply by the use of slang or vernacular as opposed to dominant discourse but as a question of linguistic inclusivity and polyvocality. The workers in *The Disinherited*, and the narrative that takes up their cause, accommodate the variety of tones and slangs belonging to the bum, the farmer boy, and men on the street. The novel resists the monologic language of the bosses by way of its insistence on this vernacular variety.

The strike becomes one of the organizing principles of the novel, trying the patience of the workers even as it tests the capacity of this open narrative style. As it drags on, scabs become long-term members of the community, and the distinctions among local residents are difficult to maintain. Some, like Larry's brother-in-law, Rollie, insist on dividing scabs from strikers absolutely, even to the point of insisting that his children not talk to the scab children who live next door, and this dooms him to disaster. Others in town, like the butcher, the teacher, and, eventually, Larry, must accept the permanent presence of the strikebreakers.

The narrative threatens to fall apart while describing Rollie's obsession with the scabs, as though the vexing problem of the divided community of workers were impossible to narrate. It veers into a second-person aside about the rats that infiltrated the town of Hamelin in the story of the Pied Piper. Attributable to no one, this interpolation is an outbreak of *skaz* in the middle of another episode, as though we are overhearing a random character (or perhaps the narrator) interrupting the story to add an instructive example. "You remember how the rats inundated Hamelin," it begins, creating an analogy with the entrance of the scab workers into town. Descending deeper into the example, it draws a nightmarelike scene in which rats appear like "squirming maggots" their "scratching, scurrying claws" everywhere (118). The second-person perspective places us there: "rising asweat with terror, you felt hairy bodies writhing under your bare feet. Close your eyes to blot them out . . . go where you would—there was no escape and they closed you in on every hand" (118–19). But where do we enter this nightmare town? How can we respond to the command to "close [our] eyes to blot them out"? What happens when we drop back into the present of narration and to the workers as they try to make sense of a dying strike? Through the structure of this aside, the reader is forced to enter an almost surreal dialogue with the text, one that threatens to upset further the already disrupted texture of the narrative. This overtly dialogic and disruptive moment endangers the tenuous unity of this immensely heteroglossic narrative and the inclusive politics it promulgates.

This episode clearly participates in what Joseph Entin has recently termed "sensational modernism," a practice among leftist writers of the period who employ "striking images of pain, prejudice, crime and violence to create avant-garde aesthetics of astonishment." Rather than realistically represent the conditions of poverty, risking a sentimental or romanticized response, writers of sensational modernism confront readers with the grotesque or the shocking, often presented in experimental prose. They "deploy arresting images of disfigured bodies to depict the poor and dispossessed in ways that challenge the sense of moral authority and cultural control" typically granted the middle and upper classes.[67] Seen in this light, this nightmare scene takes on even more power; it shocks us into acknowledging the horror of the failed strike and the resulting poverty and disillusionment, as well as the fiercely contested right to call oneself a worker. This nightmarish passage thus accomplishes what the rest of the episode cannot—it brings readers into direct contact with the strikers and insists on their collaboration. The reader becomes the confidante of the speaker, someone who knows that no scab is good, no matter how long he remains in town, and, ultimately, someone who knows that in the nightmare world of the prolonged strike, the "rats" are there to stay. The second-person perspective of this passage insists that we acknowledge our connection to the terror of this experience, no matter where we stand on the matter of the strike itself. In Derek Attridge's terms, we are forced not only to acknowledge the radical singularity of the striker and the terror of his ultimate powerlessness but also to come into contact with the materiality of its consequences. We are trapped, like Larry and Rollie, in a situation from which "there [is] no escape and they close ... in on you on every hand" (119). We cannot close our ears to the voices of this dream or the nightmarish conditions of workers' lives and still continue to read the book.

The poetic quality of this passage also marks its ability to counter a potentially sentimental, realist reading of this scene. On its surface, the narrative seems to present Rollie as a failure, a character later shot while chasing the scab who took his job. But the speaker of this aside, in abandoning realism, releases himself from this rigid way of thinking as well as from the unified consensus of the world of the strikers. The poetic language introduces another sensibility into the narration, one almost as shocking as the references to rats and maggots, and which pushes the narrative beyond the conventional. Like the Russian *skaz* discussed by Bakhtin, this interpolated passage marks a shift in orientation within the narrative toward *someone else's speech* and, by virtue of that, toward someone else's perspective, which transforms Rollie's obsession with the scabs into a nightmare/fantasy that is larger than life, dangerous, and, ultimately, absurd. This interpolated passage thus marks the impossibility of reading Rollie's obsession in realistic terms or judging the scabs according to his logic. The narrative cannot return to Rollie's rigid either/or ethics or a politics that does not recognize the harsh choices faced by all the workers, strikers and scabs alike. The speaker of this passage, then, is like Larry, a rebel poet, using poetic language to interrupt the consensus point of view, to insist on the absurdity of the choices these cornered workers must face, and to force us to recognize the injustice of their entrapment. At this moment Conroy generates modernist narrative out of the confluence of antirealism and ethical recognition, and he positions this narrative as the avant-garde of a movement toward workers' rights.

Toward the end of the book, another parenthetical episode allows the narrative's many voices to speak back to the consensus of opinion around it and to the accepted perception of "reality." Larry and his friends have found hard and dirty work paving a new highway near his hometown of Monkey's Nest, Missouri. They are desperate for the employment after a long, lean winter, but the job of laying rows of bricks and pouring hot asphalt in the height of summer is brutal. As Larry puts it, in his more sophisticated narrative voice, "To sit in the shade for a minute would have been a glorious boon. At the ends of our rows we straightened as quickly as we could to ease the sharp pain in our spines" (285). One businessman standing in the street wonders how the men can stand it, when "'I'm all a-lather jist settin' under the 'lectric fan.'" His companion replies in a similar colloquial tone, "'Aw, they're *used* to it! It don't hurt *them* like it would you or me. That kind of work is good for a man if you're *used* to it'" (286).

This comment, from one of the many vernacular voices that populate this text, is given no summary power or special consideration. Its colloquial rhythm is not much different from many of the workers' statements captured in the novel, though it is of a noticeably different register from Larry's narrating voice. Yet the import of the speech is to distinguish the businessman from the street pavers, to delimit the group of men for whom hard manual labor is an unfair burden and to define another class of men for whom such work is a benefit. The purpose of this kind of delimiting of classes of men, in this instance, is to absolve the businessman from responsibility for the workers. If he can imagine that they are so supremely "other" that they not only do not suffer from the heat or the hard work but actually benefit from it, then he need not involve himself in caring for or about them.

Defining workers in this way was not uncommon in the period; many of the worker-writers of the late 1920s and 1930s come to their vocation in part to combat such easy distancing of working men and women from "mainstream" America. It is therefore ironic that the sophisticated voice in this episode belongs to the working man. But what is most unusual here is not the comment but the response—as in the Hamelin episode, the text almost rips open, allowing Larry's (and Conroy's) anger at this "othering" to tear through its surface in a parenthetical interpolation: "('I'd like to see *you* stooping over, red in the face, puffing like a steamboat, your belly folding into huge hairy ridges, bursting the seams in the seat of your pants!' I thought savagely)" (286). The violence of this response bespeaks a commonality between classes of men that the businessman cannot possibly imagine. That is, Larry's anger is the counterpart of the businessman's derision, and his comment reflects the same distancing impulse. He pokes fun at the businessman, imagining him incapable of the work, unable to bear the heat, and too fat to lean into the job. He may reject the idea that heavy labor in the scorching sun is good for one class of men and not another, but he accepts the claims that these men are so unlike each other as to leave no possibility of mutual understanding. The moment is a refusal of ethical understanding; there can be no being-toward-an-other who is represented as a brute or faced with savagery. This is almost the obverse of the ethical sensibility of Bakha in Anand's *Untouchable*, who cannot comprehend why his caste status should require him to abandon a hurt child. If Bakha comes to understand his commonality with those of higher status through recognition of his ethical responsibility toward the child, Larry experiences it through what seems to be a repudiation of his ethical sensibility.

Yet this passage appears just before the often-quoted moment in the narrative when Larry throws in his lot with the disinherited once and for all and accepts the challenge to organize his fellows. He says,

> I no longer felt shame at being seen at such work as I would have once, and I knew that the only way for me to rise to something approximating the grandiose ambitions of my youth would be to ride with my class, with the disinherited: the bricklayers, the flivver tramps, boomers, and outcasts pounding their ears in flophouses.

> Every gibe at any of the paving gang, every covert or open sneer by prosperous looking bystanders infuriated me but did not abash me.
>
> (286)

Daniel Aaron describes this moment as a weakness in the narrative; the slow awakening to class consciousness on the part of the hero "was already hardening into a stereotype" of the proletarian novel in the 1930s.[68] Yet I would argue that this scene, with its rent narrative texture and its savage anger, is anything but pat. The necessity of self-definition in the face of extreme othering, combined with Larry's sense of angry resignation, make this a deeply compelling moment. Further, the statement of purpose that might, in some contexts, seem maudlin or trite represents a step past the reciprocal hatred of the parenthetical comment and a new recognition of ethical obligation. While Larry continues to feel "infuriated" by the jeers of bystanders, he directs his attention to developing the community of his fellows rather than widening the rift with those who deride him. His ethical step here is to move from mockery and hatred toward commonality and political purpose. The hole in the narrative occasioned by his savage outburst represents Larry's shift from a questionable ethics of mutual derision and distrust to a nascent politics of community and class solidarity.

Thus the unusual narrative structure of the novel, characterized by a compendium of folk voices, emphasis on the *skaz* form, use of textual disruption, and incorporation of orality, helps move it past struggle with the ethics of a specific worker identity toward the effort to build an open, empowering class politics. The novel rejects the desire, represented by the middle-class man in the street, to set the workers in their places and to circumscribe their difficulties, even as it sets aside the workers' impulses to close their borders against hostile outsiders.

A late episode in the novel makes this anti-exclusionary, anti-foundationalist position even clearer by raising the situation of black workers, who were often the target of anger on the part of the unemployed in the period and who are often out of sight in white proletarian fiction of the early 1930s. In the paving episode, blacks and whites both work on the highway, but not together. The water boy keeps separate cups for whites and blacks; one worker is overheard saying, "'Damned if *I'd* drink after one of the black baboons'" (292). Larry, who insists on drinking from whichever cup comes his way, resigns himself to the racism around him and narrates his admiration for "Steamboat" Mose, a "huge, raw-boned Negro of sixty," the pace setter for the crew, and a bricklayer of prodigious ability, "who could still make the young bucks beg for mercy" (290). When Mose collapses one afternoon, strikes his head on a curb and is unable to rise, the foreman is ready to leave him for dead. "Well, it was only an old nigger played out. That was the way it appeared to the boss and many of the others" (293). Appalled, Larry insists on calling a doctor and refuses to work until one is brought. Others take up the call, and an impromptu strike forces the foreman to bring in a doctor. This scene echoes the railroad strike earlier in the novel but from a changed perspective; instead of a battle against a class-defined other or an effort to divide the righteous workers from the scabs, this strike arises from solidarity with an outsider. The novel makes no sentimental claims to having reversed the workers' racism, but Larry no longer has to choose between class loyalty and interracial solidarity. As in his work later in the decade, when he would write about the Great Migration in collaboration with Arna Bontemps, Conroy creates an unusually multiracial picture of the working world and elaborates a model of class solidarity across racial lines that was prescient for his time.[69]

Conroy's work, which was marginalized in the late 1920s by the dominance of the Communist Party and was later eclipsed by the ascendancy of Philip Rahv's *Partisan Review*, exemplifies an important modernist strain of radical writing. In the work he championed among the Radical Poets, in his own writing, and in the work of many of the writers he nurtured, Conroy placed priority on narrative strategies that incorporate working-class voices, rhythms, and experiences into fiction, without acceding to a dominant, unified perspective or politics. At the same time, he built a disseminated, multifaceted, and often anarchic workers' politics of solidarity and resistance that was both the source of and the context for the narrative innovations he championed. Conroy commented that "our task is to vivify the daily struggles, the aspirations, triumphs, despairs of the future masters of life—the workers."[70] By developing texts that challenged the sentimental representation of the poor and foregrounded the aesthetic dimension of the conditions of modernity for workers in the United States, Conroy, rebel poet, editor, and activist, not only vivified the proletarian struggle but also used it to animate a version of narrative modernism committed to the radical demands of working-class justice.

Writing on the Breadline: Meridel Le Sueur's World of Work

If *The Disinherited* brought together a compendium of (mostly male) voices, Meridel Le Sueur's most celebrated essay "Women on the Breadlines" begins with women together: "I am sitting in the city free employment bureau. It's the women's section. We have been sitting here now for four hours. We sit here everyday, waiting for a job. There are no jobs."[71] The narrator of the essay, alone at first, merges quickly into the "we" that dominates the rest of the text. The short declarative sentences emphasize the text's iterative movement; the statement "we sit here everyday" is repeated throughout the essay. The ability to sit calmly defines the women in the essay, who wait, endlessly, for jobs that don't come, and the "everyday" here becomes not only a marker of stalled temporality but also a sign of the essay's concern with the ordinary. The essay seems purposefully not to build toward anything or to move beyond the mundane, and it declines to grant special significance to the anecdotes it offers. Le Sueur asks us to recognize that understanding the experience of poor women on a breadline in 1932 means attending to the unremarkable, repeated events and unceasing labor of women's daily lives. "It is appalling to think that these women sitting so listless in the room may work as hard as it is possible for a human being to work, may labor night and day. . . . The endless labor, the bending back, the water-soaked hands. . . . It is not the suffering of birth, death, love that the young reject, but the suffering of endless labor without a dream."[72] In this essay, the repeated motion of endless labor casts up a myriad of bent backs and ruined hands that stand metonymically for the working women of the American Midwest.

Like many other contributors to *The Anvil* and *The New Masses*, where "Women on the Breadlines" first appeared, Le Sueur seeks to shift attention to the material reality of the world of work and uses her narratives to engage her readers with workers' lives, both public and private. Like Jack Conroy, who was her friend and colleague, Le Sueur was a lifelong Midwesterner; she was a member of the *Anvil* circle of writers and the editor of a short-lived journal called *Midwest*. However, Le Sueur's focus on the bodily experiences of women working at both domestic and wage labor brings a set of concerns to the fore that are not often highlighted in proletarian fiction as conceived by those like Mike Gold or even Conroy.[73] Like Agnes Smedley and Tillie Olsen, Le Sueur inserts the travails of the farmer's daughters and rural wives into proletarian fiction and develops a progressive regionalism that focuses on the unacknowledged power of Midwestern women. She insists that a materialist understanding of the working class recognize the everyday suffering of the woman who performs labor. This is labor that is largely unseen and is rarely the subject of a mass movement—the woman who washes the streetcars overnight or pours coffee for striking workers or prostitutes herself in order to live. Countering the sentimental depiction of woman as long-suffering mother, which is a common trope in much male-authored proletarian fiction, the bodily experience of women in relation to the land and their suffering in hunger, domestic abuse, pregnancy, childbirth, and abortion become central to Le Sueur's depiction of the Midwestern world of work, both rural and urban, and to the structure of narratives like *I Hear Men Talking* and *The Girl*. Further, by focusing on the status of women's bodies under conditions of modernity, Le Sueur illuminates the role of what Foucault calls biopolitics—the attempt to rationalize and contain "the phenomena characteristic of a set of living beings forming a population: health, hygiene, birthrate, life expectancy, race"—in the oppression and regulation of working people during the Depression.[74] Foucault's concept helps us move from the ethical notion of embodiment or of "lived embodied experience" that we have seen particularly in the work of other women writers, such as Woolf and Rhys, to an understanding of how the bodily experience of the world comes into contact (and often conflict) with state regulation of groups by way of their bodies. Further, Le Sueur's use of the embodied experiences of working-class women to foreground their intimate ethical communities and to resist this regulation shows how the ethical and political merge in her narratives. The sheer physicality of Le Sueur's writing—the abundance of body parts, the swirl of female desire, the representation of hunger, childbirth, and death—not only brings the embodied experiences of working women to the center of modernist narrative but also uses them to highlight the ways that workers' bodies are crucial both to their constraint in the United States during the Depression era and to their efforts at liberation.

Le Sueur's mature writing and her commitment to a progressive Midwestern regionalism grows out of a lifetime of involvement with radical politics and the reporting she undertook throughout the 1930s and beyond. Born in 1900 to a family of active social reformers whose homes were "meeting places for Wobblies, anarchists, socialists, and union organizers,"[75] she first attempted an acting career, living in an anarchist commune with Alexander Berkman and Emma Goldman in New York City and later moving to Hollywood. She eked out a living through the late 1910s and 1920s while beginning to contribute occasional pieces to left-leaning publications. Her writing from the 1920s often focuses on young girls struggling for autonomy; the Persephone figure appears as a ravished and manipulated girl who must struggle to emerge from a period of darkness. Yet by 1927 she found an innovative and evolving narrative style and turned from exploring the challenges she faced as a young woman to an attempt to document the lives of women she had come to know and the power relationships that often defined them.

Her short story "The Laundress," published in 1927 in Mencken's *American Mercury*, where Conroy's writing career was also launched, creates a link between the personal and physical strength of lone women. It describes a young girl's fascination with the laundress, Mrs. Kretch, who washes her family's clothes: "It was fine to see her work, so thoroughly, with a hardy pride in working well with her hands." The story narrates the girl's growing recognition of the laundress's life beyond the ironing table and her ability to raise her children on her own. There is hardly a man in the story; Mrs. Kretch is neither widowed nor abandoned but purposefully and successfully single. She "worked like a drudge" for her husband, "but when he bullied the children she brought them to town, and, to his surprise, earned their living until they were large enough, one by one, to add to the family budget."[76] Rather than either the saintliness or victimhood attached to the female characters in much proletarian fiction of the time, single motherhood and a life of hard work brings Mrs. Kretch the opportunity for shared purpose and feminist sensibility. As Laura Hapke puts it, "Le Sueur's artistic celebration of the solo mother who had no nostalgia for or much memory of a marital past was a form of rebellion against Ma Joadism."[77] Later, Le Sueur would document the lives of laundresses, waitresses, farm wives, and the unemployed, focusing on the physicality of their labor and their bodily experiences in order to create new narratives of female agency and to place female experience at the center of modernist critique.

In this manner Le Sueur's writing elaborates a complex notion of female experience as both embodied and structured by the material realities of class and gender and generates a narrative practice defined by this "contact." Critics such as Constance Coiner and Paula Rabinowitz have long pointed to the way that her reportage brings the bodies and narratives of women together and highlights the material differences between women's and men's experiences of poverty: "As a narrator of working-class women's lives, Meridel Le Sueur theorizes the relationship of bodies and texts, of labor and desire, suggesting that we need to understand the working class as both embodied and textualized. Moreover she insists that we read both bodies and texts as gendered." Yet Rabinowitz's reading too easily essentializes the bodily experiences of women and men, equating men with lost labor and women with the desire for pregnancy: "The body of the working-class man of the 1930s . . . is hungry, an empty space once filled by his labor; the body of the working-class woman, as well as her text, is pregnant with desire for 'children' . . . [and] for 'history' to change the world for them."[78] If, on the other hand, Le Sueur's writing challenges the absence of women from standard accounts of the proletariat by casting them as workers, for pay or not, it is not in order to ignore the real hunger they suffer on the breadlines or to replace it with a idealized maternity. The main character in her most celebrated novel, *The Girl*, is both hungry *and* pregnant at the end of the novel.

The notion of embodiment that has emerged more recently in the feminist theory of Elizabeth Grosz, Toril Moi, Iris Marion Young, and others offers another way of understanding the complex interplay of body, gender, class, and text in Le Sueur's work. Drawing on the phenomenological tradition of Merleau-Ponty and Simone de Beauvoir, Moi and Young in different ways propose a notion of the "lived body" as crucial to understanding the importance to identity of physical experience: "The lived body is a unified idea of a physical body acting and experiencing in a specific sociocultural context; it is the body-in-situation" and in contact with its material conditions of existence.[79] The experiences of a lived body are specific, material, and concrete rather than expressions of generalized, biological notions of sex or more abstract cultural performances of gender. At the intersection of the biological and the social, the notion of the lived body accounts for the way that bodily experiences record and exhibit the sexed and gendered identities of women and men. The lived body arises from the human subject's everyday experience of her or his specific body in a particular material environment and provides a background or context for the subject's performance of being-in-the-world.

While Moi seeks to use this idea of embodiment to dismantle the sex/gender division, Young describes the ways the lived body intersects with sociocultural structures of gender. As such, the lived body is both the place where gender is played out and, in its particular biological constitution, a potential source of resistance to gender's social strictures. Young claims that "the body as lived is always enculturated" and inscribed within gendered systems of social organization, such as the division of labor into public and private, male and female realms. "Gender structures . . . are historically given and . . . precede action and consciousness. Each person experiences aspects of gender as facticity, as sociohistorical givens with which she or he must deal." Those gender structures, clearly, also intersect with the "givens" of a class identity so that any lived body experience always already encounters the sociohistorical constraints of a particular class/gender structure. Gendered subjects, seen in such a light, become "habituated bodies, reacting to, reproducing, and modifying structures."[80] Still, the gendered body, as a nexus of sensibilities and relationships to the world and the site of specific and personal response to the material situations, divisions of labor, and hierarchies of power within specific social settings, also has the potential to resist or modify those structures. This is what Elizabeth Grosz (following Merleau-Ponty) calls the body's "duplicity . . . [which] is necessary to account for its complex emergence from the world and its capacity to live in and remake the world."[81] The body is the place of contact between the self and the world, where subject and object become intertwined. But it is also the locus of the self's coming into being, its creation of itself as a subject that exists physically within the world, and the basis of both ethics and politics. As such, lived experiences of sex and gender can also gesture beyond their prescribed roles in the sex/gender system. They represent the potential model of activity that Beauvoir would say is the "situation" crucial to a woman's "becoming," and the beginning of what I would call her constitution of an "as if" justice.[82]

Le Sueur's writing often highlights just such a process of embodied becoming even as it documents the degree to which this potential freedom is constrained by the historical situation of the Depression-era American Midwest and the biopolitics of U.S. modernity. Her collection of stories from the early 1930s, *I Hear Men Talking*, a series of interconnected vignettes bound together by its young heroine, Penelope, might well be characterized as an alternative female bildungsroman where bodily experiences guide and constrain spiritual development.[83] Penelope wanders in and out of farm kitchens and milking sheds, visiting the old spinster whose youth is the subject of town gossip and helping a newcomer in difficult childbirth. Early chapters describe her awakening to female desire, her watching a young boy stacking sacks of potatoes (15), her becoming aware of her own reflection in the plate-glass windows of the town (14), and the townspeople's noticing her. She is enraptured by the arm of her girlfriend across her shoulder: "Pen was lost in agony [*sic*] of love and the swift repulsion of Jenny's sharp, sensuous body, the strong feel and odor of her" and delighted by the close friendship driven by this touch (15–16).

Later stories increase Penelope's personal understanding through the collective life histories of the townspeople and the moments of suffering among its women, both inserting her into the gendered power structure of town life, made more rigid by its entrance into a modernizing capitalist economy, and expanding her own bodily experience by extension through theirs. While helping during a difficult childbirth, Penelope feels the boundaries drop away between herself and the expectant mother, who is lying etherized in her arms as the doctor applies the forceps: "Penelope lifted the heavy shoulders against her and then she felt the tearing stricture, the pressure, the weight away from her, taut, then falling back lax against her, repeated and repeated, until she was swaying with a rhythm transmitted to her . . . and she thought: she's crying! but saw it was her own tears" (97). By the end of the narrative, having experienced the death of the young boy she admired in the opening scenes, Penelope seems to have attained the status of woman by way of shared bodily suffering. As Le Sueur puts it in her afterword, written in 1984, "The image is of the new child within the body of us all. This must include . . . Penelope and the corrupt town. The image the writer must now develop is the synthesis" (239). Against the structuring power of the division of labor, gender conformity, and the "corruption" of increasingly commodified economic life in town, the events of Penelope's life offer the possibility of shared sensibilities, joined emotions, and common embodied experiences as the basis for an oppositional biopolitics.

The development of embodied female experience in *I Hear Men Talking* is also constantly linked to pastoral descriptions of the rural Midwestern landscape in opposition to the images of consumption and privation in the life of the town. Le Sueur employs a pastoral mode in which the idyllic countryside and its simpler people serve to highlight the corruption of town life. Penelope's growing bodily awareness and sexuality become connected to the rural idyll and its potential for love and human interconnection. The pastoral thus becomes a vehicle for resistance to the social structures of class and gender, as well as a means of placing Penelope in a context beyond the town's corrupt values.[84] Penelope moves into the narrative with the smell of spring (14). While the sometimes overly lyrical language later displeased Le Sueur, who criticized it as "too beautiful" (243), it nonetheless creates a context of plenitude where Penelope's growing awareness of and pleasure in her body becomes a source of power and being-in-the-world rather than a means for her insertion into the town's corrupt systems of desire.[85]

Le Sueur also employs pastoral elements in *I Hear Men Talking* to align Penelope with the growing political activism of the farmers. Paul Alpers discusses the coming together of rural figures, often as the occasion for songs and colloquies that address, and seek to redress, separation, absence, and loss in pastoral.[86] The central conceit of *I Hear Men Talking* functions in much the same way. The conversations Penelope overhears in her aunts' speakeasy produce a rural idyll and communal colloquy that move toward the political power to redress grievances directly. For example, during a milk strike Penelope overhears the men: "The talk went on in the market that so and so had such a stand of wheat, or timothy, that the corn was so high, that the hogs were cramming their insides until they had drums of bellies from the mash that couldn't be sold anyway" (78). The too-full hogs and high-grown corn in this passage demonstrate the disruption of farm life during the strike even as they also become signs and sources of the rural resistance. "In a little while the corn will be high and a thousand men could hide in the corn and you couldn't see them, a thousand men in the corn. And Penelope saw the corn growing up and the thousand men like the corn growing tall ... saw them waving like good soil planted with fat ripe corn, marching corn, all moving together" (79). Penelope's growing awareness of the plight of the impoverished farmers, the purpose of their strike, and the meaning of their combined resistance are bound up in the power of the rural colloquy and the connection between the people and the landscape.

Thus the pastoral mode here shows the landscape as not only the locus of rural communion but also the impetus toward that gathering and the source of the speech (or song) that emerges from it. The pastoral demonstrates the potential strength and solidarity of the embattled farm people, and, as Le Sueur puts it, "the lyrical is used as a reaction to the deathly action of the economics and history of the town" (242). Rather than rely on a sentimental depiction of Penelope's coming of age in relation to maternity and the fertility of the earth, Le Sueur gives her access, by way of the strike, to the more direct, political power that the rural life of the land provides for its people and that the pastoral mode can create in narrative.[87]

This rural power, symbolized by the milk strike, also revolves around the concept of "contact" that Le Sueur introduces in a later essay. For Le Sueur contact can mean the kind of connection between people and their land evident in the language and imagery of *I Hear*

Men Talking as well as the human solidarity that might derive from this connection. Contact also stands for the interconnections among the population, its material situation, and its local history, which for Le Sueur become the source of political activism. Contact of this sort is thus key to Le Sueur's belief in the potential power of the rural Midwest and to the importance that both she and Conroy accord to the little magazines and local writers' communities they helped promote in the 1930s.

> The regionalism which can now be effective is one not of isolation but of contact. In the middle west the historical movement of pioneering, of the Populist movement, the great agrarian revolts against the piracy of eastern capital, against the looting of the prairies, and the forests, against the wanton destruction that has destroyed now the land . . . has started in upon the people themselves, taking toll of their rich, obscure, and anonymous lives.[88]

Over and against the alienating forces of urban capitalism, which conspire not only to pit workers against one another but also to rob the land of its natural resources, Le Sueur grounds a progressive populism in the regional history and geography of the Midwest.[89] Those who lay claim to this vital, progressive history, even though they lead anonymous lives of the obscure, become the inheritors of the pioneer spirit and carry with them the potential for a renewed future.

At the same time, Le Sueur's writing exhibits no certainty that this positive kind of contact will arise from the difficult material circumstances of Midwestern farm life. Her 1930 essay "Corn Village," a gut-wrenching description of the violence and deprivation of Kansas farm life, makes clear the tenuousness of this power of connection. In the opening sentence, Le Sueur says, "I will never recover from my sparse childhood in Kansas" (9), and at the end she claims, "I have come from you mysteriously wounded. I have waked from my adolescence to find a wound inflicted in my heart" (24). Over and over, the words "terror," "terrifying," "violence," and "horror" appear, describing the deprivations of the rural poor: "I am filled with terror when I think of the emptiness and ghostliness of mid-America" (10); even the plains are described as having a "terrifying beauty" (11). The horror is a horror of isolation, of a hardscrabble land that yields very little and a long bleak winter under a "leaden sky" that offers "no vista, no shaking out, no revelation" (12). The effort to make a living pits farmers against one another in a competition to survive, and the way the landscape is used in this competition leads to its "ruin and desolation" (140). "What does an American think about the land, what dreams come from the sight of it, what painful dreaming? Are they only money dreams, power dreams?" (12). The essay suggests that the pioneer history of conquering the land in this competitive dream of power leads to the terrifying isolation and devastation of Midwestern farm life, and more directly to the near-collapse of family farming in 1929 and the early 1930s.

Le Sueur here locates the lived experiences of her characters specifically in the transition to economic modernity and capitalized agriculture in the American Midwest. Following the increased demand for commodities caused by World War I, farmers on the prairie began to shift production practices, often mortgaging their farms to make the transition from horse-drawn cultivation to mechanized practices requiring capitalization. Tractor use demanded investments of capital in the form of fuel and new equipment, and new developments in fertilization and seed production also required the investment of cash. In the late 1920s, even before the crash, a series of bumper crops and high production began to drive commodity prices down. The price of wheat dropped from $1.05 per bushel in 1929 to 38 cents per bushel in 1932, and corn dropped from 77 to 32 cents per bushel. It seemed to some that "tractor farming during the 1930s was actually a losing investment, since the climate and the sometimes anemic commodity markets canceled any profits." As Michael Johnston Grant puts it in *Down and Out on the Family Farm*, "The period between the Wall Street crash and the end of World War Two was a time when agricultural, economic, and environmental trends thwarted farm families from making the jump into the middle income level."[90] For Le Sueur, capital-intensive trends in farming meant not only hard times for farm families and increased competition among them but also increased degradation of the land. Her interest in political organizing and rural activism arose out of recognition that the trend toward a mechanized and capital-intensive farming practice was unsustainable and directly linked to the poverty and farm failures of the early 1930s.

Her 1929 short story "Harvest," in which a newly married young woman quarrels with her husband over the purchase of a threshing machine, links this conflict not only to the issue of embodiment and the matter of "contact" but also, thereby, to the commodification of desire that, according to Le Sueur, threatens farm culture and ultimately subordinates the rural poor to the biopolitics of the capitalist state. The young wife, Ruth, enters the narrative, like Penelope, surrounded by pastoral images that represent her own body and sexuality. "She thought: *And my body in the sun, root-alive, opening in the sun dark at its deep roots*, and it pained her now that she had quarreled with her husband." The husband, Winji, walking back from the fields sways like a stalk of corn.[91] The story makes clear the connection between farming and sexuality: "He strode the sun-scarred earth laying it open, the seed falling in the shadows; then at evening he came from them to her" (8). Ruth understands that the threshing machine puts this connection in jeopardy ("She knew how men came in from riding that monster all day . . . not in a column of mounting heat as her husband came to her now" [7]).

The thresher not only changes the man's relationship to the land (and therefore to her) but also becomes an object of desire, linked to the couple's financial situation and position within the town. Once Winji becomes enamored of the images of the thresher in the catalogue, he spends his evenings turning the pages rather than talking with Ruth. His obsession with the thresher and, by extension, with the commodity culture that it represents, divides the couple. Their easy, lyrical communion described in the first pages devolves into arguments made up of a stuttering pattern of single repeated words, uttered while the characters have their backs turned to each other (14). Buying the thresher disrupts their assumption of communal marital property. Winji asks Ruth to come with him to buy the machine, saying, "It's your money, in a way." But Ruth replies, "No, no. . . . It's your money. Do with it as you like. It's yours. You're the master of the house" (12). The appeal of the machine to Winji is also bound up with commodified notions of individual success that are foreign to Ruth. He tells her that the thresher will help them advance and that they will be "powerful people in this neighborhood" (14), and Ruth can only respond by clenching her hands to keep from tearing him to pieces. In the end, Winji buys the thresher he so desires, repeating the phrase, "We have got to get ahead" (6), and Ruth, pregnant, hates him for it.

Thus Le Sueur incorporates the modernization of Midwestern farming practices into the development of the characters in "Harvest" and creates a narrative depiction of the way that this shift links an artificially created commodified desire, like Winji's for the thresher, to the pursuit of individual gain and capitalist power. Though Ruth is pregnant throughout, the story does not mobilize the sentimental trope of the maternal except as a sign of what Winji's desire for the thresher displaces. He does not appear moved by his impending parenthood, nor does the prospect of the baby change his purchasing plans. Once again, the subtlety of Le Sueur's handling of matters of sexuality and fertility takes her well beyond what critics too often connect to a simple notion of the maternal in her work.[92] Here priority is given to *male* fecundity and its importance to this couple's balance. It is undermined not by movement away from the land itself or by direct misuse of it but rather by making it subservient to the desire for money and power that is projected onto the thresher. The mechanization of farming practice in the Midwest during the 1920s is shown not only to dismantle the habits and attitudes associated with rural life but also to disrupt the balanced economy of gender relations and sexuality among rural people.

The twentieth-century challenge to the gender economy becomes even more salient in the more complex narration of the novel *The Girl*. Written out of bits and pieces of Le Sueur's Depression-era reporting, published in fragments during the 1930s, and only completed in the 1970s, the novel seems to have relinquished the assumptions about the potential of human-landscape contact and the pastoral hope of "human fullness in a rural world" present in her earlier work.[93] The eponymous girl of the story, whom we follow throughout the novel without knowing her name, has come to the city from a life of poverty in rural Wisconsin. Her father had moved to the farm looking for "something better."[94] But agriculture does not produce enough capital to sustain them, and the pastoral scene no longer provides community or colloquy. Instead, the commodified farm and the impoverished, isolated families who must scrape together funds from their depleted fields become the backdrop for the girl's escape into the city. The demise of the rural idyll is even more apparent and clearly connected to issues of bodily integrity later in the novel as the girl and her boyfriend, Butch, try to escape a botched bank robbery by driving away into the snowy landscape. The beauty of the scenery and its potential for escape from the threat of the police gives way to Butch's rants, delirious from his gunshot wounds: "What have they done to us. . . . Where are the oats, the wheat, I was sure they were planted. . . . What are they doing to you now honey? They own the town. They own the earth and the sweet marrow of your body" (95). Despite the doomed love that grows between these characters as they hide out in the country, the landscape here calls up Butch's bodily integrity, his lack of autonomy, and his conviction that "they" own the town, the earth, and, especially, the girl, rather than the countryside's connection to rebirth or its role as the site of meaningful contact between human life and its material sources.

The novel revolves around the issue of bodily autonomy, especially for women, who are subject to surveillance by the men around them as well as by police and relief workers in Depression-era St. Paul. Naïve as she arrives in the city, the girl is befriended by a prostitute and a bootlegger's wife who give her work in their restaurant. In sharp, dialogue-driven vignettes, Le Sueur narrates the growing relationship among the women that develops as the girl experiences the hard work, deprivation, and subservience to men that characterize their lives in a doubly supervised and disciplined arena, with the police on the outside, picking up wandering women in order to "give them tests and sterilize [them] or send [them] to the woman's prison," and the men on the inside of the speakeasy, trying to "make a home run or a strike" (1). The gangster Ganz, who provides the booze, also provides "protection," but he entices the girl into a hotel room by promising money, then cheats, beats, and rapes her. By the end of the novel, the women are hounded by relief workers, whose supervision includes cutting off funding to women who behave badly with men and threatening sterilization for the girl, who by that point is pregnant. The connection among surveillance, violence, and women's bodies is unavoidable; the frequent moments when the men strike these women serve merely as occasional reminders.

Yet the book also opens up a realm of bodily experience alive with pleasure, "contact," and the potential resistance of the pastoral situation even under conditions of modernity in the Depression-era city. Though she is wasting away from disease, Clara, the woman who works as a prostitute, enters the novel as a bodily force of hope and autonomy for the girl. "I kept as close to Clara as I could. Something was in her so sure as if she knew everything I would ever know. She made the hollowness of my flesh fill with people" (1). Beautiful and enticing to the girl as well as the men, Clara's presence in the novel is connected to moments of interrelationship and generosity. She believes that "everybody can get along if they try" and harbors dreams of middle-class existence, saying that eventually "she will get married and sing in the choir and play bridge on Sundays with the best people" (8). In the terms of Le Sueur's book, the work she does to provide this money is no worse than any other wage labor within a commodified economy and offers a means for personal generosity: "You come and stay with me, Clara said. I make enough money off the johns to pay the rent and something over. You could make it good kid, it ain't nothing . . . and you meet nice men too, that's give you lace tablecloths and peasant pottery" (39). The novel elaborates sexual activity as a realm where women might exert some kind of autonomy within modern commodity culture and also where lived body experience opens up a gap within the existing economy of gender that might provide resistance to the dominant biopolitics. Clara's prostitution is juxtaposed with the girl's growing desire for Butch, who makes her feel "all [her] body opening little smiles" (40). The girl's growing awareness of the pleasure and pain of sex, its place in the regimes of labor and surveillance, and its potential to shift those regimes contribute to a complex narrative of embodied experience that is integral to the novel's Depression-era reportage.

That reportage, crucial from the outset, encompasses more and more of the narrative as the book proceeds. The narration swerves back and forth between the first-person story of the girl's coming of age among the down and out in Depression-era Saint Paul and the presentation of the stories told her by others. Belle, the bootlegger's wife, tells her tales of the gangsters and their rackets and of the violent men she has known. Clara recounts stories of the places she has lived and the times when she almost ended her own life. The union worker Amelia describes the six children she has lost and the dangerous practices of the local relief workers. The proliferation of these stories in the otherwise dialogue-driven text sets them apart from the more naturalistic tale of the girl, her relationship with Butch, and her developing pregnancy. They become detached from their speakers, as though Clara, Belle, and Amelia serve as vehicles for the memories and life experiences of the many women that Le Sueur met and interviewed during the early years of the Depression. Like those of the women on the breadlines, the women's experiences recounted in this novel become repeating examples of the hidden poverty among Midwestern urban and rural working women in the early 1930s and of the seemingly endless proliferation of their spiritual and bodily suffering.

Le Sueur's merging of reportage and embodied experiences in this novel creates abortion and sterilization as repeated events in the narratives of women's lives. If the iterative structure of "Women on the Breadlines" emphasizes women's lives of working and waiting, repetition in *The Girl* underscores the iterative everydayness of both pregnancy and abortion. The women's tales of abortion in *The Girl* stand in for those of the anonymous women Le Sueur interviewed over many years as well as for others who suffered the real threat of forced sterilization during the period.[95] We never learn how Amelia lost all six of her children, but Belle reports that she has had thirteen abortions (9) and Clara has knowledge of the "pills for an abortion" (100) and remembers the smell of the man who provides the pseudosurgical procedure (72). Butch insists that the girl abort the child she is carrying, saying "you've got to do it that's all" (72), though she interrupts the book's series of abortions by refusing his demand. The girl's escape from the abortion room becomes a singular act of ethical independence and defiance that breaks the repeated practice of bodily violence and abortions. After Butch's death she will say, "Now I know the whole city and the way it is and the way those in it can be together.... Now I am at home with my own body and the bodies of others and I will do whatever there is to do" (102). The shift to the possibility of a chosen pregnancy and a joyful childbirth provide the focus for the final sections of the novel, shifting the politics surrounding the fecundity of working women's bodies under regimes of surveillance. If the biopolitics of the state casts these bodies as unruly, sexualized, and deviant, the novel celebrates this iterative unruliness as the source of a celebratory and fecund impropriety.

The last sections of the novel become dominated by a sometimes-chaotic assortment of voices and bodies from the urban community of women, serving to underscore the pleasurable and productive deviance that Le Sueur endorses in *The Girl*. The women's stories pepper the narrative, becoming, much like the incidents of *skaz* in Conroy's *The Disinherited*, moments when the voices of others disrupt or divert the narrative proper, forcing it to move toward its end in fits and starts, by way of a series of different voices. As in Conroy's novel, these moments sometimes emerge from a seemingly irrational perspective or carry the potential to rend the logic of the main narrative. For example, Butch's senile mother, who lives with Clara and the girl, often tells stories about her dead sons as though they are still alive. While the girl comments on the fact that Butch's mother is "goony" (105), the dividing line between memory ("she remembers her mother and her dead daughter and the orchard where the boys played" [106]) and delusion ("she'll say, Don't make a noise now, Butch is sleeping" [106]) is thin. When Clara begins to succumb to illness, she also reinhabits the past, writing letters about an old boyfriend as though he were still with her.

These letters introduce another narrative and temporal dimension into the text, disrupting the progress of the narrative. Amelia, who is the representative of the Worker's Alliance, tells the girl story after story, but it is hard to know whether we are meant to understand her tales of police on the prowl or the enforced sterilization of young women as factually true or as propaganda in service of the union, thereby further confusing the novel's distinctions between fiction and reportage. The girl says, "Amelia has been telling me things for a long time and now it gets clearer and clearer, yes clearer" (112), but until the girl is forced by the police into a maternity home, destined to be sterilized after giving birth, it is not clear that we can trust these stories. When Clara is whisked away for electroshock treatments, the narrative finally appropriates the women's horrific stories into its main plotline. The use of multiple voices and communal perspectives, *skaz*, reported speech, and intertexts in the final chapters creates a sensational modernism based on a refusal of the border between fact and fiction and a commitment to the narrative heightening of reality in the service of political resistance. The novel's structural unruliness— its persistent unwillingness to segregate reportage and overheard stories—keeps the final episode of political awakening among the women from subsiding into a stock moment and generates a powerful critique of Depression-era biopolitics from within the nexus of narrative and embodied experience.

Feminist critics read the ending of *The Girl*, in which Belle, Amelia, Butch's mother, and the other women attend simultaneously to Clara's death and the birth of the girl's child, as support for the ideal of women's communal politics as opposed to male-centered political organizations and the Communist Party in particular.[96] But this moment of solidarity appears to other critics to support the role of communist politics in Le Sueur's work.[97] Viewed from within the development of her life's work, however, the ending of *The Girl* may be understood as an extension of Le Sueur's notion of "contact" into a multivoiced, modernist critique of the biopolitics of Depression-era America rather than an endorsement of a unified party line. At the end, the women of the novel recreate the pastoral idyll under the circumstances of modernity, their abandoned warehouse standing in for the natural landscapes of Le Sueur's earlier work. The interweaving of their communal voices, speaking from the abandoned spaces of modern industrial life, generates a radically engaged modernism from the lived bodily experiences of working women.

Le Sueur's most famous essay, "I Was Marching," published in 1934 in *The New Masses*, exhibits the same kind of narrative innovation. Laura Hapke takes her to task for this essay, decrying the way that Le Sueur seems to countenance the traditional role of woman as helpmeet to the more activist male strikers.⁹⁸ Yet like most readers, Hapke misses the importance of Le Sueur's narrative experimentation in this essay. "I Was Marching" is not an autobiographical sketch but rather a hybrid text, like *The Girl* and "Women on the Breadlines," that helps establish the trajectory of Le Sueur's work into a new mode of narrative modernism on the border between fact and fiction, political tract and aesthetic narration.⁹⁹ "I Was Marching" follows the narrator's development from isolated individual to a participant in a strike, emphasizing her fear not only of the bloodiness of the event but also of the deep chaos and bodily violence involved in the march. "I knew my feelings to be those belonging to disruption, chaos and disintegration and I felt their direct and awful movement, mute and powerful, drawing them into a close and glowing cohesion like a powerful conflagration in the middle of the city."¹⁰⁰ Like the girl or the other young heroines in Le Sueur's fiction, the narrator's bodily experiences propel her towards communal sensibility and direct action:

> In these terrible happenings you cannot be neutral now. No one can be neutral in the face of bullets.
> The next day, with sweat breaking out on my body, I walked past the three guards at the door.
>
> (161)

The bodies of the narrator, the women strike workers, and the men on the picket line merge in the amalgamation of body parts that forms the final march scene of the essay. If the women marching forward are a "million hands, movements, faces" with "the open mouth crying, the nostrils stretched apart" (171), they have become part of the communal body whose labor propels the strike. Their movement is important because it is "repeating again and again," multiplied not only by the many who participate in the march but also by those who had gone before and would come after (171). Like the women waiting in the relief office in the essay "Women on the Breadlines," the woman worker in "I Was Marching" becomes important to Le Sueur not in spite of her hidden status but because of it, and her understanding of their power comes not from avoiding the bent backs and ruined hands of endless labor or the "gaping wounds [and] . . . crying mouths" of the picket line but in and through these threatening bodily experiences. Like the chaotic and deviantly fecund bodies of the women in *The Girl*, Le Sueur's strikers challenge not only the obvious oppression of U.S. working people in the thirties but also the biopolitics that generates this oppression from the surveillance, containment, and suppression of lived bodily experience among the working classes.

The *skaz*, collective voices, merging of fact and fiction, focus on "contact," and emphasis on women's repeated bodily experiences in Le Sueur's work become, like the multiple voices and representations of folkways in Conroy's writing, vehicles for both narrative experimentation and resistance to the conditions of working-class people in the Midwest of the 1920s and 1930s. Though usually described in the context of hard-boiled realism, writings by Conroy and Le Sueur use innovative narrative practices to present the experiences of working-class people in response to the developing conditions of modernity in the rural Midwest, and therefore they ask to be read as a radical stream of American modernism that makes politics a central concern of literary experimentalism. Like Harlem Renaissance writers, Conroy and Le Sueur create a modernism based on vernaculars and folkways, which inscribes resistance to the political oppression of workers in the United States during the Depression era into the sound, shape, and texture of their narratives. Still, while textual practice, editorial work, and community activism often converge for Conroy and Le Sueur, their writings do not succumb to crass instrumentalism or subservience to a particular party line. Rather, by representing the complex mosaic composed of the bodies and voices of working-class women and men, their writings not only demonstrate the crucial link between the private lives of the poor and their public identities as workers but also build an alternative politics out of the narrative community of those lives.

Afterword

On December 10, 2009, Barack Obama delivered his much-anticipated speech accepting the Nobel Peace Prize. In it he created a complex argument, based on the theology of Reinhold Neibuhr, about the moral necessity of political action in a flawed and dangerous world. His remarks describe the fine line between just and unjust war, evoking the principle that warfare is justified "if it is waged as a last resort or in self-defense; if the force used is proportional; and if, whenever possible, civilians are spared from violence." But the speech also asked its audience "to think in new ways about the notions of just war and the imperatives of a just peace."[1] Accepting the necessity of military action in the threatening contemporary world, Obama describes peace as a matter of pragmatic negotiation rather than absolute moral imperative. In this sense he also evokes Martin Luther King's 1964 Nobel speech, which calls for "the positive affirmation of peace" as more than the simple absence of war.[2] In a nod to the principles of Gandhi and King, Obama characterizes himself as "living testimony to the moral force of non-violence." Yet, he continues, "I face the world as it is," unable to turn away from the forces of evil and violence against America. By characterizing his position in terms of realism—a reluctant acquiescence to the world as it is rather than as it ought to be—Obama seems to echo Hume's law, limiting himself to those matters he can affect through pragmatic action in the world as it exists.

Yet by the end of the speech Obama returns to the connection between ought and is, reminding his audience that the division between the two has never been absolute and that our moral "passions, motives, volitions, and thoughts" can guide our path to new experiences of the world.[3] He cites King, who refused "to accept the idea that the 'isness' of man's present condition makes him morally incapable of reaching up for the eternal 'oughtness' that forever confronts him," and calls us to reaffirm our commitment to human possibility and to the creation of the world "as it ought to be." Having acknowledged the difficulty of achieving a true and lasting peace and enumerated the conditions—economic, religious, and legal—that stand in the way, Obama reaches for his "moral compass," drawing out of the context of the here and now the path to a future justice:

> Let us reach for the world that ought to be—that spark of the divine that still stirs within each of our souls.
>
> Somewhere today, in the here and now, in the world as it is, a soldier sees he's outgunned, but stands firm to keep the peace. Somewhere today, in this world, a young protestor awaits the brutality of her government, but has the courage to march on. Somewhere today, a mother facing punishing poverty still takes the time to teach her child, scrapes together what few coins she has to send that child to school—because she believes that a cruel world still has a place for that child's dreams. . . . We can acknowledge that oppression will always be with us, and still strive for justice.

Striving for justice, in Obama's speech, means taking the circumstances of the world as it is and recognizing their potential to move toward what ought to be. In an imperfect world, the pragmatic actions of individuals standing firm, marching in protest, or educating a child can raise their ethical claims vis-à-vis the surrounding society and begin the conversation about how to instantiate justice. From the soldier armed and ready for battle and the rough life of an impoverished child Obama helps us imagine the possibilities of a future peace based not on the absence of war but on the eradication of violence, political oppression, and poverty. It is no surprise that these were also the cornerstones of Martin Luther King's Nobel lecture, "The Quest for Peace and Justice" and that the just peace Obama imagines rests on King's link between the end of oppression and the beginning of true nonviolence.

Even more than King, however, Obama manages this transition from what "is" to what "ought to be" by way of narrative. The few words chronicling the struggles of the soldier, the teachings of the impoverished mother, or the steps of the protestors create simple life stories that generate characters, order a sequence of events, and recount it from a particular perspective. The narrative works its own process of innovation, synthesizing events into plots, however short, that lead toward possible future consequences while generating relationships among character, listener, and speaker that carry their own future effects. The narrative dimension of Obama's text thus helps posit the problem of justice as a temporal one, governing the transition from the impoverished here and now of our present to an imagined world of a just future, in which these plots would end in a reversal of circumstance. The brief narrative moments in Obama's speech underscore his message of hope for a future peace and work to enact it by the narrative construction of an "as if" justice. Hume's law thus retreats before Obama's imaginative act of storytelling. The possibility of what ought to be grows out of the experience of what is, transformed by the ethical and aesthetic work of narration into a potential new political reality.

I refer to Obama's Nobel speech neither to signal my agreement with his politics nor to appropriate his theoretical grounding. I do not share Obama's trust in the military as a means toward peace and justice, nor do I rest my belief in the possibility of a more just future on his measure of religious faith and trust in the divine. Certainly, many of the modernists whose texts have inspired this book would have been equally suspicious of such grounds for progressive politics. At the same time, Obama's contemporary use of narrative to bridge between "ought" and "is" makes clear the ongoing force of this storytelling power and the function it continues to play in current efforts to imagine justice. Obama's Nobel speech also spirals back toward the questions that, I have argued, lie at the heart of both narration and justice: Who speaks, and from what location? For, as he points out, even the granting of the Peace Prize to a single individual, self-admittedly at "the beginning, and not the end, of [his] labors on the world stage," raises questions about how we understand the plot of Obama's political life and his relationship to "the men and women around the world who have been jailed and beaten in the pursuit of justice." Obama's actions "on the world stage" place him in contact with the stories and political claims of these men and women across the world, yet, as his speech makes clear, his framework for political justice remains tied to national aims and fortunes and the ongoing defense of America's global position.

But questions of justice in the contemporary world seem to require an end to that national perspective, at least as the absolute locus of political belonging, and to demand a new way of imagining the "who" of global politics. Nancy Fraser argues that in the face of globalizing regimes of human rights and networks of political governance, the Westphalian "posit of exclusive, undivided state sovereignty is no longer plausible . . . equally questionable is the notion of a sharp division between domestic and international space." This challenge to the national horizon for politics demands that we reframe our understanding of who counts as a political subject with rights to claim redress and political standing in matters of justice. "The 'who' of justice is itself unjustly defined . . . when for example, the claims of the global poor are shunted into the domestic political arenas of weak or failed states and blocked from confronting the offshore sources of their dispossession."[4] Thus the matter of who speaks and from what location emerges more forcefully as a key question for contemporary law and politics while the process of reframing our understanding of sovereignty and citizenship depends on the new narrative construction of a transnational "who."

Even at this late moment in the history of globalization, then, we return to the concerns with which I began this book. Narratives create "as if" realms that not only respond to the exigence of their rhetorical situations but also carry implications for action in the world and for the establishment of real-world justice within the domain of politics. The crucial matter of "who speaks" and the linked problem of accounting for oneself in narrative become central to the text's activity in the world, especially when it foregrounds matters of ethical relationship, national belonging, geographical positioning, and economic status. These concerns emerge again and again in modernist writing, linking formal experimentation irrevocably to matters of ethics and politics and shifting our understanding of the stakes and claims of modernism worldwide. If we look with the kind of transnational optic I've proposed in this book, investigating modernism as a global range of relationships, practices, problematics, and cultural engagements with modernity rather than an established set of works, however capacious, we discover new political synergies and social commitments that are fueled rather than derailed by narrative experimentation, and an array of global perspectives that question the dogma of the Westphalian worldview. Caught up in the challenges posed by economic, political, and social modernity, transnational modernism engages inexorably with matters of justice and politics. In this way, I've hoped to suggest, it opens up a vantage point not only on a new world of twentieth-century commitment but also on the global imperatives of the present.

NOTES

Introduction: Imagining Justice

1. Mulk Raj Anand, *Untouchable* (1940; New York: Penguin, 1986), 142; further references cited in the text.

2. In this sense, the representation of Gandhi here might be called a version of "virtue ethics" in which the matter of individual character is the starting point for morality.

3. Rita Felski, *The Gender of Modernity* (Cambridge, Mass.: Harvard University Press, 1995), 9.

4. For Foucault on the attitude of modernity, see "What Is Enlightenment?" in *The Foucault Reader*, ed. Paul Rabinow (New York: Pantheon, 1984), 32–50. I rely on Frederic Jameson's definition of modernization as "the transfer and/or implementation of industrial technology already developed," the new social impulses that accompany that implementation, and the forms of social and political control that arise in response to it (*A Singular Modernity: Essay on the Ontology of the Present* [London: Verso, 2002], 166).

5. E. M. Forster, preface to *Untouchable*, by Mulk Raj Anand (New York: Penguin, 1940), vi. Forster, interestingly enough, emphasizes the modernity of the "flush toilet" solution in this preface, posits it as a rational solution ("no god is needed to rescue the Untouchables"), and thereby reinforces a problematic equation of modernity with rationality (as opposed to religion) (viii).

6. Simon Critchley, *Ethics, Politics, Subjectivity* (New York: Verso, 1999), 275. Derrida elaborates the link between hospitality and Levinasian ethics

in *Adieu to Emmanuel Levinas*, trans. Pascale-Anne Brault and Michael Naas (Stanford, Calif.: Stanford University Press, 1999).

7. See Sumit Sarkar's classic study of the earlier Bengali movement, *The Swadeshi Movement in Bengal, 1903–1908* (Delhi: People's, 1977) in which he discusses the tension between modernism and traditionalism in the movement (24). Dipesh Chakrabarty, *Habitations of Modernity: Essays in the Wake of Subaltern Studies* (Chicago: University of Chicago Press, 2002), explores a number of ways in which the history of India complicates the binary between tradition and modernity, among other dichotomies (26).

8. Ashis Nandy, qtd. in Chakrabarty, *Habitations of Modernity*, 39; Chakrabarty, *Habitations of Modernity*, 62.

9. For another approach to the relationship between ethics and justice, or "ought" and "is," in modernism, see Ravit Reichman, *The Affective Life of Law: Legal Modernism and the Literary Imagination* (Stanford, Calif.: Stanford University Press, 2009).

10. A large body of contemporary scholarship addresses the ethics of narration. See, for example, Adam Zachary Newton, *Narrative Ethics* (Cambridge, Mass.: Harvard University Press, 1997); and, from a different perspective, Dorothy J. Hale, "Aesthetics and the New Ethics: Theorizing the Novel in the Twenty-first Century," *PMLA* 124, no. 3 (May 2009): 896–905. Recently, scholars have begun to focus on the particular narrative demands of modernist texts. See for example, Melba Cuddy-Keane, "Inside and Outside the Covers: Beginnings, Endings, and Woolf's Non-coercive Ethical Texts," in *Woolfian Boundaries: Selected Papers from the Sixteenth Annual International Conference on Virginia Woolf*, ed. Anna Burrells, Steve Ellis, Deborah Parsons, and Kathryn Simpson (Clemson, S.C.: Clemson University Digital Press, 2007), 172–81.

11. Derek Attridge, "Ethical Modernism: Servants as Others in J. M. Coetzee's Early Fiction," in *Poetics Today* 25, no. 4 (Winter 2004): 654.

12. Newton, *Narrative Ethics*, 11.

13. I here draw on the definition of "exigence" as it is used in contemporary genre theory. See, for example, Lloyd F. Bitzer, "The Rhetorical Situation," *Philosophy and Rhetoric* 1 (1968): 1–14; and Arthur B. Miller, "Rhetorical Exigence," *Philosophy and Rhetoric* 2 (1972): 111–18. I am indebted to Jennifer Harrison for calling my attention to this concept.

14. Hannah Arendt, *The Human Condition* (Chicago: University of Chicago Press, 1958), 184.

15. On genre as social action, see Carolyn Miller, "Genre as Social Action," *Quarterly Journal of Speech* 70 (1984): 151–67; and Kenneth Burke, *A Grammar of Motives* (Berkeley: University of California Press, 1969).

16. Paul Ricoeur, *Time and Narrative*, vols. 1 and 3, trans. Kathleen Blamey (Chicago: University of Chicago Press, 1984), 1:xi.

17. Kenneth Burke, *Permanence and Change* (New York: New Republic, 1936), 329–30.

18. Gayatri Chakravorty Spivak, "Ethics and Politics in Tagore, Coetzee, and Certain Scenes of Teaching," *Diacritics* 32, no. 3–4 (Fall–Winter 2002): 18, 24.

19. Chakrabarty, *Habitations of Modernity*, 114.

20. Paul Ricoeur, *Oneself as Another*, trans. Kathleen Blamey (Chicago: University of Chicago Press, 1992), 159. Also see Ricoeur, "On Interpretation," in *From Text to Action*, trans Kathleen Blamey (Evanston, Ill.: Northwestern University Press, 1991), 1–22. In *Time and Narrative*, Ricoeur refers to an "as if past" that can be shared between fiction and history (3:189–90). The philosopher Hans Vaihinger employs the phrase "as if" in a slightly different though related sense, to refer to the way in which discourse in all branches of human knowledge relies upon useful fictions to advance thought. See Vaihinger, *The Philosophy of 'As-If,'* trans. C. K. Ogden (London: Routledge and Keegan Paul, 1924; reprint, New York: Barnes and Noble, 1968).

21. I do not here use the term "possible worlds" in the exact manner of possible world philosophers or as in the literary criticism of those like Marie-Laure Ryan (*Possible Worlds, Artificial Intelligence, and Narrative Theory* [Bloomington: Indiana University Press, 1991]). Still, like them I mean to indicate the interactive relationship between the actual world and the other possible ones we can imagine.

22. Susan Stanford Friedman, "Definitional Excursions: The Meanings of Modern/Modernity/Modernism," *Modernism/Modernity* 8, no. 3 (2001): 503.

23. The literature that attempts to define modernity is vast and varied. Modernity as I refer to it is a social, historical, and economic situation of late capitalism, characterized in part by advancing industrialization, expanding division of labor, and the increasing globalization of capital, as well as a range of attitudes associated with that situation as it emerges in different shapes and guises worldwide. However, I also share Eric Rothstein's understanding of the term as a practice-based label for a variety of experiences, habits, practices, and ideologies that emerge in conjunction with that situation and resist the effort to reduce it to a short nominal list (Eric Rothstein, "Broaching a Cultural Logic of Modernity," *MLQ* 61, no. 2 [June 2000]: 359–95). Important approaches to modernity include Jameson, *A Singular Modernity*; Felski, *The Gender of Modernity*; Zygmunt Bauman, *Modernity and the Holocaust* (Cambridge: Polity Press, 1989); Anthony Giddens, *The Consequences of Modernity* (Stanford, Calif.: Stanford University Press, 1990); Arjun Appadurai, *Modernity at Large: Cultural Dimensions of Globalization* (Minneapolis: University of Minnesota Press, 1996); Chakrabarty, *Habitations of Modernity*.

24. Peter Childs, *Modernism*, 2nd ed. (London: Routledge, 2008), 20. David Harvey makes a similar claim about the possible worlds of narrative fiction in relation to justice. See "The Cartographic Imagination: Balzac in Paris," in *Cosmopolitan Geographies: New Locations in Literature and Culture*, ed. Vinay Dharwadker (New York: Routledge, 2001), 64.

25. Baudelaire, qtd. in Walter Benjamin, "The Paris of the Second Empire in Baudelaire," in *Charles Baudelaire: A Lyric Poet in the Era of High Capitalism*, trans. Harry Zohn (London: Verso, 1983), 82.

26. Antoine Compagnon, *The Five Paradoxes of Modernity* (New York: Columbia University Press, 1994). Compagnon discusses this paradox as the tension between the modern and the avant-garde (31–57).

27. Elleke Boehmer, *Colonial and Postcolonial Literature* (New York: Oxford University Press, 1995), 7.

28. Jahan Ramazani, "A Transnational Poetics," *American Literary History* 18, no. 2 (2006): 339.

29. Jameson, *A Singular Modernity*, 180.

30. In a different way, Matt Hart also attempts to increase the political valence of Ramazani's use of the term "transnational." See *Nations of Nothing but Poetry: Modernism, Transnationalism, and Synthetic Vernacular Poetry* (New York: Oxford University Press, 2010). For an overview of the ways that transnationalism has transformed literary study, see Paul Jay, *Global Matters: The Transnational Turn in Literary Studies* (Ithaca, N.Y.: Cornell University Press, 2010).

31. Jay, *Global Matters*, 333.

32. Françoise Lionnet and Shu-Mei Shih, eds., *Minor Transnationalism* (Durham, N.C.: Duke University Press, 2005), 5.

33. Mulk Raj Anand, *Conversations in Bloomsbury* (1981; Oxford: Oxford University Press, 1995).

34. Susan Stryker and Stephen Whittle, *The Transgender Studies Reader* (New York: Routledge, 2006), 3. I wish to make clear that by making this comparison I in no way wish to elide the specificity of the transgender or transsexual voice but rather to listen to what the power of its critique can teach.

35. John Rawls, *A Theory of Justice* (Cambridge, Mass.: Belknap Press/Harvard University Press, 1971); Amartya Sen, *The Idea of Justice* (Cambridge, Mass.: Harvard University Press, 2009). Molly Hite also notes the absence of contemporary critical commentary on the relationship between ethics and politics in "Tonal Cues and Uncertain Values: Affect and Ethics in *Mrs. Dalloway*," *Narrative* 18, no. 3 (October 2010): 249–75.

36. Aristotle, *The Ethics of Aristotle: The Nicomachean Ethics*, trans. J. A. K. Thomson, rev. Hugh Tredennick (New York: Penguin, 1976), I.i (64), I.iii (65).

37. Ibid., 5.i (173); 5.vi (188).

38. David Hume, *A Treatise of Human Nature*, ed. L. A. Selby-Biggem, rev. 2nd ed., ed. P. H. Nidditch (New York: Oxford University Press, 1978), 3.1.1 468, 3.1.2 470, 3.1.1 468; further references cited in the text.

39. R. M. Hare, *The Language of Morals* (Oxford: Clarendon Press, 1952). In many ways it is this distinction between "ought" and "is" that prompts my effort to think about the connection between ethics and politics.

40. David Hume, *An Enquiry Concerning the Principles of Morals* (1777; reprint, 1912, Project Gutenberg e-book, 2010), section 3, part 1, accessed 28 September 2010, http://www.gutenberg.org/ebooks/4320.

41. Immanuel Kant, *On History*, ed. Louis White Beck (Indianapolis: Bobbs-Merrill, 1963), appendix 1, "On the Opposition Between Morality and Politics with Respect to Perpetual Peace," 117.

42. Kant, *On History*, 117.

43. See the discussion of rulers in the section "Public Rights" in Kant, *The Metaphysics of Morals*, trans. Mary Gregor (Cambridge: Cambridge University Press, 1996), 93–95.

44. Kant, *On History*, 128 For a discussion of the relationship between ethics and politics in Kant, also see, Marguerite La Caze, "At the Intersection: Kant, Derrida, and the Relation Between Ethics and Politics," *Political Theory* 35, no. 6 (2007): 781–805.

45. G. E. Moore, *Principia Ethica* (1903; Fair Use Repository, n.d.), 1.2, accessed 30 July 2009, http://fair-use.org/g-e-moore/principia-ethica/chapter-I.

46. Ibid., 1.7.

47. Emmanuel Levinas, "Ethics as First Philosophy" in *The Levinas Reader*, ed. Seán Hand (Malden, Mass.: Blackwell, 1989), 75–88; Robert Bernasconi, "The Third Party: Levinas on the Intersection of the Ethical and the Political," *Journal of the British Society for Phenomenology* 30, no. 1 (1999): 81. There is a growing body of work that addresses the question of politics in Levinasian thought, most of it focused on his notion of the "third" person who is always present at the scene of encounter between self and other. See Levinas, *Ethics and Infinity: Conversations with Philippe Nemo*, trans. Richard A. Cohen (Pittsburgh, Penn.: Duquesne University Press, 1985), "Being-for-the-Other," 115–16.

48. Levinas, "Ethics as First Philosophy," 84, 86.

49. Levinas, *Ethics and Infinity*, 95.

50. Emmanuel Levinas, *Totality and Infinity*, trans. Alphonso Lingis (Pittsburgh, Penn.: Duquesne University Press, 1969), 194, 43.

51. Though Derrida, in his emphasis on the notion of hospitality and the figure of the "third," will attempt to point Levinas in the direction of justice, his commentary in *Adieu to Levinas* serves mainly to highlight the gap in Levinas's writing on the question of the passage from ethics to politics (Critchley, *Ethics, Politics, Subjectivity*, 274).

52. There is an enormous body of work that elaborates on or revises Rawls's liberal theory of justice from a variety of perspectives. See, for example, Michael Walzer, *Spheres of Justice* (New York: Basic Books, 1983); Iris Marion Young, *Justice and the Politics of Difference* (Princeton, N.J.: Princeton University Press, 1990); Michael Sandel, *Justice: What's the Right Thing to Do?* (New York: Farrar Straus, 2009); Sen, *The Idea of Justice*; Nancy Fraser, *Scales of Justice: Reimagining Political Space in a Globalizing World* (New York: Columbia University Press, 2009).

53. John Rawls, "Justice as Fairness: Political Not Metaphysical" (1985), reprint, in *Twentieth-Century Political Theory*, 2nd ed., ed. Stephen Eric Bronner (New York: Routledge, 2005), 15, 16.

54. Rawls, *A Theory of Justice*, 61.

55. Chantal Mouffe, *The Return of the Political* (1993; New York: Verso, 2005), 44.

56. See Sen's chapter "Rawls and Beyond" in *The Idea of Justice*, 52–74. He also makes an important argument about the reach of justice beyond political institutions.

57. Among current theorists outside the communitarian camp, K. Anthony Appiah and Martha Nussbaum are among the few to grapple directly with this issue, Appiah from a pragmatic standpoint and Nussbaum through a neo-Aristotelian perspective. See Appiah, *The Ethics of Identity* (Princeton, N.J.: Princeton University Press, 2005); and Nussbaum, *Poetic Justice: The Literary Imagination and Public Life* (Boston: Beacon, 1995). As I've argued previously, I do not find the communitarian position generally convincing, not least because it describes community more as an entity rather than a process and develops a normative model of ethics based in a shared set of assumptions rather than attitudes toward others. See my *Modernist Fiction, Cosmopolitanism, and the Politics of Community* (2001; Cambridge: Cambridge University Press, 2006).

58. While it is clear that the confluence of ethics and politics flows through many varieties of narrative, it is my argument that it becomes particularly visible in transnational modernism.

59. See Luce Irigaray, *An Ethics of Sexual Difference* (Ithaca, N.Y.: Cornell University Press, 1984); Irigaray, *Sexes and Genealogies*, trans. Gillian Gill (New York: Columbia University Press, 1993; Tina Chanter, *The Ethics of Eros: Irigaray's Rewriting of the Philosophers* (New York: Routledge, 1995); and Chanter, *Feminist Interpretations of Emmanuel Levinas* (University Park: Penn State University Press, 2001).

60. Jacques Derrida, *On Cosmopolitanism and Forgiveness*, trans. Mark Dooley and Michale Hughes (New York: Routledge, 2001), 22–23.

61. This is Aristotle's definition. The philosopher Kelly Oliver takes ethics in the direction of the social in this manner: Kelly Oliver, *Family Values: Subjects Between Nature and Culture* (New York: Routledge), 1997.

62. Nancy calls this vision "philosophy-politics": Jean-Luc Nancy, *Being Singular Plural*, trans. Robert Richardson and Anne O'Byrne (Stanford, Calif.: Stanford University Press/Meridian, 2000), 25, 27.

63. I borrow the phrase "virile subject" from Oliver, *Family Values*, 119–33.

64. Oliver, *Family Values*, 231.

65. Jean-Luc Nancy, *The Sense of the World*, trans. Jeffrey Librett (Minneapolis: University of Minnesota P, 1997); Nancy, *Being Singular Plural*.

66. See Jean-Jacques Lecercle's definition of politics as "the form our being in society takes" ("Return to the Political," *PMLA* 125, no. 4 [October 2010]: 917).

67. Appiah, *The Ethics of Identity*, xvii.

68. Roland Barthes, *Mythologies*, cited in Mouffe, *Return of the Political*, 51.

69. These implications have been the subject of a number of critiques of Rawls in the many years since the *Theory of Justice* was published.

70. See, for example, Drucilla Cornell's and Iris Marion Young's critiques of Rawls along feminist lines: Cornell, *At the Heart of Freedom: Feminism, Sex, and Equality* (Princeton, N.J.: Princeton University Press, 1998); Young, *Justice and the Politics of Difference*.

71. See Fraser, *Scales of Justice*. Fraser argues convincingly that the problem of the "who" of political justice in a post-Westphalian world ought to concern us as much as the "what." Amartya Sen also takes up the question of global justice as a crucial question for liberal theory in *The Idea of Justice*, 140–45.

72. Chanter, *The Ethics of Eros*, 81. The passage in question appears in G. W. F. Hegel, *Phenomenology of Spirit*, trans. A. V. Miller (New York: Oxford University Press, 1977), 274.

73. Hegel, *Phenomenology*, 274–75.

74. David Harvey, *Justice, Nature, and the Geography of Difference* (Malden, Mass.: Blackwell, 1996), 330.

75. Charles Taylor, *Modern Social Imaginaries* (Durham, N.C.: Duke University Press, 2004), 23.

76. I use the term "radical democracy" as formulated by Ernesto Laclau and Chantal Mouffe in *Hegemony and Socialist Strategy: Towards a Radical Democratic Politics* (London: Verso, 1985). According to Mouffe, "radical and plural democracy rejects the very possibility of a non-exclusive public sphere of rational argument where a non-coercive consensus could be attained" (*The Democratic Paradox* [New York: Verso, Phronesis, 2000], 33).

77. On the importance of "situation" and its supplement in thought, see Alan Badiou, *Ethics: An Essay on the Understanding of Evil*, trans. Peter Hallward (New York: Verso, 2001), 41–42.

78. Cornell, *At the Heart of Freedom*, 8. Harvey makes a similar point (*Justice*, 332–33).

79. Vaihinger, *The Philosophy of 'As-If,'* viii.

80. Cornell, *At the Heart of Freedom*, 15–16; Badiou, *Ethics*, 42; the subtitle of Fraser's *Scales of Justice* is *Reimagining Political Space in a Globalizing World*; Jacques Rancière, *Dissensus: On Politics and Aesthetics*, ed. and trans. Steven Corcoran (New York: Continuum, 2010), 152.

81. In this book I rely primarily on imaginative prose narratives such as fiction, memoir, autobiography, reportage, creative essay, and short story, but I also delve briefly into photo essay and film. I have not investigated narrative poetry, in part because it was a less common mode among modernist writers and because it seems somewhat less preoccupied with the ethical and political relationships that develop in narrative prose, at least in the period in question. I do believe, however, that many of the attributes I examine in

imaginative narrative also apply in other narrative situations (e.g., history, testimony, song, drama).

82. On accountability as the link between ethics and narration, see Ricoeur, *Oneself as Another*, 165. For the importance of the question "who are you?" as the basis for narration, see Adriana Cavarero, *Relating Narratives: Storytelling and Selfhood*, trans. Paul A. Kottman (New York: Routledge, 2000).

83. I am here drawing on Derek Attridge's notion of the ethical basis of reading. See Attridge, *The Singularity of Literature* (New York: Routledge, 2004).

84. Mouffe, *The Return of the Political*, 52–53.

85. Or *kairos*.

86. Arendt, *The Human Condition*, 77; Arendt, *Responsibility and Judgment*, ed. Jerome Kohn (New York: Schocken, 2003), 153.

87. Arendt, *The Human Condition*, 183. She is here extending and revising Heidegger's notion of "being-in-the-world." Jean-Luc Nancy's more recent notion of "being-in-common" is a similar attempt to revise Heidegger on this point and to posit relationship or community as crucial to being and central to any description of the political. See *Being Singular Plural*.

88. Arendt, *The Human Condition*, 145; Hannah Arendt, *Lectures on Kant's Political Philosophy*, ed. Ronald Beiner (Chicago: University of Chicago Press, 1989), 43.

89. Arendt, *Lectures on Kant's Political Philosophy*, 184.

90. Adriana Cavarero, *Relating Narratives*, 20, 92.

91. Arendt, *Responsibility and Judgment*, 106. Indeed, as Seyla Benhabib puts it, "[Arendt] regarded plurality as the political principle par excellence" (*Situating the Self: Gender, Community, and Postmodernism in Contemporary Ethics* [New York: Routledge, 1992], 138).

92. Arendt, *The Human Condition*, 180.

93. Arendt, *Responsibility and Judgment*, 139.

94. For a discussion of this relationship, see Ricoeur, *Oneself as Another*, 19–20.

95. Ricoeur, *Oneself as Another*, "Imagination in Discourse and Action," 179.

96. Ricoeur, *Oneself as Another*, 74.

97. Ricouer frequently uses the word "laboratory" to describe fictional or literary narrative in *Oneself as Another*.

98. I here draw on Ricouer's refusal of Hume's famous claim that one cannot derive an "ought" from an "is" (*Oneself as Another*, 170).

99. Miller, "Genre as Social Action," 152.

100. Attridge, *The Singularity of Literature*, 63.

101. Many scholars have pointed to the ways that British laws against untouchability may have been especially counterproductive. See, most famously,

Gayatri Chakravorty Spivak, *A Critique of Postcolonial Reason* (Cambridge, Mass.: Harvard University Press, 1999).

102. Harvey, *Justice*, 330.

103. Attridge, *The Singularity of Literature*, 131.

104. Kenneth Burke, "Literature as Equipment for Living," in *The Philosophy of Literary Form* (1941; Berkeley: University of California Press, 1973).

105. Nussbaum, *Poetic Justice*, 2.

106. Jean-Paul Sartre, *What Is Literature and Other Essays*, trans. Bernard Frechtman (Cambridge Mass.: Harvard University Press, 1988), 34.

107. Ibid., 37.

108. Ibid., 28.

109. Theodor Adorno, "Commitment," in *Notes to Literature*, vol. 2, trans. Shierry Weber Nicholson (New York: Columbia University Press, 1992), 77.

110. Ibid., 89.

111. Theodor Adorno, *Aesthetic Theory*, trans. C. Lenhardt (New York: Rouledge, 1984), 7.

112. Franco Moretti, *Signs Taken for Wonders: On the Sociology of Literary Forms* (1983; New York: Verso, 2005), 185. I do not want to suggest, however, that Moretti follows Adorno in his method of analysis.

113. Adorno, *Aesthetic Theory*, 327.

114. Adorno, *Aesthetic Theory*, 2.

115. To be clear, Adorno constantly posits and undermines the notion of the autonomous work of art throughout his *Aesthetic Theory*.

116. Williams, *The Politics of Modernism* (London: Verso, 1996), "Media, Margins, and Modernity," 178.

117. Williams, *The Politics of Modernism*, "The Politics of the Avant-garde," 56–57.

118. Williams, *The Politics of Modernism*, "When Was Modernism?" 35.

119. Williams, *The Politics of Modernism*, "When Was Modernism?" 34.

120. Williams, *The Politics of Modernism*, "When Was Modernism?" 32.

121. I applaud the renewed work being done on "thirties" writers under the moniker of "intermodernism" by Kristen Bluemel and others (see Bluemel, *Intermodernism: Writing and Culture in Interwar and Wartime Britain* [Edinburgh: Edinburgh University Press, 2009]). Still, by calling this work by another name and describing it as occupying the position between modernism and postmodernism, Bluemel is necessarily distinguishing it from the modernism of an earlier period.

122. Williams, *The Politics of Modernism*, "The Politics of the Avant-garde," 60.

123. Friedman, "Definitional Excursions," 508–9.

124. Pascale Casanova, *The World Republic of Letters*, trans. M. B. DeBevoise (Cambridge, Mass.: Harvard University Press, 2004). I discuss the limitations of Casanova's model in my "Imagining World Literatures: Modernism

and Comparative Literature," in *Disciplining Modernism*, ed. Pamela Caughie (London: Palgrave, 2009), 53–71.

125. David Lodge, *The Modes of Modern Writing* (London: Bloomsbury, 1977); Franco Moretti, *Modern Epic: The World System from Goethe to Garcia Marquez* (New York: Verso, 1996), 2; Jameson, *A Singular Modernity*, part 2: "Modernism as Ideology," 139–210.

126. Indeed, a growing group of scholars is now approaching modernism from something like this vantage point. See, for example, Friedman, "Definitional Excursions"; Brent Hayes Edwards, *The Practice of Diaspora* (Cambridge, Mass.: Harvard University Press, 2003); Melba Cuddy Keane, "Modernism, Geopolitics, Globalization," *Modernism/Modernity* 10, no. 3 (2003): 539–58; Anita Patterson, *Race, American Literature, and Transnational Modernism* (New York: Cambridge University Press, 2008); Laura Winkiel, *Modernism, Race, and Manifestos* (New York: Cambridge University Press, 2008); Jahan Ramazani, *A Transnational Poetics* (Chicago: University of Chicago Press, 2009); Hart, *Nations of Nothing but Poetry*; as well as work in progress by Jed Esty, Paul Saint-Amour, and many others. Recent and forthcoming essay collections focusing on the intersecting problematics of transnational modernism include Laura Doyle and Laura Winkiel, eds., *Geomodernisms: Race, Modernism, Modernity* (Bloomington: Indiana University Press, 2005); Richard Begam and Michael Valdez Moses eds., *Modernism and Colonialism: British and Irish Literature, 1899–1939* (Durham, N.C.: Duke University Press, 2007); Astradur Eysteinsson and Vivian Liska eds., *Modernism*, 2 vols. (Philadelphia: Benjamins, 2007); Pamela Caughie, ed., *Disciplining Modernism* (New York: Palgrave, 2010); Mark Wollaeger, ed., *The Oxford Handbook of Global Modernism* (Oxford: Oxford University Press, forthcoming). For an overview of the recent shifts toward a more temporally and geographically expansive view of modernism, see Doug Mao and Rebecca Walkowitz, "The New Modernist Studies," *PMLA* 123, no. 3 (May 2008): 737–48.

127. Lionnet and Shih, *Minor Transnationalism*, 8

128. Rebecca Walkowitz, "Comparison Literature," *NLH* 40, no. 3 (Summer 2009): 567.

129. See for example, David Damrosch, *What Is World Literature* (Princeton, N.J.: Princeton University Press, 2003); Martin Puchner, *Poetry of the Revolution: Marx, Manifestos, and the Avant-gardes* (Princeton, N.J.: Princeton University Press, 2006); and Ramazani, *A Transnational Poetics*.

130. This is not to say that Anand somehow "completes" Joyce but rather that his work allows us to see Joyce differently.

131. I here also reference the movement towards transnationalism as a critique of globalization within contemporary political theory. See James Anderson, ed., *Transnational Democracy: Political Spaces and Border Crossings* (New York: Routledge, 2002).

132. Hart, *Nations of Nothing but Poetry*, 19.

133. Franco Moretti, "Conjectures on World Literature," in *Debating World Literature*, ed. Christopher Prendergast (London: Verso, 2004), 148–63.

134. See note 139.

135. I here reference Bill Ashcroft, Gareth Griffiths, and Helen Tiffin, *The Empire Writes Back: Theory and Practice in Post-Colonial Literature* (New York: Routledge, 1989). Important recent work on Asian literature has made clear the multiple origination points and complexity of global flows of modernism. See, for example, Steven Yao, *Translation and the Languages of Modernism* (New York: Palgrave, 2002); Priya Joshi, *In Another Country: Colonialism, Culture, and the English Novel in India* (New York: Columbia University Press, 2002); Eric Hayot, *The Hypothetical Mandarin: Sympathy, Modernity, and Chinese Pain* (Oxford: Oxford University Press, 2009); Christopher Bush, *Ideographic Modernism: China, Writing, and Media* (Oxford: Oxford University Press, 2009).

136. On the interconnection between twentieth-century writing and international justice, see, especially, Joseph Slaughter, *Human Rights, Inc.* (New York: Fordham University Press, 2007).

137. Jameson, *A Singular Modernity*, 13.

138. Rothstein, "Broaching a Cultural Logic," 359.

139. The scholarly exploration of Bengali modernism has already been well begun, especially in regard to the study of Tagore. See for example, Spivak, "Ethics and Politics"; Chakrabarty, *Habitations of Modernity*; Sangeeta Ray, *En-gendering India: Woman and Nation in Colonial and Postcolonial Narratives* (Durham, N.C.: Duke University Press, 2000); Susan Stanford Friedman, "Planetarity: Musing Modernist Studies," *Modernism/Modernity* 17, no. 3 (2010): 471–99; Amardeep Singh, "Veiled Strangers: Rabindranath Tagore's America, in Letters and Lectures," *Journeys* 10, no. 1 (2009): 51–68; and forthcoming work by Ben Conisbee Baer. Scholarship in English that treats Japanese or Portuguese modernism has been slower to emerge. For overviews, see the relevant chapters in Eysteinsson and Liska, *Modernism*.

1. Intimate and Global: Ethical Domains from Woolf to Rhys

1. Virginia Woolf, *The Death of the Moth and Other Essays* (New York: Harcourt, 1970), 114. See also the extended discussion of this essay in Melba Cuddy-Keane, *Virginia Woolf, the Intellectual, and the Public Sphere* (Cambridge: Cambridge University Press, 2003), 22–34.

2. Woolf, *The Death of the Moth*, 113.

3. Virginia Woolf, "Introductory Letter," in *Life as We Have Known It*, ed. Margaret Llewelyn Davies (New York: Norton, 1975), xx–xxi. For a more complete discussion of this introductory letter and its implications for Woolf's notions of community, see my *Modernist Fiction, Cosmopolitanism,*

and the Politics of Community (2001; Cambridge: Cambridge University Press, 2006), 117–20.

4. Virginia Woolf, "Mr. Bennett and Mrs. Brown," in Woolf, *Collected Essays*, vol. 1 (London: Hogarth, 1966), 319.

5. See Iris Marion Young, *On Female Body Experience* (New York: Oxford University Press, 2005). I will discuss this theory at more length in chapter 5.

6. Immanuel Kant, *The Critique of Judgment*, trans. J. H. Bernard (New York: Hafner, 1951), section 40, 135–38. I will take up the importance of Arendt's revision of Kant's "enlarged thinking" for reading narrative politics in the next chapter.

7. Gilles Deleuze, *The Fold: Leibniz and the Baroque*, trans. Peter Conley (Minneapolis: University of Minnesota Press, 1993).

8. See, for example, Ewa Plonowska Ziarek's discussion of what she calls the "futural dimension of democratic politics" (*An Ethics of Dissensus: Postmodernity, Feminism, and the Politics of Radical Democracy* [Stanford, Calif.: Stanford University Press, 2001), 8.

9. I use the term "radical democracy" following Chantal Mouffe and Ernesto LaClau's elaborations in *Hegemony and Socialist Strategy: Towards a Radical Democratic Politics* (London: Verso, 1985), and further writings.

10. Hannah Arendt, *The Human Condition* (Chicago: University of Chicago Press, 1958), 176.

11. Gayatri Chakravorty Spivak, *A Critique of Postcolonial Reason* (Cambridge, Mass.: Harvard University Press, 1999), 125. To be clear, Spivak is very critical of Rhys's writing about the Caribbean.

12. Lee Edelman, *No Future: Queer Theory and the Death Drive* (Durham, N.C.: Duke University Press, 2004).

13. See Edward Said, *Culture and Imperialism* (New York: Vintage, 1994); and Frederic Jameson, "Modernism and Imperialism," in *Nationalism, Colonialism, and Literature*, by Terry Eagleton, Fredric Jameson, Edward W. Said (Minneapolis: University of Minnesota Press, 1990), 43–69. Also see the discussion of Jameson's essay in the editors' introduction to Richard Begam and Michael Valdez Moses, eds., *Modernism and Colonialism: British and Irish Literature, 1899–1939* (Durham, N.C.: Duke University Press, 2007), 1–5.

14. One notable exception is Melba Cuddy-Keane, "Modernism, Geopolitics, Globalization," *Modernism/Modernity* 10, no. 3 (2003): 539–58.

15. Kelly Oliver, *Family Values: Subjects Between Nature and Culture* (New York: Routledge, 1997), 156.

16. Ibid., 157–58.

17. See Luce Irigaray, *An Ethics of Sexual Difference*, trans. Carolyn Burke (Ithaca, N.Y.: Cornell University Press, 1984); Irigaray, *Sexes and Genealogies*, trans. Gillian Gill (New York: Columbia University Press, 1993); Tina Chanter, *The Ethics of Eros: Irigaray's Rewriting of the Philosophers* (New York: Routledge, 1995); and Chanter, *Feminist Interpretations of Emmanuel Levinas* (University Park: Penn State University Press, 2001). The list of feminist

philosophical texts on the matter of care in the years since Carol Gilligan, *In a Different Voice: Psychological Theory and Women's Development* (Cambridge: Cambridge University Press, 1982), is long. See, for example, Virginia Held, *The Ethics of Care: Personal, Political, and Global* (Oxford: Oxford University Press, 2005). On the link between the ethics of care and justice, see Robin West, *Caring for Justice* (New York: New York University Press, 1997).

18. See Irigaray, *Sexes and Genealogies*; Judith Butler, *Antigone's Claim: Kinship Between Life and Death* (New York: Columbia University Press, 2000). For a cogent analysis of the position of women within the traditions of moral philosophy, see Margaret Urban Walker, *Moral Understandings: A Feminist Study of Ethics* (New York: Routledge, 1998).

19. Irigaray, *Ethics*, 204. Levinas rather notoriously raises the question of procreation—or, in *Totality and Infinity*, trans. Alphonso Lingis (Pittsburgh, Penn.: Duquesne University Press, 1969), of filiation or paternity—within his ethics, employing the patriarchal coding of the lover as masculine and the beloved as feminine. This problematic relation with the feminine other is "resolved in paternity" without fully accounting for the participation of the feminine, who is always other (Levinas, *Totality*, 271). On this problem, also see Vicki Bell, "On Ethics and Feminism: Reflecting on Levinas' Ethics of Non-(in)difference," *Feminist Theory* 2, no. 2 (2002): 163.

20. Oliver, *Family Values*, 196, 232, 231.

21. Jean-Luc Nancy, *Being Singular Plural*, trans. Robert Richardson and Anne O'Byrne (Stanford, Calif.: Stanford University Press/Meridian, 2000), 30, 79.

22. As Nancy describes it, "being-with" can be seen "as just measure, as justness and justice" (ibid., 81).

23. Adriana Cavarero, *Relating Narratives: Storytelling and Selfhood*, trans. Paul A. Kottman (New York: Routledge, 2000), 90.

24. Ibid., 20. Cavarero is drawing on Arendt here.

25. This is more complex and intertwined process than the empathy between writer and reader that Martha Nussbaum emphasizes in, for example, "The Narrative Imagination" chapter in Nussbaum, *Cultivating Humanity: A Classical Defense of Reform in Liberal Education* (Cambridge, Mass.: Harvard University Press, 1997).

26. Cavarero, *Relating Narratives*, 87.

27. See Jacques Rancière, *The Politics of Aesthetics*, trans. Gabriel Rockhill (London: Continuum, 2004), 13,

28. Cavarero, *Relating Narratives*, 87.

29. John Dewey, *Art as Experience* (1934; New York: Penguin, 2005), 50–51.

30. In a different way Dewey also understands the aesthetic object as a sort of "external embodiment" of an aesthetic experience (*Art as Experience*, 53).

31. Kant, *Critique of Judgment*, 1.9 (53).

32. Kant, *Critique of Judgment*, 2.59 (198).

33. Kant, *Critique of Judgment*, 2.59 (199).

34. This is the title of Moore's 1903 essay.

35. For a systematic treatment of philosophical realism and its connection to postimpressionism and to Woolf, see Ann Banfield, *The Phantom Table: Woolf, Fry, Russell, and the Epistemology of Modernism* (Cambridge: Cambridge University Press, 2000). For the connection of Woolf to the continental philosophical tradition, see Mark Hussey, *The Singing of the Real World: The Philosophy of Virginia Woolf's Fiction* (Columbus: Ohio State University Press, 1986).

36. Kant, *The Critique of Judgment*, introduction, 27.

37. See G. E. Moore, *Principia Ethica* (1903; Fair Use Repository, n.d.), accessed 30 July 2009, http://fair-use.org/g-e-moore/principia-ethica.

38. Roger Fry, "An Essay in Aesthetics" (1909), in *Vision and Design*, ed. J. B. Bullen (New York: Oxford University Press, 1990), 15.

39. Ibid., 22, 24.

40. Banfield, *The Phantom Table*, 247.

41. Virginia Woolf, *Letters of Virginia Woolf*, vol. 6 (New York: Harcourt, 1980), 419.

42. Jane Goldman, *The Feminist Aesthetics of Virginia Woolf* (Cambridge: Cambridge University Press, 1998), 116; Virginia Woolf, *Letters of Virginia Woolf*, vol. 2 (New York: Harcourt, 1976), 257. For a more extensive account of the connection between the work of Vanessa Bell and Virginia Woolf, see Diane Gillespie, *The Sisters' Arts: The Writing and Painting of Virginia Woolf and Vanessa Bell* (Syracuse, N.Y,: Syracuse University Press, 1988).

43. Goldman, *The Feminist Aesthetics of Virginia Woolf*, 257.

44. Virginia Woolf, *To The Lighthouse* (1927; New York: Harcourt, 1955), 23 (further references cited in the text); Banfield, *The Phantom Table*, 50–51.

45. Martha Nussbaum, "The Window: Knowledge of Other Minds in Virginia Woolf's *To the Lighthouse*," *NLH* 26 (1995): 742.

46. The "fold" is a concept borrowed from Deleuze, but the way I use it in this chapter is inspired by Mieke Bal; see "Enfolding Feminism," in *Feminist Consequences: Theory for the New Century*, ed. Elisabeth Bronfen and Misha Kavka (New York: Columbia University Press, 2001), 321–52.

47. I resist, however, calling this "dissensus" as do both Ewa Plonowska Ziarek and Jacques Rancière, among others (see most recently Rancière, *Dissensus: On Politics and Aesthetics*, ed. and trans. Steven Corcoran [New York: Continuum, 2010]).

48. Bal, "Enfolding Feminism," 324.

49. Bal, "Enfolding Feminism," 330.

50. Bal, "Enfolding Feminism," 333.

51. Deleuze, *The Fold*, 115.

52. Deleuze, *The Fold*, 120.

53. Bal, "Enfolding Feminism," 330.

54. Bal, "Enfolding Feminism," 333.

55. Virginia Woolf, *Orlando* (1928; New York: Harcourt, 1956), 158; further references cited in the text.

56. I here differ significantly from Martha Nussbaum's understanding of empathy between individuals as the source of ethics in fiction. See *Cultivating Humanity*, 85–113.

57. See Chanter, *The Ethics of Eros*, 218.

58. The question of the distinction between the saying and the said is a fraught one in Levinas.

59. Emmanuel Levinas, *Otherwise Than Being; Or, Beyond Essence*, trans. Alphonso Lingis (Dordrecht: Kluwer Academic Publishers, 1991), 40.

60. Deleuze, *The Fold*, 115.

61. Virginia Woolf, *Mrs. Dalloway* (1925; New York: Harcourt, 1981), 126; further references cited in the text.

62. An exception here is Ravit Reichman, who reads this scene as an ethical moment "defined by strangerness rather than knowledge" (*The Affective Life of Law* [Stanford, Calif.: Stanford University Press, 2009], 61.

63. Woolf, *Letters*, 6:414.

64. Jane Marcus, "'No More Horses': Virginia Woolf on Art and Propaganda," *Women's Studies* 4, no. 2/3 (1977): 265–90; Brenda Silver, "The Authority of Anger: *Three Guineas* as Case Study," *Signs* 16, no. 2 (Winter 1991): 340–70.

65. Virginia Woolf, *Three Guineas*, ed. Naomi Black (1938; Oxford: Shakespeare Head Press of Blackwell Publishers, 2001), appendix D, appendix E, 246–53; further references cited in the text. As Naomi Black points out, "Woolf supplied bibliographic references with great care" and also used the notes to provide background detail that did not fit into the text proper (246).

66. The three original scrapbooks are in the University of Sussex and are available online by subscription at the California State University–Bakersfield. Brenda Silver, *Virginia Woolf's Reading Notebooks* (Princeton, N.J.: Princeton University Press, 1983), examines the contents of these scrapbooks and notebooks.

67. Susan Sontag takes issue with the very claim that atrocity photographs engender resistance to war (*Regarding the Pain of Others* [New York: Picador, 2003], 9).

68. As John Whitter-Ferguson makes clear, Woolf's essay appears in a "deliberately broken form" that opens itself out into passages that are epistolary, biographical, historical, argumentative, and literary" (*Framing Pieces: Designs of the Gloss in Joyce, Woolf, and Pound* [New York: Oxford University Press, 1996], 90, 92).

69. Sontag, *Regarding the Pain of Others*, 26.

70. Holly Henry, *Virginia Woolf and the Discourse of Science* (Cambridge: Cambridge University Press, 2003), 146.

71. Sontag, *Regarding the Pain of Others*, 9.

72. The letter was dated 4 November 1936 (*Three Guineas*, 174n10).

73. Emily Dalgarno, *Virginia Woolf and the Visual World* (Cambridge: Cambridge University Press, 2001), 164. These photos were part of a large group sent out of Spain and published in greater number in the French press. See also Caroline Brothers, *War and Photography: A Cultural History* (New York: Routledge, 1997).

74. Woolf, *The Diary of Virginia Woolf*, vol. 5: *1936–41*, ed. Anne Olivier Bell and Andrew McNeillie (New York: Harcourt Brace, 1984), 32.

75. Sontag, *Regarding the Pain of Others*, 9.

76. The nonintervention pact was an agreement signed on 9 September 1936 by Great Britain, France, Russia, Italy, and Germany and eventually by twenty-seven countries, pledging not to supply materials of war to either side in the conflict in Spain. It quickly became clear that Hitler and Mussolini were aiding the Nationalists and in France and Great Britain there was strong pressure from the left to abandon the pact.

77. Sontag, *Regarding the Pain of Others*, 24.

78. Henry, *Woolf and the Discourse of Science*, 143.

79. Dalgarno, *Woolf and the Visual World*, 169.

80. Louis Delaprée, "The Martyrdom of Madrid," (Madrid, 1937), 21, 15, in *The Reading Notes for* Three Guineas*: An Archival Edition*, ed. Merry M. Pawlowski and Vara S. Neverow, accessed 11 February 2009, http://www.csub.edu/woolf/tgs_home.html (subscription required).

81. George Orwell, *Homage to Catalonia* (1938; Boston: Beacon, 1967), 231. I will treat Orwell's statement and his response to the Civil War at length in chapter 5.

82. Delaprée, "The Martyrdom of Madrid," 21, 20, 21, 14.

83. W. E. Dougherty and Morris Janowitz, *A Psychological Warfare Casebook* (Baltimore, Md.: Johns Hopkins University Press, 1956), 2.

84. Virginia Woolf, *The Diary of Virginia Woolf*, vol. 4: *1931–35*, ed. Anne Olivier Bell (New York: Harcourt: 1983), 300; Susan Suleiman, *Authoritarian Fictions: The Ideological Novel as a Literary Genre* (New York: Columbia University Press, 1983); Marcus, "'No More Horses,'" 103.

85. Laura Winkiel, *Modernism, Race, and Manifestos* (Cambridge: Cambridge University Press, 2008), 202–3.

86. Janet Gurkin Altman, *Epistolarity: Approaches to a Form* (Columbus: Ohio State University Press, 1982), 89, 88.

87. Judith Butler, *Giving an Account of Oneself* (New York: Fordham University Press, 2005), 8, 64.

88. Cavarero, *Relating Narratives*, 24.

89. Paul Ricoeur, *Oneself as Another*, trans. Kathleen Blamey (Chicago: University of Chicago Press, 1992), 16; Arendt, *The Human Condition*, 183.

90. Arendt, *The Human Condition*, 176–78.

91. Arendt, *The Human Condition*, 180.

92. Sontag, *Regarding the Pain of Others*, 10, 12.

93. In this way they exhibit some of the attributes that Jed Esty ascribes to the colonial bildungsroman. See Jed Esty, "Virginia Woolf's Colony and the Adolescence of Modernist Fiction," in *Modernism and Colonialism: British and Irish Literature, 1899–1939*, ed. Richard Begam and Michael Valdez Moses (Durham, N.C.: Duke University Press, 2007), 70–90; and Esty, "The Colonial Bildungsroman: The Story of an African Farm and the Ghost of Goethe," *Victorian Studies* 49, no. 3 (Spring 2007): 407–30.

94. Edelman, *No Future*, 6.

95. Jean Rhys, *Smile Please* (New York: Penguin, 1979), 8, 10.

96. As Maren Linett puts it, "Jean Rhys's novels present an intriguing case study for thinking about the status and meaning of fragmented text" ("'New Worlds, New Everything': Fragmentation and Trauma in Jean Rhys," *Twentieth-Century Literature* 51, no. 4 [Winter 2005]: 437).

97. Spivak, *A Critique of Postcolonial Reason*, 125.

98. Delia Caparoso Konzett, *Ethnic Modernisms: Anna Yezierska, Zora Neale Hurston, Jean Rhys, and the Aesthetics of Dislocation* (New York: Palgrave, 2002), 156.

99. See, for example, Judith Raiskin, *Snow on the Cane Fields: Women's Writing and Creole Subjectivity* (Minneapolis: University of Minnesota Press, 1996), 129–30; and Veronica Gregg, *Jean Rhys's Historical Imagination: Reading and Writing the Creole* (Chapel Hill: University of North Carolina Press, 1995). Kamau Brathwaite claims the category of "Creole" primarily for black people from the region; see "History of the Voice," in Brathwaite, *Roots: Essays in Caribbean Literature* (Ann Arbor: University of Michigan Press, 1993), 259–304. The debate between Gayatri Spivak and Benita Parry about how to read the racial politics of *Wide Sargasso Sea* also surrounds this point. See Spivak, "Three Women's Texts and Critique of Imperialism," *Critical Inquiry* 12, no. 1 (Autumn 1985): 243–61; Spivak, *Critique of Postcolonial Reason*; and Parry, *Postcolonial Studies: A Materialist Critique* (New York: Routledge, 2004).

100. Raiskin, *Snow on the Cane Fields*, 108.

101. Parry, *Postcolonial Studies*, 21.

102. Jean Rhys, interview with Ned Thomas, qtd. in Gregg, *Jean Rhys's Historical Imagination*, 2.

103. Ford Madox Ford, qtd. in Gregg, *Jean Rhys's Historical Imagination*, 6.

104. Rhys, *Smile Please*, 165, 169, 165.

105. The Geography Working Group's Interim Report (1990), qtd. in Brendan Bartley, Rob Hitchin, and Phil Hubbard, *Thinking Geographically: Space, Theory, and Contemporary Human Geography* (New York: Continuum, 2002), 11.

106. David Harvey, *Justice, Nature, and the Geography of Difference* (Malden, Mass.: Blackwell, 1996), 5, 211.

107. Jean Rhys, *Letters, 1931–66*, ed. Francis Wyndham and Diana Melly (New York: Penguin, 1985), 171, 24.

108. See the original ending of *Voyage in the Dark*, where Anna's death is made clear, in Bonnie Kime Scott, ed., *The Gender of Modernism* (Indianapolis: Indiana University Press, 1990), 381–89.

109. In the letter just cited Rhys vacillates about the madness described in the book: "Perhaps I was simply trying to describe a girl going potty," she writes, and then a few lines later, "I expect I've made it sound even pottier than it is" (Rhys, *Letters, 1931–66*, 24). The early critical reception of Rhys's work made much of the madness and self-destructive behavior of her heroines.

110. Jean Rhys, *Voyage in the Dark* (1934; New York: Norton, 1982); further references cited in the text.

111. Peter Kalliney, "Jean Rhys: Left Bank Modernist as Postcolonial Intellectual," in *Oxford Handbook of Global Modernisms*, ed. Mark Wollaeger (Oxford: Oxford University Press, forthcoming). Most critics agree that Rhys employs a highly suspect typology of blackness.

112. Homi Bhabha, *The Location of Culture* (New York: Routledge, 1994), 92.

113. Susan Stanford Friedman, *Mappings: Feminism and the Cultural Geographies of Encounter* (Princeton, N.J.: Princeton University Press, 1998), 28–29.

114. Butler, *Giving an Account of Oneself*, 39.

115. Mary Lou Emery, "The Politics of Form: Jean Rhys's Social Vision in *Voyage in the Dark* and *Wide Sargasso Sea*," *Twentieth-Century Literature* 28, no. 4 (Winter 1982): 422.

116. Jean Rhys, *Good Morning, Midnight* (1939; New York: Norton, 1986), 15; further references cited in the text.

117. Here also see Rhys's early short story "Learning to Be a Mother," which rehearsed similar events.

118. Jean Rhys, *Quartet* (1929; New York: Norton, 1997), 72, 77, 118. Indeed, one of the most interesting aspects of the sexual scenario in *Quartet* is the voyeurism of Heidler's wife, Lois, who watches their lovemaking from the hallway, putting Marya literally on display.

119. Konzett, *Ethnic Modernisms*, 152–53.

120. Levinas, *Otherwise*, 75.

2. Comparative Colonialisms: Joyce, Anand, and the Question of Engagement

1. Mulk Raj Anand, *Conversations in Bloomsbury* (1981; Oxford: Oxford University Press, 1995), 7.

2. Ibid, 32.

3. Jean-Paul Sartre, *What Is Literature and Other Essays*, trans. Bernard Frechtman (Cambridge Mass.: Harvard University Press, 1988), 40.

4. Kristen Bluemel, *George Orwell and the Radical Eccentric* (New York: Palgrave, 2004), calls this writing "intermodernsm." Yet I want to resist the tendency to exclude the work of "thirties writers" from modernism.

5. James Joyce, *A Portrait of the Artist as a Young Man* (1917), Case Studies in Contemporary Criticism (New York : Bedford Books, 1992), 214; further references will be cited in the text.

6. Franco Moretti, *The Way of the World* (New York: Verso, 2000), 16.

7. See Hannah Arendt, *Lectures on Kant's Political Philosophy*, ed. Ronald Beiner (Chicago: University of Chicago Press, 1989), 43.

8. Elleke Boehmer, *Empire, the National, and the Postcolonial* (Oxford: Oxford University Press, 2002), 3.

9. See Joseph Lennon, *Irish Orientalism: A Literary and Intellectual History* (Syracuse, N.Y.: Syracuse University Press, 2004); and Gauri Viswanathan, "Ireland, India, and the Poetics of Internationalism," *Journal of World History* 15, no. 1 (2004), accessed 3 January 2006, http://www.historycooperative.org/journals/jwh/15.1/viswanathan.html.

10. See, for example, James Connolly, "The Coming Revolt in India: Its Political and Social Causes," *The Harp* (January 1908), accessed 3 January 2006, http://www.marxists.org/archive/connolly/1908/01/india1.htm.

11. Elleke Boehmer, *Colonial and Postcolonial Literature* (New York: Oxford University Press, 1995), 129.

12. Kristen Bluemel, *George Orwell and the Radical Eccentric*, 81.

13. Richard Ellmann, *James Joyce* (1959; Oxford: Oxford University Press, 1982), 28.

14. See for example, Edward Soja, *Postmodern Geographies: The Reassertion of Space in Critical Social Theory* (New York: Verso, 1989).

15. David Harvey, "The Cartographic Imagination: Balzac in Paris," in *Cosmopolitan Geographies: New Locations in Literature and Culture*, ed. Vinay Dharwadker (New York: Routledge, 2001), 64.

16. Ibid., 74.

17. See, for example, Franco Moretti, *An Atlas of the European Novel, 1800–1900* (New York: Verso, 1998), 87–110, which includes several maps of Paris with the locations of events in Balzac's novels marked on them.

18. Harvey, "The Cartographic Imagination," 66.

19. Harvey, "The Cartographic Imagination," 83, 84.

20. James Joyce, *Ulysses* (1922; New York: Random House, 1986), 96, 61, 96; further references cited in the text.

21. Humboldt was perhaps the greatest geographer of his era and a pioneer in global thinking. Robert E. Dickinson, *The Makers of Modern Geography* (London: Routledge, 1969), 23; David Harvey, "Cosmopolitanism and the Banality of Geographical Evils," *Public Culture* 12, no. 2 (2000): 548.

22. The French Societé de Géographie, the oldest in the world, was founded in 1821; the British Royal Geographical Society, in 1859; and the American Geographic Society, in 1851.

23. Harvey, "Cosmopolitanism," 549.

24. See William Davis, "The Essential in Geography," *American Geographical Society of New York Bulletin* 36, no. 8 (1904): 470; and Marion I. Newbigin, *Modern Geography* (London: Williams and Norgate, 1911).

25. Halford John MacKinder, "On the Scope and Methods of Geography" (1887), in *Human Geography: An Essential Anthology*, ed. John Agnew, David N. Livingstone, and Alistair Rogers (Malden, Mass.: Blackwell, 1996), 157, 165, 172.

26. Halford John MacKinder, "The Geographical Pivot of History" (1904), in *Human Geography: An Essential Anthology*, ed. John Agnew, David N. Livingstone, and Alistair Rogers (Malden, Mass.: Blackwell, 1996).

27. Halford John MacKinder, *Democratic Ideals and Reality* (New York: Henry Holt, 1919), 79, 40.

28. It was also ultimately used to support arguments of geographical necessity in Nazi expansionism.

29. Mackinder, "On the Scope and Methods of Geography," 235.

30. See Dickinson, *The Makers of Modern Geography*, 209.

31. Vidal's influence on the famed midcentury American geographer Carl O. Sauer has been credited for the development of ecology in the United States. Fernand Braudel's concept of the *"longue durée"* comes directly out of Vidal's geography.

32. Paul Vidal de la Blache, *Principles of Human Geography*, trans. Millicent Todd Bingham (New York: Henry Holt, 1926), 6, 20.

33. Ibid., 16.

34. Harvey, "Cosmopolitanism," 532.

35. Seamus Deane, *Strange Country: Modernity and Nationhood in Irish Writing Since 1790* (Oxford: Oxford University Press, 1997), 95.

36. Marjorie Howes, "'Goodbye Ireland I'm going to Gort': Geography, Scale, and Narrating the Nation," in *Semicolonial Joyce*, ed. Derek Attridge and Marjorie Howes (Cambridge: Cambridge University Press, 2000), 75; Enda Duffy, *The Subaltern* Ulysses (Minneapolis: University of Minnesota Press, 1994), 48; also see Emer Nolan, *James Joyce and Nationalism* (London: Routledge, 1995); Vincent Cheng, *Joyce, Race, and Empire* (Cambridge: Cambridge University Press, 1995); Joseph Valente, *James Joyce and the Problem of Justice: Negotiating Sexual and Colonial Difference* (Cambridge: Cambridge University Press, 1995).

37. Deane, *Strange Country*, 95; Michael Seidel, *Epic Geography: James Joyce's* Ulysses (Princeton, N.J.: Princeton University Press, 1976).

38. James Joyce, *Dubliners* (1914; New York: Modern Library, n.d.), 288, my emphasis.

39. As Vincent Cheng points out, the notion of the Celtic West relies on a construction of the national "soil" as the locus of an "authentic" Irishness that is oversimplified and elusive (*Inauthentic: The Anxiety Over Culture and Identity* [New Brunswick, N.J.: Rutgers University Press, 2004], 48–49).

40. See Jessica Berman, *Modernist Fiction, Cosmopolitanism, and the Politics of Community* (2001; Cambridge: Cambridge University Press, 2006).

41. Cheng, *Inauthentic*, 48.

42. Bruce Robbins points out that because weather does not stop at national borders, this snow is necessarily cosmopolitan ("The Newspapers Were Right: Cosmopolitanism, Forgetting, and 'The Dead,'" *Interventions* 5, no. 1 [2003]: 106).

43. See Ellmann, *James Joyce*, 249.

44. See Weldon Thornton, *Allusions in* Ulysses: *An Annotated List* (Chapel Hill: University of North Carolina Press, 1961), 70. The bank's position on the green makes the sun appear to be rising in the northwest.

45. See David Lloyd on the importance of adulteration for Joyce's engagement with nationalism and colonialism (*Anomalous States: Irish Writing and the Post-Colonial Moment* [Durham, N.C.: Duke University Press, 1993], 108–10).

46. Seidel, *Epic Geography*, xiii.

47. Seidel, *Epic Geography*, xi.

48. Daniel R. Schwarz, *Reading Joyce's* Ulysses (London: Macmillan, 1987), 22

49. Cheryl Herr, "Walking in Dublin," in *A Portrait of the Artist as a Young Man*, ed. R. B. Kershner, Case Studies in Contemporary Criticism, 2nd ed. (Boston: Bedford/Saint Martin's, 2006), 423.

50. Joyce, "Ireland, Island of Saints and Sages" (1907), in *The Critical Writings of James Joyce* ed. Ellsworth Mason and Richard Ellman (New York: Viking Press, 1959), 34, 154.

51. Nolan, *Joyce and Nationalism*, 74.

52. See http://www.litscape.com/author/Thomas_Moore/Let_Erin_Remember_The_Days_Of_Old.html (accessed 27 January 2010).

53. On the other hand, Zack Bowen claims that "the song suits Stephen's train of thought" (*Musical Allusions in the Works of James Joyce* [Albany: SUNY Press, 1978], 78).

54. Joyce, "Ireland," 166.

55. Declan Kiberd, *Inventing Ireland* (Cambridge, Mass.: Harvard University Press, 1995), 337.

56. Joyce, "Ireland," 165.

57. Mulk Raj Anand, *Untouchable* (1940; New York: Penguin, 1986), 43; further references cited in the text.

58. Mulk Raj Anand, *Coolie* (1936; New York: Liberty Press, 1952), 287; further references cited in the text.

59. One of the most bloody and infamous conflicts in the history of the Raj, in which soldiers opened fire on 10,000 civilians (Saros Cowasjee, *So Many Freedoms: A Study of the Major Fiction of Mulk Raj Anand* [Oxford: Oxford University Press, 1977], 9).

60. Quoted in Marlene Fisher, *The Wisdom of the Heart: A Study of the Works of Mulk Raj Anand* (New Delhi: Sterling, 1985), 17.

61. For another approach to the question of Anand's relationship to metropolitan modernism, see Ben Conisbee Baer, "Shit Writing: Mulk Raj Anand's *Untouchable*, the Image of Gandhi, and the Progressive Writers' Association," *Modernism/Modernity* 16, no. 3 (September 2009): 575–95.

62. Arvind Krishna Mehrotra, ed., *A History of Indian Literature in English* (New York: Columbia University Press, 2003), 175.

63. Paul Saint-Amour, "From *Ulysses* to *Untouchable*: Mulk Raj Anand's Joycean Transmigrations," unpublished paper, International James Joyce Symposium, Dublin, June 2004, 5.

64. Anand, qtd. in Fisher, *The Wisdom of the Heart*, 30.

65. Mehrotra, *A History of Indian Literature*, 177.

66. Fisher, *The Wisdom of the Heart*, 26.

67. For more on the connection between Joyce and Anand, see Jessica Berman, "Comparative Colonialisms: Joyce, Anand, and the Question of Engagement," *Modernism/Modernity* (Fall 2006): 465–85.

68. This is not to say that Anand somehow completes Joyce.

69. Boehmer, *Colonial and Postcolonial Literature*, 129.

70. Paul Saint-Amour, "From *Ulysses* to *Untouchable*."

71. Mulk Raj Anand, *Roots and Flowers* (Dharwar: Karnatak University Press, 1972), 19, 18. To be clear, many critics who trace the rise of the novel in India demonstrate its emergence in the nineteenth century from an amalgam of narrative traditions. See, for example, Sangeeta Ray, *En-gendering India: Woman and Nation in Colonial and Postcolonial Narratives* (Durham, N.C.: Duke University Press, 2000), 11–12.

72. Anand, *Roots and Flowers*, 21–23, 19.

73. E. M. Forster, preface to *Untouchable*, by Mulk Raj Anand (New York: Penguin, 1940), vi.

74. Fisher, *The Wisdom of the Heart*, 26.

75. Anand, qtd. in Fisher, *The Wisdom of the Heart*, 17.

76. Anand, *Roots and Flowers*, 12, 15.

77. Anand, *Roots and Flowers*, 17, 11.

78. Harvey, "Cosmopolitanism," 557–58.

79. See Bruce Robbins, "Introduction Part I: Actually Existing Cosmopolitanism," in *Cosmopolitics: Thinking and Feeling Beyond the Nation*, ed. Pheng Cheah and Bruce Robbins (Minneapolis: University of Minnesota Press, 1998); and K. Anthony Appiah, "Cosmopolitan Patriots," in *For Love of Country: Debating the Limits of Patriotism*, by Martha C. Nussbaum et al. (Boston: Beacon Press, 1996).

80. Mulk Raj Anand, "The World I Hope For No. 4," BBC Eastern Service, broadcast 28 October 1943, 1515–1530 GMT, typescript, BBC Written Archives Centre.

81. Immanuel Kant, *On History*, ed. Lewis White Beck (Indianapolis: Bobbs-Merrill, 1963), "Idea for a Universal History from a Cosmopolitan Point of View," 20.

82. Kant, *On History*, "On the Opposition Between Morality and Politics with Respect to Perpetual Peace," 105.

83. Anand, *Roots and Flowers*, 23, 21.

84. K. Anthony Appiah, *Cosmopolitanism: Ethics in a World of Strangers* (New York: Norton, 2006), 78.

85. This idea of a unified India is not unlike the "inauthentic" Ireland of conquest and migration that Joyce describes in "Ireland, Island of Saints and Sages."

86. Mulk Raj Anand, "The Search for National Identity in India," in *Cultural Self-Comprehension of Nations*, ed. Han Köchler, International Progress Organisation, Studies in International Cultural Relations 1 (Tubingen: Erdmann, 1978), 74.

87. Mulk Raj Anand, "The Sources of Protest in My Novels," *Literary Criterion* 18, no. 4 (1983): 5.

88. Anand, *Conversations in Bloomsbury*, 32.

89. Anand, *Roots*, 21, 18–19.

90. Anand, *Conversations in Bloomsbury*, 7.

91. Marc Redfield, *Phantom Formations: Aesthetic Ideology and the Bildungsroman* (Ithaca, N.Y.: Cornell University Press, 1996), 43, 47.

92. Franco Moretti, *The Way of the World: The Bildungsroman in European Culture* (London: Verso, 2000), 227.

93. See, for example, the notion of *Bildung* in Friedrich Schiller, *On the Aesthetic Education of Man*, ed. Elizabeth Wilkinson and L. A. Willoughby (Oxford: Oxford University Press, 1967).

94. Jed Esty, "Virginia Woolf's Colony and the Adolescence of Modernist Fiction," in *Modernism and Colonialism: British and Irish Literature, 1899–1939*, ed. Richard Begam and Michael Valdez Moses (Durham, N.C.: Duke University Press, 2006), 74.

95. Mikhail M. Bakhtin, "The *Bildungsroman* and Its Significance in the History of Realism: Toward a Historical Typology of the Novel," in *Speech Genres and Other Late Essays*, trans. Vern W. McGee (Austin: University of Texas Press, 1986), 22.

96. Moretti, *The Way of the World*, 16.

97. For David Lloyd, writing about the Irish twentieth century, the genre is inherently tied to "major" literature, which presumes a certain commonality between writer and reader (*Nationalism and Minor Literature: James Clarence Mangan and the Emergence of Irish Cultural Nationalism* [Berkeley and Los Angeles: University of California Press, 1987], 20).

98. Bakhtin, "The *Bildungsroman* and Its Significance," 23

99. Lloyd, *Nationalism*, 20.

100. Jerome Buckley, *Season of Youth: The Bildungsroman from Dickens to Golding* (Cambridge Mass.: Harvard University Press, 1974), 226. Tobias Boes characterizes *Portrait* as an important twentieth-century extension of the tradition from Goethe ("*The Portrait of the Artist as a Young Man* and the 'Individuating Rhythm' of Modernity," *ELH* 75 [2008]: 770).

101. Esty, "Virginia Woolf's Colony," 76.

102. Breon Mitchell, "*A Portrait* as *Bildungsroman*: A Novel of Development," in *Readings on* A Portrait of the Artist as a Young Man, ed. Clarice Swisher (New York: Greenhaven Press, 2000), 56.

103. See Jane Marcus, *Hearts of Darkness: White Women Write Race* (New Brunswick, N.J.: Rutgers University Press, 2004). Bluemel, *George Orwell and the Radical Eccentric*, also discusses Munoo's character from a feminist perspective.

104. Mehrotra, *A History of Indian Literature*, 177.

105. Trevor Williams, *Reading Joyce Politically* (Gainesville: University Press of Florida. 1997), 106.

106. Ibid., 107.

107. It is nonetheless surprising to note how infrequently *Portrait* appears in studies of Joyce and colonialism. In Attridge and Howes's edited collection, *Semicolonial Joyce* (Cambridge: Cambridge University Press, 2000), only Marjorie Howes treats *Portrait* at any length ("'Goodbye Ireland'"). Other exceptions are: Nolan, *Joyce and Nationalism*; Duffy, *The Subaltern* Ulysses; and Cheng, *Joyce, Race and Empire*.

108. The longer passage reads: "And so in Sion was I established, and in the holy city I likewise rested, and in Jerusalem was my power. And I took root in an honourable people, and in the glorious company of the saints was I detained. I was exalted like a cedar in Lebanus, and as a cypress in Mount Sion" (John Henry Newman, "The Glories of Mary for the Sake of Her Son," in *Discourses to Mixed Congregations*, from *Newman Reader*, accessed 21 June 2006, http://www.newmanreader.org/works/discourses/discourse17.html. Newman does not identify the source of his quotation, beyond calling it an antiphon, yet it is nearly identical to most translations of Ecclesiasticus 12.15–16. Interestingly enough, the word most often missing from other translations is the very word in question here: "detain."

109. J. Otten, "Antiphon" (1907), in *The Catholic Encyclopedia* (New York: Robert Appleton), accessed 10 March 2011, http://www.newadvent.org/cathen/01575b.htm.

110. Lloyd, *Nationalism*, 21. Though I find Lloyd's discussion useful on this point, I resist the dichotomy he draws between "major" and "minor" literature.

111. See Arendt, *Lectures on Kant's Political Philosophy*, 43.

112. Charles Taylor, *Sources of the Self: The Making of the Modern Identity* (Cambridge, Mass.: Harvard University Press, 1989), 159.

113. Hannah Arendt, *Responsibility and Judgment*, ed. Jerome Kohn (New York: Schocken, 2003), 153.

114. Ibid., 146.

115. Ibid., 141.

116. Lloyd, *Nationalism*, 20–21.

117. Derek Attridge, *Joyce Effects: On Language, Theory, and History* (Cambridge: Cambridge University Press, 2000), 66, 68.

118. Anand, *Conversations in Bloomsbury*, 7.

119. This is not to claim that *all* extra-semiotic uses of language will necessarily work in this political fashion.

120. Feroza Jussawalla, *Family Quarrels: Towards a Criticism of Indian Writing in English* (New York: Peter Lang, 1985), 70–75.

121. As one critic puts it, "Narayan's novels are so satisfyingly Indian perhaps because they are so authentically South Indian . . . through skillful use of the English language he delineates people whose actions, behaviour, and responses are shaped by a language different from English" (qtd. in Jussawalla, *Family Quarrels*, 74).

122. Baer, "Shit Writing," 580.

123. Anand, qtd. in Jussawalla, *Family Quarrels*, 84.

124. Mulk Raj Anand, "Pigeon-Indian: Some Notes on Indian-English Writing," *World Literature Written in English* 21, no. 2 (Summer 1982): 325–36.

125. Mehrotra, *A History of Indian Literature*, 179.

3. Modernism in the Zenana: The Domestic Spaces of Sorabji, Hussain, and Ishvani

1. Krupabai Satthianadhan, *Kamala*, intro. Chandani Lokugé (Oxford: Oxford University Press, 1998), 141.

2. For a discussion of the prevailing model for narrating female agency in the nineteenth century, see Meenakshi Mukherjee, *The Perishable Empire: Essays on Indian Writing in English*, (New York: Oxford University Press 2000), 77–78.

3. Most readers of this novel read the ending as a problematic reinscription of *pativrata*. See, for example, Chandani Lokugé, introduction to *Kamala*, by Krupabai Satthianadhan (Oxford: Oxford University Press, 1998), 13–15. Lokugé uses the metaphor of the threshold to describe Satthianadhan's inability to take her heroine beyond traditional domesticity at the end of the novel. I employ it as a transitional zone rather than a barrier to progress.

4. Priya Joshi and others have focused our attention on the nineteenth century, when several strong Indian woman poets began writing in English

and other English women living in India were writing sophisticated novels about Indian life (*In Another Country: Colonialism, Culture, and the English Novel in India* [New York: Columbia University Press, 2002]). Sangeeta Ray spans the period in her important study of the representation of women in fiction, but she does not linger there (*En-gendering India: Woman and Nation in Colonial and Postcolonial Narratives* [Durham, N.C.: Duke University Press, 2000]). The historian Antoinette Burton focuses on the 1920s and 1930s in *Dwelling in the Archives: Women Writing House, Home, and History in Late Colonial India* (New York: Oxford University Press, 2003), but the only fiction in this book, which makes strong claims for the value of literary texts as historical "evidence," was written in the 1960s looking back on the 1930s.

5. K. R. Srinivasa Iyengar, *Indian Writing in English*, 3rd ed. (New Delhi: Sterling, 1983), 438.

6. Sir Ramalinga Reddy, foreword to *Purdah and Polygamy*, by Iqbalunissa Hussain (Bangalore: Hosali Press, 1944), 1. Though Oxford University Press has reprinted a laudable number of women's texts in their Oxford India Paperbacks series, few women writers from the first half of the twentieth century appear. Even Eunice de Souza and Lindsay Pereira, the editors of the 2002 anthology *Women's Voices: Selections from Nineteenth and Early-Twentieth Century Indian Writing in English* (Oxford: Oxford University Press, 2002), working in Bombay, found it difficult to retrieve texts and resurrect biographies for the forty women included in the volume.

7. In Arvind Krishna Mehrota, ed., *A History of Indian Literature in English* (New York: Columbia University Press, 2003), discussion of the origins of the novel in English gives prominent place to Krupabai Satthianadhan, and a section is devoted to Sarojini Naidu and Cornelia Sorobji. But subsequent chapters barely mention a woman author. Susie Tharu and Ke Lalita's two-volume anthology of Indian women writers was a crucial corrective to this record, but even they barely treat the early twentieth century (*Women Writing in India: 600 B.C. to the Present*, 2 vols. [New York: Feminist Press, 1993]).

8. Burton, *Dwelling in the Archives*, 10.

9. Qtd. in Burton, *Dwelling in the Archives*, 9

10. Qtd. in Geraldine Forbes, *Women in Modern India* (Cambridge: Cambridge University Press, 1996), 94.

11. Child marriage was already a widespread concern because of the introduction in 1927 of what would be the Sarda Act, finally passed in 1929, raising the age of consent.

12. See Burton, *Dwelling in the Archives*, chapter 1, "Memory Becomes Her," for an excellent discussion of the role of the home and domesticity in the debates over national reform and independence.

13. Mrinalini Sinha, *Specters of Mother India: The Global Restructuring of an Empire* (Durham, N.C.: Duke University Press, 2006), 8.

14. Ibid., 10.

15. Sinha ties the period of retrenchment to the debate surrounding Katherine Mayo's *Mother India*, which was widely discussed throughout the early 1930s.

16. Contrary to common assumption, women writers in the first half of the twentieth century were sufficiently in command of their craft to be able to generate formally complex narratives. Diaries and autobiographical accounts of educated women demonstrate their familiarity the British literary tradition as well as contemporary European and American writers. Sorabji's personal diaries show that in 1903 she read novels by Edith Wharton, Maxim Gorky, and C. K. Chesterton; in February 1904 alone she read Shaw's *Man and Superman*, *Rebecca of Sunnybrook Farm*, and five other books (Cornelia Sorabji papers, India Office Selected Papers: Private Papers Collection, British Library, Mss EUR 165/63, 64, 65).

17. Reddy, foreword to *Purdah and Polygamy*, 4.

18. Philippe Lejeune, *On Autobiography*, ed. Paul John Eakin, trans. Katherine Leary, History and Theory of Literature 52 (Minneapolis: University of Minnesota Press, 1988).

19. R. K. Narayan, qtd. In S. K. Desai, ed., *Experimentation with Language in Indian Writing in English Fiction* (Kolhapur: Shivaji University, 1974), iii.

20. M. K. Bhatnagar, *Political Consciousness in Indian English Writing* (New Delhi: Bahri, 1991), 8.

21. Cornelia Sorabji, *India Calling* (1934), ed. Chandani Lokugé (New York: Oxford University Press, 2001), 19–20.

22. Critics often read this Sorabji family dictum as an expression of a certain noblesse oblige. However, I wish to take the phrase seriously in its rhetorical dimension as a indication of the way that Sorabji approaches the intersection of narration and social life.

23. Cornelia Sorabji, *Sun Babies: Studies in the Child-Life of India* (London: John Murray, 1904), 9.

24. As will be even clearer thirty years later in her autobiographies *India Calling* and *India Recalled* (London: Nisbet 1936).

25. Though Burton, *Dwelling in the Archives*, makes a strong case for the removed ethnographic gaze in Sorabji's autobiographical texts of the 1930s, I would argue that her early fiction exhibits a complexity of narrative structure that challenges the distance of both narrator and reader.

26. James Phelan discusses this sort of relationship between readers and characters as an essential component of narrative (*Narrative as Rhetoric: Techniques, Audiences, Ethics, Ideology* [Columbus: Ohio State University Press, 1996], 27).

27. Paul Ricoeur, *Oneself as Another*, trans. Kathleen Blamey (Chicago: University of Chicago Press 1990), 17, 140.

28. Lejeune, *On Autobiography*, 131–32.

29. Sorabji, *Sun Babies*, 50; further references cited in the text.

30. I am grateful to Sonita Sarker for this insight.

31. Sonita Sarker, "Unruly Subjects: Cornelia Sorabji and Ravinder Randhawa," in *Trans-Status Subjects: Gender in the Globalization of South and Southeast Asia*, ed. Sonita Sarker and Esha Niyogi De (Durham, N.C.: Duke University Press, 2002), 267–88.

32. See the "Chronology of Cornelia Sorabji" in *India Calling* and the description of this period of her life in chapter 3.

33. It is important to note the impressiveness of her career, given the critical tendency to dismiss Sorabji as the product of privilege and an elite education because she had many ties to the British aristocracy and was a lifelong friend of Princess Beatrice.

34. British Library mss. EUR/165 work diary folder #108.

35. British Library mss. EUR/165, Folder #80, Letter 15 April 1919.

36. Sorabji's papers exist in a large holding in the British Library and include several unpublished talks as well as diaries and letters.

37. Sorabji, *India Recalled*, 194.

38. Sorabji, "The Role of Indian Women," *Lyceum Magazine* (1919); "Tea-Time Talks," in British Library collection mss. EUR/165/114, 10–11.

39. On the matter of purdah, I rely on Eunice de Souza's broad use of the term as "not just the burqua of whatever design worn by some Muslim women, . . . but the elaborate codes of seclusion and feminine modesty used to protect and control the lives of women" (Eunice de Souza, ed., *Purdah: An Anthology* [New York: Oxford University Press, 2004], xi). There is difference of opinion about whether purdah existed in Hindu society before the Muslims, but in the nineteenth and early twentieth centuries purdah was a sign of status among upper- and middle-class families across India and widely practiced.

40. In this sense, as in Woolf's *Three Guineas*, the epistolary form introduces a high degree of narrative uncertainty.

41. Cornelia Sorabji, *Love and Life Behind the Purdah*, ed. Chandani Lokugé (New Delhi: Oxford University Press, 2003), 70–72; further references cited in the text. There was demand for female doctors in India in this period since secluded women could not consult with a male physician.

42. Burton, *Dwelling in the Archives*, 95.

43. See De Souza, ed., *Purdah: An Anthology*, for a compelling collection of these writings.

44. Ray, *En-Gendering India*, 103, 107.

45. The phrase is Victoria Rosner's. See her *Modernism and the Architecture of Private Life* (New York: Columbia University Press, 2005), 5.

46. See the chapter "Women in the Nationalist Movement" in Forbes, *Women in Modern India*: "It was possible to help the movement without leaving home or neglecting the family" (125).

47. Rabindranath Tagore, letter to Charles Freer Andrews, 7 September 1920, *Selected Letters of Rabindranath Tagore*, ed. Krishna Dutta and Andrew Robinson (Cambridge: Cambridge University Press, 1997), 237.

48. Lorna Ellis, *Appearing to Diminish: Female Development and the British Bildungsroman, 1750–1850* (Lewisburg, Penn.: Bucknell University Press, 1999), 10; also see Susan Fraiman, *Unbecoming Women: British Women Writers and the Novel of Development* (New York: Columbia, 1993).

49. Jed Esty, "Virginia Woolf's Colony and the Adolescence of Modernist Fiction," in *Modernism and Colonialism*, ed. Richard Begam and Michael Valdez Moses (Durham, N.C.: Duke University Press, 2007).

50. Iqbalunissa Hussain, *Purdah and Polygamy* (Bangalore: Hosali Press, 1944), 1; further references cited in the text.

51. Reddy, foreword to *Purdah and Polygamy*, 1; de Souza, *Purdah*, 507.

52. Sakinatul Fatima Wazir Hassan, "Indian Muslim Women—a Perspective," in *Our Cause: Symposium by Indian Women*, ed. Shaym Nehru (Allahabad, Kitabistan, 1938?), 24. It is interesting to note that the essay preceding this one in the collection is from Cornelia Sorabji.

53. Teresa Hubel, "The Missing Muslim Woman in Indo-Anglian Literature: Iqbalunnisa Hussain's *Purdah and Polygamy*," in *Perspectives on South Asia*, ed. V. A. Pai Panandiker and Navnita Chadha Behera (Delhi: Konark, 2000), 147.

54. Rosner, *Modernism and the Architecture of Private Life*, 2.

55. Eunice de Souza has described her efforts to discover biographical details of the lives of women writers from the period in de Souza and Pereira, eds., *Women's Voices*.

56. Iqbalunissa Hussain, *Changing India: a Muslim Woman Speaks* (Bangalore: Hosali Press, 1940), 3, iii; further references cited in the text.

57. Many commentators from the period, both Hindu and Muslim, discuss the bodily effects of early marriage and seclusion on women, citing higher statistics for female mortality in childbirth and infant mortality among teenage mothers and tracing the prevalence of tuberculosis and other communicable diseases among secluded women. See Shayam Nehru, ed., *Our Cause: A Symposium by Indian Women* (Allahabad, Kitabistan, 1938?).

58. The little biographical information that can be found comes from a single entry in National Council of Women of India, *Women in India: Who's Who* (Bombay: National Council of Women, 1935); from records of her publications; and from the foreword to *Changing India*.

59. Raja Rao and Iqbal Singh, *Changing India* (London: George Allen and Unwin, 1939), 9; further references cited in the text.

60. Zuhra "determined that Nazni should be punished for having . . . been treated by a surgeon" (65).

61. Zuhra will not touch her clothing.

62. G. Ishvani, *Girl in Bombay* (London: Pilot Press, 1947), v.

63. Leigh Gilmore, *Autobiographics: A Feminist Theory of Women's Self-Representation* (Ithaca, N.Y.: Cornell University Press, 1994), 13.

64. Gayatri Chakravorty Spivak, *Death of a Discipline* (New York: Columbia University Press, 2003).

65. As described in the text, Ishvani's family belonged to a splinter group of Kojas who had rebelled against the Aga Khan's influence, become Shias, and been persecuted for it. Thus her membership in the Aga Khani community is a particular affront.

66. Pakistan Resolution of the Lahore Session of the all India Muslim League, 22 February–4 March 1940, accessed 11 April 2011, http://www.kashmir-information.com/LegalDocs/68.html.

67. One of the first presidents of the Indian National Congress, Rahimtulla M. Sayani, was a Koja from the same group.

68. Kamala Sathianadhan is the second wife of W. T. Sathianadhan, Krupabai's husband.

69. Padmini Sengupta, *Portrait of an Indian Woman* (Calcutta: YMCA Publishing House, 1956). See also Eunice de Souza, *Sathianadhan Family Album* (New Delhi: Sahitya Akademi, 2005).

70. Kamala Sathianadhan, *Detective Janaki* (Bombay: Thacker and Company, 1944), 24.

4. Commitment and the Scene of War: Max Aub and Spanish Civil War Writing

1. George Orwell, *Homage to Catalonia* (1938; Boston: Beacon, 1967), 198.

2. Peter Monteath, *Writing the Good Fight: Political Commitment in the International Literature of the Spanish Civil War* (Westport, Conn.: Greenwood, 1994), suggests that there may be as many as 700 novels and more than 20,000 eye-witness accounts, histories, memoirs, and propaganda publications (xiv).

3. The Pulitzer Prize committee nominated the novel but the board rejected it, and no prize was given in that year.

4. Including Peter Carroll, *The Odyssey of the Abraham Lincoln Brigade: Americans in the Spanish Civil War* (Stanford, Calif.: Stanford University Press, 1994); Peter Carroll and James D. Fernández, *Facing Fascism: New York and the Spanish Civil War* (New York: New York University Press, 2007); Cary Nelson and Jefferson Hendricks, eds., *Madrid 1937: Letters of the Abraham Lincoln Brigade from the Spanish Civil War* (New York: Routledge, 1996).

5. Anthony Geist and José Monleón, eds., *Modernism and Its Margins: Reinscribing Cultural Modernity from Spain and Latin America* (New York: Garland, 1999), xix.

6. Peter Nicholls, *Modernisms: A Literary Guide* (Berkeley: University of California Press, 1995); Peter Conrad, *Modern Times, Modern Places* (New York: Knopf, 1999); David Bradshaw, *Concise Companion to Modernism* (Malden, Mass.: Blackwell, 2003). Even Pericles Lewis's admirably broad *Cambridge Introduction to Modernism* (Cambridge: Cambridge University Press, 2007) neglects Spain. Mark Wolleager's forthcoming edited collection on global

modernism (Oxford University Press) will include an essay by Gayle Rogers focused on modernism in Spain.

7. Mary Lee Bretz, *Encounters Across Borders: The Changing Visions of Spanish Modernism, 1890–1930* (Lewisburg, Penn.: Bucknell University Press, 2001), 21.

8. Ibid.

9. The use of the term "modernism" within Spanish and Latin American literary traditions is fraught. The term *"modernismo"* was used as early as the 1880s (Bretz, *Encounters Across Borders*, 24) but its connection to the generation of 1898 sometimes made it a term to rebel against in the twentieth century by those like Ortega y Gasset (Gayle Rogers, personal communication). In the twentieth century, *"modernismo"* is often associated with early-twentieth-century Latin American writers such as Rubén Darío and José Martí, rather than the Spanish literary vanguard. Nonetheless, I will claim along with Bretz that modernism "evolves over time and even synchronically carries multiple, contradictory significations" (*Encounters Across Borders*, 28). I also follow such critics as Bretz and Geist and Monleón in employing the terms "modernism" and "modernist" to refer to vanguardist and experimental writers in both Spain and Latin America after 1898 and through the mid- to late twentieth century.

10. See Derek Harris, ed., *The Spanish Avant-garde* (New York: Manchester University Press, 1995).

11. It bears noting here that women were also significant in the Spanish vanguard of this period, though they have been often sidelined by critics. See Roberta Johnson's chapter "Vanguard Feminists Dream the Nation," in her *Gender and Nation in the Spanish Modernist Novel* (Nashville, Tenn.: Vanderbilt University Press, 2003), 224–80.

12. Pascale Casanova, *The World Republic of Letters*, trans. M. B. DeBevoise (Cambridge, Mass.: Harvard University Press, 2005), 111.

13. This is Max Aub's term. It also is important to note its connection to the development of a Latin American "hyper-realism" that emerges along with "magical realism" in the 1970s.

14. On the relationship between total war and modernism, see Paul Saint-Amour, "Airwar Prophecy and Interwar Modernism," *Comparative Literature Studies* 42, no. 2 (2005): 130–61.

15. Sender's narrative was published first (1937) in London in translation and only afterward (1938) in Spanish.

16. Qtd. in Gareth Thomas, *The Novel of the Spanish Civil War (1936–1975)* (Cambridge: Cambridge University Press, 1990), 97.

17. Michael Eaude, "Obituary: José María Gironella," *The Guardian*, 30 January 30 2003, accessed 17 July 2007, http://www.guardian.co.uk/spain/article/0,2763,885201,00.html.

18. José María Gironella, *One Million Dead*, trans. Joan MacLean (New York: Doubleday, 1963), ix.

19. Janet Perez, "Prose in Franco's Spain," in *The Cambridge History of Spanish Literature*, ed. David Thatcher Gies (Cambridge: Cambridge University Press, 2004), 632.

20. See his *El rey y la reina* (1949) or *Los cinco libros de Ariadne* (1957).

21. Gironella, *One Million Dead*, x.

22. Gerald Martin, "Translator's Note," in *Field of Honour*, by Max Aub (New York: Verso, 2009), xii. *Field of Honour* is a translation of the first volume of the sequence, *Campo cerrado*. None of the other volumes has been translated.

23. Jordana Mendelson, *Documenting Spain: Artists, Exhibition Culture, and the Modern Nation, 1929–1939* (University Park: Pennsylvania State University Press, 2005), xxvii–xxviii.

24. Still, many of the generation of 1898 (Unamuno, Baroja, and so on) retained primarily antimodern attitudes and looked to Spain's past rather than European models of the future for solutions to social ills.

25. "Vanguardism" is the term commonly used to indicate the broad modernist and avant-garde movements of the 1920s and 1930s. The interaction of Spanish trends in art and literature with Parisian developments, which Derek Harris calls "hybridization," is one of the hidden stories of the development of modernism in Europe. See Harris, "Squared Horizons: The Hybridisation of the Avant-garde in Spain," in *The Spanish Avant-garde*, ed. Harris (New York: Manchester University Press, 1995), 1–14. On the reception and influence of Joyce in Spain, see Gayle Rogers, introduction to "James Joyce in His Labyrinth" (1924), by Antonio Marichalar, trans. Rogers, *PMLA* 124, no. 3 (2009): 926–28.

26. Critics disagree about how to characterize the generation in the period before the war. It is important to note that women's writing often does not fit into these "generations." Roberta Johnson points out that men and women in the 1920s often wrote in "different spheres and for different audiences" (*Gender and Nation in the Spanish Modernist Novel*, viii), but the construction of the "generation" model was generally derived from the work of male writers.

27. Johnson's *Gender and Nation* is a notable exception.

28. Francisco Longoria, *El arte narrativo de Max Aub* (Madrid: Playor, 1977), 11; all translations in this chapter are my own except where otherwise noted.

29. Ibid., 12.

30. There is critical debate on the matter of whether Ortega meant this essay to serve as a manifesto or was describing the existing situation among Spanish writers. Either way, *La deshumanización del arte* (2nd ed. [Madrid: Revista de Occidente, 1928]), served as a touchstone for many younger writers like Benjamin Jarnes. See, for example, Paul Ilie, "Benjamín Jarnés: Aspects of the Dehumanized Novel," *PMLA* 76, no. 3 (June 1961): 247–53. I am indebted to Gayle Rogers for his insight into Ortega and his influence.

31. Joan Ramon Resina, "The Catalan Avant-garde," in *The Cambridge History of Spanish Literature*, ed. David Thatcher Gies (Cambridge: Cambridge University Press, 2004), 543.

32. José Ortega y Gasset, *The Dehumanization of Art and Other Writings on Art and Culture*, trans. Willard Trask (New York: Doubleday Anchor, 1956), 14.

33. G. G. Brown, *A Literary History of Spain: The Twentieth Century* (London: Ernest Benn, 1971), 13.

34. José Ortega y Gasset, "Doestoievsky y Proust" (1925), in *Ideas sobre el teatro y la novela* (Madrid: Alianza, 1982), 31.

35. José Ortega y Gasset, *The Revolt of the Masses* (New York: Norton, 1932).

36. Longoria, *El arte narrativo de Max Aub*, 29.

37. Ignacio Soldevila Durante, preface to *Geografía, prehistoria, 1928*, by Max Aub (Segorbe: Ayuntamiento, 1996), 17.

38. Ibid. I am indebted to Ignacio Soldevila Durante for this interpretation of this poem.

39. He became the director of a theater in Valencia in 1935.

40. Josefina Alix, "From War to Magic: The Spanish Pavilion, Paris 1937," in *Barcelona and Modernity: Picasso, Gaudí, Miró, Dalí*, ed. William H. Robinson, Jordi Falgàs, and Carmen Belén Lord (New Haven, Conn.: Yale University Press, 2006), 450; Gijs Van Hensbergen, *Guernica: The Biography of a Twentieth-Century Icon* (London: Bloomsbury, 2004), 25.

41. Max Aub, *Discurso de la novela española contemporánea* (Mexico City: Colegio de Mexico 1945), 102. See also Longoria, *El arte narrativo de Max Aub*, 71. Manuel Aznar Soler calls this "testimonial realism," though I cannot trace his use of that term to any source in Aub (*Los laberintos del exilio: Diecisiete estudios sobre la obra literaria de Max Aub* [Seville: Renacimiento: Biblioteca del Exilo, 2003], 31).

42. Aub, *Discurso*, 102–3.

43. Max Aub, "Una carta," in *Hablo como hombre* (Mexico: Joaquin Mortiz, 1967), 36.

44. Max Aub, "De la novela de neustros dias y de la Española en particular," in *Hablo como hombre*, 157

45. This novel was actually completed third, in 1948, and was not published until 1951, but it is composed partially from fragments Aub had written in 1939: Aub, *Campo abierto* (1951), 2nd ed. (Madrid: Punto de lectura, 2004); translations are my own.

46. Antony Beevor, *The Battle for Spain: The Spanish Civil War, 1936–1939* (New York: Penguin, 2006), 55.

47. Saint-Amour, "Airwar Prophecy and Interwar Modernism," 131–32.

48. There is a gap of more than ten years between the publication of *Campo abierto* (1951) and last three volumes, *Campo de moro* (1963), *Campo*

francés (1965), and *Campo de los almendros* (1968). This chapter focuses primarily on the first three volumes, the last of which was published in 1951.

49. The fifth volume of the series, *Campo francés*, takes up the period after 1939.

50. Max Aub, qtd. in Luis Llorens Marzo, "Génesis del Laberinto mágico: Los autógrafos de Max Aub entre 1938 y 1942," *Bulletin of Spanish Studies* 80, no. 4 (2003): 457.

51. See especially Michael Ugarte, "Max Aub's Magical Labyrinth of Exile," *Hispania* 68, no. 4 (December 1985): 733–39; and Ignacio Soldevila Durante, *La obra narrativa de Max Aub (1929–1969)* (Madrid: Biblioteca Románica Hispánica, editorial Gredos, 1973), which in many ways is still unsurpassed.

52. Ugarte, "Max Aub's Magical Labyrinth," 734.

53. As Longoria claims, one of Aub's major concerns is to create an allegory of human incommunication (*El arte narrativo de Max Aub*, 101).

54. Longoria, *El arte narrativo de Max Aub*, 102, though Longoria claims that this perspective mellows as the cycle moves on.

55. Max Aub, *Campo cerrado* (Xalapa: Universidad Veracruzana, 1968), 78; *Field of Honour*, trans. Gerald Martin (New York: Verso, 2009), 85 (translation modified); further references cited in the text, with references to the Spanish citation given first, the published translation afterward.

56. Aub, *Hablo como hombre*, 35.

57. Aub, *Hablo como hombre*, 38.

58. Beevor, *The Battle for Spain*, 67.

59. Buenaventura Durruti, qtd. in Abel Paz, *Durruti in the Spanish Revolution*, trans. Chuck Morse. (Oakland, Calif.: AK Press, 2007), 401.

60. Ugarte, "Max Aub's Magical Labyrinth," 735.

61. Longoria, *El arte narrativo de Max Aub*, 53.

62. Thomas, *The Novel of the Spanish Civil War*, 113.

63. Thomas, *The Novel of the Spanish Civil War*, 113.

64. Hemingway, preface to Regler, *The Great Crusade*, qtd. in Thomas, *The Novel of the Spanish Civil War*, 10.

65. Allen Josephs, "Hemingway and the Spanish Civil War; Or, The Volatile Mixture of Politics and Art," in *Rewriting the Good Fight: Critical Essays on the Literature of the Spanish Civil War*, ed. Frieda S. Brown et al. (East Lansing: Michigan State University Press, 1989), 183.

66. Orwell, *Homage to Catalonia*, 4–5; further references cited in the text.

67. W. E. Dougherty and Morris Janowitz, *A Psychological Warfare Casebook* (Baltimore, Md.: Johns Hopkins University Press, 1956), 2.

68. Mark Wollaeger, *Modernism, Media, and Propaganda: British Narrative from 1900–1945* (Princeton, N.J.: Princeton University Press, 2006), xiv.

69. Ibid., 10.

70. Susan Rubin Suleiman, *Authoritarian Fictions: The Ideological Novel as a Literary Genre* (New York: Columbia University Press, 1983).

71. Philip M. Taylor, *Munitions of the Mind: A History of Propaganda from the Ancient World to the Present Era* (Manchester: Manchester University Press, 1995), 6.

72. Suleiman, *Authoritarian Fictions*, 54–56.

73. See, for example, Hugh Thomas, review of *Homage to Catalonia*, by George Orwell, *The Nation*, 20 April 1962; reprint, in *George Orwell: The Critical Heritage*, ed. Jeffery Meyers (London: Routledge, 1975), 150–51.

74. See Herbert Matthews, review of *Homage to Catalonia*, by George Orwell, *The Nation*, 27 December 1952; reprint, in *George Orwell: The Critical Heritage*, ed. Jeffery Meyers (London: Routledge, 1975), 143–49.

75. Clifford Geertz, *The Interpretation of Cultures* (New York: Basic, 1973); James Clifford, *The Predicament of Culture: Twentieth-Century Ethnography, Literature, and Art* (Cambridge, Mass.: Harvard University Press, 1988); Mary Louise Pratt, *Imperial Eyes: Travel Writing and Transculturation* (New York: Routledge, 1992).

76. Clifford, *The Predicament of Culture*, 14.

77. Orwell, "Why I Write" (1946), in *George Orwell: A Collection of Essays* (New York: Harcourt, Brace and Company, 1946), 314–15; Orwell, "The Frontiers of Art and Propaganda" (1941), *My Country Right or Left: 1940–43, The Collected Essays, Journalism, and Letters*, vol. 2, ed. Sonia Orwell and Ian Angus (Boston: Godine, 1968), 126.

78. In 1622 Pope Gregory XV created a committee of cardinals called the Congregatio de Propaganda Fide to supervise the spread of the faith through missionaries. On the history of propaganda, see Taylor, *Munitions of the Mind*; and Robert Jackall, ed., *Propaganda* (New York: New York University Press, 1995).

79. Trudi Tate, "Rumour, Propaganda, and *Parade's End*," *Essays in Criticism* 47, no. 4 (1997): 335.

80. The first "actuality film" of the war, about the Battle of the Somme, had 2,000 bookings during its first two months of release in 1915 (Cate Haste, "The Machinery of Propaganda," in *Propaganda*, ed. Robert Jackall [New York: New York University Press, 1995], 131).

81. Qtd. in Tate, "Rumour, Propaganda, and *Parade's End*," 336.

82. Mirta Nuñez Díaz-Balart, *La prensa de guerra en la zona republicana durante la Guerra Civil Española*; and Eduardo González Galleja et al., "Catálogo de las publicaciones periódicas localizados en la zona franquista durante la Guerra Civil Española": both cited in Mendelson, *Revistas y guerra: 1936–39* (Madrid: Museo Nacional Centro de la Reina Sofía, 2007), 344.

83. I am deeply indebted to Mendelson's scholarship on these materials and to her generosity in sharing it (*Revistas*, 344).

84. Mendelson, *Revistas*, 342.

85. Mendelson, *Revistas*, 283, 275, 374, 304.

86. Mendelson, *Revistas*, 369.

87. Virginia Woolf, *Three Guineas*, ed. Naomi Black (Oxford: Shakespeare Head of Blackwell Publishers, 2001), 10. According to Gayle Rogers, archival

materials held in Northwestern University's special collections show that the second republic was especially adept at getting such photographs and information to the U.K. (private communication).

88. Thomas Waugh, "'Men Cannot Act Before the Camera in the Presence of Death': Joris Ivens' *The Spanish Earth*," in *Documenting the Documentary: Close Readings of Documentary Film and Video*, ed. Barry Keith Grant and Jeannette Sloniowski (Detroit: Wayne State University Press, 1998), 136.

89. Joris Ivens, *The Camera and I* (New York: International Publishers, 1969), 211–12.

90. Waugh, "'Men Cannot Act Before the Camera,'" 142. Also see Ivens's description of his process of shooting the film in *Camera and I*, 103–38. Ivens discusses the decision to re-create events in *The Spanish Earth* in several of the essays included in Kees Bakker, ed., *Joris Ivens and the Documentary Context* (Amsterdam: Amsterdam University Press, 1999).

91. Waugh, "'Men Cannot Act Before the Camera,'" 141. This line appears at the beginning of reel 2 in the film and in the book version of the commentary (Ernest Hemingway, *The Spanish Earth*, intro. Jasper Wood [Cleveland, Ohio: J. B. Savage Company, 1938; facsimile ed., Ann Arbor, Mich.: University Microfilms, 1970], 12).

92. Waugh, "'Men Cannot Act Before the Camera,'" 143.

93. Credit for the superb editing of the film, under strict time constraints, goes to Helen van Dongen.

94. Ivens, *The Camera and I*, 133.

95. In this way, the film bears an uncanny similarity to Woolf's original project for the "essay-novel" that was to become the novel *The Years* and the essay *Three Guineas*.

96. Ivens, *The Camera and I*, 107–8.

97. This stands in direct contrast with the introduction to the 1938 book version of the film's commentary, which tries to hide the fact that Ivens recreated events and crafted scenes, claiming, "It is not a wasted propaganda film to teach us much useless theory. It is a picture which tells us the truth and not a pack of dirty lies. It wasn't acted out or posed for . . . it is what is real and true and horrible" (Jasper Wood, introduction to *The Spanish Earth*, by Ernest Hemingway, 11).

98. Ivens, "Documentary: Subjectivity and Montage," in *Documenting the Documentary: Close Readings of Documentary Film and Video*, ed. Barry Keith Grant and Jeannette Sloniowski (Detroit: Wayne State University Press, 1998), 251, 258.

99. Hemingway, *The Spanish Earth*, 46.

100. The history of Malraux's efforts to get France to donate planes to the Republic and to help organize the Republican air force has been discussed from many perspectives. Though Malraux was celebrated for his efforts at the time, it is clear that the planes that he brought to Spain were out of date;

the pilots, likely mercenaries; and Malraux's own involvement in the fighting, minimal. See Beevor, *The Battle for Spain*, 140.

101. Jean-François Lyotard, *Soundproof Room: Malraux's Anti-Aesthetics*, trans. Robert Harvey (Stanford, Calif.: Stanford University Press, 2001), 56.

102. Ibid., 68.

103. This connection may also explain the collaboration between the two writers on the film. Aub's personal writings are full of admiration for Malraux.

104. Theodor Adorno, *Aesthetic Theory*, trans. C. Lenhardt (New York: Rouledge, 1984), 6; Elizabeth Grosz, *Time Travels: Feminism, Nature, Power* (Durham, N.C.: Duke University Press, 2005), 75.

5. Arising from the Cornlands: The Working-Class Voices of Conroy and Le Sueur

1. Agnes Smedley, *Daughter of Earth* (New York: Feminist Press, 1973), 3, 4.

2. Ibid., 4.

3. In this sense her work bears some affinity with Aub's "transcendental realism."

4. Nonetheless, I resist the impulse to call this "crazy-quilt" narrative "crazy" and to connect it to the heroine's breakdown at the end of the novel, as does Paula Rabinowitz in her otherwise superb *Labor and Desire: Women's Revolutionary Fiction in Depression America* (Chapel Hill: University of North Carolina Press, 1991), 11.

5. Meridel Le Sueur, afterword to *I Hear Men Talking and Other Stories* (Minneapolis: West End, 1984), 237.

6. David Kadlec, *Mosaic Modernism: Anarchism, Pragmatism, Culture* (Baltimore, Md.: Johns Hopkins University Press, 2000).

7. Rita Barnard, "Modern American Fiction," in *The Cambridge Companion to American Modernism*, ed. Walter Kalaidjian (New York: Cambridge University Press 2005), 43. Barnard is here writing about Frank Asch's' novel *Pay Day*, but her comments also apply to the many other novels she considers in this essay. See also her *Great Depression and the Culture of Abundance* (New York: Cambridge, 1995) for more in-depth treatment of this issue in the work of Kenneth Fearing and Nathaniel West. The preponderance of scholarship on the cultural production of the Depression era has come out of American studies, following such pioneering work as Warren Susman, ed., *Culture and Commitment, 1929–1945* (New York: G. Braziller, 1973); and Michael Denning, *The Cultural Front: The Laboring of American Culture in the Twentieth Century* (New York: Verso, 1997), and is not focused on modernism per se. Some who have argued specifically for the social engagement of American modernism include Walter Kalaidjian, *American Culture*

Between the Wars: Revisionary Modernism and Postmodern Critique (New York: Columbia University Press, 1993); Alan Filreis, *Modernism from Right to Left: Wallace Stevens, the Thirties, and Literary Radicalism* (New York: Cambridge University Press, 2005); Rabinowitz, *Labor and Desire*; Michael Szalay, *New Deal Modernism* (Durham, N.C.: Duke University Press 2000); Joseph Entin, *Sensational Modernism: Experimental Fiction and Photography in Thirties America* (Chapel Hill: University of North Carolina Press, 2007). Forthcoming work by Ann Mattis addresses the connections between modernism and domestic service, particularly in work by Gertrude Stein, Jessie Redmon Fauset, and Zora Neale Hurston ("Dirty Work: Domestic Service and the Making of the Middle Class in Modern Women's Fiction," in progress).

8. Barnard, "Modern American Fiction," 46; Entin, *Sensational Modernism*, 4; Szalay, *New Deal Modernism*, 55.

9. The meaning of this term has been debated ever since Michael Gold first used it in 1921, with some attaching it to explicitly Marxist writers while others tie it to any text that treats working-class experience. See David Madden, *Proletarian Writers of the Thirties* (Carbondale: Sothern Illinois University Press, 1968), xv–xli.

10. See Morris Dickstein, *Dancing in the Dark: A Cultural History of the Great Depression* (New York: Norton, 2009), for a discussion of the crucial role of culture, especially film, in responding to the Depression.

11. Philip Rahv, qtd. in Barbara Foley, *Radical Representations: Politics and Form in U.S. Proletarian Fiction, 1929–1941* (Durham, N.C.: Duke University Press 1993), 17.

12. Foley, *Radical Representations*, 19.

13. For a look at the interconnections between Harlem Renaissance writing and transnational modernisms, see the chapter on Langston Hughes in Anita Patterson, *Race, American Literature, and Transnational Modernism* (Cambridge: Cambridge University Press, 2008), 93–130.

14. *The Midwest: A Review*, issue 1 (1936).

15. Daniel Aaron, *Writers on the Left: Episodes in American Literary Communism* (1961; New York: Columbia University Press, 1992), 84.

16. Michael Gold, "Towards Proletarian Art," *Liberator* 4 (February 1921), reprint, *Mike Gold: A Literary Anthology*, ed. Michael Folsom (New York: International Publishers, 1972), 64–65, 69.

17. Michael Gold, qtd. in Aaron, *Writers on the Left*, 85.

18. Six novels were written in the period about this important strike.

19. William Empson, *Some Versions of Pastoral* (1935; New York: New Directions, 1974), 6.

20. Rabinowitz, *Labor and Desire*, 73; As Barbara Foley puts it, "From its beginnings American cultural proletarianism was explicitly linked with the Proletkult (1918–20) movement that sprang up in the Soviet Union in the wake of the Bolshevik Revolution. Indeed, the very terms 'proletarian art' and 'proletarian literature' were derived from the Soviet model" (Foley, *Radi-*

cal Representations, 63). Foley's chapter 3, "Defining Proletarian Literature" (86–128) goes into depth on the controversies surrounding the term.

21. Empson, *Some Versions of Pastoral*, 6. His chapter also connects pastoral and proletarian writing by remarking on its humility of tone, its emphasis on the humble protagonist as, like the shepherd of pastoral, a symbol of heroic values, and the ability of proletarian fiction to represent complexity within a simple setting (3–23).

22. M. Keith Booker, *The American Novel of the Left: A Research Guide* (Westport, Conn.: Greenwood Press, 1999), 7. There has long been debate about whether working-class literature must be written by those from the class. Laura Hapke, ed. *Labor's Text: The Worker in American Fiction* (New Brunswick, N.J.: Rutgers University Press, 2001), discusses the difficulty of defining "working class" (xii) and takes a broad view, examining texts about workers. For purposes of this chapter, however, I will restrict myself to those writers who considered themselves to be working class.

23. Philip Rahv, "Valedictory on the Propaganda Issue," *The Little Magazine* 1, no. 5 (September 1934): 1–2.

24. See Daniel Aaron's brilliant though all-male *Writers on the Left*, for example.

25. Rabinowitz, *Labor and Desire*, 73.

26. Booker claims that "the sheer volume of leftist cultural production in America in the twentieth century has been far greater than most accounts of modern literary history would acknowledge" (*The American Novel of the Left*, 6).

27. Douglas Wixson refers to the period between 1928 and 1933 as the "proletarian bull market" (*Worker-Writer in America: Jack Conroy and the Tradition of Midwestern Literary Radicalism, 1898–1990* [Urbana: University of Illinois Press, 1994], 290–324).

28. Daniel Aaron, introduction to *The Disinherited*, by Jack Conroy (1933; New York: Hill and Wang, 1963), xiv.

29. See Kadlec, *Mosaic Modernism*.

30. These are a few of the many little magazines, of no specific political doctrine or literary school, that began to publish worker's writing in the 1920s. See Wixson, *Worker-Writer in America*, 119. Conroy's papers at the Newberry Library contain his extensive collection of little magazines.

31. Jack Conroy papers, Newberry Library, Conroy MSS, Box 41, Folder 1859, "Literary Underworld of the Thirties," interview, 17 April 1969, 3.

32. Wixson, *Worker-Writer in America*, 138.

33. Leonard Spier, editorial, *The Rebel Poet* 15 (August 1932): 3.

34. Jack Conroy papers, Newberry Library, Conroy MSS, Box 41, Folder 1862, "Memories of Arna Bontemps"; Guggenheim recipients in 1935 included Kenneth Burke, Lola Ridge, Langston Hughes, and Edmund Wilson.

35. Arna Bontemps and Jack Conroy, preface to *Anyplace but Here* (1966; Columbia: University of Missouri Press, 1997); originally published as *They*

Seek a City. Conroy and Bontemps collaborated over thirty years and published a series of children's books together.

36. Despite his harsh words about proletarian literature, Mencken was extraordinarily open to a variety of writing and offered words of encouragement and, crucially, publication, to many young working-class writers in the late 1920s and early 1930s (Wixson, *Worker-Writer in America*, 190–91).

37. Wixson, *Worker-Writer in America*, 143, 263.

38. Jack Conroy, introduction to *Writers in Revolt: The Anvil Anthology*, ed. Conroy and Curt Johnson (New York: Lawrence Hill, 1973), xii–xiii.

39. See Denning, *The Cultural Front*, his classic depiction of the role of culture in the period of the Popular Front, which followed the Third Period in 1935.

40. Wixson, *Worker-Writer in America*, 273, 283.

41. Jack Conroy papers, Newberry Library, Conroy MSS, Box 5, Folder 251, letter from Walter Carmon, 12 November 1932.

42. Jack Conroy, qtd. in Wixson, *Worker-Writer in America*, 273, 288.

43. Conroy, "Literary Underworld of the Thirties," interview.

44. Jack Conroy, introduction to *The Jack Conroy Reader*, ed. Jack Salzman and David Ray (New York: Burt Franklin, 1979), xi.

45. For example, Conroy published two stories by Erskine Caldwell, "Daughter" and "Blue Boy," that others had declined because their content was too risky or off-color (Conroy, introduction to *The Jack Conroy Reader*, xv–xvi).

46. Conroy, introduction to *The Jack Conroy Reader*, xviii.

47. Derek Attridge, *The Singularity of Literature* (London: Routledge, 2004), 125.

48. Derek Attridge, "Ethical Modernism: Servants as Others in J. M. Coetzee's Early Fiction," *Poetics Today* 25, no. 4 (Winter 2004): 654.

49. Also see Ewa Plonowska Ziarek, *An Ethics of Dissensus: Postmodernity, Feminism, and the Politics of Radical Democracy* (Stanford, Calif.: Stanford University Press, 2001).

50. Kadlec, *Mosaic Modernism*, 208.

51. Peter Childs, *Modernism*, 2nd ed. (London: Routledge, 2008), 20.

52. Nelson Algren, "Within the City" (1935), in *Writers in Revolt: The Anvil Anthology*, ed. Jack Conroy and Curt Johnson (New York: Lawrence Hill, 1973), 8. The story ultimately became part of Algren's novel *Somebody in Boots* (1935; New York: Thunder's Mouth Press, 1987).

53. Caldwell's stories often condescend toward their characters, especially the black ones, but in this story the community support for Jim seems to mitigate against this condescension, at least in part.

54. Erskine Caldwell, "Daughter" (1933), in *Writers in Revolt: The Anvil Anthology*, ed. Jack Conroy and Curt Johnson (New York: Lawrence Hill, 1973).

55. See Boris Eichenbaum, "How Gogol's 'Overcoat' Works," in *Gogol from the Twentieth Century*, ed. Robert A. Maguire (Princeton, N.J.: Princeton University Press, 1974), 267–92; Wixson, *Worker-Writer in America*, 299.

56. Joe Kalar, qtd. in Wixson, *Worker-Writer in America*, 298.

57. Eichenbaum, "How Gogol's 'Overcoat' Works," 272.

58. Mikhail M. Bakhtin, *Problems of Dostoevsky's Poetics*, ed. and trans. Caryl Emerson (Minneapolis: University of Minnesota Press, 1984), 191, 192.

59. Mencken told Conroy "that an autobiography would make a far better book than a collection of sketches, and that it would sell better.... You have a good story to tell, and you will tell it effectively. Maybe parts of it will fit into The American Mercury ... I hope you tackle it" (Jack Conroy papers, Newberry Library, Conroy MSS, Box 20, Folder 1043, Mencken correspondence, 21 December 1933[?]).

60. Wixson, *Worker-Writer in America*, 310.

61. As Daniel Aaron puts it, "Conroy's critics in the thirties ... pointed out the obvious literary weakness of this book: its awkward unhinged episodes, its flat and undeveloped characterization, its pat conclusion. Undoubtedly Conroy might have profited had he been a more self-conscious writer" (introduction, xii). More recently, Laura Hapke calls the novel "episodic" and criticizes its "flat labor characters" (*Labor's Text*, 226).

62. Adriana Cavarero, *Relating Narratives: Storytelling and Selfhood*, trans. Paul A. Kottman (New York: Routledge, 2000).

63. Jack Conroy, *The Disinherited* (1933; New York: Hill and Wang, 1963), 108; further references cited in the text.

64. Hapke *Labor's Text*, 226.

65. Matthew Hart, *Nations of Nothing but Poetry: Modernism, Transnationalism, and Synthetic Vernacular Writing* (New York: Oxford University Press, 2010), 13.

66. This is a representation of the famous strike in 1922.

67. Entin, *Sensational Modernism*, 2–3.

68. Aaron, introduction, xii.

69. See Bontemps and Conroy, *Anyplace but Here*.

70. Jack Conroy, "The Worker as Writer" (1935), in *The Jack Conroy Reader*, ed. Jack Salzman and David Ray (New York: Burt Franklin, 1979), 221.

71. Meridel Le Sueur, "Women on the Breadlines"(1932), in *Ripening: Selected Work*, ed. and intro. Elaine Hedges, 2nd ed. (New York: The Feminist Press, 1990), 136.

72. Ibid., 142–43.

73. See Rabinowitz, *Labor and Desire*, 22, for a discussion of Mike Gold's "construction of the proletariat and proletarian literature as masculine."

74. Michel Foucault, *The Birth of Biopolitics: Lectures at the College de France, 1978–79*, ed. Michel Senellart, trans. Graham Burchell (New York: Palgrave, 2008), 317.

75. Elaine Hedges, introduction to Le Sueur, *Ripening*, 2.

76. Le Sueur, "The Laundress" (1927), in *Ripening*, 109.

77. Laura Hapke, *Daughters of the Great Depression: Women, Work, and Fiction in the American 1930s* (Athens: University of Georgia Press, 1995), 89.

78. Rabinowitz, *Labor and Desire*, 2–3.

79. Iris Marion Young, *On Female Body Experience: "Throwing Like a Girl" and Other Essays* (New York: Oxford University Press, 2005), 16.

80. Ibid., 17, 25, 26.

81. Elizabeth Grosz, *Time Travels: Feminism, Nature, Power* (Durham, N.C.: Duke University Press, 2005), 120–21.

82. Toril Moi, *What Is a Woman? And Other Essays* (Oxford: Oxford University Press, 1999), 65. The focus on women's bodies "in situation" within current feminist thought comes primarily from Beauvoir, as Moi points out.

83. Meridel Le Sueur, *I Hear Men Talking* (Minneapolis: West End, 1984); further references cited in the text. Like much of Le Sueur's work, individual stories were published in the 1930s but were not collected in book form until much later.

84. I here rely not only on Empson but also on Paul Alpers, *What Is Pastoral?* (Chicago: University of Chicago Press, 1996).

85. For another way into the relationships among sexuality, class, and modernity in the period, see Michael Trask, *Cruising Modernism: Class and Sexuality in American Literature and Social Thought* (Ithaca, N.Y.: Cornell University Press, 2003).

86. Alpers, *What Is Pastoral?* 81.

87. Here I take issue with the critical tendency, most visible in Paula Rabinowitz's work, to describe Le Sueur's writing about women mainly in relation to maternity.

88. Meridel Le Sueur, "The American Way," *Midwest* 1, no. 1 (November 1936): 6.

89. Michael Johnston Grant, *Down and Out on the Family Farm: Rural Rehabilitation in the Great Plains, 1929–1945* (Omaha: University of Nebraska Press, 2002), 3.

90. Ibid, 14, 3.

91. Meridel Le Sueur, "Harvest" (1929) in *Harvest and Song for My Time* (Minneapolis: West End, 1977), 7; further references cited in the text. "Harvest" was written in 1929 but not published until 1977.

92. See, for example, Rabinowitz, *Labor and Desire*; and Hapke, *Daughters of the Great Depression*.

93. Alpers, *What Is Pastoral?* 398.

94. Meridel Le Sueur, *The Girl*, rev. ed. (Albuquerque: West End Press, 1990), 37; further references cited in the text.

95. On Le Sueur's reporting, see Hedges, introduction to Le Sueur, *Ripening*, 9–10.

96. See, Hedges, introduction to Le Sueur, *Ripening*, though Hedges makes clear that Le Sueur also found much of value in the Communist Party.

97. Alan Wald, *Exiles from a Future Time: The Forging of the Mid-Twentieth Century* (Chapel Hill: University of North Carolina Press, 2002), 98.

98. Hapke, *Daughters of the Depression*, 91.

99. Though it appears that Le Sueur participated in the 1934 Minneapolis truckers strike that is its source (Hedges, in Le Sueur, *Ripening*, 136).

100. Meridel Le Sueur, "I Was Marching" (1934), in *Salute to Spring* (New York: International Publishers, 1977), 160; further references cited in the text.

Afterword

1. Barack Obama, "A Just and Lasting Peace," Nobel speech, 10 December 2009, http://nobelprize.org/nobel_prizes/peace/laureates/2009/obama-lecture_en.html.

2. Martin Luther King, "The Quest for Peace and Justice," Nobel speech, http://nobelprize.org/nobel_prizes/peace/laureates/1964/king-lecture.html.

3. David Hume, *A Treatise of Human Nature*, ed. L. A. Selby-Biggem, rev. 2nd ed., ed. P. H. Nidditch, (New York: Oxford University Press, 1978), 3.1.1.468.

4. Nancy Fraser, *Scales of Justice: Reimagining Political Space in a Globalizing World* (New York: Columbia University Press, 2009), 5–6.

BIBLIOGRAPHY

Archival Sources

BBC Written Archives Centre. BBC Eastern Service, typescripts.
Jack Conroy papers. Newberry Library.
Jean Rhys papers. University of Tulsa, McFarlin Library.
Neala Schleuning Meridel Le Sueur Collection. Special Collections, University of Delaware Library.
Cornelia Sorabji papers. India Office Selected Papers: Private Papers Collection, British Library.
Spanish Civil War Poster Collection. Library of Congress.

Other Sources

Aaron, Daniel. Introduction to *The Disinherited*, by Jack Conroy. New York: Hill and Wang, 1963.
———. *Writers on the Left: Episodes in American Literary Communism*. 1961. New York: Columbia University Press, 1992.
Adorno, Theodor. *Aesthetic Theory*. Trans. C. Lenhardt. New York: Rouledge, 1984.
———. "Commitment." In *Notes to Literature*, vol. 2, trans. Shierry Weber Nicholson, 76–94. New York: Columbia University Press, 1992.

Algren, Nelson. *Somebody in Boots.* 1935. New York: Thunder's Mouth Press, 1987.

———. "Within the City." 1935. In *Writers in Revolt: The Anvil Anthology*, ed. Jack Conroy and Curt Johnson. New York: Lawrence Hill, 1973.

Alix, Josefina. "From War to Magic: The Spanish Pavilion, Paris 1937." In *Barcelona and Modernity: Picasso, Gaudí, Miró, Dalí*, ed. William H. Robinson, Jordi Falgàs, and Carmen Belén Lord, 450–57. New Haven, Conn.: Yale University Press, 2006.

Alpers, Paul. *What Is Pastoral?* Chicago: University of Chicago Press, 1996.

Altman, Janet Gurkin. *Epistolarity: Approaches to a Form.* Columbus: Ohio State University Press, 1982.

Anand, Mulk Raj. *Conversations in Bloomsbury.* 1981. Oxford: Oxford University Press, 1995.

———. *Coolie.* 1936. New York: Liberty Press, 1952

———. "Pigeon-Indian: Some Notes on Indian-English Writing." *World Literature Written in English* 21, no. 2 (Summer 1982): 325–36.

———. *Roots and Flowers.* Dharwar: Karnatak University Press, 1972.

———. "The Search for National Identity in India." In *Cultural Self-Comprehension of Nations*, ed. Hans Köchler, 73–98. International Progress Organisation, Studies in International Cultural Relations 1. Tubingen: Erdmann, 1978.

———. "The Sources of Protest in My Novels." *Literary Criterion* 18, no. 4 (1983): 1–12.

———. *Untouchable.* 1940. New York: Penguin, 1986.

———. "The World I Hope For No. 4." BBC Eastern Service. Broadcast 28 October 1943, 1515–1530 GMT. Typescript, BBC Written Archives Centre.

Anderson, James, ed. *Transnational Democracy: Political Spaces and Border Crossings.* New York: Routledge, 2002.

Appadurai, Arjun. *Modernity at Large: Cultural Dimensions of Globalization.* Minneapolis: University of Minnesota Press, 1996.

Appiah, K. Anthony. *Cosmopolitanism: Ethics in a World of Strangers.* New York: Norton, 2006.

———. "Cosmopolitan Patriots." In *For Love of Country: Debating the Limits of Patriotism*, by Martha C. Nussbaum et al., 21–29 Boston: Beacon Press, 1996.

———. *The Ethics of Identity.* Princeton, N.J.: Princeton University Press, 2005.

Arendt, Hannah. *The Human Condition.* Chicago: University of Chicago Press, 1958.

———. *Lectures on Kant's Political Philosophy.* Ed. Ronald Beiner. Chicago: University of Chicago Press, 1989.

———. *Responsibility and Judgment.* Ed. Jerome Kohn. New York: Schocken, 2003.

Aristotle. *The Ethics of Aristotle: The Nicomachean Ethics.* Trans. J. A. K. Thomson. Rev. Hugh Tredennick. New York: Penguin, 1976.
Ashcroft, Bill, Gareth Griffiths, and Helen Tiffin. *The Empire Writes Back: Theory and Practice in Post-Colonial Literature.* New York: Routledge, 1989.
Attridge, Derek. "Ethical Modernism: Servants as Others in J. M. Coetzee's Early Fiction." *Poetics Today* 25, no. 4 (Winter 2004): 653–71.
———. *Joyce Effects: On Language, Theory, and History.* Cambridge: Cambridge University Press, 2000.
———. *The Singularity of Literature.* New York: Routledge, 2004.
Attridge, Derek, and Marjorie Howes, eds. *Semicolonial Joyce.* Cambridge: Cambridge University Press, 2000.
Aub, Max. *Campo abierto.* 1951. 2nd ed. Madrid: Punto de lectura, 2004.
———. *Campo cerrado.* 1943. Xalapa: Universidad Veracruzana, 1968.
———. *Discurso de la novela española contemporánea.* Mexico City: Colegio de Mexico, 1945.
———. *Geografía, prehistoria, 1928.* Segorbe: Ayuntamiento, 1996
———. *Field of Honour.* Trans. Gerald Martin. New York: Verso, 2009.
———. *Hablo como hombre.* Mexico: Joaquin Mortiz, 1967.
Aznar Soler, Manuel. *Los laberintos del exilio: Diecisiete estudios sobre la obra literaria de Max Aub.* Seville: Renacimiento: Biblioteca del Exilio, 2003.
Badiou, Alan. *Ethics: An Essay on the Understanding of Evil.* Trans. Peter Hallward. New York: Verso, 2001.
Baer, Ben Conisbee. "Shit Writing: Mulk Raj Anand's *Untouchable*, the Image of Gandhi, and the Progressive Writers' Association." *Modernism/Modernity* 16, no. 3 (September 2009): 575–95.
Bakhtin, Mikhail M. "The *Bildungsroman* and Its Significance in the History of Realism: Toward a Historical Typology of the Novel." In *Speech Genres and Other Late Essays*, trans. Vern W. McGee, 10–59. Austin: University of Texas Press, 1986.
———. *Problems of Dostoevsky's Poetics.* Ed. and trans. Caryl Emerson. Minneapolis: University of Minnesota Press, 1984.
Bakker, Kees, ed. *Joris Ivens and the Documentary Context.* Amsterdam: Amsterdam University Press, 1999.
Bal, Mieke. "Enfolding Feminism." In *Feminist Consequences: Theory for the New Century*, ed. Elisabeth Bronfen and Misha Kavka, 321–52. New York: Columbia University Press, 2001.
Banfield, Ann. *The Phantom Table: Woolf, Fry, Russell, and the Epistemology of Modernism.* Cambridge: Cambridge University Press, 2000.
Barnard, Rita. *The Great Depression and the Culture of Abundance.* New York: Cambridge University Press, 1995.
———. "Modern American Fiction." In *The Cambridge Companion to American Modernism*, ed. Walter Kalaidjian, 39–67. New York: Cambridge University Press, 2005.

Bartley, Brendan, Rob Hitchin, and Phil Hubbard. *Thinking Geographically: Space, Theory, and Contemporary Human Geography*. New York: Continuum, 2002.

Bauman, Zygmunt. *Modernity and the Holocaust*. Cambridge: Polity Press, 1989.

Beevor, Antony. *The Battle for Spain: The Spanish Civil War, 1936–1939*. New York: Penguin, 2006.

Begam, Richard, and Michael Valdez Moses, eds. *Modernism and Colonialism: British and Irish Literature, 1899–1939*. Durham, N.C.: Duke University Press, 2007.

Bell, Vicki. "On Ethics and Feminism: Reflecting on Levinas' Ethics of Non-(in)difference." *Feminist Theory* 2, no. 2 (2002): 143–276.

Benhabib, Seyla. *Situating the Self: Gender, Community, and Postmodernism in Contemporary Ethics*. New York: Routledge, 1992.

Benjamin, Walter. "The Paris of the Second Empire in Baudelaire." In *Charles Baudelaire: A Lyric Poet in the Era of High Capitalism*, trans. Harry Zohn. London: Verso, 1983.

———. "The Storyteller." In *Illuminations*, ed. Hannah Arendt, trans. Harry Zohn, 83–110. New York: Schocken, 1969.

Berman, Jessica. "Comparative Colonialisms: Joyce, Anand, and the Question of Engagement." *Modernism/Modernity* (Fall 2006): 465–85.

———. "Imagining World Literatures: Modernism and Comparative Literature." In *Disciplining Modernism*, ed. Pamela Caughie, 53–71. London: Palgrave, 2009.

———. *Modernist Fiction, Cosmopolitanism, and the Politics of Community*. 2001. Cambridge: Cambridge University Press, 2006.

Bernasconi, Robert. "The Third Party: Levinas on the Intersection of the Ethical and the Political." *Journal of the British Society for Phenomenology* 30, no. 1 (1999): 76–87.

Bhabha, Homi. *The Location of Culture*. New York: Routledge, 1994.

Bhatnagar, M. K. *Political Consciousness in Indian English Writing*. New Delhi: Bahri, 1991.

Bitzer, Lloyd F. "The Rhetorical Situation." *Philosophy and Rhetoric* 1 (1968): 1–14.

Bluemel, Kristen. *George Orwell and the Radical Eccentric*. New York: Palgrave, 2004.

———. *Intermodernism: Writing and Culture in Interwar and Wartime Britain*. Edinburgh: Edinburgh University Press, 2009.

Boehmer, Elleke. *Colonial and Postcolonial Literature*. New York: Oxford University Press, 1995.

———. *Empire, the National, and the Postcolonial*. Oxford: Oxford University Press, 2002.

Boes, Tobias. "*The Portrait of the Artist as a Young Man* and the 'Individuating Rhythm' of Modernity," *ELH* 75 (2008): 767–85.

Bontemps, Arna, and Jack Conroy. *Anyplace but Here*. 1966. Columbia: University of Missouri Press, 1997. Originally published as *They Seek a City*.

Booker, M. Keith. *The Modern American Novel of the Left: A Research Guide*. Westport, Conn.: Greenwood Press, 1999.

Bowen, Zack. *Musical Allusions in the Works of James Joyce*. Albany: SUNY Press, 1978.

Bradshaw, David. *Concise Companion to Modernism*. Malden, Mass.: Blackwell, 2003.

Brathwaite, Kamau. "History of the Voice." In Brathwaite, *Roots: Essays in Caribbean Literature*, 259–304. Ann Arbor: University of Michigan Press, 1993.

Bretz, Mary Lee. *Encounters Across Borders: The Changing Visions of Spanish Modernism, 1890–1930*. Lewisburg, Penn.: Bucknell University Press, 2001.

Brothers, Caroline. *War and Photography: A Cultural History*. New York: Routledge, 1997.

Brown, G. G. *A Literary History of Spain: The Twentieth Century*. London: Ernest Benn, 1971.

Buckley, Jerome. *Season of Youth: The Bildungsroman from Dickens to Golding*. Cambridge, Mass.: Harvard University Press, 1974.

Burke, Kenneth. *A Grammar of Motives*. Berkeley: University of California Press, 1969.

———. "Literature as Equipment for Living." 1941. In *The Philosophy of Literary Form*, 293–304. Berkeley: University of California Press, 1973.

———. *Permanence and Change*. New York: New Republic, 1936.

Burton, Antoinette. *Dwelling in the Archives: Women Writing House, Home, and History in Late Colonial India*. New York: Oxford University Press, 2003.

Bush, Christopher. *Ideographic Modernism: China, Writing, and Media*. Oxford: Oxford University Press, 2009.

Butler, Judith. *Antigone's Claim: Kinship Between Life and Death*. New York: Columbia University Press, 2000.

———. *Giving an Account of Oneself*. New York: Fordham University Press, 2005.

Caldwell, Erskine. "Daughter." In *Writers in Revolt: The Anvil Anthology*, ed. Jack Conroy and Curt Johnson, 26–31. New York: Lawrence Hill, 1973.

Carroll, Peter. *The Odyssey of the Abraham Lincoln Brigade: Americans in the Spanish Civil War*. Stanford, Calif.: Stanford University Press, 1994.

Carroll, Peter, and James D. Fernández. *Facing Fascism: New York and the Spanish Civil War*. New York: New York University Press, 2007.

Casanova, Pascale. *The World Republic of Letters*. Trans. M. B. DeBevoise. Cambridge, Mass.: Harvard University Press 2005.

Caughie, Pamela, ed. *Disciplining Modernism*. New York: Palgrave, 2010.

Cavarero, Adriana. *Relating Narratives: Storytelling and Selfhood*. Trans. Paul A. Kottman. New York: Routledge, 2000.

Chakrabarty, Dipesh. *Habitations of Modernity: Essays in the Wake of Subaltern Studies*. Chicago: University of Chicago Press, 2002.

Chanter, Tina. *The Ethics of Eros: Irigaray's Rewriting of the Philosophers.* New York: Routledge, 1995.

———. *Feminist Interpretations of Emmanuel Levinas.* University Park: Penn State University Press, 2001.

Cheng, Vincent. *Inauthentic: The Anxiety Over Culture and Identity.* New Brunswick, N.J.: Rutgers University Press, 2004.

———. *Joyce, Race, and Empire.* Cambridge: Cambridge University Press, 1995.

Childs, Peter. *Modernism.* 2nd ed. London: Routledge, 2008.

Clifford, James. *The Predicament of Culture: Twentieth-Century Ethnography, Literature, and Art.* Cambridge, Mass.: Harvard University Press, 1988.

Compagnon, Antoine. *The Five Paradoxes of Modernity.* New York: Columbia University Press, 1994.

Connolly, James. "The Coming Revolt in India: Its Political and Social Causes." *The Harp* (January 1908). Accessed 3 January 2006. http://www.marxists.org/archive/connolly/1908/01/india1.htm.

Conrad, Peter. *Modern Times, Modern Places.* New York: Knopf, 1999.

Conroy, Jack. *The Disinherited.* 1933. Intro. Daniel Aaron. New York: Hill and Wang, 1963.

———. *The Jack Conroy Reader.* Ed. Jack Salzman and David Ray. Intro. Conroy. New York: Burt Franklin, 1979.

Conroy, Jack, and Curt Johnson, eds. *Writers in Revolt: The Anvil Anthology.* New York: Lawrence Hill, 1973.

Cornell, Drucilla. *At the Heart of Freedom: Feminism, Sex, and Equality.* Princeton, N.J.: Princeton University Press, 1998.

Cowasjee, Saros. *So Many Freedoms: A Study of the Major Fiction of Mulk Raj Anand.* Oxford: Oxford University Press. 1977.

Critchley, Simon. *Ethics, Politics, Subjectivity.* New York: Verso, 1999.

Cuddy-Keane, Melba. "Inside and Outside the Covers: Beginnings, Endings, and Woolf's Non-Coercive Ethical Texts." In *Woolfian Boundaries: Selected Papers from the Sixteenth Annual International Conference on Virginia Woolf,* ed. Anna Burrells, Steve Ellis, Deborah Parsons, and Kathryn Simpson, 172–81. Clemson, S.C.: Clemson University Digital Press, 2007.

———. "Modernism, Geopolitics, Globalization." *Modernism/Modernity* 10, no. 3 (2003): 539–58.

———. *Virginia Woolf, the Intellectual, and the Public Sphere.* Cambridge: Cambridge University Press, 2003.

Dalgarno, Emily. *Virginia Woolf and the Visual World.* Cambridge: Cambridge University Press, 2001.

Damrosch, David. *What Is World Literature?* Princeton, N.J.: Princeton University Press, 2003.

Davis, William. "The Essential in Geography." *American Geographical Society of New York Bulletin* 36, no .8. (1904): 470–73.

Deane, Seamus. *Strange Country: Modernity and Nationhood in Irish Writing Since 1790*. Oxford: Oxford University Press, 1997.
Delaprée, Louis. "The Martyrdom of Madrid." Madrid, 1937. In *The Reading Notes for* Three Guineas: *An Archival Edition*, ed. Merry M. Pawlowski and Vara S. Neverow. Accessed 11 February 2009. http://www.csub.edu/woolf/tgs_home.html.
Deleuze, Gilles. *The Fold: Leibniz and the Baroque*. Trans. Peter Conley. Minneapolis: University of Minnesota Press, 1993.
Denning, Michael. *The Cultural Front: The Laboring of American Culture in the Twentieth Century*. New York: Verso, 1997.
Derrida, Jacques. *Adieu to Emmanuel Levinas*. Trans. Pascale-Anne Brault and Michael Naas. Stanford, Calif.: Stanford University Press, 1999.
———. *On Cosmopolitanism and Forgiveness*. Trans. Mark Dooley and Michale Hughes. New York: Routledge, 2001.
Desai, S. K., ed. *Experimentation with Language in Indian Writing in English Fiction*. Kolhapur: Shivaji University, 1974.
Dewey, John. *Art as Experience*. 1934. New York: Penguin, 2005.
Dickinson, Robert E. *The Makers of Modern Geography*. London: Routledge, 1969.
Dickstein, Morris. *Dancing in the Dark: A Cultural History of the Great Depression*. New York: Norton, 2009.
Dougherty, W. E., and Morris Janowitz. *A Psychological Warfare Casebook*. Baltimore, Md.: Johns Hopkins University Press, 1956.
Doyle, Laura, and Laura Winkiel, eds. *Geomodernisms: Race, Modernism, Modernity*. Bloomington: Indiana University Press, 2005.
Duffy, Enda. *The Subaltern* Ulysses. Minneapolis: University of Minnesota Press, 1994.
Edelman, Lee. *No Future: Queer Theory and the Death Drive*. Durham, N.C.: Duke University Press, 2004.
Edwards, Brent Hayes. *The Practice of Diaspora*. Cambridge, Mass.: Harvard University Press, 2003.
Eichenbaum, Boris. "How Gogol's 'Overcoat' Works." In *Gogol from the Twentieth Century*, ed. Robert A. Maguire, 267–92. Princeton, N.J.: Princeton University Press, 1974.
Ellis, Lorna. *Appearing to Diminish: Female Development and the British Bildungsroman, 1750–1850*. Lewisburg, Penn.: Bucknell University Press, 1999.
Ellmann, Richard. *James Joyce*. 1959. Oxford: Oxford University Press, 1982.
Emery, Mary Lou. "The Politics of Form: Jean Rhys's Social Vision in *Voyage in the Dark* and *Wide Sargasso Sea*." *Twentieth-Century Literature* 28, no. 4 (Winter 1982): 418–31.
Empson, William. *Some Versions of Pastoral*. 1935. New York: New Directions, 1974.
Entin, Joseph. *Sensational Modernism: Experimental Fiction and Photography in Thirties America*. Chapel Hill: University of North Carolina Press, 2007.

Esty, Jed. "The Colonial Bildungsroman: The Story of an African Farm and the Ghost of Goethe." *Victorian Studies* 49, no. 3. (Spring 2007): 407–30.

———. "Virginia Woolf's Colony and the Adolescence of Modernist Fiction." In *Modernism and Colonialism: British and Irish Literature, 1899–1939*, ed. Richard Begam and Michael Valdez Moses, 70–90. Durham, N.C.: Duke University Press, 2007.

Eysteinsson, Astradur, and Vivian Liska, eds. *Modernism*. 2 vols. Philadelphia: Benjamins, 2007.

Felski, Rita. *The Gender of Modernity*. Cambridge, Mass.: Harvard University Press, 1995.

Filreis, Alan. *Modernism from Right to Left: Wallace Stevens, the Thirties, and Literary Radicalism*. New York: Cambridge University Press, 2005.

Fisher, Marlene. *The Wisdom of the Heart: A Study of the Works of Mulk Raj Anand*. New Delhi: Sterling, 1985.

Foley, Barbara. *Radical Representations: Politics and Form in U.S. Proletarian Fiction, 1929–1941*. Durham, N.C.: Duke University Press, 1993.

Forbes, Geraldine. *Women in Modern India*. Cambridge: Cambridge University Press, 1996.

Forster, E. M. Preface to *Untouchable*, by Mulk Raj Anand. New York: Penguin, 1940.

Foucault, Michel. *The Birth of Biopolitics: Lectures at the College de France, 1978–79*. Ed. Michel Senellart. Trans. Graham Burchell. New York: Palgrave, 2008.

———. "What Is Enlightenment?" In *The Foucault Reader*, ed. Paul Rabinow, 32–50. New York: Pantheon, 1984.

Fraiman, Susan. *Unbecoming Women: British Women Writers and the Novel of Development*. New York: Columbia, 1993.

Fraser, Nancy. *Scales of Justice: Reimagining Political Space in a Globalizing World*. New York: Columbia University Press, 2009.

Friedman, Susan Stanford. "Definitional Excursions: The Meanings of *Modern/Modernity/Modernism*." *Modernism/Modernity* 8, no. 3 (2001): 493–513.

———. *Mappings: Feminism and the Cultural Geographies of Encounter*. Princeton, N.J.: Princeton University Press, 1998.

———. "Planetarity: Musing Modernist Studies, "*Modernism/Modernity* 17, no. 3 (2010): 471–99.

Fry, Roger. "An Essay in Aesthetics." 1909. In *Vision and Design*, ed. J. B. Bullen, 12–27. New York: Oxford University Press, 1990.

Geertz, Clifford. *The Interpretation of Cultures*. New York: Basic, 1973.

Geist, Anthony, and José Monleón, eds. *Modernism and Its Margins: Reinscribing Cultural Modernity from Spain and Latin America*. New York: Garland, 1999.

Giddens, Anthony. *The Consequences of Modernity*. Stanford, Calif.: Stanford University Press, 1990.

Gies, David Thatcher, ed. *The Cambridge History of Spanish Literature*. Cambridge: Cambridge University Press, 2004.

Gillespie, Diane. *The Sisters' Arts: The Writing and Painting of Virginia Woolf and Vanessa Bell.* Syracuse, N.Y.: Syracuse University Press, 1988.

Gilligan, Carol. *In a Different Voice: Psychological Theory and Women's Development.* Cambridge: Cambridge University Press, 1982.

Gilmore, Leigh. *Autobiographics: A Feminist Theory of Women's Self-Representation.* Ithaca, N.Y.: Cornell University Press, 1994.

Gironella, José María. *One Million Dead.* Trans. Joan MacLean. New York: Doubleday, 1963.

Gold, Michael. "Towards Proletarian Art." *Liberator* 4 (February 1921). Reprint, in *Mike Gold: A Literary Anthology*, ed. Michael Folsom, 64–70. New York: International Publishers, 1972.

Goldman, Jane. *The Feminist Aesthetics of Virginia Woolf.* Cambridge: Cambridge University Press, 1998.

Grant, Michael Johnston. *Down and Out on the Family Farm: Rural Rehabilitation in the Great Plains, 1929–1945.* Omaha: University of Nebraska Press, 2002.

Gregg, Veronica. *Jean Rhys's Historical Imagination: Reading and Writing the Creole.* Chapel Hill: University of North Carolina Press, 1995.

Grosz, Elizabeth. *Time Travels: Feminism, Nature, Power.* Durham, N.C.: Duke University Press, 2005.

Hale, Dorothy J. "Aesthetics and the New Ethics: Theorizing the Novel in the Twenty-first Century." *PMLA* 124, no. 3 (May 2009): 896–905.

Hapke, Laura. *Daughters of the Great Depression: Women, Work, and Fiction in the American 1930s.* Athens: University of Georgia Press, 1995.

———, ed. *Labor's Text: The Worker in American Fiction.* New Brunswick, N.J.: Rutgers University Press, 2001.

Hare, R. M. *The Language of Morals.* Oxford: Clarendon Press, 1952.

Harris, Derek, ed. *The Spanish Avant-garde.* New York: Manchester University Press, 1995.

———. "Squared Horizons: The Hybridisation of the Avant-garde in Spain." In *The Spanish Avant-garde*, ed. Harris, 1–14. New York: Manchester University Press, 1995.

Hart, Matthew. *Nations of Nothing but Poetry: Modernism, Transnationalism, and Synthetic Vernacular Poetry.* New York: Oxford University Press, 2010.

Harvey, David. "The Cartographic Imagination: Balzac in Paris." In *Cosmopolitan Geographies: New Locations in Literature and Culture*, ed. Vinay Dharwadker, 63–88. New York: Routledge, 2001.

———. "Cosmopolitanism and the Banality of Geographical Evils." *Public Culture* 12, no. 2 (2000): 529–64.

———. *Justice, Nature, and the Geography of Difference.* Malden, Mass.: Blackwell, 1996.

Hassan, Sakinatul Fatima Wazir. "Indian Muslim Women—a Perspective." In *Our Cause: Symposium by Indian Women.* Ed. Shaym Nehru, 22–26. Allahabad, Kitabistan, 1938?.

Haste, Cate. "The Machinery of Propaganda." In *Propaganda*, ed. Robert Jackall. 105–36. New York: New York University Press, 1995.

Hayot, Eric. *The Hypothetical Mandarin: Sympathy, Modernity, and Chinese Pain.* Oxford: Oxford University Press, 2009.

Hegel, G. W. F. *Phenomenology of Spirit*. Trans. A. V. Miller. New York: Oxford University Press, 1977.

Held, Virginia. *The Ethics of Care: Personal, Political, and Global.* Oxford: Oxford University Press, 2005.

Hemingway, Ernest. *The Spanish Earth*. Intro. Jasper Wood. Cleveland, Ohio: J. B. Savage Company, 1938. Facsimile ed., Ann Arbor, Mich.: University Microfilms, 1970.

Henry, Holly. *Virginia Woolf and the Discourse of Science*. Cambridge: Cambridge University Press, 2003.

Hensbergen, Gijs Van. *Guernica: The Biography of a Twentieth-Century Icon.* London: Bloomsbury, 2004.

Herr, Cheryl. "Walking in Dublin." In *A Portrait of the Artist as a Young Man*, by James Joyce, ed. R. B. Kershner, Case Studies in Contemporary Criticism, 2nd ed., 415–29. Boston: Bedford/Saint Martin's, 2006.

Hite, Molly. "Tonal Cues and Uncertain Values: Affect and Ethics in *Mrs. Dalloway*." *Narrative* 18, no. 3 (October 2010): 249–75.

Howes, Marjorie. "'Goodbye Ireland I'm Going to Gort': Geography, Scale, and Narrating the Nation." In *Semicolonial Joyce*, ed. Derek Attridge and Marjorie Howes, 58–77. Cambridge: Cambridge University Press, 2000.

Hubel, Teresa. "The Missing Muslim Woman in Indo-Anglian Literature: Iqbalunnisa Hussain's *Purdah and Polygamy*." In *Perspectives on South Asia*, ed. V. A. Pai Panandiker and Navnita Chadha Behera, 141–51. Delhi: Konark, 2000.

Hume, David. *An Enquiry Concerning the Principles of Morals.* 1777. Reprint, 1912. Project Gutenberg e-book, 2010. Accessed 28 September 2010. http://www.gutenberg.org/ebooks/4320.

———. *A Treatise of Human Nature*. Ed. L.A. Selby-Biggem. Rev. 2nd ed., ed. P. H. Nidditch. New York: Oxford University Press, 1978.

Hussain, Iqbalunnisa. *Changing India: A Muslim Woman Speaks*. Bangalore: Hosali Press, 1940.

———. *Purdah and Polygamy*. Intro. Sir Ramalinga Reddy. Bangalore: Hosali Press, 1944.

Hussey, Mark. *The Singing of the Real World: The Philosophy of Virginia Woolf's Fiction.* Columbus: Ohio State University Press, 1986.

Ilie, Paul. "Benjamín Jarnés: Aspects of the Dehumanized Novel." *PMLA* 76, no. 3 (June 1961): 247–53.

Irigaray, Luce. *An Ethics of Sexual Difference*. Trans. Carolyn Burke. Ithaca, N.Y.: Cornell University Press, 1984.

———. *Sexes and Genealogies*. Trans. Gillian Gill. New York: Columbia University Press, 1993.

Ishvani, G. *Girl in Bombay*. London: Pilot Press, 1947.
Ivens, Joris. *The Camera and I*. New York: International Publishers, 1969.
———. "Documentary: Subjectivity and Montage." 1939. In *Joris Ivens and the Documentary Context*, ed. Kees Bakker, 250–61. Amsterdam: Amsterdam University Press, 1999.
Iyengar, K. R. Srinivasa. *Indian Writing in English*. 3rd ed. New Delhi: Sterling, 1983.
Jackall, Robert, ed. *Propaganda*. New York: New York University Press, 1995.
Jameson, Frederic. "Modernism and Imperialism." In *Nationalism, Colonialism, and Literature*, by Terry Eagleton, Fredric Jameson, and Edward W. Said, 43–69. Minneapolis: University of Minnesota Press, 1990.
———. *A Singular Modernity: Essay on the Ontology of the Present*. New York: Verso, 2002.
Jay, Paul. *Global Matters: The Transnational Turn in Literary Studies*. Ithaca, N.Y.: Cornell University Press, 2010.
Johnson, Roberta. *Gender and Nation in the Spanish Modernist Novel*. Nashville, Tenn.: Vanderbilt University Press, 2003.
Josephs, Allen. "Hemingway and the Spanish Civil War; Or, The Volatile Mixture of Politics and Art." In *Rewriting the Good Fight: Critical Essays on the Literature of the Spanish Civil War*, ed. Frieda S. Brown et al., 175–84. East Lansing: Michigan State University Press, 1989.
Joshi, Priya. *In Another Country: Colonialism, Culture, and the English Novel in India*. New York: Columbia University Press, 2002.
Joyce, James. *Dubliners*. 1914. New York: Modern Library, n.d.
———. "Ireland, Island of Saints and Sages." 1907. In *The Critical Writings of James Joyce*, ed. Ellsworth Mason and Richard Ellman, 153–74. New York: Viking Press, 1959.
———. *A Portrait of the Artist as a Young Man*. 1917. Case Studies in Contemporary Criticism. New York: Bedford Books, 1993.
———. *Ulysses*. 1922. New York: Random House, 1986.
Jussawalla, Feroza. *Family Quarrels: Towards a Criticism of Indian Writing in English*. New York: Peter Lang, 1985.
Kadlec, David. *Mosaic Modernism: Anarchism, Pragmatism, Culture*. Baltimore, Md.: Johns Hopkins University Press, 2000.
Kalaidjian, Walter. *American Culture Between the Wars: Revisionary Modernism and Postmodern Critique*. New York: Columbia University Press, 1993.
Kalliney, Peter. "Jean Rhys: Left Bank Modernist as Postcolonial Intellectual." In *Oxford Handbook of Global Modernisms*, ed. Mark Wollaeger. Oxford: Oxford University Press, forthcoming.
Kant, Immanuel. *The Critique of Judgment*. Trans. J. H. Bernard. New York: Hafner, 1951.
———. *The Metaphysics of Morals*. Trans. Mary Gregor. Cambridge: Cambridge University Press, 1996.

———. *On History*. Ed. Louis White Beck. Indianapolis: Bobbs-Merrill, 1963.

Kiberd, Declan. *Inventing Ireland*. Cambridge, Mass.: Harvard University Press, 1995.

King, Martin Luther. "The Quest for Peace and Justice." Nobel speech. http://nobelprize.org/nobel_prizes/peace/laureates/1964/king-lecture.html.

Konzett, Delia Caparoso. *Ethnic Modernisms: Anna Yezierska, Zora Neale Hurston, Jean Rhys, and the Aesthetics of Dislocation*. New York: Palgrave, 2002.

La Caze, Marguerite. "At the Intersection: Kant, Derrida, and the Relation Between Ethics and Politics." *Political Theory* 35, no. 6 (2007): 781–805.

Laclau, Ernesto, and Chantal Mouffe. *Hegemony and Socialist Strategy: Towards a Radical Democratic Politics*. London: Verso, 1985.

Lecercle, Jean-Jacques. "Return to the Political." *PMLA* 125, no. 4 (October 2010): 916–19.

Lejeune, Philippe. *On Autobiography*. Ed. Paul John Eakin. Trans. Katherine Leary. History and Theory of Literature 52. Minneapolis: University of Minnesota Press, 1988.

Lennon, Joseph. *Irish Orientalism: A Literary and Intellectual History*. Syracuse, N.Y.: Syracuse University Press, 2004.

Le Sueur, Meridel. "The American Way." *Midwest* 1, no. 1 (November 1936): 5–6.

———. *The Girl*. Rev. ed. Albuquerque: West End Press, 1990.

———. "Harvest." 1929. In *Harvest and Song for My Time*, 7–17. Minneapolis: West End, 1977.

———. *I Hear Men Talking and Other Stories*. Minneapolis: West End, 1984.

———. *Ripening: Selected Work*. 2nd ed. Ed. and intro. Elaine Hedges. New York: The Feminist Press, 1990.

———. *Salute to Spring*. New York: International Publishers, 1977.

Levinas, Emmanuel. "Ethics as First Philosophy." In *The Levinas Reader*, ed. Seán Hand, 75–88. Malden, Mass.: Blackwell, 1989.

———. *Ethics and Infinity: Conversations with Philippe Nemo*. Trans. Richard A. Cohen. Pittsburgh, Penn.: Duquesne University Press, 1985.

———. *Otherwise Than Being; Or, Beyond Essence*. Trans. Alphonso Lingis. Dordrecht: Kluwer Academic Publishers, 1991.

———. *Totality and Infinity*. Trans. Alphonso Lingis. Pittsburgh, Penn.: Duquesne University Press, 1969.

———. "Uniqueness." In *Entre Nous: On Thinking-of-the-Other*, trans. Michael B. Smith and Barbara Harshav, 162–68. New York: Columbia University Press, 1998.

Lewis, Pericles. *The Cambridge Introduction to Modernism*. Cambridge: Cambridge University Press, 2007.

Linett, Maren. "'New Worlds, New Everything': Fragmentation and Trauma in Jean Rhys." *Twentieth-Century Literature* 51, no. 4. (Winter 2005): 437–66.

Lionnet, Françoise, and Shu-Mei Shih, eds. *Minor Transnationalism*. Durham, N.C.: Duke University Press, 2005.

Llorens Marzo, Luis. "Génesis del Laberinto mágico: Los autógrafos de Max Aub entre 1938 y 1942." *Bulletin of Spanish Studies* 80, no. 4. (2003): 449–76.

Lloyd, David. *Anomalous States: Irish Writing and the Post-Colonial Moment*. Durham, N.C.: Duke University Press, 1993.

———. *Nationalism and Minor Literature: James Clarence Mangan and the Emergence of Irish Cultural Nationalism*. Berkeley and Los Angeles: University of California Press, 1987.

Lodge, David. *The Modes of Modern Writing*. London: Bloomsbury, 1977.

Lokugé, Chandani. Introduction to *Kamala*, by Krupabai Satthianadhan, 13–15. Oxford: Oxford University Press, 1998.

Longoria, Francisco. *El arte narrativo de Max Aub*. Madrid: Playor, 1977.

Lyotard, Jean-François. *Soundproof Room: Malraux's Anti-Aesthetics*. Trans. Robert Harvey. Stanford, Calif.: Stanford University Press, 2001.

MacKinder, Halford John. *Democratic Ideals and Reality*. New York: Henry Holt, 1919.

——— "The Geographical Pivot of History." 1904. In *Human Geography: An Essential Anthology*, ed. John Agnew, David N. Livingstone, and Alistair Rogers, 536–51. Malden, Mass.: Blackwell, 1996.

———. "On the Scope and Methods of Geography." 1887. In *Human Geography: An Essential Anthology*, ed. John Agnew, David N. Livingstone, and Alistair Rogers, 155–72. Malden, Mass.: Blackwell, 1996.

Madden, David. *Proletarian Writers of the Thirties*. Carbondale: Southern Illinois University Press, 1968.

Mao, Doug, and Rebecca Walkowitz. "The New Modernist Studies." *PMLA* 123, no. 3 (May 2008): 737–48.

Marcus, Jane. *Hearts of Darkness: White Women Write Race*. New Brunswick, N.J.: Rutgers University Press, 2004.

———. "'No More Horses': Virginia Woolf on Art and Propaganda." *Women's Studies* 4, no. 2/3 (1977): 265–90.

Martin, Gerald. Translator's note to *Field of Honour*, by Max Aub. New York: Verso, 2009.

Matthews, Herbert. Review of *Homage to Catalonia*, by George Orwell. *The Nation*, 27 December 1952. Reprint, in *George Orwell: The Critical Heritage*, ed. Jeffery Meyers, 143–49. London: Routledge, 1975.

Mehrotra, Arvind Krishna, ed. *A History of Indian Literature in English*. New York: Columbia University Press, 2003.

Mendelson, Jordana. *Documenting Spain: Artists, Exhibition Culture, and the Modern Nation. 1929–1939*. University Park: Pennsylvania State University Press, 2005.

———. *Revistas y guerra: 1936–39*. Madrid: Museo Nacional Centro de la Reina Sofía, 2007.

Meyers, Jeffery, ed. *George Orwell: The Critical Heritage.* London: Routledge, 1975.
Miller, Arthur B. "Rhetorical Exigence." *Philosophy and Rhetoric* 2 (1972): 111–18.
Miller, Carolyn. "Genre as Social Action." *Quarterly Journal of Speech* 70 (1984): 151–67.
Mitchell, Breon. "*A Portrait* as *Bildungsroman*: A Novel of Development." In *Readings on* A Portrait of the Artist as a Young Man, ed. Clarice Swisher, 52–58. New York: Greenhaven Press, 2000.
Moi, Toril. *What Is a Woman? And Other Essays.* Oxford: Oxford University Press, 1999.
Monteath, Peter. *Writing the Good Fight: Political Commitment in the International Literature of the Spanish Civil War.* Westport, Conn.: Greenwood, 1994.
Moore, G. E. *Principia Ethica.* 1903. Fair Use Repository, n.d. Accessed 30 July 2009. http://fair-use.org/g-e-moore/principia-ethica.
Moretti, Franco. *An Atlas of the European Novel, 1800–1900.* New York: Verso, 1998.
———. "Conjectures on World Literature." In *Debating World Literature,* ed. Christopher Prendergast, 148–63. London: Verso, 2004.
———. *Modern Epic: The World System from Goethe to Garcia Marquez.* New York: Verso, 1996.
———. *Signs Taken for Wonders: On the Sociology of Literary Forms.* 1983. New York: Verso, 2005.
———. *The Way of the World: The Bildungsroman in European Culture.* New York: Verso, 2000.
Mouffe, Chantal. *The Democratic Paradox.* New York: Verso, Phronesis, 2000.
———. *The Return of the Political.* 1993. New York: Verso. 2005.
Mukherjee, Meenakshi. *The Perishable Empire: Essays on Indian Writing in English.* New York: Oxford University Press, 2000.
Nancy, Jean-Luc. *Being Singular Plural.* Trans. Robert Richardson and Anne O'Byrne. Stanford, Calif.: Stanford University Press/Meridian, 2000.
———. *The Sense of the World.* Trans. Jeffrey Librett. Minneapolis: University of Minnesota Press, 1997.
National Council of Women of India. *Women in India: Who's Who.* Bombay: National Council of Women, 1935.
Nehru, Shayam, ed. *Our Cause: A Symposium by Indian Women.* Allahabad, Kitabistan, 1938(?).
Nelson, Cary, and Jefferson Hendricks, eds. *Madrid 1937: Letters of the Abraham Lincoln Brigade From the Spanish Civil War.* New York: Routledge, 1996.
Newbigin, Marion I. *Modern Geography.* London: Williams and Norgate, 1911.
Newman, John Henry. "The Glories of Mary for the Sake of Her Son." In *Discourses to Mixed Congregations.* From *Newman Reader.* Accessed 21 June 2006. http://www.newmanreader.org/works/discourses/discourse17.html.

Newton, Adam Zachary. *Narrative Ethics.* Cambridge, Mass.: Harvard University Press, 1995.
Nicholls, Peter. *Modernisms: A Literary Guide.* Berkeley: University of California Press, 1995.
Nolan, Emer. *James Joyce and Nationalism.* London: Routledge, 1995.
Nussbaum, Martha. *Cultivating Humanity: A Classical Defense of Reform in Liberal Education.* Cambridge, Mass.: Harvard University Press, 1997.
———. *Poetic Justice: The Literary Imagination and Public Life.* Boston: Beacon, 1995.
———. "The Window: Knowledge of Other Minds in Virginia Woolf's *To the Lighthouse.*" *NLH* 26 (1995): 731–53.
Obama, Barack. "A Just and Lasting Peace." Nobel speech, 10 December 2009. http://nobelprize.org/nobel_prizes/peace/laureates/2009/obama-lecture_en.html.
Oliver, Kelly. *Family Values: Subjects Between Nature and Culture.* New York: Routledge, 1997.
Ortega y Gasset, José. *The Dehumanization of Art and Other Writings on Art and Culture.* Trans. Willard Trask. New York: Doubleday Anchor, 1956.
———. "Doestoievsky y Proust." 1925. In *Ideas sobre el teatro y la novella.* Madrid: Alianza, 1982.
———. *La deshumanización del arte.* 2nd ed. Madrid: Revista de Occidente, 1928.
———. *The Revolt of the Masses.* New York: Norton, 1932.
Orwell, George. "The Frontiers of Art and Propaganda." 1941. In George Orwell, *My Country Right or Left: 1940–43, The Collected Essays, Journalism, and Letters,* vol. 2, ed. Sonia Orwell and Ian Angus, 123-26. Boston: Godine, 1968.
———. *Homage to Catalonia.* 1938. Boston: Beacon. 1967.
———. "Why I Write." 1946. In *George Orwell: A Collection of Essays,* 309–16. New York: Harcourt, Brace and Company, 1946.
Otten, J. "Antiphon." 1907. In *The Catholic Encyclopedia.* New York: Robert Appleton. Accessed 10 March 2011. http://www.newadvent.org/cathen/01575b.htm.
Parry, Benita. *Postcolonial Studies: A Materialist Critique.* New York: Routledge, 2004.
Patterson, Anita. *Race, American Literature, and Transnational Modernisms.* New York: Cambridge University Press, 2008.
Paz, Abel. *Durruti in the Spanish Revolution.* Trans. Chuck Morse. Oakland, Calif.: AK Press, 2007.
Perez, Janet. "Prose in Franco's Spain." In *The Cambridge History of Spanish Literature,* ed. David Thatcher Gies, 628–42. Cambridge: Cambridge University Press, 2004.
Phelan, James. *Narrative as Rhetoric: Techniques, Audiences, Ethics, Ideology.* Columbus: Ohio State University Press, 1996.

Pratt, Mary Louise. *Imperial Eyes: Travel Writing and Transculturation.* New York: Routledge, 1992.
Puchner, Martin. *Poetry of the Revolution: Marx, Manifestos, and the Avant-gardes.* Princeton, N.J.: Princeton University Press, 2006.
Rabinowitz, Paula. *Labor and Desire: Women's Revolutionary Fiction in Depression America.* Chapel Hill: University of North Carolina Press, 1991.
Rahv, Philip. "Valedictory on the Propaganda Issue." *The Little Magazine* 1, no. 5. (September 1934): 1–2.
Raiskin, Judith. *Snow on the Cane Fields: Women's Writing and Creole Subjectivity.* Minneapolis: University of Minnesota Press, 1996.
Ramazani, Jahan. "A Transnational Poetics." *American Literary History* 18, no. 2 (2006): 332–59.
———. *A Transnational Poetics.* Chicago: University of Chicago Press, 2009.
Rancière, Jacques. *Dissensus: On Politics and Aesthetics.* Ed. and trans. Steven Corcoran. New York: Continuum, 2010.
———. *The Politics of Aesthetics.* Trans. Gabriel Rockhill. London: Continuum, 2004.
Rao, Raja, and Iqbal Singh. *Changing India.* London: George Allen and Unwin, 1939.
Rawls, John "Justice as Fairness: Political Not Metaphysical." 1985. Reprint, in *Twentieth-Century Political Theory,* 2nd ed., ed. Stephen Eric Bronner, 37–58. New York: Routledge, 2005.
———. *A Theory of Justice.* Cambridge, Mass.: Belknap Press/Harvard University Press, 1971.
Ray, Sangeeta. *En-gendering India: Woman and Nation in Colonial and Postcolonial Narratives.* Durham, N.C.: Duke University Press, 2000.
Reddy, Sir Ramalinga. Foreword to *Purdah and Polygamy,* by Iqbalunnisa Hussain. Bangalore: Hosali Press, 1944.
Redfield, Marc. *Phantom Formations: Aesthetic Ideology and the Bildungsroman.* Ithaca, N.Y.: Cornell University Press, 1996.
Reichman, Ravit. *The Affective Life of Law: Legal Modernism and the Literary Imagination.* Stanford, Calif.: Stanford University Press, 2009.
Resina, Joan Ramon. "The Catalan Avant-garde" In *The Cambridge History of Spanish Literature,* ed. David Thatcher Gies, 543. Cambridge: Cambridge University Press, 2004.
Rhys, Jean. *Good Morning, Midnight.* 1939. New York: Norton, 1986.
———. *Letters, 1931–66.* Ed. Francis Wyndham and Diana Melly. New York: Penguin, 1985.
———. *Quartet.* 1929. New York: Norton, 1997.
———. *Smile Please.* New York: Penguin, 1979.
———. *Voyage in the Dark.* 1934. New York: Norton, 1982.
Ricoeur, Paul. *Oneself as Another.* Trans. Kathleen Blamey. Chicago: University of Chicago Press, 1992.

———. "On Interpretation." In *From Text to Action*, trans. Kathleen Blamey, 1–22. Evanston, Ill.: Northwestern University Press, 1991.

———. *Time and Narrative*. Vols. 1 and 3. Trans. Kathleen Blamey. Chicago: University of Chicago Press, 1984, 1988.

Robbins, Bruce. "Introduction Part I: Actually Existing Cosmopolitanism." In *Cosmopolitics: Thinking and Feeling Beyond the Nation*, ed. Pheng Cheah and Bruce Robbins. Minneapolis: University of Minnesota Press, 1998.

———. "The Newspapers Were Right: Cosmopolitanism, Forgetting, and 'The Dead.'" *Interventions* 5, no. 1 (2003): 101–12.

Rogers, Gayle. Introduction to "James Joyce in His Labyrinth," by Antonio Marichalar, trans. Rogers. *PMLA* 124, no. 3 (2009): 926–28.

Rosner, Victoria. *Modernism and the Architecture of Private Life*. New York: Columbia University Press, 2005.

Rothstein, Eric. "Broaching a Cultural Logic of Modernity." *MLQ* 61, no. 2 (June 2000): 359–95.

Ryan, Marie-Laure. *Possible Worlds, Artificial Intelligence, and Narrative Theory*. Bloomington: Indiana, 1991.

Said, Edward. *Culture and Imperialism*. New York: Vintage, 1994.

Saint-Amour, Paul. "Airwar Prophecy and Interwar Modernism." *Comparative Literature Studies* 42, no. 2 (2005): 130–61.

———. "From *Ulysses* to *Untouchable*: Mulk Raj Anand's Joycean Transmigrations." Unpublished paper, International James Joyce Symposium, Dublin, Ireland, June 2004.

Sandel, Michael. *Justice: What's the Right Thing to Do?* New York: Farrar Straus, 2009.

Sartre, Jean-Paul. *What Is Literature and Other Essays*. Trans. Bernard Frechtman. Cambridge Mass.: Harvard University Press, 1988.

Sarkar, Sumit. *The Swadeshi Movement in Bengal, 1903–1908*. Delhi: People's, 1977.

Sarker, Sonita. "Unruly Subjects: Cornelia Sorabji and Ravinder Randhawa." In *Trans-Status Subjects: Gender in the Globalization of South and Southeast Asia*, ed. Sonita Sarker and Esha Niyogi De, 267–88. Durham, N.C.: Duke University Press, 2002.

Sathianadhan, Kamala. *Detective Janaki*. Bombay: Thacker and Company, 1944.

Satthianadhan, Krupabai. *Kamala*. Intro. Chandani Lokugé. Oxford: Oxford University Press, 1998.

Schiller, Friedrich. *On the Aesthetic Education of Man*. Ed. Elizabeth Wilkinson and L. A. Willoughby. Oxford: Oxford University Press, 1967.

Schwarz, Daniel R. *Reading Joyce's* Ulysses. London: Macmillan, 1987.

Scott, Bonnie Kime, ed. *The Gender of Modernism*. Indianapolis: Indiana University Press, 1990.

Seidel, Michael. *Epic Geography: James Joyce's* Ulysses. Princeton, N.J.: Princeton University Press, 1976.

Sen, Amartya. *The Idea of Justice*. Cambridge, Mass.: Harvard University Press, 2009.

Sengupta, Padmini. *Portrait of an Indian Woman*. Calcutta: YMCA Publishing House, 1956.

Silver, Brenda. "The Authority of Anger: *Three Guineas* as Case Study." *Signs* 16, no .2 (Winter 1991): 340–70.

———. *Virginia Woolf's Reading Notebooks*. Princeton, N.J.: Princeton University Press, 1983.

Singh, Amardeep. "Veiled Strangers: Rabindranath Tagore's America, in Letters and Lectures." *Journeys* 10, no. 1 (2009): 51–68.

Sinha, Mrinalini. *Specters of Mother India: The Global Restructuring of an Empire*. Durham, N.C.: Duke University Press, 2006.

Slaughter, Joseph. *Human Rights, Inc*. New York: Fordham University Press, 2007.

Smedley, Agnes. *Daughter of Earth*. New York: Feminist Press, 1973.

Soja, Edward. *Postmodern Geographies: The Reassertion of Space in Critical Social Theory*. New York: Verso, 1989.

Soldevila Durante, Ignacio. *La obra narrativa de Max Aub (1929–1969)*. Madrid: Biblioteca Románica Hispánica, editorial Gredos, 1973.

———. Preface to *Geografía, prehistoria, 1928*, by Max Aub, 10–52. Segorbe: Ayuntamiento, 1996.

Sontag, Susan. *Regarding the Pain of Others*. New York: Picador, 2003.

Sorabji, Cornelia. *India Calling*. 1934. Ed. Chandani Lokugé. New York: Oxford University Press, 2001.

———. *India Recalled*. London: Nisbet, 1936.

———. *Love and Life Behind the Purdah*. 1902. Ed. Chandani Lokugé. New York: Oxford University Press, 2003.

———. "The Role of Indian Women." *Lyceum Magazine* (1919).

———. *Sun Babies: Studies in the Child-Life of India*. London: John Murray, 1904.

Souza, Eunice de. *Sathianadhan Family Album*. New Delhi: Sahitya Akademi, 2005.

———. ed. *Purdah: An Anthology*. New York: Oxford University Press, 2004.

Souza, Eunice de, and Lindsay Pereira, eds. *Women's Voices: Selections from Nineteenth and Early-Twentieth Century Indian Writing in English*. Oxford: Oxford University Press, 2002.

Spier, Leonard. Editorial. *The Rebel Poet* 15 (August 1932): 3.

Spivak, Gayatri Chakravorty. *A Critique of Postcolonial Reason*. Cambridge, Mass.: Harvard University Press, 1999.

——— *Death of a Discipline*. New York: Columbia University Press, 2003.

———. "Ethics and Politics in Tagore, Coetzee, and Certain Scenes of Teaching." *Diacritics* 32, no. 3–4. (Fall–Winter 2002): 17–31.

——— "Three Women's Texts and Critique of Imperialism." *Critical Inquiry* 12, no. 1 (Autumn 1985): 243–61.

Stryker, Susan, and Stephen Whittle, eds. *The Transgender Studies Reader.* New York: Routledge, 2006.

Suleiman, Susan. *Authoritarian Fictions: The Ideological Novel as a Literary Genre.* New York: Columbia University Press, 1983.

Susman, Warren, ed. *Culture and Commitment, 1929–1945.* New York: G. Braziller, 1973.

Szalay, Michael. *New Deal Modernism.* Durham, N.C.: Duke University Press, 2000.

Tagore, Rabindranath. *Selected Letters of Rabindranath Tagore.* Ed. Krishna Dutta and Andrew Robinson. Cambridge: Cambridge University Press, 1997.

Taylor, Charles. *Modern Social Imaginaries.* Durham, N.C.: Duke University Press, 2004.

———. *Sources of the Self: The Making of the Modern Identity.* Cambridge, Mass.: Harvard University Press, 1989.

Taylor, Philip M. *Munitions of the Mind: A History of Propaganda from the Ancient World to the Present Era.* Manchester: Manchester University Press, 1995.

Tharu, Susie, and Ke Lalita. *Women Writing in India: 600 B.C. to the Present.* 2 vols. New York: Feminist Press, 1993.

Tate, Trudi. "Rumour, Propaganda, and *Parade's End*." *Essays in Criticism* 47, no. 4 (1997): 332–54.

Thomas, Gareth. *The Novel of the Spanish Civil War (1936–1975).* Cambridge: Cambridge University Press, 1990.

Thomas, Hugh. Review of *Homage to Catalonia*, by George Orwell. *The Nation*, 20 April 1962. Reprint, in *George Orwell: The Critical Heritage*, ed. Jeffery Meyers, 150–51. London: Routledge, 1975.

Thornton, Weldon. *Allusions in* Ulysses: *An Annotated List.* Chapel Hill: UNC P, 1961.

Trask, Michael. *Cruising Modernism: Class and Sexuality in American Literature and Social Thought.* Ithaca, N.Y.: Cornell University Press, 2003.

Ugarte, Michael. "Max Aub's Magical Labyrinth of Exile." *Hispania* 68, no. 4 (December 1985): 733–39.

Vaihinger, Hans. *The Philosophy of 'As-If.'* Trans. C. K. Ogden. London: Routledge and Keegan Paul, 1924; reprint, New York: Barnes and Noble, 1968.

Valente, Joseph. *James Joyce and the Problem of Justice: Negotiating Sexual and Colonial Difference.* Cambridge: Cambridge University Press, 1995.

Vidal de la Blache, Paul. *Principles of Human Geography.* Trans. Millicent Todd Bingham. New York: Henry Holt, 1926.

Viswanathan, Gauri. "Ireland, India, and the Poetics of Internationalism." *Journal of World History* 15, no. 1 (2004). Accessed 3 Janaury 2006. http://www.historycooperative.org/journals/jwh/15.1/viswanathan.html.

Wald, Alan. *Exiles from a Future Time: the Forging of the Mid-Twentieth Century.* Chapel Hill: University of North Carolina Press, 2002.

Walker, Margaret Urban. *Moral Understandings: A Feminist Study of Ethics.* New York: Routledge, 1998.
Walzer, Michael. *Spheres of Justice.* New York: Basic Books, 1983.
Walkowitz, Rebecca. "Comparison Literature." *NLH* 40, no. 3 (Summer 2009): 567–82.
Waugh, Thomas. "'Men Cannot Act Before the Camera in the Presence of Death:' Joris Ivens' *The Spanish Earth.*" In *Documenting the Documentary: Close Readings of Documentary Film and Video,* ed. Barry Keith Grant and Jeannette Sloniowski, 136–53. Detroit: Wayne State University Press, 1998.
West, Robin. *Caring for Justice.* New York: New York University Press, 1997.
Whitter-Ferguson, John. *Framing Pieces: Designs of the Gloss in Joyce, Woolf, and Pound.* New York: Oxford University Press, 1996.
Williams, Raymond. *The Politics of Modernism.* London: Verso, 1996.
Williams, Trevor. *Reading Joyce Politically.* Gainesville: University Press of Florida, 1997.
Winkiel, Laura. *Modernism, Race, and Manifestos.* New York: Cambridge University Press, 2008.
Wixson, Douglas. *Worker-Writer in America: Jack Conroy and the Tradition of Midwestern Literary Radicalism. 1898–1990.* Urbana: University of Illinois Press, 1994.
Wollaeger, Mark. *Modernism, Media, and Propaganda: British Narrative from 1900–1945.* Princeton, N.J.: Princeton University Press, 2006.
———, ed. *The Oxford Handbook of Global Modernism.* Oxford: Oxford University Press, forthcoming.
Woolf, Virginia. *The Death of the Moth and Other Essays.* New York: Harcourt, 1970.
———. *The Diary of Virginia Woolf.* Vol. 4: *1931–35.* Ed. Anne Olivier Bell. New York: Harcourt, 1983.
———. *The Diary of Virginia Woolf.* Vol. 5: *1936–41.* Ed. Anne Olivier Bell and Andrew McNeillie. New York: Harcourt, 1984.
———. "Introductory Letter." In *Life as We Have Known It,* ed. Margaret Llewelyn Davies, xv–xxxix. New York: Norton, 1975.
———. *Letters of Virginia Woolf.* Vol. 2. New York: Harcourt, 1976.
———. *Letters of Virginia Woolf.* Vol. 6. New York: Harcourt, 1980.
———. "Mr. Bennett and Mrs. Brown." In Woolf, *Collected Essays,* vol. 1, ed. Leonard Woolf, 319–37. London: Hogarth, 1966.
———. *Mrs. Dalloway.* 1925. New York: Harcourt, 1981.
———. *Orlando.* 1928. New York: Harcourt, 1956.
———. *Three Guineas.* 1938. Ed. Naomi Black. Oxford: Shakespeare Head Press of Blackwell Publishers, 2001.
———. *To The Lighthouse.* 1927. New York: Harcourt, 1955.
Yao, Steven. *Translation and the Languages of Modernism.* New York: Palgrave, 2002.

Young, Iris Marion. *Justice and the Politics of Difference*. Princeton, N.J.: Princeton University Press, 1990.

———. *On Female Body Experience: "Throwing Like a Girl" and Other Essays*. New York: Oxford University Press, 2005.

Ziarek, Ewa Plonowska. *An Ethics of Dissensus: Postmodernity, Feminism, and the Politics of Radical Democracy*. Stanford, Calif.: Stanford University Press, 2001.

INDEX

Aaron, Daniel, 237, 243, 245, 262
abortion, 276–77
Adorno, Theodor W., 24–26, 184, 236
aesthetics: aesthetic dimension of modernism, 8, 26; Bloomsbury aesthetics, 49; and ethics/ethical folds, 46–62; Fry and, 48–49; and Kantian idealism, 47–48; Levinas and, 57–58; Moore and, 13, 48; "negative dialectics," 27; Ortega and, 194–97; Orwell and, 216; and partisanship, 8–9; and propaganda, 212; Smedley and, 237–38; Woolf and, 48–62
Aga Khan, 178–79, 316n65
Algren, Nelson, 247, 249, 251
All Soviet Writers Union, 248–49
Alpers, Paul, 270
Altman, Janet Gurkin, 71
American Mercury (magazine), 247, 266
Anand, Mulk Raj: background of, 90, 109–10; and bildungsroman tradition, 28, 34, 91, 93, 118–25, 130–35; on choice of language, 134; compared to Conroy, 260; *Conversations in Bloomsbury*, 10, 90; and cosmopolitanism, 91, 108–18, 132, 134; and defamiliarization, 10; and "enlarged thinking" (Arendt's concept), 93; experimentalism of, 34, 92–93, 119, 122; geographic sensibility, 91, 108–18; Harvey and, 116; on Indian cultural and religious syncretism, 118; Joyce and, 9, 30–31, 34, 90–94, 110, 112, 119; Lloyd and, 131; modernism and, 23, 111–15; narrative style, 134–35; "Pigeon-Indian" (essay), 134; "Roots and Flowers" lecture, 112; "The Search for National Identity in India" (essay), 118; self-description, 112; "The World I Hope For" (essay), 117; and transnationalism, 30–31, 33, 34, 91–135, 134–35; use of language,

Anand, Mulk Raj (*continued*)
28, 93, 119, 131–33; Woolf and, 110–11. *See also Coolie*; *Untouchable*
Anderson, Sherwood, 247
Anthill, Diana, 78
Antigone (Sophocles), 17
antiphon, 125–26, 310n108
Anvil, The (magazine), 244, 246, 249, 253–54, 264; *Writers in Revolt* anthology, 250–53. *See also New Anvil, The*
Appardurai, Arjun, 8
Appiah, Anthony, 16, 118, 292n57
Arendt, Hannah, 39, 90; "enlarged thinking," 19, 93, 128–29; and intersubjectivity and community, 19, 294n87; on link between speech and action, 75; on narrative action, 19–21; and representative man, 129; on self-narration and "web of human relations," 6, 20, 75; and "Who are you?" question, 75
Aristotle, 11–12
art, 231–32; Adorno and, 24–26; Ivens and, 230–32; Ortega's dehumanized art, 194–97; Orwell and, 216; and partisanship, 231–32; proletarian art, 243–44; Sartre and, 92. *See also* propaganda
"as if" realm, 18, 283–84; Algren and, 251; Anand and, 117; Aub and, 198–99; and ethics-politics connection, 22; and geography, 95; and Kantian view of aesthetics, 47–48; and narrative engagement with politics, 7; Obama and, 283–84; Ricoeur and, 289n20; Smedley and, 238; and transnational optic, 29, 32; Vaihinger and, 289n20; and warfare, 236. *See also* imagination
At Home in the World (Tagore), 161
Attridge, Derek, 6, 23, 131, 249, 259

Aub, Max, 28, 34–35, 189–210, 235–36; background of, 193–94; compared to Camus, 204; compared to Woolf, 198; early writing, 193–95; and *L'espoir: Sierra de Teruel* (film), 233–36; and existentialism, 205–6; experimentalism of, 31, 187–88; *Fábula verde*, 195; Faulkner and, 198; *Geografía*, 195; geographies, 28; Malraux and, 235, 323n103; modernism of, 192; narrative style, 198, 202, 210; and Ortega y Gasset, 193–95; and other Civil War writers, 189–96; and partisanship, 198; poetry, 195–96; political allegiance, 190–91, 195; and problem of political engagement, 196–210; and separation of art from social concerns, 195–96; and Spanish modernism, 191–96; and transcendental realism, 187, 188–89, 196–210, 317n13; and transnationalism, 31; use of metaphor, 208–9; and Vichy concentration camps, 202. *See also El laberinto mágico*
Austen, Jane, 240; Hussain compared to, 140, 164–65, 176
autobiography, 7, 8; autobiographical pact, 148; border between fiction and autobiography in Indian writing, 141–45, 148, 177–80; Conroy and, 255–56; Gilmore and, 177; Ishvani and, 177–80; Lejeune and, 148; and *skaz* (sketch) form, 242; Smedley and, 238; Sorabji and, 145, 148, 155–56; violations of the autobiographical pact, 144, 148, 177

Baartman, Sara, 85
Badiou, Alan, 18
Baer, Ben Conisbee, 133–34

Bakhtin, Mikhail, 120, 254
Bal, Mieke, 50–51, 300n46
Balzac, Honoré de, 96–97, 101
Banfield, Ann, 50
Barnard, Rita, 240
Baroja, Pío, 186
Baudelaire, Charles, 96
Beauvoir, Simone de, 237, 267, 328n82
Beevor, Antony, 184
"Behind the Purdah" (Sorabji), 157–60
Bell, Clive, 49
Bell, Vanessa, 49
Benet, Juan, 186–87
Bengal famine of 1943, 182
Berkman, Alexander, 265
Bernays, Edward, 217
Bernini, Gian Lorenzo, 52
Bhabha, Homi, 83
bildungsroman: Anand and, 28, 34, 91, 93, 118–25, 130–35; Bakhtin and, 120; British female bildungsroman, 164, 172; Conroy and, 255–56; Esty and, 119–21, 164; and experimental modes of narration, 8; Hegel and, 120; Hussain and, 141, 161–77; Ishvani and, 141, 161–63, 179–80; Joyce and, 34, 91, 119–31, 135, 310n100; Le Sueur and, 268, 270; Lloyd and, 126, 309n97; Moretti and, 119–20; Redfield and, 119; roots of genre, 119–20; Sathianadhan, Kamala and, 161–64, 180–81; Sathianadhan, Krupabai and, 161; Smedley and, 237–38; Sorabji and, 141, 161; Tagore and, 161; Wilde and, 120; Woolf and, 120
biopolitics (Foucault's term), 265, 268, 275, 277–78, 280
Black, Naomi, 301n65
Bloomsbury aesthetics, 49
Bluemel, Kristen, 295n121
Boehmer, Elleke, 93, 94, 111

Boes, Tobias, 310n100
Bontemps, Arna, 247, 263
Bourgeois, Louise, 51
bourgeois culture, critique of, 25, 26, 27, 168, 173, 244
Bowen, Zack, 307n53
Bradshaw, David, 185
Braudel, Fernand, 100
Bretz, Mary Lee, 185, 317n9
Buñuel, Luis, 186
bureaucracy, 4
Burke, Kenneth, 6, 23
Burton, Antoinette, 141, 159, 160
Butler, Judith, 84; and narrative incoherence, 74; and self-narration, 74, 78

Caldwell, Erskine, 251–53, 326nn 45, 53
Campo abierto (Aub), 199–201, 319nn 45, 48
Campo cerrado (Aub), 204–10, 318n22
Camus, Albert, 204
capitalism, 4, 25, 111, 116, 118, 289n23
Caravaggio, Michelangelo Merisi da, 51, 53
Caribbean, 79–86
Carmon, Walt, 248
Casanova, Pascale, 186–87
caste. *See* untouchability; *Untouchable*
Cavarero, Adriana, 20, 45–47, 255; and narratable self, 46; and "Who are you?" question, 46, 74
Chakrabarty, Dipesh, 5, 7, 8
Changing India (Hussain), 169–71, 175–76
Changing India (Rao and Singh), 170–71
Chanter, Tina, 44
Chen, Vincent, 103
Cheney, Lucia and Ralph, 247
Cheng, Vincent, 307n39

citizenship, 12, 14–17, 62, 284; Anand and, 91–92, 130; and bildungsroman, 120; and cosmopolitanism, 103, 117; female citizen-subject in India, 35, 142–43, 156–57, 160, 162, 169, 175, 181–82; Fraser and, 284; Joyce and, 91. *See also* "representative man," modernist critique of

Clifford, James, 214

Coiner, Constance, 266

colonialism: and India, 1, 5, 28, 116 (*see also* Anand, Mulk Raj; women in India); Rhys and, 41–42, 77–89; and transnational reading of Joyce and Anand, 31, 93–135

Communist Party, 241–43, 247–48, 263, 278

community: Arendt and, 19, 128–29, 294n87; Aub and, 205–6, 208–10; communitarian position, 292n57; and conflict between private and public values, 240; contrast to warfare, 75; and ethics-politics connection, 15–16, 20–21; Heidegger and, 294n87; and intimate ethics, 43–45; Kant's *sensus communis*, 21, 129; and link between speech and action, 75; Nancy and, 16, 294n87; the self in community with itself, 128–29; and social imaginaries (Taylor's term), 17; and women, 16

Concise Companion to Modernism (Bradshaw), 185

Conrad, Peter, 185

Conroy, Jack, 36, 238, 243–63; and All Soviet Writers Union, 248–49; and anarchist political culture, 248; background and career, 245–49; and Bontemps, 247; compared to Anand, 260; compared to Le Sueur, 277; and editorial work, 246, 249, 255, 271; Guggenheim award, 245, 246; Hapke and, 327n61; and literary magazines, 245–54, 326n45; Mencken and, 255, 327n59; network of literary contacts, 246–47; poetry, 246; and Rebel Poets organization, 247–49; and rural Midwest, 242; and *skaz* (sketch) form, 253–54; and vernacular style, 249–54; work marginalized, 245, 263. *See also Anvil, The*; *Disinherited, The*; *New Anvil, The*; *Rebel Poet*

"contact" (Le Sueur's concept), 18, 36, 239, 240, 242, 249, 252, 270, 272, 275, 280

Contraataque (Sender), 189

Conversations in Bloomsbury (Anand), 10, 90

Coolie (Anand): and bildungsroman tradition, 121–24, 130–35; geographic sensibility and cosmopolitanism, 109, 116–17; irony in, 123; and narrative focalization, 122–23; use of language, 131–33

Cornell, Drucilla, 18, 39

"Corn Village" (Le Sueur), 271–72

cosmopolitanism: Anand and, 91, 108–18, 132, 134; Harvey and, 101, 117; Joyce and, 101, 103, 307n42; Kant and, 117

Cosmos (von Humboldt), 97

Cousins, James, 93

Covici, Pascal, 245

Crane, Hart, 255

Creole identity, 79–81, 83–85

Critchley, Simon, 5

Critique of Judgment (Kant), 47

Cypresses Believe in God, The (*Los cipreses creen en Dios*; Gironella), 189–90

Dalí, Salvador, 186

dalit literature, and *Untouchable*, 111

Darío, Rubén, 317n9

"Daughter" (Caldwell), 251–53, 326n45
Daughter of Earth (Smedley), 237–38, 323n4
"Dead, The" (Joyce), 102–3, 107
Deane, Seamus, 101
Death of a Discipline (Spivak), 30
Death of the Virgin (Caravaggio painting), 53
defamiliarization: Anand and, 3, 10, 23; Orwell and, 27, 214–15; as preoccupation of modernism, 7; radical estrangement, 27–28; and stories in *The Anvil*, 250
Delaprée, Louis, 69–70
Deleuze, Gilles, 50–51. *See also* "fold, the"
Depression, the, 239, 241, 242, 265, 268, 274. *See also* working-class narratives, U.S.
Derrida, Jacques, 15, 291n51
Desai, Anita, 139
Detective Janaki (Kamala Sathianadhan), 162–64, 180–82
différend (Lyotard's concept), 234–35
Disinherited, The (Conroy), 36, 238, 239, 254–63; Aaron and, 262; autobiographical component, 255–56; and awaking to class consciousness, 261–62; compared to Anand's *Untouchable*, 260; compared to Le Sueur's *The Girl*, 239–40, 277; conflict between private and public values, 240; criticisms of, 327n61; decentered narrative structure, 29, 36, 255–57, 262; fall into obscurity, 245, 263; Hapke and, 327n61; and Harlem Renaissance, 255; Mencken and, 255, 327n59; multiple perspectives, 254–63; and racism, 262–63; and "sensational modernism," 259–60; and *skaz* (sketch) form, 254, 255, 258, 262; and vernacular style, 254–63

"distant reading" (Moretti's term), 31
"Documentary: Subjectivity and Montage" (Ivens), 231–32
domestic space. *See* women in India; zenana
Dominica, 79–83
Dos Passos, John, 229, 245
Dougherty, W. E., 212
Down and Out on the Family Farm (Grant), 272
Dubliners (Joyce), 102
Dunham, Katherine, 247

Ecstasy of St. Theresa, The (Bernini sculpture), 52
Edelmen, Lee, 41, 78
Eichenbaum, Boris, 253, 254
Ellis, Lorna, 164
embodiment, 8, 45, 267–68; Cavarero and, 46, 74; Grosz and, 268; Le Sueur and, 36, 239, 242, 264–69, 272, 276, 278; Levinas and, 44; Moi and, 267; Rhys and, 79, 87–88; Woolf and, 39–40, 43, 62, 73. *See also* feminism
Emery, Mary Lou, 85
Empson, William, 243–44, 325n21
engagement: Adorno and, 24–25; Anand and, 134–35; Arendt and, 129; and transnational reading of Joyce and Anand, 92
"enlarged thinking" (Arendt's concept), 19, 93, 128–30, 135
Entin, Joseph, 241
"epic geography" (Seidel's term), 102, 104
epistolary form: Sorabji and, 157–60; Woolf and, 62, 71–74, 213, 301n68
essays, 7; Anand's essays, 117, 118; Le Sueur's essays, 264, 271–72, 278–79; Orwell's "Why I write," 216; Woolf's essays, 39, 40, 71, 87 (*see also Three Guineas*)
Esty, Jed, 119–21, 164

ethics, 43–44; and aesthetics, 46–62; Arendt and, 19; Aristotle's definition, 11–12; Attridge and, 6; Derrida and, 15; ethical obligations as structural principle of narrative, 5; fact/value split, 12, 26, 29, 64; Gandhi and, 2–3, 5, 166, 287n2; Hume and, 12; intimate ethics, 43–48, 76, 78, 89, 242 (*see also* Le Sueur, Meridel; Rhys, Jean; Woolf, Virginia); intimate ethics and figure of the fold, 33, 40–41, 48–62; Kant and, 12–13; Levinas and, 13–15, 57; Moore and, 13, 48; Nancy and, 15–16; Nussbaum and, 301n56; Rawls and, 14–15; and social imaginaries, 17; "virtue ethics," 287n2; women's experiences marginalized in traditional philosophy, 17. *See also* ethics-politics connection; good, the; virtue; *specific writers and works*

Ethics of Sexual Difference, The (Irigaray), 57

ethics-politics connection, 4–9, 11–19; Anand and, 2–6, 15, 22–23; Appiah and, 16; Arendt and, 19–21, 128–29; Aristotle and, 11–12; avoidance of discourse on, 11, 13, 15, 290n35, 291n51; and experimental modes of narration, 23; Gandhi and, 5; Hume and, 12; and imagination/"as if" realm, 7, 20–22; Kant and, 12–13; and narration, 6–7, 23; and narrative action, 19–23; and Obama's Nobel Peace Prize speech, 36; Rawls and, 14; and the self in community with others, 15–16, 20–21, 43–45; and transnationalism, 292n58. *See also* "is" and "ought to be," connection between; *specific writers and works*

exigence, 6, 17, 21, 26, 284, 288n13; Anand and, 109; and "enlarged thinking" (Arendt's concept), 128

existentialism, 205–6

Eysteinsson, Astradur, 185

Fábula verde (Aub), 195

fact/fiction boundary, play with, 26; and Indian narratives, 23, 141–47, 154, 177–80; and *The Spanish Earth* (film), 228–31, 322n95; and U.S. working-class narratives, 239, 278, 279

fact/value split: Hume and, 12, 26, 29, 64; Obama and, 283. *See also* Hume's Guillotine; Hume's law

Falange and Francoist propaganda posters, 221, 223, *224–25*

family values (Oliver's term), 45

farming, 271–74. *See also* working-class narratives, U.S.

Farrell, James, 249

Faulkner, William, 198

Fearing, Kenneth, 247

Febvre, Lucian, 100

feminism: and ethics-politics connection, 15; and intimate ethics, 33, 40–41, 48–62; and notion of embodiment, 267–69, 328n82; and traditional ethical philosophy, 17

fiction: double valence with respect to reference (Ricoeur's observation), 21; and experimental modes of narration, 8; as type of narrative form, 7. *See also* "as if" realm; fact/fiction boundary, play with; imagination; *specific writers and works*

Field of Honour (*Campo cerrado*; Aub), 204–10, 318n22

Flaubert, Gustave, 96

"Fleetfoot" (Sorabji), 149–50

"fold, the" (Deleuze's concept): Bal and, 50–51, 300n46; described, 51; intimate ethics and figure of

the fold, 33, 40–41, 48–62, 71;
    Woolf and, 51–62
Foley, Barbara, 324n20
folkways. *See* vernacular and
    folkways
Ford, Ford Madox, 80
Forster, E. M., 4, 114, 187n5
For Whom the Bell Tolls (Hemingway), 184, 210–11
Foucault, Michel, 4, 265. *See also*
    biopolitics
Fraiman, Susan, 164
Fraser, Nancy, 18, 284
Friedman, Susan Stanford, 7, 28, 32
Fry, Roger, 48–49

Galdós, Benito Pérez, 198
Gandhi, Mahatma, 1–3, 5, 22, 110,
    114–15, 162, 179; Anand and, 1–3,
    5, 154; Ishvani and, 179; Sorabji
    and, 154; and virtue, 2–3, 5, 166,
    287n2. *See also* Swadeshi program; *swaraj* principle
Geertz, Clifford, 214
Geist, Anthony, 185
Geografía (Aub), 195
geographic sensibility: Anand and,
    28, 91, 108–18; Aub and, 28;
    Balzac and, 96–97, 101; center/
    periphery model, 99, 104; Cheng
    and, 307n39; and delimitation
    of modernism, 28–33; "epic
    geography" (Seidel's term), 102,
    104; geographical "possibilism,"
    99–100, 108; Harvey and, 95–96,
    98, 108, 116–17; Joyce and, 34, 91,
    94–108, 134, 307n39; and justice,
    81–82; MacKinder and, 98–99,
    101, 105; modernist geography,
    99–108; and redescription, 95;
    Rhys and, 80–86; statist geography, 98–99; Vidal de la Blache
    and, 99–101, 102; von Humboldt
    and, 97; "world island" concept,
    99, 100. *See also* cosmopolitanism
Gilmore, Leigh, 177

Ginsberg, Louis, 247
Girl, The (Le Sueur), 36, 238,
    274–78; compared to Conroy's
    The Disinherited, 277; conflict
    between private and public values, 240; and embodied female
    experience, 242, 267, 275–76;
    narrative style, 276–77; and "sensational modernism," 278; and
    skaz (sketch) form, 277
Girl in Bombay (Ishvani), 145,
    162–63, 177–80, 182; and coming
    of age, 179–80; and distinction
    between fiction and autobiography, 177–80; religious conflict,
    178–80, 316n65
Gironella, José María, 189–90
Gold, Michael, 243, 245, 248, 249,
    324n9. *See also New Masses, The*
Goldman, Emma, 265
Goldman, Jane, 49
good, the: Aristotle and, 11–12;
    Moore and, 13, 48; Rawls and, 14
Good Morning, Midnight (Rhys), 33,
    41–42, 77, 79, 86–87
Grant, Michael, 272
Great Britain: British audience
    for Indian works, 154, 170;
    and early propaganda, 216–17;
    English novel tradition, 164–65,
    172; similarities between British
    workers and untouchables in
    India, 110; and Spanish Civil War,
    65, 68, 70, 215, 227–28. *See also*
    colonialism; India; Joyce, James;
    Orwell, George; Rhys, Jean;
    Woolf, Virginia
Great Migration, 246, 263
Gregg, Veronica, 80
Grosz, Elizabeth, 184, 236, 267–68
Guernica (Picasso), 228

Ha estallado la paz (Gironella), 189
Hapke, Laura, 266, 278–79, 327n59
"Harlem Dancer, The" (McKay),
    251

Harlem Renaissance, 29, 242, 255, 280
Harris, Derek, 318n25
Hart, Matthew, 255
"Harvest" (Le Sueur), 272–74
Harvey, David, 90; and cosmopolitanism, 101; and geography, 95–96, 98, 108, 116–17; on justice, 17, 22, 81
Hasan, Sakinatul Fatima Wazir, 167
Heart Divided, A (Nawaz), 178
Hegel, G. W. F., 17, 120
Heidegger, Martin, 294n87
Hellman, Lillian, 229
Hemingway, Ernest, 35; as narrator for *The Spanish Earth*, 228–29, 233; *For Whom the Bell Tolls*, 184, 210–11
Herr, Cheryl, 105
Hite, Molly, 290n35
Hitler, Adolf, 302n76
Homage to Catalonia (Orwell), 35, 188, 211–16, 235–36; and defamiliarization, 27, 214–15; narrative style, 213–14; and propaganda, 215–16
Homer, 47
Hottentot Venus, 85, 86, 88
Howes, Marjorie, 310n107
Hughes, Langston, 246, 247, 249
Hume, David, 12, 29, 294n98
Hume's Guillotine, 12. *See also* Hume's law
Hume's law, 12, 281, 283. *See also* Hume's Guillotine
Hurston, Zora Neale, 240, 255
Hussain, Iqbalunnisa, 34–35, 140, 142–43, 161–77; background of, 168–69; and bildungsroman/coming of age, 141, 161–77; *Changing India*, 169–71, 175–76; compared to Austen, 140, 164–65, 176; experimentalism of, 175–77; narrative "disorder," 174–77; use of language, 143, 176. *See also Purdah and Polygamy*
hyper-realism, 317n13

idealism, Kantian, 47–48
I Hear Men Talking (Le Sueur), 268–71
Illinois Writers Project, 247
imagination: and ethics-politics connection, 20–22; and interconnection of action and story, 21; Kant and, 47; and narration, 18–21; and politics, 18; social imaginaries (Taylor's term), 17–18. *See also* "as if" realm; "is" and "ought to be," connection between
India: Anand on Indian cultural and religious syncretism, 118; Bengal famine of 1943, 182; colonialism and connection between Joyce and Anand, 93–135; colonial status, 1, 5, 116; contrast between Hussain's *Changing India* and Rao and Singh's *Changing India*, 170–71; English-language literary tradition, 140, 144, 182, 313n16; as feminine ("Mother India"), 141–42, 180; Indian modernity, 1–5, 111, 114–19, 140–47, 153, 155, 160–62, 166–67, 169–70, 182–83, 287n5; religious conflict, 178–80, 316n65; Swadeshi program, 5, 115, 162; *swaraj* principle, 162, 171; traditional "recitalist" narrative, 112, 119; women in (*see* women in India). *See also* Anand, Mulk Raj; Gandhi, Mahatma; Hussain, Iqbalunnisa; Ishvani, G.; Rao, Raja; Sathianadhan, Kamala; Satthianadhan, Krupabai; Sorabji, Cornelia; Tagore, Rabindranath
India Recalled (Sorabji), 154, 156
intermodernism (Bluemel's term), 295n121
Ireland: colonialism and transnational reading of Joyce and Anand, 93–135; and geographic sensibility in Joyce's work, 94–108. *See also* Joyce, James

Irigaray, Luce, 44, 57
"is" and "ought to be," connection between, 12, 36, 64, 281–83, 290n30, 294n98
Ishvani, G., 34–35, 140, 161–62; and bildungsroman, 141, 161–63, 179–80; and border between fiction and autobiography, 177–80; link between public and domestic life, 142–43. *See also Girl in Bombay*
Islam, 165–80, 314n39, 316n65
Ivens, Joris, 35, 228–33, 322n97. *See also Spanish Earth, The*
"I Was Marching" (Le Sueur), 278–79

Jameson, Frederic, 1, 9, 29, 32, 287n4
Janowitz, Morris, 212
Jews Without Money (Gold), 243
Johnson, Curt, 250
Johnson, Roberta, 318n26
Joseph, Allen, 211
Joyce, James, 33, 240; Anand and, 9, 30–31, 90–94, 110, 112, 119; Attridge and, 131; and bildungsroman tradition, 119–31, 135; and cosmopolitanism, 101, 103; *Dubliners*, 102–3; and "enlarged thinking" (Arendt's concept), 93; experimentalism of, 34, 92–93, 122, 126–29; geographic sensibility, 34, 91, 94–108, 134, 307n39; Lloyd and, 131; and transnationalism, 30–31, 34, 91–135; use of language, 25, 93, 124–27, 130–31. *See also Portrait of the Artist as a Young Man, A*; "Dead, The"; *Ulysses*
justice: Anand and, 108, 117; Aristotle and, 12; and "as if" realm, 7, 18, 236; Cornell and, 18; Gandhi and, 2; and geography, 81–82; Harvey and, 17, 22, 81; Hume and, 12; and intimate ethics, 45, 242; Kant and, 13; and modernism, 9, 26; Mouffe and, 19; Nancy and, 15–16; narrative's role in imagining justice, 7 (*see also specific writers and works*); Obama and, 281–84; Rawls and, 14–15; and the self in community with others, 16; and social imaginaries, 17; warfare and, 281–83; and "who" question in political justice, 16–17, 293n71 (*see also* citizenship). *See also* "is" and "ought to be," connection between; women in India; working-class narratives, U.S.; *specific writers and works*
"Justice as Fairness: Political Not Metaphysical" (Rawls), 14–15

Kadlec, David, 240
Kafka, Franz, 25
Kalar, Joe, 247, 253
Kamala (Krupabai Satthianadhan), 139, 147, 161, 311n3
Kant, Immanuel: and aesthetics, 47–48; and cosmopolitanism, 117; and distinction between ethics and politics, 12–13; idealism, 47–48; and imagination, 47; Moore and, 48; *sensus communis*, 21, 129
Kiberd, Declan, 107
King, Martin Luther, Jr., 281–83
Koja sect, 177–79, 316n65
Konzett, Delia Caparosa, 88

Laberinto mágico, El (Aub), 35, 188–210, 235–36; *Campo abierto*, 199–201, 319nn 45, 48; *Campo cerrado (Field of Honour)*, 204–10, 318n22; complexity of perspective, 191–92; home front vs. battlefront, 28, 192; and incarceration and exile, 202–3; and justice, 192, 210; labyrinth device,

Laberinto mágico, El (Aub) *(continued)* 202–3; narrative style, 198, 202; and partisanship, 198; political engagement and ethics, 201–10; and propaganda, 192; publication dates, 319n48; and transcendental realism, 188–89, 198–210; Ugarte and, 203; use of metaphor, 208–9. See also modernism, Spanish; Spain, modernism in
Laclau, Ernesto, 293n76
La Revista de Occidente (magazine), 186, 194. See also Ortega y Gasset, José
"Laundress, The" (Le Sueur), 266
Lefebvre, Henri, 90
Lejeune, Philippe, 148
L'espoir (Malraux novel), 233–35
L'espoir: Sierra de Teruel (film), 35, 188, 233–36
Le Sueur, Meridel, 36, 238, 264–80; background of, 265–66; and bildungsroman tradition, 268, 270; and biopolitics, 265, 268, 275, 277–78, 280; Coiner and, 266; Communist Party membership, 241; compared to Conroy, 277; compared to Woolf and Rhys, 265; and "contact," 239, 270–72, 275; "Corn Village" (essay), 271–72; and embodied female experience, 264–69, 272, 276, 278, 280; Hapke and, 266, 278–79; "Harvest," 272–74; *I Hear Men Talking*, 268–71; "I Was Marching" (essay), 278–79; and literary magazines, 249, 264; narrative style, 276–80; and pastoral mode, 268–69; Rabinowitz and, 266–67, 328n87; and rural Midwest, 242, 264–65, 271–74; "The Laundress," 266; "Women on the Breadlines" (essay), 264, 279. See also *Girl, The*
Levinas, Emmanuel, 1, 21, 291nn47, 51, 295n121; ethical theory of, 13–15; and intimate ethics, 43–44, 299n19; reticence on politics, 11, 13
Linett, Maren, 303n96
Lionnet, Françoise, 10, 30
Lippman, Walter, 217
Liska, Vivian, 185
"lived body," 267–68
Lloyd, David, 126, 130, 309n97
Lodge, David, 29
Lokugé, Chandani, 311n3
Longoria, Francisco, 193
Los ciprese screen en Dios (Gironella), 189–90
Love and Life Behind the Purdah (Sorabji), 145, 146, 156–60; "Behind the Purdah," 157–60; compared to Woolf's *Three Guineas*, 159; narrative style and form, 157–59; and revision of perspective, 149; and trope of the intermediary, 156–57; and "Who are you?" question, 159
Lyotard, Jean-François, 234–35

Machado, Antonio, 186
MacKinder, Halford John, 98–99, 101, 105
MacLeish, Archibald, 229
madness, 82, 304n109
Madrid, siege of, 65–70
magical realism, 317n13
Magic Labyrinth, The. See *Laberinto mágico, El*
Malraux, Andre, 35, 188, 233–35, 322n100, 323n103
Marcus, Jane, 70–71
marriage: in India, 141–42, 162–64, 170–76, 178, 180–81, 312n11, 315n57; Woolf and, 50, 57, 59–60
Martí, José, 317n9
"Martyrdom of Madrid, The" (Delaprée), 69–70
Mayo, Katherine, 141–42
McKay, Claude, 251

Mencken, H. L., 245, 247, 266, 326n36, 327n59
Mendelson, Jordana, 192, 217–18
Merleau-Ponty, Maurice, 267–68. *See also* embodiment
"Middlebrow" (Woolf), 39, 71, 87
Million Dead, A (*Un millón de muertos*; Gironella), 189–90
"minor" (Lloyd's term), 126–27, 130
Mitchell, Breon, 122
modernism, 266; aesthetic dimension, 8, 26; connection between politically engaged writing and experimental, 9, 26; defined/described, 7–8; delimitation of, 26–27, 32; formal preoccupations of, 7, 26, 185; and geography, 28–33, 99–108; Indian, 23 (*see also* Anand, Mulk Raj; women in India); modernist commitments, 23–28; "new deal," 241; and proletarian literature, 241; and propaganda, 212; rhetorical actions, 7–9; role in imagining justice, 9, 26; selection of time period for, 25–26; "sensational," 259–60, 278; Spanish, 184–89, 192–95, 317n9; transnational, 28–33 (*see also* transnational reading of modernism); and U.S. working-class narratives of the 1920s and 1930s, 240–43, 259–60, 266; vanguardism, 192, 318n25; Williams and, 26–27. *See also* defamiliarization; fact/fiction boundary, play with; narrative focalization; narrative forms; temporality; transcendental realism; verisimilitude
Modernisms (Nicholls), 185
modernity: defined/described, 287n4, 289n23; and Dublin, 101–2, 105; and India, 1–5, 111, 114–19, 140–47, 153, 155, 160–62, 166–67, 169–70, 182–83, 287n5 (*see also* women in India); and Paris, 96–97; as "practice-based" (Rothstein's term), 32; and rationality, 187n5; and Spain, 189, 192, 221, 233, 236 (*see also* Spanish Civil War); and the United States, 238, 240, 265, 272–74 (*see also* working-class narratives, U.S.)
Modern Times, Modern Places (Conrad), 185
Moi, Toril, 267, 328n82. *See also* embodiment
Monleón, José, 185
Moore, G. E.: and the good, 13, 28; Kant and, 48
Moore, Marianne, 240
Moore, Thomas, 106
Moretti, Franco, 25, 29, 31, 119–20
Mosaic Modernism: Anarchism, Pragmatism, Culture (Kadlec), 240
Mother India (Mayo), 141–42
Mouffe, Chantal, 18–19, 293n76
"Mr. Bennett and Mrs. Brown" (Woolf), 40
Mrs. Dalloway (Woolf), 25; and Anand's *Untouchable*, 110–11; and Aub's *Campo cerrado*, 205; and critique of propaganda and advertising, 25; experimentalism of, 40; and intimate ethics and figure of the fold, 40–41, 50, 60–62
Mussolini, Benito, 302n76
"My Master's Slave" (Sorabji), 150–52

Nancy, Jean-Luc, 15–16, 21, 45, 294n87
Nandy, Ashis, 5
Narayan, R. K., 133, 140, 144, 311n121
narratable self (Cavarero's term), 46; Conroy and, 255; and intimate ethics, 46–47; and relationship and reciprocity, 74–75. *See also* self-narration; "Who are you?" question

narration, act of: Arendt on, 6; and ethics-politics connection, 6–7, 19–23; and imagination, 18–19; and reciprocal relation of teller and reader/listener, 6–7, 18–19, 46, 71–72, 145–46. *See also* self-narration/accounting for self
narrative action, 19–23, 96; Arendt on, 19–21
narrative focalization: Anand and, 1, 23, 111, 122–23, 135; Aub and, 202; Joyce and, 91, 93, 122–23, 127, 130; and propaganda, 212
narrative forms (genres), 7–9, 25–26; Anand and, 23, 34, 92–93, 119, 122; and ethics-politics connection, 7, 23; hybrid genres in India, 141–47, 177–82; Ishvani and, 177–80; Joyce and, 34, 92–93, 122, 126–29; mosaic form in U.S. working-class narratives, 238, 240, 246, 256, 280; Orwell and, 213–14; Rhys and, 43; Kamala Sathianadhan and, 180–82; Sorabji and, 157–58; and transnationalism, 29; Woolf and, 33, 43, 62, 71–75. *See also* autobiography; epistolary form; essays; reportage; *skaz* (sketch)
narrative structures of address, 26; Rhys and, 43, 84, 88; Woolf and, 41, 62, 74, 76, 213
narrative style. *See specific writers and works*
nationality: and Indian writers, 109, 118, 141, 169–70; Joyce and, 95, 97, 101, 103, 109; MacKinder and, 99; Rhys and, 80, 86
Nawaz, Mumtaz Shah, 178
Neiburh, Reinhold, 281
New Anvil, The (magazine), 245, 246
Newman, John Henry, 125, 310n108
New Masses, The (magazine), 245, 247, 248, 278. *See also* Gold, Michael
Nicholls, Peter, 185

Nobel Peace Prize, 281–84
Nolan, Emer, 106
Novel of the Spanish Civil War, The (Thomas), 184–85
Nussbaum, Martha, 50, 292n57, 301n56

Obama, Barack, 36, 281–84
Oliver, Kelly, 16, 45
Olsen, Tillie, 264
One Million Dead (Gironella), 189–90
orality. *See* vernacular and folkways
Orlando (Woolf), 33; experimentalism of, 40; and intimate ethics and figure of the fold, 40–41, 50, 51–56; "Orlando on her return to England," 54, 55
Ortega y Gasset, José, 186, 193–95, 317n9, 318n30; Aub and, 193–94
Orwell, George, 184, 235–36; and aesthetics, 216; and delimitation of modernism, 27; narrative style, 213–14; on partisanship, 69; and propaganda, 213–16; and transnationalism, 31; "Why I Write" (essay), 216. *See also Homage to Catalonia*

Pakistan, 179
Parker, Dorothy, 229
Parry, Benita, 80
Partisan Review (magazine), 241, 245, 249, 263. *See also* Rahv, Philip
partisanship, 210–16; Aub and, 198; Ivens and, 231–32; Orwell and, 211–15, 236
pastoral imagery: Empson and, 243, 325n21; Le Sueur and, 269–70, 273–75, 278; and proletarian literature, 244, 325n21; and Spanish Civil War, 232–33
patriarchy, Woolf's critique of, 41, 63, 72, 73, 76, 77, 89
Peace Has Broken Out (*Ha estallado la paz*; Gironella), 189

"personalization" (Ivens's term), and filmmaking, 229–30, 234–35
Phelan, James, 313n26
photojournalism, 65–68, 217; and documentary technique in *The Spanish Earth* film, 229–32
Picasso, Pablo, 186, 228
poetry, 24, 293n81; Aub and, 195–96; Conroy and, 246
politics: Arendt and, 19–20; and encounter between text and reader, 18–19; and ethical assumptions about identity, community, and citizenship, 16–17; Fraser and, 18; Gandhi and, 2–3; and imagination/"as if" realm, 18; Kant and, 13; Levinas and, 11, 13, 291nn 47, 51; marginalized groups and construction of the citizen, 16–17; and modernism, 9, 27; and modernist commitments, 23–28; and postimpressionism, 49; Rancière's definition, 18; and transnational reading of Joyce and Anand, 92–135; and "Who are you?" question, 75. *See also* ethics-politics connection; propaganda; Spanish Civil War; warfare; women in India; *specific issues, writers, and works*
polygamy, 165–77
Portrait of an Indian Woman (Sengupta), 180
Portrait of the Artist as a Young Man, A (Joyce): and bildungsroman tradition, 121–28, 310n100; and coloniality, 125–26, 310n107; and "enlarged thinking" (Arendt's concept), 128–30; and geography, 105, 107; influence on Anand, 90–94, 110, 119; Mitchell and, 122; and narrative focalization, 122–23; and politics, 122, 129–30; use of language, 25, 124–27, 131; voice and narrative perspectives, 126–29; Williams and, 123

postimpressionism, 48–49
poverty: and cosmopolitanism in Anand's work, 109; differences between men's and women's experiences of poverty, 266; and Rhys's characters, 76–89; and "sensational modernism," 259–60; and *Untouchable*, 109. *See also* Anand, Mulk Raj; working-class narratives, U.S.
Pratt, Mary Louise, 214
pregnancy and childbirth, 269, 276–77, 315n57. *See also* Le Sueur, Meridel
Pride and Prejudice (Austen), 165
Principia Ethica (Moore), 13, 48
Problems of Dostoevsky's Poetics (Bahktin), 254
proletarian literature, 241, 243–44, 256, 264, 325n21; debate over term, 324n9 (*see also* Gold, Michael)
propaganda, 35, 65–68, 188, 190–92, 210–36; and aesthetics, 212, 216; Aub and, 192; changing meanings of, 216–17; Dougherty and Janowitz's definition, 212; Falange and Francoist propaganda posters, 223, *224–25*; and *L'espoir: Sierra de Teruel* (film), 233–36; Malraux and, 233–35; and manipulation of perspective, 191–92; and modernism, 212; official Republican propaganda in the Spanish Civil War, 217–21, *219–22*, 226, 227–28; origins of, 216–17; Orwell and, 213–16; and proletarian art, 243; as prophecy, 227–28; Sender and, 190; and *The Spanish Earth* (Ivens film), 228–33; and Spanish Pavilion at Paris World Fair, 228–29; Suleiman and, 211–12; and verisimilitude, 35–36, 211, 212; Woolf and, 25, 70–71, 191, 218, 223
prose writing, Sartre on, 23–24

prostitution, 42, 274–75
purdah, 161–82, 314n39; Hussain and, 165–77; Ishvani and, 178–80; overview of coming-of-age narratives, 161–64; Sathianadhan, Kamala and, 180–82; Sorabji and, 145–46, 152–61. *See also Love and Life Behind the Purdah*; *Purdah and Polygamy*; zenana
Purdah and Polygamy (Hussain), 145, 162–77, 182; and coming of age, 163–64, 172; and English novel tradition, 164–65, 172; forward to, 143; irony in, 165–66, 176; and Islam, 165–77; multiple perspectives, 175–76; narrative "disorder," 174–77; and politics of everyday life, 166, 171; use of language, 143, 176

Quartet (Rhys), 33, 77, 79, 87, 304n118
queer theory, 78

Rabinowitz, Paula, 266–67, 323n4, 328n87
race: Joyce and, 106; and modernist geography, 100–101; Rhys and, 83–85, 89; and working-class narratives, 246–47, 262–63
radical alterity, 40, 44, 50
radical democracy, 17, 293n76
radical estrangement, 27–28
Rahv, Philip, 241, 248, 263
Raiskin, Judith, 80
Ramazani, Jahan, 9–10
Rancière, Jacques, 18
Rao, Raja, 140, 170–71, 178
Rawls, John, 11, 14
Ray, Sangeeta, 139, 161
realism, 135; and aesthetics, 48; Anand and, 110; Aub and, 200; disruption of, 9, 25; hyper-realism and magical realism, 317n13; Obama and, 281; and proletarian literature, 241; Sartre and, 24; socialist realism, 29; testimonial realism, 319n41; Tolstoy and Galdós and, 198; and U.S. working-class narratives, 36, 237–39. *See also* transcendental realism
Rebel Poet (magazine), 245–49. *See also* Conroy, Jack
Rebel Poets organization, 247–49, 253, 263
Reddy, Sir Ramalinga, 143
redescription, 7, 21, 25, 95, 144
Redfield, Marc, 119
Regarding the Pain of Others (Sontag), 65
religion: Islam in Hussain's *Purdah and Polygamy*, 165–77; religious conflict in Ishvani's *Girl in Bombay*, 178–80, 316n65; Sorabji and, 155
reportage: and Aub's *El laberinto mágico*, 200; and Conroy's *The Disinherited*, 255; and documentary technique in *The Spanish Earth* (film), 229–32; early use of film in, 217; and experimental modes of narration, 8; and Le Sueur's *The Girl*, 276, 278; and Orwell's *Homage to Catalonia*, 214; and Smedley's *Daughter of Earth*, 238; tension between documentary reporting and propaganda during Spanish Civil War, 210–36; as type of narrative form, 7
"representative man," modernist critique of: Anand and, 34, 91, 93, 118–25, 130–35; Joyce and, 34, 91, 119–31, 135
Republican propaganda posters (Spanish Civil War), 217–21, *219–22*, *226*, *227–28*
Revolt of the Masses (Ortega), 195
Rhys, Jean, 33, 65–70, 76–89, 303n96; background of, 79–81; and coloniality, 77–79; and commodification of women's

bodies, 87–88; compared to Le Sueur, 265; compared to Woolf, 41–43, 76–78, 84, 87, 89; and figure of the fold, 78; Ford and, 80; geographic sensibility, 80–86; Konzett and, 88; and narrative incoherence and hiatus, 78, 303n96; plots, 86; political argument and futureless borderwalking characters, 76–89; and race, 83–85; self-destructive heroines, 82, 304n109; Spivak and, 79; structure of address, 88–89; "Vienne" (story), 86. *See also Good Morning Midnight*; *Quartet*; *Voyage in the Dark*; *Wide Sargasso Sea*
Ricoeur, Paul, 1, 289n20, 294n98; "as if" realm, 7 (*see also* "as if" realm); and dialectic of selfhood and otherness, 75; on fiction's double valence with respect to reference, 21; and self-reflexivity, 147
Robbins, Bruce, 307n42
Rosner, Victoria, 167
Rothstein, Eric, 32, 289n23

Said, Edward, 28
Saint-Amour, Paul, 200
Sarkar, Sumit, 5
Sartre, Jean-Paul, 23–24, 88, 92
Sathianadhan, Kamala, 35, 161–64, 316n68; *Detective Janaki*, 162–64, 180–82
Sathianadhan, W. T., 316n68
Satthianadhan, Krupabai, 34–35, 316n68; *Kamala*, 139, 147, 161, 311n3
"Search for National Identity in India, The" (Anand), 118
Seidel, Michael, 102, 104
self: Arendt and, 128–29; and Deleuze's concept of the fold, 51; and intimate ethics, 44–46; Leibniz and, 51

self-narration/accounting for self, 284; Arendt and, 6, 20; Butler and, 74, 78, 84; Cavarero and, 46–47; and connection between aesthetics and ethics, 46; Conroy and, 255; and ethics-politics connection, 20, 284; incomplete accounts of self, 84; Rhys and, 77, 78, 79, 83, 84, 86, 88; Sorabji and, 147–48; Woolf and, 63, 74–76. *See also* autobiography; narratable self
Sen, Amartya, 11, 15
Sender, Ramón, 189, 190
Sengupta, Padmini, 180
sensational modernism (Entin's term), 259–60, 278
Sentimental Education (Flaubert), 97
sexuality: Joyce and, 124; Le Sueur and, 269, 273–74; Rhys and, 85–88, 304n118
Shakespeare, William, 47
sharecropping, 252
Shu-Mei Shih, 10, 30
Singh, Iqbal, 170–71
skaz (sketch), 242, 253–54; and Conroy's *The Disinherited*, 29, 36, 255, 258, 262; and experimental modes of narration, 8; and Le Sueur's *The Girl*, 277; Russian origins of genre, 253, 260
slavery and servitude: enslavement to narrative, 145–46, 148–49; and Sorabji's narratives, 145–61
Smedley, Agnes, 237–38, 264; Communist Party membership, 241; *Daughter of Earth*, 237–38, 323n4; and mosaic structure, 238, 240; and transcendental realism, 323n3
"social imaginaries" (Taylor's term), 17–18
Soler, Manuel Aznar, 319n41
Some Versions of Pastoral (Empson), 243–44
Sontag, Susan, 64–65, 68, 71, 76, 301n67

Sophocles, 47
Sorabji, Cornelia, 34–35, 140, 142–43, 145–61, 182, 313nn 16, 25, 26; and autobiography, 145, 148, 154–56; background and career, 145–46, 153, 314n33; and bildungsroman, 141, 161; British audience, 154; Burton and, 159, 160; compared to Woolf, 159; enslavement to narrative, 145–46, 148–49; Gandhi and, 154; *India Recalled*, 154, 156; modernism of, 153, 158; narrative style and form, 146–47, 149, 157–59; and religion, 155; "Tea-Time Talks," 154–55; trope of the intermediary, 153, 155–56, 160. *See also Love and Life Behind the Purdah; Sun Babies*

Soundproof Room: Malraux's Anti-Aesthetics (Lyotard), 234–35
Souza, Eunice de, 314n39
Soviet Union: and proletarian art and literature, 248–49, 324n20; *skaz* (sketch) form, 253, 260
Spain: experimental narrative and war writing, 187; modernity, 189, 192, 221, 233, 236; modernism in, 184–89, 192–95, 317n9; surrealism and Dada, 186, 192; tradition of literary criticism, 192–93, 318n26; war with the United States (1898), 192–93. *See also* Aub, Max; Ortega y Gasset, José; Spanish Civil War
Spanish Civil War, 35, 184–236, 316n68, 318n26; European non-intervention pact, 68, 301n76; Hemingway's *For Whom the Bell Tolls*, 184; images of dead children, 65, 66, 67, 68; "The Martyrdom of Madrid" (Delaprée pamphlet), 69–70; and modernist writing, 185–89; and objectivity vs. partisanship in writing, 190–91; and partisanship, 210–16; and propaganda, 35, 65–70, 188, 190–92, 210–36; siege of Madrid, 65–70; transcendental realism and political engagement, 196–210; and transnationalism, 31; writings about, 184–88, 316n2. *See also* Aub, Max; Gironella, José María; Hemingway, Ernest; *L'espoir: Sierra de Teruel* (film); Orwell, George; Sender, Ramón; *The Spanish Earth* (film); *Three Guineas* (Woolf)

Spanish Earth, The (film), 188, 228–33, 235–36; camera work, 230, 232–33; change in original plans for, 229; and documentary technique, 229–32; and emotional response of the viewer, 232; as half-fictional, half-documentary, 228–31, 322n95; and "personalization," 229–30; and propaganda, 230–32; staged scenes, 229, 322n97; and transnationalism, 31
Spivak, Gayarti, 31; and modernism, 8; and narration, 7; on Rhys, 41, 79; and transnationalism, 30
sterilization, 275–76, 278
Stories of Indian Christian Life (Kamala Sathianadhan and W. T. Sathianadhan), 180
Stranger, The (Camus), 204
suffrage movement, 49
Suleiman, Susan Rubin, 71, 212–13
Sun Babies (Sorabji), 146–56; and challenge to autobiographical pact, 148; compared to Satthianadhan's *Kamala*, 147; "Fleetfoot" (story), 149–50; "My Master's Slave" (story), 150–52; narrative style and form, 146–47; quasi-fictive stance, 146–48; and revision of perspective, 149; and self-narration, 147–48

Swadeshi program, 5, 115, 162. *See also* Gandhi, Mahatma
swaraj principle, 162, 171. *See also* Gandhi, Mahatma
Szalay, Michael, 241

Tagore, Rabindranath, 161, 162
Taylor, Charles, 17–18
"Tea-Time Talks" (Sorabji), 154–55
technology, 2–4, 111, 287n4. *See also* farming
temporality: Anand and, 4; Aub and, 187, 189, 200–203; Foucault's "attitude toward time," 4; Gironella and, 190; Hussain and, 175; Joyce and, 104; Le Sueur and, 264, 277; play with time and space as preoccupation of modernism, 7, 26; and propaganda, 227; Rhys and, 33, 41, 77; Woolf and, 61
Terkel, Studs, 247
testimonial realism, 319n41. *See also* transcendental realism
Theory of Justice (Rawls), 14
Thomas, Gareth, 184–85, 209
Thornton, Weldon, 103
Three Guineas (Woolf), 33, 62–76, 301n65; documentary impulse, 63, 301n65; and "essay-novel" project, 322n95; experimentalism of, 62, 71–75, 301n68; and fact/value split, 64; and feminism, 70–71; Marcus on, 70–71; mock epistolary structure of, 71–72; political argument and narrative incoherence, 41, 62–63, 72–75; and propaganda, 70–71, 191, 223; Sontag on, 64–65, 68, 71; structure of address, 62, 74–76, 191; use of images, 63–73, 76
Tolstoy, Leo, 198
total war, 28, 62–63, 65, 185, 187, 236; Aub and, 189, 191, 199–203; Delaprée and, 70; and partisanship, 213; and photojournalism, 68; and propaganda, 227–28; and *The Spanish Earth* (film), 233; and Spanish modernism, 193; Woolf and, 69, 72, 76
To the Lighthouse (Woolf), 33; Banfield on, 50; experimentalism of, 40; and intimate ethics and figure of the fold, 40–41, 50, 56–60; and Levinas's ethics, 57; Nussbaum on, 50; use of color, 57–58
transcendental realism, 187–89, 196–210, 317n13, 323n3
transgender, transexual theory, 11
transnational reading of modernism, 28–33, 284, 292n58; defined/described, 9–11, 30–31; nodes of modernism, 31–33, 192, 90n1; reading Aub with Orwell and *The Spanish Earth* (film), 31; reading Joyce and Anand together, 30–31, 34, 91–135. *See also* cosmopolitanism
travel narrative, 213–14. *See also* *Homage to Catalonia*

Ugarte, Michael, 203
Ulysses (Joyce): Anand and, 110–11; and Aub's *Campo cerrado*, 205; and critique of bourgeois Dublin, 25; and geography, 96–97, 102–8, 135; Nolan and, 106; and principle of wandering, 105, 107; Thornton and, 103; use of language, 25
Unamuno, Miguel de, 186
United States. *See* women in the U.S.; working-class narratives, U.S.
untouchability: British laws against, 294n101; and "flush toilet" solution, 3, 187n5; Gandhi and, 1–3, 5, 154. *See also* Anand, Mulk Raj

Untouchable (Anand), 1–5; Baer and, 133–34; and bildungsroman tradition, 28; compared to Conroy's *The Disinherited*, 260; and cosmopolitanism, 114–15; and ethics-politics connection, 2–6, 15, 22–23; experimentalism of, 23; Forster's preface, 4, 114, 187n5; Gandhi and, 110; and gaps in narrative consistency, 3–4; and geography, 108–9; and Joyce's *Ulysses*, 110–11; and justice, 22–23; as modernist text, 111–15; touch in, 113–14; and transnationalism, 10, 29; use of language, 28, 133–34; variety of styles and modes, 112; voice, 23; and Woolf's *Mrs. Dalloway*, 110, 112

Vaihinger, Hans, 18, 289n20
vanguardism, 192, 318n25. See also Aub, Max; Ortega y Gasset, José
verisimilitude: Anand and, 134; Aub and transcendental realism, 187–89, 196–210; Hemingway and, 210–11; Orwell and, 211; and propaganda, 35–36, 211, 212; refusal of, as preoccupation of modernism, 7, 26; Sorabji and, 147
vernacular and folkways, 239, 242, 280; and Conroy's *The Disinherited*, 254, 255–63; and someone else's speech, 254, 260; and stories in *The Anvil*, 249–54
Vidal de la Blache, Paul, 99–101, 102
"Vienne" (Rhys), 86
virtue, 45; Aristotle and, 12; Gandhi and, 2–3, 5, 166, 287n2; Hume and, 12; Hussain and, 166; Levinas and, 15; Moore and, 13; Woolf and, 59
von Humboldt, Alexander, 97, 305n21

Voyage in the Dark (Rhys), 33, 77, 79, 82–88, 304n109; Emery and, 85; and ethics-politics connection, 41–42; and geographic sensibility, 82–86; heroine's lack of future, 84; Kalliney on, 83; and race, 83–85; and sexuality, 85–88; structure of address, 84

Walker, Margaret, 246
Walkowitz, Rebecca, 30
warfare: battle as *différend*, 234–35; contrast to community, 75; Hemingway and, 210–11; and Obama's Nobel Peace Prize speech, 281–83; and propaganda, 210–16; and "Who are you?" question, 76; and Woolf's *Three Guineas*, 62–76. See also partisanship; Spanish Civil War; total war
War in Spain, The (Sender), 189
Waugh, Thomas, 229
West, Rebecca, 27
"When Was Modernism?" (Williams), 26–27
Whittier-Ferguson, John, 301n68
"Who are you?" question: Arendt and, 75; Cavarero and, 46, 74; and intimate ethics, 46; and political engagement, 75; Rhys and, 33, 43, 77, 88; and warfare, 76; Woolf and, 41, 74–76
"Who speaks?" question, 147, 283–84
"Why I Write" (Orwell), 216
Wide Sargasso Sea (Rhys), 41, 79–80
Wilde, Oscar, 120
Williams, Raymond, 26–28; "When Was Modernism?" (essay), 26–27
Williams, Trevor, 123
Williams, William Carlos, 240, 249
Wilson, Woodrow, 217
"Within the City" (Algren story), 251
Wixson, Douglas, 247, 253, 325n27

Wollaeger, Mark, 212
women: biopolitics in the U.S., 265, 268, 275, 277–78, 280; commodification of women's bodies in Rhys's work, 87–88; Hottentot Venus, 85, 86, 88; and intimate ethics, 44, 299n19; pregnancy and childbirth, 269, 276–77, 315n57. *See also* marriage; women in India; women in the United States
women in India, 34–35, 139–83; and coloniality, 141–42; and English-language narrative tradition, 140, 144, 313n16; and experimental narrative styles, 143; husband worship, 139; hybrid narrative genres, 141; and Krupabai Satthianadhan's *Kamala*, 139; and marriage, 141–42, 162–64, 170–76, 178, 180–81, 312n11, 315n57; Mayo's narratives, 141–42; and money, 167–68; and "moral mother" trope, 169–70; and national development, 169–70; politics and the home linked in Kamala Sathianadhan's *Detective Janaki*, 180–82; purdah and coming of age, 161–77; purdah and polygamy in Hussain's narratives, 165–77; purdah in Sorabji's narratives, 152–61; slavery, servitude, and domestic logic in Sorabji's narratives, 145–61; tension between modernity and traditional domestic space (zenana), 140–83; and violations of the autobiographical pact, 144; writing marginalized, 140, 182, 312nn 6, 7
women in the United States: abortion, 276–77; and biopolitics, 265, 268, 275, 277–78, 280; and embodied female experience, 242, 264–69, 280; gender relations among rural people, 274; pregnancy and childbirth, 269, 276–77; prostitution, 274–75; relationship between public and private spheres, 239; single motherhood, 266; sterilization, 275–76, 278. *See also* Le Sueur, Meridel; Smedley, Agnes
"Women on the Breadlines" (Le Sueur), 264, 279
Woolf, Virginia, 33, 49–76, 86; and aesthetics, 48–62; and bildungsroman tradition, 120; compared to Aub, 198; compared to Indian writers, 159, 162; compared to Le Sueur, 265; compared to Rhys, 41–43, 76–78, 84, 87, 89; critique of patriarchal authority, 41, 63, 72, 73, 76, 77, 89; experimentalism of, 33, 40, 50, 62; and Fry's aesthetics, 49; and gap between known and unknown life, 39–40, 87; influence on Anand, 110–11; intimate ethics and figure of the fold, 40–41, 71; intimate ethics and public politics linked in *Three Guineas*, 62–76; "Middlebrow" (essay), 39, 71, 87; "Mr. Bennett and Mrs. Brown" (essay), 40; and propaganda, 70–71, 191, 218, 223; and sister Vanessa Bell, 49; utopian optimism of, 84; *The Years*, 70, 322n95. *See also* *Mrs. Dalloway*; *Orlando*; *Three Guineas*; *To the Lighthouse*
working-class narratives, U.S., 237–80; and anarchist, pragmatist, or antifoundationalist political culture, 240, 247–49; Attridge and, 249; and biopolitics, 265, 268, 275, 277–78, 280; conflict between private values and public expectations of workers, 240; and "contact," 239, 240, 242, 249, 252, 272; and domestic concerns, 239–40; and embodied female experience of suffering, 242,

working-class narratives (*continued*) 264–69, 280; Kadlec and, 240; literary magazines, 244–54, 263–64 (*see also* Anvil, The; New Anvil, The; New Masses, The; Rebel Poet); and mosaic form, 240, 256–57; as narratives by U.S. working-class writers, 325n22; proletarian literature, 241, 243–44, 256, 264, 324n9, 325n21; and race, 246–47, 262–63; and Rebel Poets organization, 247–49, 263; and "sensational modernism," 259–60, 278; and *skaz* (sketch) form, 242, 253–55, 258; and transitions in farm life, 271–74; urban vs. rural narratives, 241–44, 264–65; vernacular and folkways, 239, 242, 249–63; *Writers in Revolt* anthology, 250–53. *See also* Conroy, Jack; Le Sueur, Meridel; Smedley, Agnes

"World I Hope For, The" (Anand), 117

"world island" concept, 99, 100

World Republic of Letters, The (Casanova), 186–87

World War I, 216–17, 272

Wright, Richard, 246, 247

Writers in Revolt (anthology), 250–53

Years, The (Woolf), 70, 322n95

Young, Iris Marion, 267–68; and embodiment, 267

zenana, 34–35; and bildungsroman tradition, 163–64; and distinction between fiction and autobiography, 144; Hussain and, 141–44, 161–77; Ishvani and, 141–44, 161–63, 178–80; Sathianadhan, Kamala and, 162–63, 180–82; Sorabji and, 141–44, 152–53, 156–60; tension between modernity and traditional domestic space, 140–83; and trope of the intermediary, 156–57, 159. *See also* women in India

GPSR Authorized Representative: Easy Access System Europe, Mustamäe tee
50, 10621 Tallinn, Estonia, gpsr.requests@easproject.com

www.ingramcontent.com/pod-product-compliance
Lightning Source LLC
Chambersburg PA
CBHW032148010526
44111CB00035B/1248